BLUE COLLAR & Proud OF IT

BLUE COLLAR
&Proud
OF IT

The All-in-One Resource
for Finding Freedom, Financial Success, and Security Outside the Cubicle

Joe Lamacchia
and Bridget Samburg

Health Communications, Inc.
Deerfield Beach, Florida

www.hcibooks.com

**Library of Congress Cataloging-in-Publication Data
is available through the Library of Congress.**

READER'S NOTE: The job statistics provided are taken from 2006–2008 data. Given economic conditions and market fluctuations, these will be subject to change.

ISBN-10: 0-7573-0778-7
ISBN-13: 978-0-7573-0778-2

Publisher: Health Communications, Inc.
      3201 S.W. 15th Street
      Deerfield Beach, FL 33442–8190

Cover design by Larissa Hise Henoch
Interior design and formatting by Lawna Patterson Oldfield

CONTENTS

INTRODUCTION

I n case you haven't guessed from the title of this book, I am blue collar and proud if it. I love to dig in the dirt, can't sit still, and totally enjoy being outside all day long. I run a million-dollar landscaping business outside of Boston in an upscale suburb. I worked my way up the ladder; have five children, a beautiful house, and a wonderful wife; and I enjoy taking vacations with my family. I read the *Wall Street Journal* religiously and as many books as I can, and most of my TV watching consists of the National Geographic Channel and business shows.

For years I've been watching as my kids and other youngsters are told by their teachers and their guidance counselors that if they don't go to college, they won't succeed. I didn't go to college, even though my family expected me to go. Frankly, I wouldn't have made it to graduation, and I know I would have hated it. I respect college and the people who go, but for some reason, our society has a hard time accepting that college simply isn't for everyone. I love learning and I haven't stopped learning, but college isn't the only way to learn.

In July 2003, I started a website called BlueCollarandProudofIt.com because I was tired of watching guidance counselors, teachers, parents, and society in general push thousands of kids out of high school and into college, while many of them went kicking and screaming. I've watched as they went off to schools with no direction and no interest. Inevitably they started feeling worse about themselves in college—all while accumulating huge amounts of debt from the loans they took out to pay for their schooling. Consider that the average cost of college in 2008, including room and board, for in-state students at a four-year state institution was $14,203, according to the U.S. Census Bureau. And if you were headed to a private university, the average annual price tag was $38,400. Then, just think, if you drop out, you still owe that money, plus you have to start over and figure out what you want to do. That's a lot of money, especially if you're unsure of why you're borrowing it in the first place.

I want more people to think about the alternatives and realize that you can be proud about going into a trade. A blue-collar career can be a choice that you feel good about as opposed to a fallback option. This is why I started my website: to provide some wisdom and encouragement and to add a different voice to the chorus of people who will tell you what to do with your life. This book persuades you to follow your own personal desires and tells you how to get the education or training *you* need, which might not be the education your parents and teachers are pushing you to get.

I've been amazed at how many people have e-mailed me from all over North America, excited to know that someone is advocating for them. I've heard from teachers who are happy to hear someone say that we should be proud of the kids who choose to make something of themselves in the trades, and I've heard from students who are afraid to tell their parents they don't want to go to college. I've heard from adults who spent years in the white-collar world only to ultimately find their passion in blue-collar work.

Blue-collar work isn't about avoiding the responsibilities that people think come only with white-collar jobs. We blue-collar workers own nice homes and run lucrative businesses. We, too, are looking to be challenged and to exceed our own expectations. We want to excel professionally. But we also love working with our hands or in nontraditional settings. How many people are sitting at a desk right now, tucked away in a cubicle, feeling boxed in and miserable, wishing they could be doing something physical instead?

Blue-collar workers are everywhere, and they are working incredibly hard to build this country, rebuild their communities, and more. We have factory workers operating equipment worth millions of dollars with technical skills that surpass the level of expertise that many people have in white-collar jobs. Why don't we take these tradespeople more seriously? It's about time we respect the skills they've acquired and the trades they are in and the work they do. We've treated many industries as if they are invisible, but we need to start paying attention to the construction industry, to automotive technicians, and to electricians, among scores of others.

I don't have anything against Shakespeare, but you don't need to get a degree in English at a four-year university if you're interested in landscape design. You don't need to be a communications major at a cost of more than $30,000 a year if all you've ever really wanted to do is become a renovation mason. We don't all want to sit in cubicles, pushing paper, working in middle-management jobs, traveling around the country for business meetings. If that's what you want, that's fine. But if you don't want that kind of life, why go to college and prepare for it?

Wall Street jobs sound sexy and being a lawyer is impressive, but what if it's not for you? There are incredible jobs available with amazing potential, challenging opportunities, and great pay. President Barack Obama has laid out a plan to create 2.5 million new jobs by January 2011, largely through rebuilding roads and bridges and refurbishing and modernizing schools across the country. In Los Angeles alone, a recent tax change was approved to fund a $1.2 billion overhaul of the city's deteriorating commuter rail, Metrolink. These are all blue-collar jobs waiting to happen. What's more, the renewable or alternative energy industries are estimating the creation of anywhere from 3 to 10 million new jobs in the next ten years.

Blue-collar workers built the United States, and we continue to build and rebuild it every day. We fix it, move it, and keep it operational twenty-four hours a day, seven days a week. We are the glue that holds the community together, the people you call when your car breaks, your roads are full of potholes, and your faucet is leaking.

We are America's backbone, and we are proud of it.

ACKNOWLEDGMENTS

I am an appreciative and grateful person and have many people to thank for helping me get to this place.

Thank you to Bridget Samburg for telling my story!

I want to thank my dad, who always told me to be aggressive; my son, Anthony, for helping me build my big business and my mother-in-law Sandy O'Brien, a successful law enforcement officer, who told me, "If you don't reach for the stars, you'll never grab one."

Thank you to Helene Taylor, who helped build my website.

Thank you to Tony, who, at my early Alcoholic Anonymous meetings, told me, "Don't drink, no matter what."

Thank you to John and Nick Sorrabella, two crazy, hyperactive elementary school drop-outs, who built a huge business and became millionaires, yelling and screaming and swearing all along the way. You've inspired me.

Thank you to my mentor Sal Balsamo, who always told me, "Joey, every day you get out of bed is a gamble. You might as well go for it."

Thank you to Richard Wright, at RTN Federal Credit Union, who trusted me all the way. To Stan Davis, for believing in me for twenty years. And thank you to Barry Steinberg, who gave me lots of his time and ideas for *Blue Collar and Proud of It* from the beginning.

Thank you Carmen, my sponsor from A.A.

Thank you to my mom for always being there.

Thank you, Rob MacDonald, for being in a lot of my media events.

And most of all, I want to thank my wife, Dawn, for helping me be a better person. Thank you, for my life.

Thank you to John Pouliot for his research and hard work and helping to compile the guide to postsecondary training in apprenticeship.

Chapter 1

Success Outside the Cubicle

Imagine not being able to find a plumber to install your new dishwasher or a car mechanic to fix your broken carburetor. What if there weren't enough welders to repair our nation's crumbling bridges? What if we woke up one day and discovered that we hadn't been training enough people in the younger generation for positions in the automotive, carpentry, manufacturing, or steel industries?

We don't have to imagine any longer. While we're not about to run out of plumbers yet, and while we still have electricians to call and construction workers to hire to build our new skyscrapers, we in the United States are running low on trained, skilled workers. Meanwhile, we're pushing more kids into college, telling them it's the only way to be successful and make a life for themselves. While they are racking

1

up massive college loans, our skilled workforce is suffering. There aren't enough trained welders or linemen or rail conductors, but we have kids in college who are miserable, who never wanted to go, and who ultimately end up dropping out.

What if we rethought the whole equation and encouraged some of these students—especially the ones who simply aren't cut out for four years of college—to go into the blue-collar workforce? What if we told high schoolers in the United States about the possibilities that exist in the blue-collar world, about the money that could be made and the exciting businesses that blue-collar workers own and run?

Baby boomers are retiring fast, and we aren't training enough youth to take over their jobs. We should be teaching students about the trades in high school, if not earlier. We should be opening doors along these other avenues, rather than only showing them the door to college. We should be telling students that unions offer incredible apprenticeships and training programs, not to mention benefits, in almost every skilled trade. By doing so, we'd not only be benefiting society but we'd also be giving hope and motivation to many young people.

The Blue-Collar Route: A Great Time to Start

This is a great time to be thinking about going blue collar. There are 309 million people in the United States right now; that's a lot of houses to build and keep in good repair and a lot of services to provide. The Bureau of Labor Statistics has estimated that between 2004 and 2014 there will be 40 million job openings for workers who are entering the workforce without a bachelor's degree.* This is more than twice the number of jobs for people who will be graduating from four-year colleges and universities.

In Canada, 48 percent of the workforce will be between the ages of forty-five and sixty-four by 2015. Nearly 3.8 million Canadians work in five skilled trade industries, but those who are retiring aren't being adequately replaced. Only 32 percent of students ages thirteen to eighteen say they would consider a career in the skilled trades.

The Canadian Council on Learning has issued reports that signal significant workforce shortages because of the rising age of workers and the shrinking pool of people entering the skilled trades. In 2002, 26 percent of small and medium-size businesses were already facing shortages, according to the Canadian Federation of Independent Businesses. Of those companies surveyed, 64 percent said they are having difficulty finding workers because of a lack of skilled applicants.

The United States and Canada are looking closely at renewable energy options, and at ways to reduce the carbon footprint and improve the environment. Gas-guzzling cars and wasteful consumption are driving all sectors to make serious changes to improve the environment and curb destructive consuming practices. Previously, only environmentalists cared about this issue. Now politicians, private-sector companies,

Statistics provided from 2006-2008 data. Due to economic conditions, these numbers are subject to change.

and all citizens are considering it. All of this talk is already resulting in significant measures, such as building solar and wind power capabilities, that in turn create job opportunities. For the first time since the 1970s, plans are in the works for the construction of various nuclear power plants around the United States—another significant source of blue-collar jobs.

Pipelines that bring water to our homes and schools and businesses all across North America are bursting. They are in desperate need of repair. We have refineries to build and coal to extract from the earth. Green-collar jobs, discussed later in this book, are cropping up everywhere as well, available in almost every industry and all parts of the country. You could be part of this next wave.

As one example of massive workforce shortages in the United States, the American Welding Society says the country could potentially face a shortage of nearly 200,000 skilled welders by 2010. The roads, bridges, and tunnels in the United States are in the worst condition ever. The infrastructure is in disarray, and there aren't enough people to do the necessary repairs. We are headed for a major revolution in terms of alternative energy and increased energy demand, but we don't have the people to build the power plants and erect the wind turbines.

"Everything is geared toward college, and in five to ten years we won't have anyone to fill these jobs," says David Marland, the training coordinator at Local 51, the plumbing and pipefitting union in Providence, Rhode Island. "These skills and trades are for life. You can always make a living." Yet Marland has a hard time even filling his apprenticeships.

These shortages are occurring for many reasons. Clearly we haven't interested enough people in the trades. "The work ethic has changed," says Jim Geisinger, president of the Northwest Forestry Association. "Kids want to sit in front of a computer." Geisinger has watched as the younger generations have left their traditional logging communities in droves. Many have moved to urban areas in search of white-collar work.

"When you talk to manufacturers across the country, the issue of skills shortages is a primary concern for all, no matter what region of Canada they are in," said Perrin Beatty, president and CEO of Canadian Manufacturers and Exporters. The gaps between jobs and the skills of the incoming workforce are being noticed. Canada's government is working to address the problem as well. "The government of Canada recognizes more and more that Canada's growth is dependent upon people entering the skilled trades—from welders and carpenters to hairstylists and chefs," said Diane Finley, minister of Human Resources and Social Development.

"The whole work world has changed dramatically," says Jan Bray, executive director of the Association for Career and Technical Education (ACTE), a national organization that works to improve technical education and better prepare youth for careers in the trades. "Our society doesn't value people who work with their hands." Bray says parents are often guilty of trying to dissuade their own children from going into the trades. "But when parents hear that you need to have a high level of math to be an auto mechanic, their perceptions start to change. You change perceptions with information." People do start to pay attention once you tell them that they need a good brain and sufficient training to do much of the available blue-collar work. Suddenly family members listen more carefully when you talk about the trades. How do we change the perceptions that have tainted almost all of these blue-collar sectors? We need to give people more information.

The entire workforce in the United States has been projected to increase by 12.8 million people between 2006 and 2016, according to the federal government. Total employment is expected to increase by 10 percent in this same time period. Transportation, warehousing, and trucking will grow rapidly, as will jobs in the utilities. Service industries are expected to increase as well. And the occupations that include installation, maintenance, and repair will increase by 9.3 percent.

Repair work is one area of rapid change, as technological advances have become prevalent in every industry. "This isn't about working on cars in your backyard," says auto technician Lori Johnson. "It's a totally different world now." If you lift up the hood of a car, Johnson points out, you're only going to find a few things you can touch and mess around with. Mostly, there are computerized diagnostic tests that must be run, and codes that must be downloaded and later interpreted. And you need training to do all of this.

In the United States, much talk is taking place about nuclear power making a comeback as people turn to it as an alternative and necessary source of energy. Canada has long been more receptive to nuclear power. In the United States, though, the industry is grappling with as much as 35 percent of its workforce retiring within the next five years. The Nuclear Energy Institute predicts needing to hire as many as 25,000 workers in that same time period. And for any new reactors that are built, the institute expects the industry to hire

> " If the traditional career and technical training does go away, the infrastructure of this country would fall apart. You wouldn't have anyone to fix your plumbing or build and repair your home. Who would be the people fixing your electricity? "
>
> —*Janet Bray, president of the Association for Career and Technical Education*

1,400 to 1,800 construction workers, including skilled tradespeople, to complete the projects. Once built, approximately 400 to 700 employees are needed to run one of these plants, at which the median salary for an electrical technician is $67,517 and a reactor operator is $77,782. Those are serious opportunities, and yet people haven't adjusted their expectation of these jobs. They haven't taken the time to learn about them.

"A lot of schoolteachers have no idea what an ironworker does," says Marco Frausto, the president and business agent of Ironworkers Local #416 in Los Angeles. He visits local high schools to talk with students about careers in the trades. "They're more interested once they hear how much you can make." In California, a journeyman is paid $31.83 an hour plus extensive health and pension benefits. Apprentices with a high school diploma and no prior experience start at $15.92 an hour plus benefits, and their wages increase 5 percent every six months. Frausto says once he actually talks about the extensive skills and training needed for welding and the techniques involved, parents are more accepting. "One does not fit all," Frausto reminds students and their parents. What works for one student won't necessarily work for another.

Wake up, Mom and Dad. Look at your child and ask, *What is good for him or her? What is going to make him or her happy and successful?* Don't think, *What college do I want to see my son or daughter in next fall?* That's not going to help. If you push what you want and your child really shouldn't be going to college, you're going to end up with one very unhappy, potentially debt-laden person. Financially, your son or daughter could be saving for his or her first house rather than paying off student loans.

Before the economy became so unpredictable in 2008, U.S. trucking companies were unable to find enough truckers and predicted that by 2014 the industry would be short nearly 110,000 drivers. Because of the increasing cost of fuel (which has slowed the trucking industry), the railroad industry is positively booming. Freight trains are moving more cargo than ever before. In 2002, the major railroads laid off about 4,700 workers. In 2006, they rehired 5,000. In 2008, the rail companies were planning to build an additional $10 billion in tracks. And according to the Transportation Department, freight tonnage is expected to increase by close to 90 percent by 2035. Where am I going with this? All of this activity means more jobs in the transportation sector and a possible shortage of jobs if we don't have well-trained individuals ready to join these industries.

People love to say that nothing is made in America anymore. But more is produced in the United States than ever before, the top-three products being food, computers and electronics, and motor vehicles. As of 2005, the manufacturing industry was producing close to $1.5 trillion in goods, and the United States exported more than $1.023 trillion as compared to the $612.1 billion in goods exported in 1996. That amount has practically doubled in less than ten years. And while the auto industry has suffered tremendously, especially in Michigan, new factories are being built in the southern states. For example, Volkswagen is building a $1 billion manufacturing plant in Chattanooga, Tennessee, which is expected to be operational in 2011.

Did You KNOW? The oil and gas industry in Canada is booming. The demand for crude oil and natural gas has risen steadily over the past twenty years, and most of it is exported. Companies are expanding, and the industry is always in need of new employees.

In Canada, the manufacturing sector employs more than 2.3 million people, or nearly 15 percent of the working population. Combined, the manufacturing, construction, automotive, and mining sectors produce half of Canada's GDP, or more than $550 billion in services. As in the United States, manufacturing and production are traditionally sources of significant employment in Canada.

Manufacturing jobs are changing, though, and many require more interpersonal and technical skills than before. Finding adequately trained and highly skilled employees is becoming increasingly difficult for the industry. Companies are constantly looking for employees who are more skilled and can perform in a more sophisticated work environment. The factories don't resemble those of yesteryear. The dark, dingy, dirty image that many people have in mind is no longer accurate. People can't go directly from high school into most of these jobs. It's a more sophisticated world, and with that comes a more sophisticated manufacturing industry. In a study conducted by the National Association of Manufacturing, 81 percent of companies interviewed said they faced a shortage of workers, and 90 percent said this comes from a lack of available skilled workers.

In 2006, the Ironworkers Union Local #3 in Pittsburgh was having a tough time recruiting new blood. So they launched an ad campaign with the slogan, "We don't go to the office, we build it." The national ironworkers organization has adopted the catchy slogan, and more people are paying attention, says William Ligetti, executive director of the Pittsburgh-based Ironworker Employers Association. The number of applicants to the Pittsburgh apprenticeship went up immediately. While there were once ninety applicants per year, the union now has about 200 applying each quarter. And in turn, Ligetti said, the quality of the new hires has dramatically increased. "This is a good-paying job," adds Ligetti. "You can go out and say, 'Hey, I built that,' and show your children."

Another source of blue-collar jobs will come from America's crumbling infrastructure. According to a 2006 study by the Federal Highway Administration, 24.5 percent of the country's bridges were deemed "structurally deficient" or "functionally obsolete." They were built shortly after World War II by blue-collar workers and were made to last about fifty years, so they're all due for an upgrade. Who is going to do all of this work? These buildings and roads don't grow from seeds. Someone has to physically go out there and build them. Infrastructure experts estimate that $2.2 trillion in work will be needed over the next decade. That's a lot of jobs. The construction of pipelines for natural gas will also create employment opportunities. As well, most cities around the country are facing leaky or corroded waste and water pipes that are in need of repair. Miles of these underground pipes are expected to cost each city several billion dollars to fix or replace.

Even the airlines are adding workers, thanks to the need for upgrading. In the summer of 2008, U.S. Airways hired one hundred mechanics in an effort to boost its performance and on-time record. The mechanics were brought in to troubleshoot, fix broken lights, and replace seats that wouldn't recline. It may sound like a small number of jobs, but it's just another way in which blue-collar America is both indispensable and always in demand.

Did You KNOW? Interestingly, Europeans don't have the same attitude about the trades as do Americans and Canadians. A study published in 2004 revealed that blue-collar workers in the United Kingdom were the happiest of all workplace employees. Hairdressers, plumbers, and chefs topped the list of the professions with the most job satisfaction. "It's a misconception that white-collar professionals have the best jobs and are therefore the happiest," said Chris Humphries, deputy director at City and Guilds, the accrediting group in England that conducted the study. "As our research proves, it's often people in vocational careers that are the most content and fulfilled." We all spend a lot of time at work, sometimes more than we should, so shouldn't we be doing something that makes us happy?

The time has come to stop turning our backs on the blue-collar jobs that have built nations. It's time to pay attention to the desires and skills of each individual, and it's past time that we put pride and value back into being a plumber, a carpenter, or a mason. We as a nation must start respecting each other for how hard we work and how well we do our work rather than by the title we have or the diplomas we hang on our walls. It's time that we as parents, teachers, businesses, and communities wake up, look around, and see the immense benefits gained and contributions made by blue-collar workers.

Did You KNOW? Many teenagers don't realize that some of the jobs in the trades actually require the same kind of hand-eye coordination that is picked up from playing video games. Most heavy equipment operators use joysticklike levers to control their machines. Hand-eye coordination is important when using backhoes and in many construction jobs. Times have changed, and many blue-collar jobs involve highly technical machinery and computers rather than purely manual labor.

Where Did the Problem Start?

A survey done in Canada about workforce readiness and attitudes revealed that 86 percent of students said their guidance counselors had not recommended the skilled trades as an option. Seventy-two percent of those same teens said their parents had not encouraged them to go into the blue-collar trades.

Many guidance counselors are totally overwhelmed by the sheer number of students they are expected to advise. Some are responsible for as many as 600 students and have little time to tailor their advice or suggestions. Plus, one way that high schools measure their own success is by the percentage of students who go on to college after graduation. As a result, counselors almost naturally find themselves pushing college and urging students to at least give it a try. Add to all of that the fact that more community colleges have open enrollment, which means almost anyone can take classes, regardless of what kind of student he or she was in high school. The result? College students are taking remedial courses in basic math and literacy skills. Something is wrong with this situation.

Some counselors admit that they hesitate to suggest anything but college for their students, because they fear the wrath of parents who are determined to see their children enroll in a four-year university. Other counselors are simply so overloaded with work that they don't have time to give personalized advice to each student. A study published by Northwestern University surveyed eighty guidance counselors around the United States and found that most were trained to respond to post–high school plans the same way: by talking about college. The study found that counselors were trained to help better students apply to four-year colleges, but they couldn't help much with students not planning on a four-year degree. Vocational teachers and counselors are simply not being encouraged to help work-bound students plan their careers.

Did You KNOW? Even though money isn't everything, you can earn a lot in the trades. Between 1997 and 2002, real wages for white-collar workers rose 1.5 percent. But the wages of blue-collar workers increased 4.8 percent over the same time period.

This book is about putting pride, excitement, and appeal back into the blue-collar industries. And it's about showing you the many lucrative, creative, challenging, and exciting options that exist in the blue-collar workforce. It's time that we all—parents, counselors, and students—take a strong look at each of the available options. With hard work and determination, anyone can build a successful career and life, even without college. I've done it, and many people around me have done it. Look around your community or your own family, and you'll see that successful blue-collar workers are all around you.

Don't think, though, that not going to college means that your education comes to an end. James Stone III is director of the National Research Center for Career and Technical Education in Kentucky, an

> " People take what used to be a respectable job and disregard it. "
>
> —*Blair Glenn,*
> *California-based arborist*

organization that works to improve career and technical education (CTE) opportunities around the country. CTE is what many of us once referred to as *vo-tech* or *technical school*. Stone's group also works to improve the transition from high school to work. He says that forgoing college is one thing, but postsecondary training is rarely optional. "To compete globally we need smarter workers." And by *smarter* Stone really means *better trained*. But Stone points out that nowadays students aren't always exposed to the trades at an early age. And in some high schools, he says, a retiring woodworking or auto mechanic teacher is likely to be replaced by an English or math teacher. "The only way kids come to know these occupations is through television," says Stone. The time for education about the trades needs to start well before high school graduation day.

My Story

If you're heading off to college because you feel pressured to go or you feel like you'll never make anything of yourself if you don't go, then you've come to the right place. I'm proof that you can, with a lot of hard work, have a very successful and fulfilling career without college.

I've been working as a landscaper for twenty-eight years in Newton, Massachusetts. I didn't go to college. My father went to Northeastern University and wore his class ring proudly every day. He worked as an executive in the finance department of a major company in the Boston area. Growing up, my two sisters and I were expected to do well in school, and college was definitely what happened after high school graduation. But I hated school. I was rebellious. I had trouble focusing and I didn't test well. And then I started to feel stupid because I wasn't keeping up with my friends; really, I wasn't all that interested in doing so. Years later I found out that I actually had attention deficit disorder and some other learning disabilities. Some of us have other problems, such as dyslexia.

Years ago people like us were called brats—kids who couldn't keep still, who were told we were fidgety or had ants in our pants. Over the years I have seen these characteristics in me, my kids, my nephew, and my friends' kids. When you try to shape people like this, as if it's a one-size-fits-all world, you are asking for trouble. As a society we're all asking for trouble when we make this move. You're going to get a reaction if you push everyone to do the same thing. Miserable, frustrated teens, being told they are not good enough, are an unpleasant, trouble-making bunch. I know, because I was one.

I'll admit that I had a bit of a bad attitude. Deep down, though, I knew that I was not a dumb person, but still I felt so lousy about myself. Then the anger started to escalate. It's a terrible cycle. You really worry that you're stupid; at least I did, and I know others who did. But I'm not stupid. I was just bored and frustrated and feeling worthless.

I barely made it out of Watertown High School with a diploma. It didn't help that my friends around me were doing okay, that my sisters were good students, and that my father wanted to know whether I was going to college or not. By ninth grade I knew I wasn't going, and when I finally told my parents my decision, I felt bad about it. But I also knew in my heart that I would be miserable if I went. On top of that, I knew it would cost my parents a ton of money that would just end up being wasted in the end.

My mother and father weren't thrilled with my decision, but they ultimately were supportive. That was 1977. When I graduated from high school, I wasn't quite sure what I wanted to do. I went to work in the Polaroid factory that was close to my hometown. It was monotonous, and I hated punching the clock and staring at the same people and sniffing the same smells every day. I needed more variety and soon landed a job working for Salvuchi Construction Company. I finally felt like I fit in. One of my first projects was helping to build Bentley College in Waltham, Massachusetts, and that's when I saw guys around me who were making great money, had cash to spend, and seemed happy.

I had grown up pretty spoiled, if not just plain lucky. I had everything I wanted, I wasn't used to going without or thinking about whether I had enough cash for dinner. But I had married very early and had a son, and I needed to support him. I wanted to give him what my parents had given me. So I spent about eighteen months working at the construction job and then went to work as a jack-of-all-trades for a local businessman, Sal Balsamo. I won't bore you with all of the details of that job—I did a little bit of everything from maintenance to errands—but I learned a lot from Sal. I didn't learn much about the trades, but I learned about life and about business. He was my first mentor, someone who inspired me to follow my dreams, take risks, and do what I wanted to do. "Every day you get out of bed is a gamble, Joey. You might as well go for it." Sal used to say that to me all the time. Now I've adopted his mantra as my own. I still repeat it a few times a week.

I knew I wanted to go for it, but it took me a while to figure out exactly what I was going after. I soon decided to start my own landscaping business. I didn't have a book to guide me and I didn't have many resources, but I decided I would figure it out as I went along. I started by going around to hair salons in affluent towns around Boston and hanging up fliers advertising my new business. "Will cut grass," my signs read. It was simple, without any fuss. I started to get a few calls.

That's all I needed. It was a start, and in the beginning I was using my old beat-up Toyota and stuffing it with my tools and lawn mower. I kept working for Sal, doing my landscaping jobs after work and on the weekends. It was hard work, but I liked it.

In 1980, when I was just twenty years old, the woman I had married way too early up and left. She wanted to be a model and took off, never to be seen again, leaving me with my son Anthony, who was just twenty-three months old at the time. I adored my son so much I barely let him out of my sight. I wanted to be the best father ever, but we were in a lousy situation. Having just started my business, I wasn't making much money yet. We were living in a small apartment that I named the Bug House since we were sharing our space with a large family of cockroaches.

I was also drinking a lot, which was how I dealt with all of the anger that had been building up over the years. The only reason I'm telling you this is to let you know that you can get through a lot and still come out on top. Even if the cards are stacked against you and it feels like you'll never get ahead, you will. If you are determined and ready to put in more than 100 percent, you can overcome all kinds of obstacles. Even though I had become an alcoholic, I was a highly functioning one, and within a few years, my business was doing really well. I'll get into some of the details later, but basically I had found my passion. I enjoyed working outside. I loved making people's lawns look beautiful, and I started adding additional services and employees to my operation.

Although my mom grew up very poor in Cambridge, Massachusetts, not far from where my father went to college, she, like my dad, had certainly hoped that I would get a degree after high school. I think it was especially hard for my father to realize that his son wasn't going to be the family lawyer or doctor. At first he tried hard through my high school years to push me to get better grades, and then one day he said,

"Joe, I wash my hands. Go ahead. Do what you want. Do what you want to do, but be the best." I was so relieved that he saw that I wasn't cut out for a career like his. But at the same time I still felt like a failure. My father also threw in one other piece of advice. "Be aggressive," he said. It took me a while, but I've built an incredible reputation, a company with fourteen employees, and a booming business because I was determined to be the best I could be. And yes, I was aggressive about it.

I often think about my father saying, "Be the best." That's my advice to anyone who will listen. "Be the best." And that is what *Blue Collar and Proud of It* is all about. Follow your *own* dreams and your *own* passions, and be the best you can possibly be. Life shouldn't be about taking the easy road, nor should it be about doing as little as you can just to get by. This statement applies to absolutely everyone out there, whether you want to be a history teacher or a landscaper, whether you want to go to school to be an architect or go through an apprenticeship to become a welder.

I'll be honest with you. I didn't always give 100 percent. I hit some rough patches after high school, and it took me a few years to figure out that I was going to go into the landscaping business. But now, each morning when I get out of bed, I love knowing that I'm going off to give my customers 100 percent.

My landscaping customers are prominent doctors, lawyers, and professors. Newton, where my business is based, is teeming with Harvard graduates and innovative businesspeople. There are investment bankers and international consultants. They understand that they need a plumber to put in their new bathtub, an auto mechanic who will fix their car, and a landscaper who will make their yard shine. And guess what? I need my chiropractor and my daughter's pediatrician and my tax accountant just as much as they need me.

What Is Best for You?

This book is about finding the right match for you and then tackling it with all that you've got. I knew I could never sit in an office. In my opinion, most people are not cut out to sit at a desk under fluorescent lights all day. Just the thought makes me itchy. A great percentage of us want to work with our hands, get dirty, be outside, be creative, or just fix stuff. We don't learn from a blackboard. Instead, we learn by trying and doing. We have to smell, touch, and feel. We learn the hands-on way, not in a classroom.

Those of us who work in the trades have immense pride. We are amazed by what we contribute to our communities, and we go home feeling that we've made a difference. This country was built by blue-collar workers, and it's going to be rebuilt and built up by blue-collar workers. We're not going away, and the work isn't going away either. You can't take your car to a call center in India to get it fixed, and you can't ship your kitchen sink overseas when it's leaking. Jobs in the building trades here can't be outsourced anywhere. And while many factory jobs are certainly being lost in the economic downturn that's taking place while this book is being written, a great many of the headline-making workforce cuts are taking place among white-collar workers.

Not Your Father's Assembly Line: Blue-Collar Goes High-Tech

Thanks to overwhelming advances in technology, blue-collar work is changing rapidly. Computerized auto body shops, high-tech construction equipment, and advanced lawn irrigation systems are what blue-collar workers are now handling on the job. Much of the work is cutting-edge, and that's why kids and twenty-somethings should feel excited and proud about choosing the blue-collar path.

Mary Stanek Wehrheim is president of Stanek Tool Corporation near Milwaukee, Wisconsin. She often hosts open houses at her company's plant to show parents, teachers, and students what her tool-making operation is all about. The people who work for Stanek are well trained, highly skilled individuals using computers and advanced machinery. As she points out, no one wants to turn over multimillion-dollar equipment to people who earned all Ds in high school and have no training. "Many kids get into the trade after they've floundered for a while," says Stanek. The reason for the floundering is that blue-collar work was not presented initially as an acceptable choice. "After they've left school and gotten confused, parents can be more receptive," to a child's decision to learn a trade, she says. Isn't it a shame we couldn't make these choices available sooner? We should be able to skip over the step that sets up so many people to fail.

Opportunities are everywhere, but training and certification are a key component to success in these fields. As technology has taken off, and largely taken over, you need the skills and the know-how to run many of the machines, diagnostic equipment, and electronics that are involved. This is the new blue-collar world. In your grandparents' generation and even your parents' generation, people could often go straight from high school into many blue-collar jobs. While this move is still possible in some sectors, more likely you will need some type of postsecondary education—an apprenticeship, on-the-job training, or classes in a particular trade. You can't just waltz out of high school and into most of these jobs. In later chapters, we go into much more detail about exactly what type of training you need to land a job in many of these blue-collar fields.

Veronica Rose, one of New York's first female master electricians, now owns her own commercial and industrial electric company. She joined the electrical union back in the late 1970s, much to the surprise of her father, who said she'd never make it. "It's easier to raise a building than it is a family," says this mother of five children. It turns out that three of her kids were college material and two were not.

She sees her own work as something that can be admired. "The world is a better place because of what I've done," says Rose. "I've created something that has brought the United States, the town, the community to another level." And she's not shy when it comes to talking about the money you can make. "It's a better income than some of the college grads will ever attain their lifetime."

Changing Times

If you've been out of high school for a while or have been working for years in the white-collar world, it's never too late to make a change. It's not too late to step out of what you are doing and start something new. That doesn't mean it's not scary or difficult, but you can definitely take the plunge. I know the saying, "You can never teach an old dog new tricks," but when it comes to the trades, it's never too late to learn a new skill. You'll find that the unions are surprisingly open to older workers, and that age can often work to your benefit. Sometimes having years under your belt in the working world signals a really serious person who has put a lot of time and thought into making this transition. This book is going to provide you with ideas, resources, and encouragement.

My mother-in-law, Sandy O'Brien, always says, "If you don't reach for the stars you'll never grab one." You see, hoping to get a star won't do you much good. But being willing to work very hard to get the star you want is what this life is all about. Sandy went from being a crossing guard to a detective on the police force in her Massachusetts town. Such change and success take time and perseverance. If you want to be a master carpenter, it won't happen overnight. It will take hours and years of patience, of trying, of learning, and, yes, of occasionally failing. If you want to own your own plumbing business, you have to spend years building up a reputation and a list of customers. If you want to be a success, you have to be willing to put in the work.

Did You KNOW?

In 1973, more than half of the workers on a factory floor in the United States had not finished high school. By 2001, one-third had training beyond high school.

Have you seen the National Geographic Channel's *Ice Road Trucker*? Or *L.A. Hard Hats*? What about *Deadliest Catch*? I'm hoping that because reality TV is shining a light on blue-collar jobs, more kids will want to go into the trades. Of all things, these reality television shows are capturing the nation's attention and highlighting some of America's most essential careers and hardest-working people.

Deadliest Catch is one of the most exhilarating shows I've seen. I'm always amazed to see the fishermen out in rough water, determined to bring in a boat full of crab or fish, no matter what. You'll actually get to meet one of the captains, Jerry Tilley, later in this book. These shows are bringing the realities of jobs straight into people's living rooms, finally illuminating their importance as well as the training required to do them.

As I've said before, training is a crucial topic in this book and an essential part of success in the trades. Before you can go off and work, you need to know what type of training is needed. Many companies and industries offer apprenticeships. Some are earn-while-you-learn programs, which means you'd be getting paid while going through training. Some are courses offered through a community college or specialized trade school. We talk more about unions in the next chapter, but for now just know that most offer outstanding apprenticeships.

If you're still reading, I'm assuming you're interested in knowing and exploring more. In the next chapter, we talk about what it means to be blue collar and try to help you determine if this path is the right one for you. Then we delve into a host of possibilities and the training required for specific jobs. We look at women in the blue-collar sector and different opportunities available to them, and we also talk about green-collar jobs, found in environmentally friendly and sustainable sectors, that will be responsible for much job growth in this country and represent some of the hottest jobs of the future. We tell you about some of the amazing organizations and programs around the country that are working to put pride back into the blue-collar sector while encouraging men and women to enter the trades. And we introduce some of the neatest people out there, men and women who are passionate about their jobs and proud to be part of the blue-collar workforce.

Stick with me, and I promise to tell you all you've ever wanted to know about getting ahead in this world while finding success outside the cubicle.

Chapter 2

What Is *Blue Collar,* Anyway?

Have you ever stopped to think about the term *blue collar*? To me, *blue collar* means skilled individuals who make the world go around. We're talking about people who are there to fix the plumbing, the leaks, and the wiring when it's broken. These same blue-collar people build skyscrapers, work as freight train conductors, and perform myriad other important jobs. Unfortunately, the term *blue collar* sometimes has a negative connotation, one that makes some people think of a person who didn't work hard enough to get a college education. We need to rethink this attitude.

The actual term *blue collar* came into everyday use in the United States around 1950 and referred to the uniforms traditionally worn in factories and other industrial work sites. You've probably seen the exact clothing I'm talking about: the durable clothes that won't tear easily and can withstand dirt and grime and grease. These blue collars were worn by plumbers, auto technicians, and service people, and while these traditional blue-collar uniforms are not obsolete, you see them a bit less nowadays. Some of you might even recognize this look since it's cropped up as fashionable retro clothing.

But beyond the color of the shirt collar, *blue collar* came to mean a certain type of worker, one who wasn't *white collar*, which basically meant an office worker or someone working in one of the professions. Blue-collar workers were traditionally paid hourly, although that's not always the case now, and many blue-collar workers are union members. *Blue collar* even came to mean a way of life. It has long defined people who don't sit in an office all day, or sit in front of a computer, with the same routine. It means a person who was often outside, in the field, or means in a shop working with his or her hands, fixing something, rebuilding a part, or operating machinery. To me, it means someone who is always looking to keep moving, doing, making, or breaking.

Traditionally, the federal government has classified all workers in the United States according to whether they were white collar, blue collar, or service workers. Chefs, police, and firefighters were grouped together as service workers, for example. But the Bureau of Labor Statistics, which tracks all these nifty jobs and counts the number of workers and the salaries in each industry, recently stopped categorizing jobs according to collar color. Apparently this approach was offending some people. It doesn't offend me, and I hope it doesn't offend you. I've said it before and you will hear me say it again: I am proud to be blue collar. But the fact is that not all jobs fit perfectly into one category anymore.

Maybe you don't even think of yourself as *blue collar*. Perhaps you use the term *tradesperson*. That's fine, too. Whatever label you apply to yourself, the point is that the non-white-collar workforce is a crucial piece of the puzzle. We are the people who like to build, scrape, hammer, carry, dig, and put our hands to use. The idea of sitting at a desk staring at a computer screen sickens us. Thinking about it makes me want to jump out of a window, actually. You see, we don't mind getting dirty, although not all of us will. But none of us are heading off to work in ironed pants and starched shirts, carrying briefcases.

The biggest change—and it's huge—in the blue-collar workforce in the past generation is that you need to be more skilled to land a job and to get ahead than fifteen, twenty, or thirty years ago. Technology is taking over, even in the blue-collar world. Every industry has been affected. Every industry has incorporated technology into its manufacturing, building processes, and overall functioning. Jobs are simply more technical than they used to be. Installing a solar panel requires training, repairing a car often involves intricate and complicated computers, and much construction work is driven by sophisticated machinery.

Did You KNOW? Have you heard the term *green collar*? The term is used to refer to careers that focus on blue-collar jobs in environmentally related careers. Green-collar jobs combine blue-collar work with green industries, and many are in the alternative energy sectors. Organic farming, sustainable fishing, and eco-friendly landscaping are all green-collar jobs. We talk in much more detail about these opportunities in Chapter 5.

In the next chapter, we give you a lot of specifics on what it takes to get started in a blue-collar job. We'll tell you a ton about what skills and disposition you need to go into a variety of jobs, and we'll go through the type of training, or preparation, you need to become successful. While we're hoping this book will put you well on your way to a successful blue-collar career, we can't guide you through every job out there. Instead we've focused on the most popular, the most lucrative, and the ones with the most projected growth. That said, we haven't included in our discussion hundreds of other blue-collar jobs .

But just to get you thinking, the blue-collar jobs I am talking about include—but are in no way limited to—plumber, logger, tool-and-die maker, shipbuilder, carpenter, electrician, forklift operator, truck driver, landscaper, mason, miner, fisher, bus driver, fabricator, auto technician, fence installer, septic builder, carpet installer, trucker, tile setter, railroad conductor, construction worker, truck driver, and air conditioner installer. I could go on for a long time, but I'm sure you get the picture. A lot of jobs are out there, but how do you figure out which one is right for you? How do you know if you are blue collar or are meant to be blue collar, or if you just want a blue-collar job? I can try to help.

I'm sure you've been asked, "So, what do you want to be?" or "What do you want to do with your life?" These questions can be frustrating, and they used to drive me crazy, especially when I was a senior in high school. If you don't know the answer, it's really okay, and even if you think you know, you may end up changing your mind. Answering the question is even harder for those of you in schools that don't offer career and technical education (CTE) classes. Thinking about your future work is tough if you've never had a chance to try auto mechanics, take a woodworking class, or test your skills at landscaping.

"Don't be afraid to jump around at first," says Joe Ross, a sheet metal contractor and owner of Ross Air Systems in Pickering, Ontario. "Try to find a trade that you are happy in." Ross says people who are just starting out in the trades may find that the field they initially started in isn't the one where they are going to settle. "You may have to change some to find what you want." Ross was fortunate that he knew what he wanted to do. He followed his father into the sheet metal industry. He had always worked with tools and cars while growing up, and he knew that he wanted to keep working with his hands.

Ross spent six years working through his apprenticeship and then worked in someone else's business for about seven years before deciding to open his own. He knew the trade well and didn't want to have a boss. At this point, Ross, who is in his early fifties, spends more of his time working with clients, landing business, and doing customer service. It's something he really enjoys. But Ross is one of those skilled trades company owners who is always happy to help out an aspiring tradesperson. He says more youth should go knock on doors, show curiosity, and ask for internships or job shadowing opportunities.

He's right. You can't just expect to waltz out of high school and start making a high salary. You have to earn it and learn the trade and get to the top with hard work. Ross suggests offering to work for free for two weeks. If you want to be a plumber or electrician or are curious about the sheet metal industry, Ross suggests begging for an unpaid job. Prove yourself and demonstrate that you are hungry to learn. The employer has nothing to lose, and you may get a great mini-introduction to a certain trade.

The Role of Unions

Unions are a crucial component of the skilled trade workforce and one of the best ways into the blue-collar industries. There are approximately 15.4 million union members in the United States and about 4.5 million in Canada. Joining a union often means that you will receive, at no cost, industry-specific training, apprenticeships, assistance landing a job, and continuing education. Unions are most well known for advocating on behalf of their members for higher or more equitable wages and benefits. They become your resource for support with contract negotiations and camaraderie among colleagues. Studies show that union workers earn, on average, 28 percent more than nonunion workers, and they are more likely to receive healthcare and pension benefits.

"Most people think of them as a place to get a job," says David Borrus, about unions. He is the business representative for the Pile Drivers Local 56 in Boston. As Borrus explains it, a large amount of his job is "selling knowledge and skills" to contractors looking to hire workers. These skills come from the apprenticeships that Borrus touts as the best aspect of union membership. Membership dues are what pay for the apprenticeship programs, which are in turn free for you. "We have a lot of money," says Borrus, who is a welder and commercial diver. "You can really buy state-of-the-art equipment." The unions are training people to be the cream of the crop, the best possible tradespeople out there. "We put a lot into training our next generation."

Unions are also in a position to know and hire the best tradespeople in the field, so the most skilled workers are typically the ones training the apprentices. "Apprenticeships are the future," says Borrus. For example, Borrus explains that apprentices are usually eased into jobs, with plenty of mentoring and coaching. They are around colleagues who have been in the field for awhile and can offer support. They won't ever be thrown into a job without the proper training. "It's not just a school," says Borrus. "There is a whole system of formal and informal mentoring going on." While trade schools are not necessarily bad places to get an education, they won't provide the mentoring or coaching available through unions. Borrus adds that once you graduate from one of these schools, you are typically on your own when it comes to finding a job.

For years, the unions had a reputation for being an old-boy network and one that was nearly impossible to get into if you didn't know someone who was already a member. "That father-son local has gone by the wayside," says Borrus. "The vast majority of our apprentices don't have a family member in the trades." Marco Frausto, the president and business agent of Ironworkers Local #416 in Los Angeles, agrees. He says the old-school attitudes have largely changed. "Now, it's more open," he says. You don't have to have connections on the inside. But you do need to be professional, demonstrate that you want to work hard, and make a good impression. Plus, the tests required to get into the unions prevent unqualified kids who have connections from gaining automatic membership.

Frausto explains that you don't need experience to apply with a union. Rather, the union is where you get the experience and training you need. "We teach you to be an ironworker," he says of his union. "We can make anybody an ironworker." When asked what skills someone should have before applying, he says that's not the most important factor. As with most unions, you mainly need to be willing to work hard and demonstrate an interest in the work. Borrus admits there are some applicants he tends to weed out. "We're not crazy about cowboy types," he explains.

Frausto, who is thirty-three and joined Local #416 more than thirteen years ago, points out that unions are integral to preserving sustainable wages. "We protect the middle class," he says. "We can't build a rich nation on the backs of poor people." That's where the union steps in. He points out that nonunion workers have to bargain their wages from job to job, whereas there are preset pay scales within unions. "It's a way to protect the worker," he explains, adding that other union benefits include health care and pensions. He also points out that unions are to thank for having created the familiar 9:00 to 5:00, eight-hour workday, which means employees can't be expected to work endless hours. "I love the trade. I love the fellowship. I love the work," says Frausto. "We've built America from coast to coast."

There are currently forty-four thousand electrical apprentices in the United States that are learning through a combined program of on-the-job training and classroom work. The industry expects this number to increase to close to 50,000 in the next several years, said Michael Callanan, the executive director of the National Joint Apprenticeship and Training Committee (NJATC). The NJATC is a joint program run by the Internal Brotherhood of Electrical Workers and the National Electrical Contractors Association. Callanan says participants work eight thousand hours alongside a trained craftsperson and spend classroom time learning theoretical approaches to wiring and electrical codes. "I can't imagine a better scenario." Once the paid training programs end, apprentices have a built-in job network.

"We've suffered under the mantra that if you don't go to college you won't be successful," says Callanan. He says the electrical industry has to work harder to demonstrate the benefits of the trade, from high wages to the specialized skills that it takes to become certified. "We haven't done a good enough job explaining to parents and guidance counselors what the trades are about," he adds. "The skill is something that can never be taken away." Plus, Callanan says that the combination of workforce shortages and the rising costs of college tuition may lead parents to see the trades as a desirable option for their children. Callanan says that throughout all of the blue-collar sectors, unions offer an unparalleled opportunity to learn, to earn, and to launch a career. "This is an opportunity to have a career, not a job," he says.

Success in the Real World

Blacksmithing Became His Passion

Robb Martin knew what he wanted to do with his life as soon as he heard about blacksmithing. As a kid, Martin, who goes by "Thak," was always building things, working with his hands, and he enjoyed creating, drawing, and sculpting. So when he learned about blacksmithing, the original metal craft, he was enthralled. He thought blacksmiths just made shoes for horses and was intrigued to see the many different applications of the trade.

The artistic, creative side of blacksmithing is definitely what appealed most to Martin, who is now forty. By the age of fourteen, Martin says he knew he wasn't going to college. He practically begged for a job at a blacksmith shop in Floradale, Ontario, near where he grew up. He started off by merely sweeping the floors, for minimum wage, and started to learn the craft from the blacksmithing couple who ran the shop.

Martin also became interested in medieval reenactments and took on a character. His is "Thak," and he's been going by that for years. Most of Martin's work in his own blacksmithing shop now includes fantasty or medieval-inspired designs. He does a lot of ornamental work for clients who are looking to create unique pieces for their home.

Martin has been struck by how many people take pride in visiting a local artisan and craftsperson who is creating something that will last hundreds of years. In what Martin calls a "throwaway culture," he sees clients who "want something with quality and personality." That's exactly what he delivers.

Although Martin has done well pursuing the creative side of blacksmithing, he said it's essential for anyone interested in the trade to learn the basics and the fundamentals and go from there. He says it's a wonderful career option for someone who has both a creative side and a willingness to work hard and pay their dues. "You need a good strong work ethic," he adds.

Having grown up on a farm, Martin was used to the hard work, so that was never a problem for him as he was learning the blacksmithing trade. There aren't many blacksmithing courses in North America—in fact, Martin teaches one of them—but someone willing to do research can find a few in Canada and the United States.

It's the primal, back-to-basics elements of blacksmithing that most appeal to Martin. That, plus the creativity and the fact that he couldn't be happier. "With some raw muscle power and some passion, you can create some amazing things."

The Service Sector

I mentioned earlier that the government stopped classifying jobs as *white collar* and *blue collar*. But the classification *service sector* still largely applies to jobs such as law enforcement, firefighters, chefs, and nurses. Cops and firefighters have historically been considered blue collar, and quite literally police officers typically wear dark-blue-collared shirts as part of their uniform. But over the past decade or so, law enforcement jobs have become extremely sophisticated as security concerns and needs have intensified. Training is rigorous, and college degrees are often required to join a police department. Many police officers continue their education to get a master's or additional training in criminal justice, terrorism prevention, or other specialties. Firefighters also face rigorous testing processes, and more and more departments are requiring college degrees. The same goes for chefs, many of whom graduate from culinary school. Some attend these culinary institutes after earning a four-year college degree.

Frankly, there are a ton of guides and resources available to anyone interested in pursuing a career as a police officer, firefighter, chef, or nurse. Therefore, we aren't going to tackle these in this book, but I did want to mention them since many people have historically thought of these jobs as blue collar. These are all incredible jobs, but if you want to go into one of these fields you won't have trouble finding much in the way of guidance, books, and support.

It's Never Too Late

I've met a lot of people who thought they had figured out a career for life in the white-collar world only to discover years into whatever they were doing that they wanted a change. Going from the white-collar world to a blue-collar job is certainly a major adjustment, but for many of the people we talked to, it's the best thing they've ever done. And really, it's never too late to start something new.

Robson Tyrer made a seemingly drastic leap when he went from professor to plumber in 1976. He was fed up with academia, didn't see a stable professional future, and decided to try his hand at something else. He wasn't even particularly mechanical. He had graduated from Princeton eleven years earlier where he majored in history. The son of physicians, Tyrer calls his move a "radical departure"; he decided to trade in the world of professorships (he was teaching Mexican history at San Francisco State at the time) for that of plumbing. "I left the academic world without any serious regrets," says the sixty-five-year-old ex-academic.

"Plumbing was entirely by accident," explains Tyrer, an Oakland, California, resident who spent seven years in a three-man plumbing partnership. He started tagging along with a self-taught friend and then the rest fell into place. Twenty-five years ago he started his own business, Mallard Plumbing, and now has eight employees who work with him. "As a plumber you are relating to people about issues that matter to them," he says. Tyrer found that while academia was incredibly interesting, there was no immediate relevancy.

But with plumbing, Tyrer says, "You are providing a very important service and one that is often linked to a real, time-sensitive need. These are bread-and-butter issues." During the 1970s, Tyrer says there were many people in the Bay Area leaving academic life to go into the trades, so having a plumber or an electrician with a Ph.D. wasn't as much of a shock as it might be in other parts of the country. Plus, the business has been lucrative. "Plumbing has been good to me," he adds. "I would never discourage anyone from going into the trades," says Tyrer, whose own son is a plumbing contractor in Denver.

Success in the Real World

When Older Is Better

Veronica Rose has been fibbing about her age for a long time. Unlike most people she tends to say she's older, not younger, than she actually is. This master electrician from Long Island, New York, is forty-eight but for years has been saying she's fifty. And when she was in her midtwenties she called herself a thirty-something. Rose knows that's not the norm, especially in white-collar America where age sometimes means you'll be edged out by a young, flashy new hire. "In the trades, it's different. Wisdom and age are valued," she says. "Age commands respect because of the wisdom and acquired knowledge."

Glenda Campbell was fifty-five when she decided to leave her job in the drafting department of a large company to become a truck driver. She had been working at the same place for twelve years, but when the company was bought out she lost her position. It's a familiar story. She could have gone looking for a similar job in a similar cubicle, but really she thought it was a good opportunity for a change.

Her twenty-one-year-old daughter had always wanted to go into trucking, so Campbell thought about it and decided she would give it a try as well. The two women went to trucking school together, which included a five-week training program that combined in-class and on-the-road preparation. They send an experienced trucker and trainer out with you for a few weeks, and then you're on your own. (Turns out with a young baby at home Campbell's daughter didn't want to stick with it.)

"I always liked driving, and I needed to do something to make money," says this grandmother and great-grandmother. "I enjoy it," she says. "Most truck drivers like the freedom. You don't have someone hanging over your shoulder." Divorced with no young children at home, Campbell, who is now fifty-nine, leaves her home in Florida for about two weeks at a time and then she has several days at home before setting out again. She's been driving for Schneider National for about five years, and she doesn't miss the office at all. On the road, Campbell gets to see a bit of the country, and if she's stopped long enough she takes time to do some exploring. Thanks to her long gray hair, Campbell says most of the male truckers she encounters just assume that she's a long-time driver and never give her grief for being a female.

Finding What Is Right for You

Just because you're interested in blue-collar work doesn't mean that every blue-collar job is the one for you. You have to figure out what is right for you, not for your mom, not for your dad, and not for your teacher or guidance counselor.

In the next chapter, we get more specific about different professions—what it means to become a logger, welder, landscaper, construction worker, and more. We'll walk you through what work you do in each of these industries and others. But before we get there, this next section is meant to help you identify your own traits or characteristics, likes or dislikes, that may be either well matched with certain jobs or surefire signs to stay away from others.

While reading through the next few pages, I recommend that you get out some paper and a pen. Write down what you like to do. What puts you in a good mood? What are you willing to work hard at doing? What are you good at doing? What is your strongest skill? These are questions that may help you start to formulate the preferences you have about jobs. Did you have a summer job that you hated? Why? What was it that didn't work for you? Maybe you are working part time, on the weekends right now, and really enjoying the work. Jot down what it is exactly that you like. The people? The money? The job sites? The skills you need to do the work? What appeals to you may not appeal to someone else, and what I like to do may be the last thing you'd enjoy doing for a job.

Here are some questions to get you thinking:

Do you like to be outside?	❏ Yes	❏ No
Do you mind getting dirty?	❏ Yes	❏ No
Do you enjoy interacting with people?	❏ Yes	❏ No
Are you creative?	❏ Yes	❏ No
Do you get seasick?	❏ Yes	❏ No
Do you prefer to follow plans and instructions, or do you prefer to work more freely?	❏ Yes	❏ No
Are you willing to move to a different part of the country?	❏ Yes	❏ No
Do you mind seasonal climate changes?	❏ Yes	❏ No
Do you prefer to work with machines rather than in the dirt or do you enjoy getting your hands dirty?	❏ Yes	❏ No
Are heavy machines something you'd enjoy using?		
Do you prefer to use your hands and muscles rather than rely on machines?	❏ Yes	❏ No
Do you prefer a combination of machine-assisted and manual work?	❏ Yes	❏ No
Do you have a fear of heights?	❏ Yes	❏ No
Do very high temperatures make you nervous?	❏ Yes	❏ No
Do you enjoy using tools?	❏ Yes	❏ No
Do you like to work alone as opposed to being on a team?	❏ Yes	❏ No
Do you mind being away from home for long periods of time?	❏ Yes	❏ No
Do you have to actually be active, as opposed to sitting long periods of time, behind the wheel of a truck, perhaps?	❏ Yes	❏ No
Do you have any physical limitations?	❏ Yes	❏ No

Some of these questions might sound strange to you, but there is a reason for my asking each one. It's really important that you plan and think ahead. You can't just decide you want to be a fisherman if you've never been on a boat or if you get seasick each time you go out. If you hate heights, you may not make the best painter and certainly you'd have to rethink welding on skyscrapers, but that doesn't mean you'd have to forgo welding altogether. If you don't like to be dirty and you don't mind being away from home for long stretches, truck driving could be a great thing for you. If you love math and are anal about measurements and enjoy working with your hands, carpentry could be a possibility for you. Do you love doing physical work? There is plenty of it out there, including logging, construction, and landscaping. Do you prefer to work alone or with a few people in a quieter environment and you love tinkering with wires? Ever thought about being a residential electrician? Do you see why I'm asking you all of these questions?

If you know that you'd hate being behind a desk every day, all day, and if you know that you'd like to be outside working or have a job that requires being physical, you've come to the right place. Do you like to get your hands into something? Do you enjoy the feeling of gripping tools and using them to make things? Just the way some people get a high from running (I don't), others get a high from working outside and sweating as part of their job (I do).

And while it is important to plan and it is important to give all that you've got to whatever you choose to do, you don't have to commit to it for life. If you think you want to be a mason now, it's okay if you end up deciding it's not for you at some point down the road. Many of these jobs have overlapping skills and sensibilities. If you decide to go into construction, you may stick with it for your whole life, or maybe you'll find a specific skill that you're excited to master. The next thing you know you could be working toward mastering carpentry or operating heavy machinery.

Hopefully you have a technical or vocational program at your school or nearby. Maybe you've taken an automotive class or a woodworking course, but many of you won't have had that opportunity. I've always called this *shop* and *vo-tech*, but now it's referred to as *career and technical education*, or *CTE*. In many school districts, those are some of the first programs to go when budgets are cut. In some areas of the country, the CTE courses are being reinstated in full force, specialized technical high schools are opening, and teens are getting the chance to experience these trades like never before. If you have had some vocational training in your school, you may be able to answer some of these questions easily. Have you enjoyed your woodworking courses? Metalsmith classes?

Unfortunately, not everyone is offered the opportunity to take CTE courses, and if you're one of those people who hasn't been exposed to the trades, you'll have to work extra hard to figure out what you want to do. I suggest finding a summer job or part-time job on the weekends with a local contractor in a field that interests you. If you can't test the waters in high school, you'll have to test them on your own. Some of you have to start from the beginning and figure out what it is you like and don't like. If you haven't had CTE courses or opportunities at the high school level, you may really be left wondering how you can possibly know if this is the path for you. I suggest getting out there and getting a job, an internship, or an apprenticeship. Knock on doors, make phone calls, and show that you are interested and hardworking. If you really love to tinker with your own car and have always wanted to be an auto mechanic, then go to your local dealership and ask if there are any part-time, weekend jobs available. Maybe you'll hate it, and maybe you'll find that you love it.

If you are a mom or dad, aunt or uncle, teacher or guidance counselor, you may be wondering how to tell if your son, daughter, or student is destined for the blue-collar workforce. Sure, they may have told you that they think they are, but maybe they haven't even figured that part out yet. There are no hard-and-fast rules about what makes someone cut out for a blue-collar job. I've spent a long time thinking about the traits that many of us blue-collar workers share in common. Maybe you've noticed these in your niece or seen some of these signs in your son. This isn't based on a scientific study, but I can tell you that the following are traits I've found in most blue-collar workers: we're very active, we like to fix and build things, we're creative, some of us have attention deficit disorder (ADD), we can be stubborn, some of us are fearless, and we can be risk takers. We act out and get very agitated in school, some of us act out at our teachers. Does your kid have what I call the blue-collar personality? It's just something to consider.

When I was in high school, I took shop and woodworking. I started to develop this blue-collar personality in my early teens. I liked shop. I liked it better than English class, which I could just never get into. When I started working for a construction company after high school, I realized just how much I enjoyed being outside. I had an easier time focusing than I did when I was at a desk, and I enjoyed the physical work. Other than some seasonal allergies, which I eventually outgrew, it was great to spend my summer days in the grass. During the winter I was shoveling sidewalks and plowing. I enjoyed that I was always moving around. I have a hard time sitting still and needed the variety. I liked meeting different clients and knowing that each job offered its own challenges.

I knew that I wanted to be outside. I knew that I couldn't be in a factory. Some people can. The idea of building something and completing one piece of the puzzle on a factory floor is very rewarding. But for me, I needed to be outside and I needed to be moving around a lot. It's hard for me to sit still and it's hard for me to stand in one place or focus on one thing. I know welders need to have total concentration, honing in on what they're doing without moving, lest they get burned, or fall or lose their place. But with landscaping I am always on the move, whether driving between jobs or out of my truck racing around yards, always with different equipment. This suits me. I love it. But it's not for everyone. That's just the point. Not everyone is cut out to eat the same things, to listen to the same music, or to do the same jobs.

Chapter 3

Show Me My Options!
The A-Z Guide to Becoming a . . .

N ow that you're thinking about your own skills and passions, I want to introduce you to what I think are some of the most interesting and challenging jobs out there. This chapter is designed to help you better understand how you can go about getting your blue-collar credentials. We'll first walk you through what each of these blue-collar jobs or industries entail, while trying to give you the nitty-gritty on what it means to be a carpenter or trucker, for example. We'll tell you what kind of training you need for these jobs and what the job market is expected to look like between now and 2016. We'll also give you a sense of how much money you can make. This is by no means a list of every single job out there, but what you'll find below is a list of twenty of the more popular, interesting, or, simply put, higher-paying blue-collar careers.

We'll answer some commonly asked questions about these trades: What is required to get these jobs? How do I get trained? Where do I start? How much can I make? We have not listed every job since there are just so many—from painter, electrician, landscaper, logger, and fabricator to heavy equipment operator, mason, cement layer, miner, and trucker. The list is nearly endless. I encourage you to use the Internet as a research tool. If you're interested in an industry, poke around online and check out some of the blogs and industry association websites for more. A wealth of information is out there. I hope you will do your own research as well, especially if you don't find anything below that appeals to you, but we're definitely going to get you started.

A lot of our information, facts, and figures come from the U.S. Bureau of Labor Statistics (BLS). They have a comprehensive list of job descriptions, training requirements, and even salary scales for every type of job registered by the Bureau of Labor. We relied heavily on the BLS's Occupational Handbook to help guide you through some of the opportunities that are available. You can access much of this information from www.bls.gov and while I haven't attributed every section to BLS, we use this resource to get many of the basics and most of the data.

As you go through this chapter and read about the various opportunities out there, think back to the last chapter and to all of the questions you answered about your own skills and personal preferences. I guarantee some of your traits will match up with what is required of the jobs in this chapter. Be on the lookout for things that interest you, appeal to you, or even totally turn you off as you read through this material. After all, narrowing down your list of options can be a good thing, too.

You'll see from what you're about to read that most—although not all—of these jobs do require postsecondary training or apprenticeships, and some of the industries that don't require it will highly recommend it. It's a way to get ahead, to become better prepared, and to join the group of skilled workers who are at an advantage when looking for a job. For many entry-level jobs, such as construction laborers, you really don't need any additional schooling, but you do need a willingness to work hard and a desire to learn. You may find a few months or years down the road that you want to work at a more advanced job. You may want to have a specialty or advance as far as you can in one of the trades. An entry-level job is an excellent way to get a front-row seat so that you can experience the many different options out there. But you can't stay in that first job forever, so keep that in mind.

I've said this before, but to find success and ultimately fulfillment, you need to go out there and be the best you can be. The best isn't going to mean staying in the same position for your whole life. Challenge yourself, develop more skills, become more valuable to your employer, and invest in yourself. If you do, you will be investing in your future. I encourage you to think about your short-term plan and long-term goals. Many of these entry-level positions are outstanding places to be in the short term; they provide an opportunity to test the waters, to learn, and to earn money. But don't get stuck in the same position forever. Do start thinking about where each of these positions can take you in the long run.

The only piece that's missing from this chapter is a list of the postsecondary programs, apprenticeships, and schools that will offer the training you need in each of these industries. We haven't forgotten that. We've included all of this information (really a gigantic list) in Chapter 11. Everything is organized alphabetically by industry and then alphabetically again by state. We haven't included every single industry, and we haven't included every single program or school or apprenticeship, but again, we wanted to help you get started. You'll find programs for the twenty-one industries listed below, and you'll have a great start on thinking about what you need for your own blue-collar credentials.

Success takes time, dedication, and patience. You have to work your way into a field or skill. Becoming a water treatment plant supervisor does not happen overnight. You need to learn the ropes and understand how all of the systems work, and you have to have experience managing an emergency, such as a burst pipeline, before you can be the one in charge. If your dream job is running a large landscaping business, you have to start at the bottom. That's what I did. For many years it was just me and a car full of equipment. Along the way, I learned and I made some mistakes, and each year I understood my customers, my trade, and my skills better.

In this chapter, you will also meet some other individuals who have successful careers in these trades. Some fell into their jobs by accident, others planned their path from early on, and all are passionate about what they do. They are hardworking as well as dedicated to helping others, like you, find their way. Many of them felt stupid in school or had a hard time telling their families that they wanted to go blue collar. All of them, though, have exciting, fulfilling careers, and none of them regret the decision to follow their passion. Be sure to read about these folks along the way.

Remember, this book is not about how to be the average you; it's about how to be the best you. It is about being the best you can possibly be. I would challenge you to look at the median salaries as a starting point, not an ending point. We can all do a little to get by, but it takes someone special to do a lot, to go over the top, to be the best at what they are doing. If you're taking the time to figure out what you want to do, what makes you tick, what gets you excited, and what you're willing to get out of bed for in the morning, then make sure you're prepared to give it 150 percent.

I hope you're starting to feel inspired to climb to the top of an industry, a company, or a skill level.

Success in the Real World

You Can't Join a Baseball Team

Craig Copeland enjoys his job, but he says the sporadic hours prevent him from joining a baseball team. A salary close to $100,000 makes it well worth the sacrifice. Copeland has worked as a bed truck operator, moving drilling rigs, and is now a dispatch operator for DC Energy Services in Crossfield, Alberta. He used to go to and from drilling sites around Alberta that required equipment deliveries or removal. "This is not a 9-to-5 job," says Copeland, explaining that an entire operation could be held up while waiting for one of his trucks to arrive.

Precision is everything in this job, says Copeland, who explains that the sometimes-eighty-thousand-pound equipment must be loaded within an inch of specification to ensure proper and safe hauling. "You feel good when you get it right." Copeland always enjoyed driving the huge rigs and appreciated the challenge in driving across rugged terrain. He says he wouldn't have enjoyed the long-haul trucking and endless open roads. He's always liked that his job didn't involve sitting in front of a computer all day, though it can involve physical labor.

Copeland says that recent workforce shortages have driven down the expertise of operators, something that he finds disappointing. He says people are promoted fairly quickly in this industry now, which is good for people getting into it, but Copeland would like to see more training. Copeland was trained by his employer and says that's the way people typically learn the industry.

Some days I wish I could try all of the jobs we talk about in this chapter. And with the way things are changing in the American workforce, I am envious of all of you who are thinking about one of these careers. This country needs enthusiastic, hardworking, trained people, and it is an exciting time to be going into the blue-collar world of work.

AUTOMOTIVE TECHNICIAN

Gone are the days of the grease monkeys who were able to tinker under the hood of a car without any training or certification. As technology has advanced, so, too, have the cars and their many moving parts. Being able to master these changes as well as stay on top of the hybrids, electric cars, and alternative-fuel sources for cars (ever heard of running a car on cooking oil?) will help you in the long run. Who knows where all of these changes will lead the industry ultimately, but one thing is for sure: things are changing rapidly, and technicians must be prepared to keep up. The more training you have in alternative cars, the better your chances for success in the future.

Not only are many car manufacturers complete sticklers for how well their mechanics are trained, some prefer to train their employees themselves. Most of the major car manufacturers, such as BMW, Ford, and Toyota, have outstanding training programs that provide specific manufacturing certification and paid positions after program completion.

⟩ The Work

As you may know, cars now roll out of the factory with their own computers onboard, which means more parts to break, but really, different parts that need servicing. In other words, this is not your grand-father's automobile. From the dashboard to the computerized antilock brake systems, there are dozens of electrical and technical components. They positively confuse me. But for a technician they open a whole new world of automotive repair. Diagnostics, computers, and troubleshooting are all key to this industry.

Technicians inspect, maintain, and repair automobiles. The increased sophistication of automobiles requires workers who can use computerized shop equipment and electronic components and still maneuver around a car's engine with basic hand tools. Automotive service technicians must be able to adapt to the constantly changing technology, and they must be detail oriented and precise in their calculations and diagnostic skills. Small parts and tiny errors can create massive problems. Technicians use a variety of tools from pneumatic wrenches to flame-cutting equipment, necessary to remove exhaust systems. High-tech tools are needed to fix the computer equipment that operates everything from the engine to the brakes and transmission.

Having physical science and math classes under your belt is considered a good thing. If you are interested in the green aspect of the automotive industry, hybrid cars add a whole other dimension to the work. Being able to service a variety of cars such as diesel, hybrids, and even electric ones will be seen as a benefit. In the next decade, technicians will need to be familiar with alternative-fuel vehicles; their job security will improve as their skills become more advanced.

Ⅲ➡ Work Setting

Generally, service technicians work indoors in repair shops; however, some shops can be drafty and noisy. Some technicians work outside or at least in bays that open to the outdoors. Although many problems can be fixed with simple computerized adjustments, technicians still frequently work with dirty, greasy parts, and in awkward positions.

⇒ Training and Certification

Most employers view vocational training programs in automotive service technology as the best preparation for trainee positions. High school programs are a great way to start training or to test the waters to see if this is something you have a knack for and enjoy. But these days, high school programs alone are not enough, and most employers require additional training. The highly regarded Automotive Youth Educational Systems (AYES) is a partnership between high school automotive repair programs and the automotive manufacturers' dealers. Students who complete these programs are prepared to take on entry-level technician positions or to go on to advanced technical education courses. Generally, courses in automotive repair, electronics, physics, chemistry, English, computers, and mathematics provide a good educational background for a career as an auto technician.

Postsecondary training programs in this industry usually provide intensive career preparation through a combination of classroom instruction and hands-on practice. Some trade and technical school programs provide concentrated training for six months to a year. Community college programs usually award a certificate or an associate's degree. Various automobile manufacturers and participating franchised dealers also sponsor two-year associate's degree programs across the country. Students in these programs typically spend two to three months at a time attending classes and then work in the service departments of participating dealers.

Blue Collar in ACTION
A New Generation of Auto Technicians

"Most kids don't grow up working on their own cars," says Vince Williams, who is a training and development specialist with General Motors. Auto mechanic wannabes must have more skills than ever before, and the ones whom Williams is looking for may seem surprising at first. He says he wants apprentices who have good reasoning and problem-solving skills. "I'm looking for a high-level thinker," he adds.

Williams works with GM's Automotive Service Educational Program (ASEP), which is a partnership between dealers, schools, and students. ASEP participants alternate between classes and hands-on technician work. Upon completion of the program, graduates are placed with dealerships. Williams says students can learn the technical and mechanical aspects of the job all through ASEP. But he's especially interested in recruiting students who have an innate sense of how to problem solve. "The more successful people, they get a hold of a problem and follow it through to solve that problem," says Williams. "You have to have that conquer attitude."

The ASEP program has a partnership with sixty-four schools around the country and graduates approximately 800 students each year. The cost to enroll is about $5,000 when all is said and done, but Williams points out that this is a small and beneficial investment considering earning potential following graduation. Because successful participants are placed with dealerships, jobs are close to guaranteed. And Williams says he knows of graduates who are making more than $70,000 after just a few years on the job. "You can make a really good living," he says.

As car technology has progressed, so have the training tools. GM now offers some of its coursework and training through iPods, the Internet, and other media. Williams says another benefit to the ASEP training is that it provides graduates with a portable skill. "No matter where you go in the country, there is a need for auto mechanics."

The National Institute for Automotive Service Excellence (ASE) has become a standard credential for automotive service technicians, and a certificate is important for those wishing to pursue a career in this field. While not mandatory for work in automotive service, certification is common for all non-entry-level technicians in most areas of the country. You can check with a local service center to find out more about what is expected in your area. Certification is granted in eight different areas of automotive service including electrical systems, engine repair, brake systems, suspension and steering, and heating and air conditioning. To become a Master Automobile Technician, you must be certified in all eight areas. This master certificate is worth considering for future growth. As with most occupations, the more you know and the more you've mastered, the more valuable and employable you become.

Employers increasingly send experienced automotive service technicians to manufacturer training centers to learn to repair newer car models or to receive special training in the repair of specific components, such as electronics, fuel injection, or air conditioners.

⯈ The Numbers

Automotive technicians and mechanics held about 773,000 jobs in 2006, according to the Bureau of Labor Statistics. Jobs are expected to increase by 14 percent between 2006 and 2016, which means an

additional 110,0(

was $16.24, with 1

per hour. Technic

mission based on

bers tend to have

counterparts.

CARPENTR

Many of you ha\

House and the pres

made carpentry and remodeling accessible to everyone, and while many of us are capable of building a small deck or making repairs around the house, a professional carpenter is a master with measurements, wood types, design, and construction.

Being a carpenter involves everything from framing a house to hand-crafting furniture and building bridges. Building something gives you an amazing feeling, and carpenters have job satisfaction in small and large proportions depending on their project. While people might specialize in industrial or residential carpentry, the neatest thing is that the job is always different. It does require a high level of patience, math skills, the ability to do precise calculations, and a willingness to work in a variety of settings on a variety of projects.

⇒ The Work

Each carpentry task is somewhat different, but most involve basic steps, such as working from blueprints while laying out, marking, and arranging material. Carpenters cut and shape wood, fiberglass, or drywall

using hand and power tools. Som
while others have a specialty.
of carpentry skills is mos
mercial projects are
ing, sewer projec
All carpen
to be su
coor

carpenters are skilled at multiple tasks
or those remodeling homes, a broad range
useful. Carpenters who work on larger com-
ore likely to have a specialty, such as tunnel brac-
, or finish work.

ers must work in accordance with local building codes, and
cessful you should have manual dexterity, excellent hand-eye
ination, a good sense of balance, and the desire to be in a physically
emanding job. The ability to solve arithmetic problems quickly and
accurately is also necessary. The bottom line is that you've got to love to
build and love what it takes to build.

ⅢⅢ➤ Work Setting

As is true of other building trades, carpentry can be strenuous. Pro-
longed standing, climbing, bending, and kneeling are just part of the gig.
Carpenters do risk injury working with sharp or rough materials, as well
as tools and power equipment, but safety precautions can prevent most
injuries. Outdoor carpentry means being in freezing temperatures some
months and sweltering heat at other times of the year.

ⅢⅢ➤ Training and Certification

Carpenters learn their trade through formal and informal training
programs. Typically, three to four years of on-the-job training and classroom instruction are needed to become a skilled carpenter. A number of
ways to train are available, including job shadowing, but a more formal
training program often improves job prospects.

You can really start your carpentry training in high school. Classes in
English, algebra, geometry, physics, mechanical drawing, blueprint read-

ing, and general shop prepare students for the trade. After high school, some people get a job as a carpenter's helper, assisting someone who is more experienced. While working as a helper you can simultaneously attend a trade school or community college to receive more formal training. Some employers offer employees formal apprenticeships, which combine on-the-job training with related classroom instruction.

On the job, apprentices learn elementary structural design and become familiar with common carpentry jobs, framing, and finish work. They also learn to use the tools, machines, equipment, and materials of the trade. In the classroom, apprentices learn safety, blueprint reading, freehand sketching, and various carpentry techniques. Both in the classroom and on the job, they learn the relationship between carpentry and the other building trades. Carpenters work closely with other building tradespeople, and while it's not necessary to have their skills, understanding how aspects such as carpentry, electrical work, and plumbing come together to complete a project is helpful.

⫸ The Numbers

Carpentry is the largest sector of the building trades, and in 2006 there were 1.5 million carpenters employed around the country. About 32 percent worked in the construction of buildings, and the same percentage was self-employed. Employment is expected to increase by 10 percent by 2016, which means another 150,000 jobs. The increase is expected largely based on the crumbling infrastructure in the United States and the need for new bridges, roads, and tunnels. Some jobs are expected to become available because of retiring workers.

CONSTRUCTION: HEAVY EQUIPMENT TECHNICIANS AND MECHANICS

Working construction is one of the most physically demanding things you can do. It's about hard hats and hard work. (And you wondered if people would think you were a slacker?) But thanks to modern equipment and machinery that does the heavy lifting for you, there are plenty of opportunities for those of us who aren't looking to haul hundreds of pounds at once.

Have you seen the television show *L.A. Hard Hats*? I can't get enough of it. On the National Geographic Channel it chronicles the construction of major metropolitan area buildings. It's so cool to watch these buildings get put together, particularly when you see that it all starts from nothing. We'll give you a sense of two different categories of construction workers, although there are indeed more. First we look at heavy vehicle and equipment technicians and mechanics. The next section addresses laborers.

⯈ The Work

Heavy vehicles are essential to many industrial projects, from construction to railroads. Various types of equipment move materials, till land, lift beams, and dig earth to pave the way for development and production. Heavy equipment technicians and mechanics repair and maintain these pieces of equipment. They work on engines, hydraulic systems, transmissions, and electrical systems. Farm machinery, cranes, bulldozers, and railcars are also considered heavy equipment and require specialized technicians and operators.

Technicians have to be able to run diagnostic tests on the computer components of these machines and discern what is broken and how it should be repaired. Handheld tools are used in repairs, as are computers. Advances in technology mean that computers are responsible for operating at least some components of the machines, so technicians must have a thorough knowledge of codes and the skills to fix electrical malfunctions, as well as be able to use standard hand tools, grinding machines, flame-cutting equipment, and more. It is common for technicians in large shops to specialize in one or two types of repair, such as engines, transmission work, electrical systems, or suspension systems. Technicians in smaller operations typically perform multiple functions. Technicians may also specialize in types of equipment, focusing only on bulldozers, cranes, or excavators, for example.

Work Setting

Repair work on heavy vehicles is often done indoors, and service technicians are usually required to lift heavy (and sometimes greasy) parts and tools. Minor cuts, burns, and bruises are common, but serious accidents are typically avoided thanks to safety regulations. Technicians usually work in well-lit, ventilated areas, and many employers provide shower facilities and locker rooms when necessary. Technicians tend to find the most jobs working for large construction companies, equipment wholesalers, or government entities.

Training and Certification

Although industry experts recommend a formal diesel or heavy equipment mechanic training program after high school, many people receive training on the job. Employers tend to look for people with mechanical aptitude who are knowledgeable about engines, electrical systems, computers, and hydraulics. High school courses in automobile repair, physics, chemistry, and mathematics provide a great foundation for getting into this line of work. When it comes to education, those who have formal postsecondary training in heavy vehicle and mobile equipment have a major advantage over those who do not.

Many employers will send their technicians to training sessions run by heavy equipment manufacturers, which often provide intensive instruction on a specific type of machinery. Industry certification can help workers advance faster. Certification from the National Institute for Automotive Service Excellence (ASE) is the recognized industry credential for heavy vehicle and mobile equipment service technicians. Certification is available for what is called master of medium or heavy truck technicians as well as in repair specialties such as brakes, electrical systems, or suspension and steering. Technicians must pass a written examination and have at least two years of experience to earn this certification.

⁞⁞➡ The Numbers

Heavy vehicle technicians and mechanics held about 188,000 jobs in 2006. Approximately 131,000 of those were mobile heavy equipment mechanics, 31,000 were farm equipment mechanics, and 27,000 were railcar repairers. According to the Bureau of Labor Statistics, employment in this area is expected to grow by about 10 percent through 2016 with the addition of more than 35,000 jobs.

Median hourly earnings for mobile heavy equipment mechanics were $19.44 in May 2006. The lowest 10 percent earned less than $12.64 and the highest 10 percent earned more than $28.18. About 23 percent of people in this industry are union members.

CONSTRUCTION: LABORER

⟹ The Work

When it comes to working at a construction site, most laborers learn on the job, but formal apprenticeship programs do exist and can provide the most thorough preparation. Laborers who have specialized skills or are willing to relocate close to new construction projects will have an advantage over other applicants. As a laborer, there is almost always room to advance and become more specialized, assuming you are a hard worker. Starting off in one job does not mean you'll be doing the same thing in five years or even five months.

Construction laborers can be found on almost all construction sites performing a wide range of tasks from the very easy to the potentially hazardous. These men and women make the small jobs happen so that the big projects are completed. Laborers typically work at building, highway, and heavy construction sites as well as on residential and commercial projects and demolition sites. Many of the jobs require physical strength, training, and experience. Other jobs require little skill and can be learned in a short amount of time. Road work and construction work entail so many different aspects, and as a laborer you will have an opportunity to try on many hats and test the waters of many different jobs without having to commit to a lifetime of the same thing.

Construction laborers clean and prepare construction sites. They remove trees and debris, monitor pumps or compressors, and build forms for pouring concrete. They load, unload, identify, and distribute building materials on a job site. They build and disassemble scaffolding, and they often assist others such as carpenters, plasterers, and masons. They may dig trenches; install sewer, water, or storm drainpipes; and place concrete and asphalt on roads. There are no shortages of jobs, and rarely is the work monotonous.

⇒ Work Setting

You have to be prepared for physically demanding work that requires multiple tools and equipment. Some computer knowledge is helpful as well, since you're bound to come across technology on these jobs. To be effective you should also be familiar or have an interest in becoming familiar with the jobs that the other workers are doing on the site.

Construction laborers often work as part of a team and should be able to get along with others, especially under pressure. Some laborers work nights and weekends, particularly on highway projects.

⇒ Training and Certification

While most of these construction laborer jobs have no specific educational qualifications, apprenticeships are available that require a high school diploma or GED. High school classes in mathematics, physics, mechanical drawing, and blueprint reading can be helpful for entry into this field. Most laborers get their first job by simply applying with a contractor who is in need of help. Some agencies place temporary laborers as well. That said, large commercial contractors with union membership often offer employees a formal apprenticeship, which may include two to four years of classroom and on-site training.

⇒ The Numbers

About 1.2 million jobs were filled by construction laborers in 2006. Employment is expected to grow by about 11 percent, or more than 130,000 jobs, between 2006 and 2016. The Bureau of Labor Statistics also predicts that opportunities will be better for laborers specializing in road construction. Median hourly earnings of construction laborers in May 2006 were $12.66, with the highest 10 percent earning more than $24.19.

Did You KNOW? The National Center for Construction Education and Research (NCCER) is an outstanding resource with information on starting a career in construction, tips on training, job boards, and salary information. The organization offers a wealth of information through its website at www.nccer.org.

ELECTRICIAN

If I had to trade in landscaping for another career, I'd become an electrician. Just think, everything is connected in some way to electricity. You have the ability to bring power to a family, a community, or a school. There are so many uses for electricity, well beyond the lightbulb. Another thing I like about this trade? Thomas Edison, who is credited with inventing the modern-day lightbulb, never even went to college. In fact, he only lasted three months in school until his teachers suggested he leave. Apparently his mind wandered too much.

Electricity is a complicated and powerful force. We wouldn't be able to do most of the things we do in a day without it. Have you ever thought about what your day would be like without electricity? Electricians bring electricity into homes, businesses, and factories. They install and maintain the wiring, fuses, and other components through which electricity flows. Some install electrical equipment. Commercial and residential electrical work are really two very different fields. Typically, electricians choose to specialize in one or the other. Codes are different, and the sheer size—let alone the types of equipment involved with wiring a commercial building—makes this a specialized section of the industry.

The Work

Electricians benefit greatly from having manual dexterity, hand-eye coordination, and a good sense of balance. Electricians usually start their work by reading blueprints that show the locations of circuits, outlets, and panel boards. To ensure public safety, electricians follow the National Electrical Code, as well as state and local building codes.

Electricians connect all types of wires to circuit breakers, transformers, outlets, and other components. When installing wiring, electricians use various hand tools as well as power tools. Electricians tend to focus on either construction or maintenance, although some do both. Electricians specializing in construction primarily install wiring systems into businesses or new homes, while maintenance electricians specialize in fixing or upgrading electrical systems or equipment.

Some electricians specialize in low-voltage wiring systems, which include voice, data, and video equipment. Telephones, computers, and even security systems are included in this work. Electricians may also install fiber optic cable for telecommunications equipment. As you've probably figured out, electrical work varies quite a bit, and the industry includes many different specialties.

Work Setting

Electricians work inside and out, at construction sites, and in homes, businesses, and factories.

Ⅲ➡ Training and Certification

Most electricians learn their trade through apprenticeship programs, which combine on-the-job training with classroom time. The unions are an excellent resource and sponsor apprenticeship programs, which have become the best way to get into this trade. These training programs usually last four years, though each program varies in length and number of requisite hours. For example, the Snohomish County Public Utility District (PUD), in the Puget Sound region in Washington, just north of Seattle, offers an apprenticeship that is seven thousand hours or three and a half years. Participants are paid $26.44 an hour, and as entry linemen that salary goes up to more than $74,000.

In general, electrical apprentices are supervised by experienced electricians, with the goal of learning bit by bit and eventually mastering all components of the trade. Some people start their classroom training before seeking an apprenticeship. Employers often hire students who complete independent postsecondary programs and usually start them at a more advanced level than those without the training. Licensing is required and varies from state to state but largely focuses on comprehension of the National Electrical Code.

Ⅲ➡ The Numbers

There were approximately 705,000 electricians employed in the United States in 2006. About 68 percent were employed in the construction industry. The Bureau of Labor Statistics is predicting good job prospects for this sector in the next decade, with an increase of about 7 percent, or 52,000 jobs. Much of the increase is attributed to retiring workers. The demand for electricians is expected in both residential and commercial projects. Electricians are expected to find work through the construction of power plants that are set to begin cropping up in the next ten years. Retrofitting and upgrading outdated electrical systems will also provide a source of employment for the industry. Those electricians who are skilled in voice, data, and video wiring are also expected to be at an advantage since these sectors are exploding. In May 2006 the median hourly earnings for electricians were $20.97 with the highest 10 percent earning more than $34.95. Apprentices usually start at half the rate paid to trained electricians.

ELEVATOR INSTALLATION AND REPAIR

Something just about everybody takes for granted is elevators. We expect them to work perfectly, become annoyed when we have to actually wait for one, and rarely stop to think about the components involved in making these machines run properly. Elevator installers and repairers are highly skilled mechanics and must be able to perform a variety of functions, from installing the parts, wiring the electrical components, constructing their frames, and then troubleshooting the various problems that happen along the way.

Ⅲ➡ The Work

Elevator installers and mechanics do a host of tasks, including assembling, installing, and replacing elevators, escalators, chairlifts, and moving walkways in buildings. Once the equipment is operational, they must conduct maintenance and repairs as well. Elevator installers put in electrical wires and controls via tubing ducts. They are also responsible for bolting or welding the steel frame of an elevator car and installing elevator doorframes on each floor. In short, they are responsible for most aspects of the elevator components you see and don't see.

Elevator installers and repairers must have a thorough knowledge of electronics, electricity, and hydraulics. Maintenance and repair workers generally need more knowledge of electricity and electronics than do installers because a large part of repair involves troubleshooting. Adjusters, the most highly skilled of all elevator installers, need a thorough knowledge of electricity, electronics, and computers. Overall, this industry requires multiple skills and a lot of training.

⮕ Work Setting

Elevator installers lift and carry heavy equipment and parts, and they may work in cramped spaces. Potential hazards include falls and electrical shock. Most of their work is performed indoors. Installers typically work standard hours, but repairs are unpredictable and service calls are made at all times of the day or night.

⮕ Training and Certification

Most elevator installers receive their education through an apprenticeship program. High school mathematics, science, and shop are quite helpful. Many of these programs can be found through unions. The apprenticeships often last for four years and combine paid, on-site training with classroom instruction. Most cities and states require installers and repairers to pass a licensing exam.

Those who complete an apprenticeship registered by their state board or by the U.S. Department of Labor can earn a journey worker certificate, an advanced certification, which is recognized nationwide and is considered an asset. As with many occupations, ongoing training is crucial for installers and repairers to keep up with technological developments in the industry.

Ⅲ➡ The Numbers

Elevator installers and repairers had about 22,000 jobs in 2006. Most were employed by specialty contractors, such as elevator companies. Employment in this industry is expected to increase by about 9 percent, or by close to 2,000 jobs, between 2006 and 2016. Demand will largely depend on growth in commercial construction, which is expected to increase. The need to update and repair older equipment also adds to the work demand.

Elevator installers and repairers are some of the highest paid in the construction trades, with median hourly wages at $30.59 as of May 2006. The top 10 percent earned more than $42.14. About 75 percent of the people working in this trade are union members.

FABRICATION AND ASSEMBLY

I've said it before, but today's factories are not your grandma's factories. For the most part, gone are the days of the dark, dingy assembly lines that you've probably seen portrayed in old movies. Instead, the plants are often pleasant environments, well-lit and clean.

Assemblers and fabricators play a crucial role in the manufacturing industry. They assemble finished products and the smaller components used to put together everything from household appliances and automobiles to computers and other electronic devices.

Ⅲ➡ The Work

Changes in technology have transformed the manufacturing and assembly process since many factories rely on automated systems, robots, computers, or programmable devices. The more advanced assemblers must be able to work with these new technologies while continuing to adapt to the inevitable changes of the future.

The job of an assembler or fabricator ranges from rather easy to quite complicated and requires a range of knowledge and skills. Those who put together complex machines must be able to read detailed blueprints or directions. Assemblers may also be responsible for basic welding or soldering. Quality control is important on assembly lines, and people must be alert and pay close attention to detail in an effort to spot defective parts. In this spirit, assemblers must follow instructions carefully, which requires excellent reading skills and the ability to understand diagrams. Manual dexterity is important, as is the ability to complete repetitive tasks quickly and methodically. It's possible that some of these positions would include heavy lifting.

Manufacturing lines are different beasts than what they used to be. An effort has been made to streamline the process so that more is accomplished at each stage. Rather than only putting together two parts, as was common years ago, an assembler may be required to perform multiple stages of the assembly process. Some experienced assemblers work with designers and engineers to build prototypes or test products. These assemblers must be able to read and interpret complex engineering specifications from text, drawings, and computer-aided drafting systems. They may also need to use a variety of tools and precision measuring instruments.

Ⅲ➡ Work Setting

The work environment for assemblers and fabricators varies. It used to be more physically demanding, but automated equipment and processes have changed that. Factory conditions can vary, but generally they are clean, well-lit places to work. Some are near sterile, if not totally dust- and dirt-free. But others require that assemblers still come in contact with oil and grease or work in loud manufacturing plants.

Ⅲ➤ Training and Certification

Typically a high school diploma or GED is sufficient for much of this industry, and on-the-job training is usually the way most people learn. But additional training is needed for advanced assembly work, such as for electronics or aircraft and motor vehicle manufacturers. As assemblers and fabricators become more experienced, they may progress to jobs that require greater skill and can be given more responsibility. Experienced assemblers often advance to become product repairers.

Ⅲ➤ The Numbers

Assemblers and fabricators held nearly 2.1 million jobs in 2006. They worked in almost every industry, but 75 percent were in manufacturing. Assembly of transportation equipment—such as aircrafts, cars, and buses—accounted for 19 percent of all jobs, while those putting together computers and electronic products accounted for another 11 percent.

Employment of assemblers and fabricators is projected to decline slowly, by about 4 percent between 2006 and 2016, primarily due to foreign competition in manufacturing and the fact that some of these jobs are being outsourced to overseas workers. That means about 80,000 jobs will be lost from the industry. That said, the manufacturing industry has been vocal about needing more skilled workers, which means that people who have training will be at an advantage. Interestingly, the aircraft industry is expected to add jobs during this same time period, thanks to the demand for new military and commercial planes.

As of May 2006, the median hourly wage of team assemblers was

$11.63, with the highest 10 percent of earners making more than $19.14. Earnings of electrical and electronic equipment assemblers were $12.29 an hour, with the highest 10 percent making more than $19.81.

FISHING

Before the reality show *Deadliest Catch*, many people probably never thought about becoming crab fishers. What with the frigid waters, dark skies, and stormy seas, the life of a fisher can be tough and wet and will often keep you out on the ocean for weeks at a time. But thanks to the show, people are talking about what it takes to reel in a hefty catch and are amazed at how brave the men and women are who fish our waters. The solace of the sea and the art of fishing certainly have their appeal.

In New England I see a lot of fisherman, whether they're out collecting lobster traps close to the shores or heading out toward the Stellwagen Bank, made famous by the book and then movie *Perfect Storm*. Commercial fishing doesn't even resemble the sport fishing many of us do on lakes, while half-watching the end of our rods and listening to a ball game on the radio. I probably don't need to say this, but to fish for a living you have to live on a coast—the Atlantic Ocean, Gulf of Mexico, or Pacific Ocean. But before you pick up and relocate, be sure you aren't prone to getting seasick and be sure that this is really a job for you.

We'll talk more in Chapter 5 about sustainable fishing and the various issues facing the fishing industry when we look at green jobs. Unfortunately, small fishing operations are having a rough time competing with the larger companies, but the hope is that more and more sustainable fishers can survive based on consumer demand for fish that have been caught responsibly.

"We talk about how we're going to recruit," says Zeke Grader, executive director of the Pacific Coast Federation of Fisherman's Association, who says it's not common to find young adults going into fishing. "For people who are willing to work hard and take on challenges, this can be very, very rewarding. It can be extremely lucrative and it can be adventuresome."

ⅢⅢ➤ The Work

Being a fisher involves strenuous work, long hours, seasonal employment, and some hazards. This work is best learned by doing. Hang around the docks, ask if you can work on board a fishing vessel, make yourself useful to the captain, and pay attention to how the lines, nets, and fish are all handled. "Make enough of a pest of yourself until you get hired" is what Grader recommends. "Either you get it out of your system, or you find out it's for you," says Grader of the desire to be a commercial fisher.

Fishers and fishing boat operators catch and trap a variety of ocean-going creatures from tuna, swordfish, and octopus to clams, lobsters, and scallops. Some boats go out hundreds of miles from shore for days at a time with multiple-person crews. These vessels tend to bring back larger hauls. Captains are responsible for overseeing the entire fishing operation and decide the location to fish, the method of doing so, and how the goods will be sold. He or she is also responsible for the ever-important safety of the crew. The first mate tends to be the captain's assistant, assumes control of the vessel when the captain is off-duty, and must be familiar with navigation equipment and the boat's overall operation. The mate also directs the crew. A boatswain, or highly experienced deckhand, will direct others as well as repair equipment and help with hauling a catch. While on board, the entire crew is working to catch, haul, clean, and preserve fish. Cleaning and securing the boat are other major ongoing tasks.

Some boats routinely stick closer to shore and spend more time in shallow waters. Although the duties of the crew are primarily the same, the day boat operations do not require preparations to be made for multinight trips, which allows everyone to spend more nights on land than at sea.

Success in the Real World

Jerry Tilley, fisher, Westport, Washington

"There are times on the ocean when life doesn't get any better," says James Tilley. At fifty-two he's seen sea turtles, a killer whale give birth, and breathtaking sunsets. But what really occupies his time are his three fishing boats and a near-constant monitoring of the sea. Depending on the season, Tilley catches king crab, tuna, prawns, or halibut.

Tilley became a bit of a household name when, as captain, he and his crew were featured on *Deadliest Catch*, the National Geographic television series about the dangers of fishing. Tilley has been working in the industry since he was a child. "It was really the only game in town," he says. "I grew up in one big fishing family." From coastal Westport, Washington, he and his family, including three sons and a daughter, became favorites on the show.

Growing up, Tilley says he pretty much hated fishing, as any kid might hate the thing his parents make him do most. Plus he used to get violently ill from seasickness. "I didn't have much of a choice," and so he went along on various expeditions with his family. And then he realized it was a great way to make a living and it was something he knew inside and out. Thirty-five years into his career as a fisher, Tilley says he loves the independence he has and enjoys running the show, calling the shots, and not having someone else tell him what to do.

Tilley says the work is rewarding, but it can be backbreaking. He even suggested to his children that they choose a different career. Still, one of his sons opted to stick with fishing, just like his dad. Tilley says there are days when the work is so tough that "you pull something out of yourself that you think isn't humanly impossible." Tilley is frank about the kind of people who shouldn't even think about getting into fishing. "A kid who's never been away from home, and who has a mom who's been doing his laundry? It won't work."

Depending on the trip, Tilley may haul between fifty thousand and one hundred thousand pounds of Dungeness crab. You'd think a fisherman might not want to ever eat what he catches, having to stare at it and smell it and handle it all day. But not Tilley. "It's my favorite. I love it," he says of crab. He used to stay out at sea for as long as twenty-eight days when he was a kid, but his trips now are more like seven to ten days. If he's had a string of long trips, his wife will often join him to break up the routine.

Tilley puts safety first, and he says it's crucial that any captain do so. "There is a fine line between being brave and being stupid." But he's never lost a single crew member, something he's proud to say. He also hasn't entirely overcome his tendency to get seasick, even after all these years. It's become less severe, and now Tilley considers it a good day if he's only dealing with a bit of nausea. Tilley is out at sea as often as possible and suspects he will continue fishing until he physically can't take it anymore. Although he makes his own schedule, Tilley admits that he's not entirely in control. "When the fish are there, you go fishing."

Work Setting

This job obviously requires that you be on the water, often in the ocean, but sometimes in protected bays or harbors. Conditions on the sea vary considerably, and fishing operations do still happen during storms, although safety is a major consideration of all captains. Storms, fog, and wind may hamper fishing vessels or cause them to suspend fishing operations, but that said, a little rain never kept a crew from going out.

Fishers and fishing vessel operators work under some of the most hazardous conditions. The crew must be on guard against the danger of injury from malfunctioning fishing gear, entanglement in fishing nets, slippery decks, or rogue waves. Fishing involves strenuous work and long hours. It's not uncommon for some commercial fishers to be out at sea for a few months at a time. Newer boats do have better accommodations, but still quarters tend to be small and sparse. Think fishing boat, not cruise ship.

Training and Certification

Fishermen and women acquire their skills on the job, and most seasoned fishers say you will know in an instant whether you're cut out for this work. There are no formal academic training requirements, but operators of large commercial fishing vessels are required to complete a U.S. Coast Guard–approved training course. Some community colleges and universities offer fishery technology and related programs that include courses in vessel operations, marine safety, navigation, and vessel repair.

Captains and mates on fishing boats that are two hundred gross tons or more must have a Coast Guard–issued license. You simply can't fish commercially without a permit, which also stipulates the type of fish you are allowed to catch, and any size or location restrictions that may exist.

ⅢⅢ➤ The Numbers

In 2006, there were 38,000 people working as fishers or fishing boat operators. About two-thirds were self-employed. Many fishermen and women are seasonal workers and tend to have other jobs throughout the year. Employment in this industry is expected to decline by 16 percent through the year 2016, which means about 6,000 less fishers by then. Many fishers blame restrictive government regulations. Others say small independent owners can no longer compete with the larger commercial fishing companies, which have the capacity and resources to go thousands of miles from shore for months on end. But that said, there are expected to be some job opportunities available as fishermen retire.

As of May 2006, the median annual earnings of fishers were $27,250 while the top 10 percent earned more than $45,480. Earnings are highest in the summer (when fish is most in demand) and lowest during the winter months. Earnings may be considerably more for those who own their own vessels or company. And remember, too, that earnings often cover only seasonal work, so many fishers have income at other times of the year as well.

FORKLIFT AND MACHINE OPERATOR

Operating large machinery can be pretty exciting. If you like to touch, feel, and move things, this could be one appealing industry for you. Material-moving workers are categorized into two groups: operators and laborers. Operators use machinery to move construction materials, earth, petroleum products, and other heavy materials. Generally, they move materials short distances at construction sites, factories, or warehouses, for example. Some move materials on or off trucks and ships. Laborers do more physical work with less assistance from heavy machinery.

ⅢⅢ➤ The Work

Machine operators control equipment by moving levers and wheels, while operating various switches and sometimes computerized components. They may also be responsible for setting up or inspecting equipment, as well as doing minor maintenance or repairs. Laborers move freight, stock, or other materials by hand and are often responsible for manning equipment.

Material-moving equipment operators need a good sense of balance, the ability to judge distances, and eye-hand-foot coordination. The equipment used in material-moving occupations requires a variety of skills. For example, forklift operators drive and control equipment used to move materials around warehouses, whereas excavating machines are equipped with scoops and shovels used to load and move earth or gravel. No two jobs are the same in this industry and the equipment is always changing, so workers must be willing to adapt.

For jobs that involve dealing with the public, such as grocery store stockers, interpersonal skills go a long way. As with many other industries, technology is revolutionizing all machinery, including the equipment used for material moving, so a familiarity with the new upgrades is extremely useful. Refuse and recyclable material collectors—or garbage collectors—also fall into this category. Most everyone is familiar with how hard they work to haul and empty garbage, all while sticking to an assigned route and sometimes a tight time schedule.

Ⅲ➤ Work Setting

Material-moving work tends to be repetitive and physically demanding. Some people in this field work at great heights, and some work outdoors, regardless of weather and climate. These jobs can expose workers to fumes, odors, loud noises, or dangerous machinery. But for the most part, the jobs are less dangerous than they used to be, thanks to safety equipment and regulations. Material movers generally work eight-hour shifts, and some work through the night depending on the company and need.

Ⅲ➤ Training and Certification

Most training for this occupation is done on the job. Some employers may require that applicants pass a physical exam due to the amount of physical lifting that is sometimes involved. Material movers generally learn skills informally from more experienced coworkers.

Workers who handle toxic chemicals or use industrial trucks receive specialized training in safety awareness and procedures. For some of these jobs, such as crane operators, there are training and apprenticeship programs available. Some states require crane or other heavy equipment operators to be licensed. You can find out more by checking with your state's motor vehicle licensing division.

Ⅲ➤ The Numbers

Despite little change in employment projections, job openings should be plentiful since there are so many of these jobs and turnover is high. In 2006, material movers held 4.8 million jobs. Out of those jobs 2,416,000 were laborers and material movers while 637,000 were industrial truck and tractor operators. Hourly earnings of material movers vary significantly, but wages can be low to start. In May 2006, median earnings for gas compressor operators were $21.83 and $18.77 for crane operators. For refuse and recyclable material collectors, it was $13.93.

GROUNDSKEEPER, LANDSCAPER, AND ARBORIST

First impressions are everything. When you drive up to a friend's house or walk past a nearby business, one of the first things you may notice is the lawn, the landscaping, the bushes, the trees, or maybe the lack of anything green. If you're looking for a new condominium, you may immediately notice whether the grounds are well maintained. A well-cared-for lawn says a lot. Landscapers, groundskeepers, and arborists—or tree experts—are the ones responsible for making sure that first impression is a good one.

Nothing relaxes me more than a perfectly cut lawn, a well-shoveled walk, and a newly mulched garden. I guess that's because I've been in the landscaping business long enough that I can spot a blade of grass out of place like a barber sees a single strand of hair that is too long. I enjoy driving away from a customer's house knowing that my crew has created something beautiful, has maintained something the owner can enjoy, and has added value to a neighborhood.

I got lucky when I started my business almost thirty years ago. That's when more and more women started working out of the house. That meant more takeout dinners, less time to mow the grass, and more landscaping business for me. As women found themselves with less time to garden, weed, and generally tend to their lawns, we landscapers found a ton of business. And now, people are busier than ever, so you can be sure there is still plenty of work available for professional landscapers.

�III➤ The Work

A groundskeeper typically refers to someone who tends to the lawns, shrubs, and flowers on residential and commercial property. Some work at estates, college campuses, and private parks. Landscapers tend to have multiple customers with different tasks or duties at each location. I always thought it would be a blast to be the groundskeeper at a Major League ball field. For those who go in this direction, it's important to understand artificial turf while knowing how to maintain the underlying soil and achieve proper drainage.

Landscapers and groundskeepers use tools ranging from mowers and shovels to bush trimmers and chain saws. Some rely on larger equipment such as tractors. Landscapers generally install and maintain plants and trees as well as tend to lawns with fertilizer and irrigation systems, for example. They grade property and build walkways, patios, and decks. Groundskeepers usually to maintain larger properties, such as athletic fields, cemeteries, and golf courses.

Tree trimmers, pruners, and arborists are charged with caring for trees, cutting away dead branches, and clearing pathways for roads or sidewalks. Specialized arborists often have advanced degrees in tree care. Some groundskeepers also have degrees in botany, the study of plants. Many arborists are employed by cities to improve urban green space or by parks to maintain healthy growth.

Success in the Real World

Blair Glenn, arborist, Los Gatos, California

"Man was not made to sit at a desk," says Blair Glenn, who has found a way to spend his workdays outside, often climbing trees. This arborist and owner of Saratoga Tree Service in Los Gatos, California, knew he didn't want to end up at a desk job. Although his mother was a teacher and his parents felt strongly about their son getting a college degree, they were supportive of Glenn's desire not to go that route. They even gave him the money they had saved for college to buy his first work truck.

"I didn't want to get stuck working indoors," says Glenn of how he ended up becoming a tree expert. He was an avid rock climber and started working for a tree expert long after graduating from high school. Glenn says he was fortunate to find a mentor who taught him the ropes, something he says remains invaluable to people just starting off in the trades. "The world is full of older people like me who want to give back." Now fifty-five, Glenn regularly mentors younger arborists and kids who show an interest in the field. As an arborist Glenn says being outside and climbing trees is what he loves, and in turn he enjoys sharing his passion.

"You have to have the desire to learn a new tree every day," he adds. Although Glenn ultimately went back to school for his degree, he spent years learning on the job while being willing, if not exuberant, to climb and work hard. "We know an awful lot about the human body, but not as much about tree management." He watches trees go through life cycles as well as seasonal changes, and he considers specific trees that he's worked on to be his own personal accomplishments. "My business is a craft. It's very creative," he says.

Glenn also enjoys the fact that on any given day he will have multiple jobs, each with its own challenges. "I enjoy spending the day at people's properties," he adds. Glenn acknowledges that this can be a tough job to sell, what with the physically demanding nature of the work and sometimes harsh weather conditions. But for Glenn it's all worth it. He doesn't need a gym membership and spends his free time hiking, fishing, and backpacking. Plus, he credits his active job for why he rarely gets sick.

Despite the fact that none of his five grown children want to take over his business, Glenn remains optimistic that his craft and trade will be passed on through generations to come. "When you step back you have job satisfaction," he says. It's something that will always appeal to people. What does he suggest for those who want to make a go at it in the trades? "Find what you love doing and make that your personal college education."

⟾ Work Setting

If you absolutely love to be outside, this could be the job for you. Much landscaping and groundskeeping work is seasonal, depending on what part of the country you are in, and it can require working throughout the colder winter months. The landscaper who was mowing grass and moving trees in the summer may end up shoveling and plowing snow come winter, if you live in a place where it snows.

Almost all of this work is performed outside, which means dealing with the elements. You experience the changing seasons firsthand, which is something I've always enjoyed. It can be physically demanding, and sometimes there is time pressure if you're racing against a coming storm or maybe a customer's big event. But I think the satisfaction of a job well done is worth the hassle of occasionally being drenched in a downpour.

⇒ Training and Certification

Most grounds maintenance workers learn on-the-job and from coworkers about how to properly plant shrubs, collect leaves, or efficiently mow a lawn. However, some occupations may require formal training in areas such as landscape design or horticulture. There are also programs and certifications that offer courses on landscaping and tree maintenance. When it comes to handling pesticides, many states require a license.

⇒ The Numbers

Landscapers and groundskeepers will see some of the largest employment growth of any sector between 2006 and 2016. It is expected that available jobs will increase 18 percent, which means an additional 270,000 positions. In 2006, there were approximately 1.5 million jobs in this field, including about 41,000 in specialized tree care. Almost 24 percent of grounds maintenance workers were self-employed, and approximately 14 percent worked part-time.

Homeowners have an increasing desire to beautify their lawns, to make a good impression, and to have an outdoor space in which to entertain. Much of this demand and industry growth is expected to come from the construction of office buildings, shopping malls, and housing developments. All of this naturally boosts the demand for landscapers. As well, it is predicted that as our country's population ages, more elderly homeowners will require lawn care services.

HEATING, AIR-CONDITIONING, AND REFRIGERATION MECHANIC AND INSTALLER

Climate control means year-round comfort, from warmth in the winter to cool air-conditioning in the summer. Controlled humidity and temperatures are found just about everywhere, from homes and commercial buildings to museums, arenas, and hotels. Installation of heating, air-conditioning, and refrigeration requires multiple skills, and the maintenance of the various systems is a crucial piece of this industry.

⟱ The Work

This industry includes heating and air-conditioning systems and refrigeration systems. More specifically it involves heating, ventilation, air-conditioning, and refrigeration and is often referred to as HVACR systems, or even just HVAC. HVAC systems include many mechanical, electrical, and electronic components, so technicians must be able to maintain, diagnose, and correct problems throughout an entire system.

Servicing air-conditioning and refrigeration equipment involves the careful recovery and recycling of refrigerants. HVAC installers and technicians should be comfortable using a variety of basic tools as well as pressure gauges and voltmeters. During the off-season, many of these systems can be updated, maintained, or cleaned. Winter is a great time for HVAC workers to clean residential or commercial air-conditioning units, and the same goes for heating systems in the summer.

High school classes in shop, math, mechanical drawing, electronics, and computer applications are all great backgrounds for anyone interested in working in the HVAC industry. Some knowledge of plumbing or

READER/CUSTOMER CARE SURVEY

We care about your opinions! Please take a moment to fill out our online Reader Survey at **http://survey.hcibooks.com.**

As a **"THANK YOU"** you will receive a **VALUABLE INSTANT COUPON** towards future book purchases as well as a **SPECIAL GIFT** available only online! Or, you may mail this card back to us.

(PLEASE PRINT IN ALL CAPS)

First Name		MI.		Last Name	
Address				Email	City
State	Zip				

1. Gender
□ Female   □ Male

2. Age
□ 8 or younger
□ 9-12   □ 13-16
□ 17-20   □ 21-30
□ 31+

3. Did you receive this book as a gift?
□ Yes   □ No

4. Annual Household Income
□ under $25,000
□ $25,000 - $34,999
□ $35,000 - $49,999
□ $50,000 - $74,999
□ over $75,000

5. What are the ages of the children living in your house?
□ 0 - 14   □ 15+

6. Marital Status
□ Single
□ Married
□ Divorced
□ Widowed

7. How did you find out about the book?
(please choose one)
□ Recommendation
□ Store Display
□ Online
□ Catalog/Mailing
□ Interview/Review

8. Where do you usually buy books?
(please choose one)
□ Bookstore
□ Online
□ Book Club/Mail Order
□ Price Club (Sam's Club, Costco's, etc.)
□ Retail Store (Target, Wal-Mart, etc.)

9. What subject do you enjoy reading about the most?
(please choose one)
□ Parenting/Family
□ Relationships
□ Recovery/Addictions
□ Health/Nutrition
□ Christianity
□ Spirituality/Inspiration
□ Business Self-help
□ Women's Issues
□ Sports

10. What attracts you most to a book?
(please choose one)
□ Title
□ Cover Design
□ Author
□ Content

BUSINESS REPLY MAIL
FIRST-CLASS MAIL PERMIT NO 45 DEERFIELD BEACH, FL

POSTAGE WILL BE PAID BY ADDRESSEE

Health Communications, Inc.
3201 SW 15th Street
Deerfield Beach FL 33442-9875

FOLD HERE

Comments

electrical work is also helpful, and a basic understanding of electronics is becoming more important. Sometimes the work can be demanding and regularly involves dealing with individual customers or institutional clients.

ⅢⅢ➤ Work Setting

HVAC mechanics and installers work in homes, retail establishments, hospitals, office buildings, and anywhere there is climate-control equipment. Technicians may work outside in cold or hot weather or in buildings that are uncomfortable. Conditions are always less desirable if the systems are broken. Safety is important when handling refrigerants and some risks are involved with the work, such as falling or getting burned.

ⅢⅢ➤ Training and Certification

Because of the increasing sophistication of HVAC systems, people who have completed postsecondary training programs are at an advantage. Some people still learn informally on the job. Many secondary and postsecondary schools offer six-month to two-year training programs. Students study theory of temperature control, equipment design and construction, and electronics. They also learn the basics of installation, maintenance, and repair. Technicians often train through these apprenticeships, many of which are offered through unions.

Some states require that HVAC mechanics and installers be licensed. Requirements for these licenses vary, and some require extensive knowledge of electrical codes. Others may require the completion of an apprenticeship program. Technicians who work with refrigerants must be certified to do so by an organization or licensing center approved by the U.S. Environmental Protection Agency.

Concern for the environment has prompted the development of new energy-saving heating and air-conditioning systems. With these there is an emphasis on better energy management, which is expected to lead residential and commercial customers to replace their existing systems. Technicians will have to become more knowledgeable about the new components, and those who are familiar with these new systems will have more job opportunities.

⮕ The Numbers

HVAC installers held about 292,000 jobs in 2006 and about 55 percent worked for contractors. Employment is projected to increase 9 percent, which is more than 26,000 jobs, between 2006 and 2016 as there continues to be a growing focus on improving indoor air quality. The need to upgrade systems will be another source of job growth as will retirement by older workers.

Median hourly earnings of HVAC mechanics and installers were $18.11 as of May 2006, with the middle 50 percent earning between $14.12 and $23.32 an hour. Apprentices usually begin at about half the wages of experienced workers.

INDUSTRIAL MACHINE MECHANIC

Industrial machine mechanics are highly skilled and specialized workers who maintain and repair machinery in a manufacturing plant or factory. They are the ones who are called in when assembly line equipment fails or when major equipment needs repair. Most start off as machine maintenance workers or as millwrights and work their way up to the mechanic level.

Ⅲ➡ The Work

The basic maintenance and repair of expensive and massive industrial machines is done by industrial maintenance workers, but the larger repairs and work are performed by the industrial mechanics. These mechanics must be able to detect the smallest of problems and correct them before they become significant. The machinery mechanics use technical manuals, understanding of equipment, and diagnostic skills to determine problems and find solutions. Computer diagnostics are increasingly a means for testing and troubleshooting problems with the machines. Industrial mechanics must also have electrical skills.

Ⅲ➡ Work Setting

Most industrial mechanics work in factories or other production facilities and may be expected to work weekends or after hours when the production plants are not operating, so as to avoid disrupting efficiency and productivity. Many mechanics will find themselves on tall ladders or in other awkward positions, although safety regulations and precautions make this a relatively safe job.

Ⅲ➡ Training and Certification

Machinery maintenance workers can typically get hired with a high school diploma or the equivalent. These entry-level positions allow for learning on the job, but machinery mechanics tend to need postsecondary training and some have skills specific to a certain machine. Employers prefer mechanics who have at least taken courses in computer programming, mechanical drawing, or electronics. Training in industrial technology is especially useful and is often offered by professional trainers or equipment manufacturers.

Mechanics typically need a year or more of formal education and training following high school. Military experience, especially on ships, is highly valued, as is a two-year associate degree in industrial maintenance. There are many apprenticeships offered by local unions as well.

⟫ The Numbers

In 2006, there were approximately 345,000 jobs for industrial machinery mechanics and maintenance workers. Of these, 261,000 were held by the more advanced mechanics. Most were employed in the manufacturing sector. Employment in this sector is expected to grow by about 7 percent, or an additional 24,000 jobs, between 2006 and 2016.

TEN OFFBEAT BLUE-COLLAR JOBS

Most of us know a painter, a plumber, and an electrician, but there are some little known, often forgotten, and pretty cool blue-collar jobs out there. The sky is the limit, and you might be surprised to learn how many unusual and interesting jobs there are in the blue-collar sector. We've put together a few of our favorite unusual jobs, but don't be shy about going out and finding the ones that most interest you.

1. **Underwater welder.** Ever think about how bridges are built or repaired, at least at their bases? Underwater welders, essential for the construction and maintenance of bridges, are required to go down deep to repair different elements of these structures. Underwater welding combines many skills, not to mention offering a unique work environment. Wet suit and oxygen tank required.

2. **Tugboat pilot**. Coast Guard training and certification are required for tanker, tugboat, and harbor boat pilots, but this occupation allows you to spend your days on the water, be it in a harbor or out on the open ocean.

3. **Chimney sweep.** They can't all dance like the chimney sweep played by Dick Van Dyke in *Mary Poppins*, but still this occupation requires quite a bit of agility. Sweeps are still the ones you call when you need a chimney inspected or cleaned. Willing to get dust up their noses and black on their faces, chimney sweeps are good at diagnosing chimney-related problems, and their days consistently include challenging jobs.

4. **Musical instrument repairer.** You don't have to go to college to become a master musical instrument repairer, although many instrument repairmen and women do have a four-year degree. Most important is an ability to play an instrument or two or three and a knack for repairing them and knowing them inside and out. Practice makes perfect.

5. **Taxi or limo driver**. Think of the places you'll go and the people you'll meet. If you like driving but don't want to drive trucks across the country, being a taxi driver or limousine driver could be an option, especially if you enjoy meeting people and providing a service.

6. **Butcher**. If you can stomach the work, you can actually have an influence over the quality of meat that you are providing to your customers. As the owner of a butcher shop, you could choose to support local farms, for example, while only offering hormone-free products. We'll leave the other job details to your imagination.

7. **Boat builder**. True craftspeople and master carpenters, the purist boat builders continue to make stunning pieces of handcrafted art. Some specialize in picnic boats and others in canoes and small sailboats. Boat builders are some of the most passionate people out there.

8. **Hot tub installer**. It would be a tough job if you had to test whether the newly installed hot tub was working properly. A plumbing background is helpful if not necessary, and installing hot tubs can be lucrative and even creative. Some people specialize in hot tub installation and become go-to experts.

9. **Critter removal**. Got a badger in your backyard? A squirrel in the attic? Pest and animal control experts are largely focused on humanely removing these animals so that you don't have to. Most pest specialists are trained by their employers, and some take courses for certification at community colleges.

10. **Blacksmith**. Although there used to be a blacksmith in every town, the art of blacksmithing is not gone. Blacksmiths are incredibly skilled with their hands and with crafting iron into railings, decorative grates, and fencing. As an art form, blacksmithing produces some of the most intricate elements still found on homes.

IRONWORKERS

Often called *cowboys in the sky*, ironworkers are regularly suspended hundreds of feet in the air as they set the steel foundation for skyscrapers. Risk and adventure are definitely part of the thrill of this job, but it comes with highly honed skills and a deep respect for safety. Being twenty stories up, perched on a steel beam, is not exactly everyone's idea of a good day at work, but for some it's just the ticket to happiness. As the ironworking industry's motto puts it, "We don't go to the office. We build it." I love that slogan.

⟾ The Work

Despite their reputation for working in the clouds, some ironworkers never leave the ground. But for those who do, a fear of heights has to be left behind. Workers must be in good physical condition and have excellent agility, balance, and depth perception.

Structural and reinforcing ironworkers place and install iron or steel girders, columns, and other construction materials to form the structure for buildings and bridges. They also position and secure steel bars prior to concrete being poured for all types of buildings, bridges, and tunnels. Before construction can begin, ironworkers must erect steel frames and assemble the cranes and derricks to move all of the steel and bars around a site. They then spend much time connecting steel columns and beams with guidance from blueprints. Ornamental ironworkers install stairs, handrails, and iron frameworks, such as those that go around windows.

⟾ Work Setting

Iron and metal workers usually work outside and in all kinds of weather. Although they have a reputation for practically tightrope walking in the sky, many find themselves at ground level on typical construction sites. For those who are outside, the weather is a major factor, and work can be suspended during severe winds or storms. Because of the possibility of falling, ironworkers use safety harnesses, scaffolding, or nets.

⟾ Training and Certification

Many learn ironworking through formal apprenticeships, and most employers recommend a three- or four-year-long apprenticeship consisting of a combination of paid on-the-job training and classroom time. Apprenticeships are often offered through unions or contractor associations.

Apprentices typically study blueprint reading, mathematics, and the basics of structural framing, reinforcing, welding, and safety. Apprentices also study the care and safe use of tools and materials. On the job, apprentices work in all aspects of the trade, starting with basic job site tasks.

Ironworkers who complete apprenticeships are certified as journey workers, which makes them more appealing when applying for jobs and promotions. Those who meet education and experience requirements can become welders certified by the American Welding Society, a highly regarded organization.

High school courses in general mathematics, mechanical drawing, and welding are beneficial for entering this industry.

ⅢⅢ➤ The Numbers

Ironworkers held about 102,000 jobs in 2006, and about 88 percent worked in construction. Although structural and reinforcing ironworkers are employed in all parts of the country, most work in metropolitan areas, where commercial construction is more prevalent. Employment of ironworkers is expected to grow 8 percent between 2006 and 2016, which means at least another 8,000 jobs. Many of these new jobs are expected to be created by retiring ironworkers.

Ironworkers tend to have high salaries compared with their counterparts in other construction trades. As of May 2006, median earnings were $19.46 an hour, with the highest 10 percent earning more than $34.78. About 31 percent of the workers in this trade are union members. Not surprisingly, those working in larger cities—such as New York, Boston, San Francisco, Chicago, and Philadelphia—earn the highest wages. Apprentices generally start at about 50 to 60 percent of the rate paid to experienced journey workers, but these salaries increase with experience.

LOGGERS AND FOREST WORKERS

The days of Paul Bunyan and his pal Babe the Blue Ox are over. Managing, harvesting, and replanting the country's forests have become a controversial but also crucial piece of this industry. Reliance on timber drives the demand for loggers, and the need to maintain the health of the forests is a daunting task that falls to forestry workers. Some are cutting while others are planting. It's an ongoing, constant cycle, and the actual jobs are quite different. That said, both would afford you an opportunity to be in some of the most beautiful and secluded places in our country.

Loggers are in such short supply right now that some logging companies in the West are offering moving expenses or even signing bonuses in hopes of luring people to the industry. At one time it was customary for these companies to recruit new blood directly from the logging communities in which they are based. But many young adults are now heading for urban areas, and logging companies are in search of people to fill openings.

⮕ The Work

Our nation's forests are a rich natural resource. Managing and harvesting them requires a variety of workers. Forest and conservation workers develop, maintain, and protect forests by growing and planting new trees, monitoring diseases, and controlling soil erosion. Loggers cut thousands of acres of forests each year for consumer and industrial products, such as building materials and paper products.

More specifically, loggers are responsible for cutting and hauling trees in large quantities along with a crew. Some will cut down trees manually, while others use sophisticated machines. A variety of equipment is used to remove and move trees, to chip the wood, and to load the hauls for transport. The industry used to require more manual labor but now relies on equipment to do much of the work. The ability to operate this equipment is beneficial for loggers looking for employment opportunities.

Some loggers are hired to scout logging sites, which means hiking through remote areas to assess accessibility and conditions. Others clear paths for crews and equipment. Most crews work for self-employed contractors who have substantial logging experience.

Some forest workers spend time physically planting trees. They may also be expected to remove trees when disease strikes. Many forestry workers clear paths, document trees, and monitor growth of areas. Some work in forest-based nurseries, forcing new growth and monitoring tree sustainability.

Forest, conservation, and logging workers must be in good health and able to work outside every day. For loggers, it's important to be able to work as part of a crew. Many loggers compare their work to that of a football team; they say you have to work as one unit, with one game plan, to succeed. Physical stamina is crucial, as is the ability to make quick decisions and have good judgment, since it's not uncommon for dangerous situations to arise. Mechanical skills are also helpful for fixing a variety of equipment used in the logging process.

⟩ Work Setting

Forestry and logging jobs are physically demanding. Workers spend almost all of their time outdoors, sometimes in poor weather and often in isolated areas. But some regard these remote areas as a perk of the job, since they have the opportunity to see and enjoy patches of the earth that haven't been explored for decades.

Most logging occupations involve lifting, climbing, and other strenuous activities, although machinery has eliminated some heavy labor. The work of logging can be hazardous, but safety precautions are taken seriously. Some of the newer equipment also includes enclosed areas for drivers or operators, making the loggers less susceptible to inclement weather. Still, loggers must be prepared to work in all conditions. Working in sparsely populated areas may mean commuting long distances to the logging sites.

The requirements of forest and conservation workers generally offer fewer hazards than those of loggers, but anyone in this sector must almost constantly be dealing with variable weather conditions.

⇒ Training and Certification

Most people in this industry, especially those at the entry level, develop skills on the job. "Ninety-nine percent of it is learn as you go," says Jim Gahlsdorf, owner of Gahlsdorf Logging, in the Salem, Oregon, area. Successful loggers must be familiar with the processes involved as well as how to operate the equipment. Safety training is a vital and required part of the instruction of all logging workers, and some states actually offer this for free. Logger training varies with each state, with some programs leading to logger certification. Logging companies and trade associations also offer training programs for workers who operate the larger equipment.

Some postsecondary schools offer two-year technical degrees in forestry, wildlife management, conservation, and forest harvesting, all of which are helpful in obtaining a job. Training programs for loggers and foresters can include sessions on encouraging the health and productivity of the country's woods. Many forestry workers have the opportunity to advance to management positions. Advanced degrees in forestry are common among conservation workers and are beneficial for those who wish to advance in the field.

Wesley Hirons, logger, Rickreall, Oregon

Wesley Hirons grew up around logging and started to learn the ropes when he was just in elementary school. His family had a logging business in Mills City, Oregon, a timber town not far from Salem. By eighth grade he was running some of the more sophisticated equipment, but after high school Hirons decided to spend four years in the navy. "I knew I would spend the rest of my life in the woods." And for the past ten years he's been working in logging full-time. For the past two years he's been with Gahlsdorf Logging in Rickreall, Oregon. "It's something I know how to do." To succeed in the business Hirons says you have to want to work hard. "With logging, you really have to perform," he says. "Your progress is immediately noticed, since you are usually working side by side with your boss." He actually loves that and enjoys the challenge.

Working outside is another aspect that has always appealed to Hirons, who can't imagine going to work in an office each day. "It's very physical work," he says of what he does, adding that he's convinced climbing mountains and hauling logs has added years to his life. At forty-one, he's fit and healthy and wouldn't consider joining a gym. But his days start as soon as light breaks, and depending on the season that can be well before 6:00 AM. Snow and rain don't stand in a logger's way either. "Weather does not dictate or determine work," says Hirons. "We're like the mailman." Only he adds that work will be delayed during lightning or severe winds for safety reasons.

The team effort is another aspect of logging that Hirons finds appealing. "Working with a group of guys to accomplish something; there's a bit of bonding there."

Hirons also enjoys the beauty of the mountains and the opportunity to see pockets of the forests that few people ever have a chance to see. The early mornings, just before sunrise, are some of his favorite times. "There's something about getting up early, you get a jump on the day," he says. "I'm seeing creeks that probably haven't been seen for eighty years."

Hirons started off in the entry-level logging positions at Gahlsdorf, but he's a supervisor now who oversees daily operations to ensure that logs are moving out at the right pace and that everyone is keeping up with their assigned jobs. He can't imagine spending his days doing anything else. "There's a lot of room to move up for people who have a lot of gumption."

⟫ The Numbers

There were about 88,000 jobs in this industry in 2006, with approximately 20,000 in forest conservation. More than one-third worked for the government, at the local or state level. Overall, employment opportunities are not expected to change through 2016, and most job openings will come from retiring loggers. But forestry workers will see as much as a 10 percent increase in job opportunities through 2016, which means another 2,000 positions. Demand is expected to increase as additional land is set aside to protect natural resources or wildlife habitats.

Earnings vary within these two sectors. When it comes to logging, the earnings often start at minimum wage. The average hourly earnings of a logging operator were $14.28 in 2006. Salaries vary significantly depending on the size and location of a logging company. For example, workers in Alaska and the Northwest earn more than those in the South, where the cost of living is also generally lower. Forestry and conservation positions often pay more than $26.00 an hour to those who are experienced.

MASON

What do the Egyptian pyramids, the Great Wall of China, and the Roman Colosseum all have in common? Masons built each of these wonders, and each one of these pieces of history has been standing for thousands of years. And another thousand years from now the work of masons will remain. Masonry is an ancient art and a craft and is often an integral part of a building, landscape, or community.

Ⅲ➡ The Work

The level of complexity in masonry varies widely from simple patios and stone walls to complex and ornate buildings. Some masons specialize in renovating antique brickwork. Masons cut and break material, design projects, and lay brick. The work can be both creative and formulaic. Masons must be adept at using specialized tools for cutting and hammering stone. After finishing laying the bricks, blocks, or stone, masons must also clean, polish, or treat the finished product. Dependability and a strong work ethic are keys to success in this field. Knowledge of basic math—including measurement, volume, mixing proportions, and geometry—are helpful.

There are a variety of specialized masons in the field. Some do a bit of everything, while others focus on honing their skills in one area. For example, refractory masons specialize in the installation of firebrick and tile in high-temperature boilers or furnaces, which are often found in industrial establishments. Brick masons and block masons build and repair walls, floors, fireplaces, and chimneys. Stonemasons tend to build stone walls, as well as set stone exteriors and floors. They work with natural material such as marble or granite as well as artificial substances such as concrete.

Masons who have versatile skills in exterior stone, brick, and concrete as well as interior tile and marble setting will have better job opportunities. The more you can do and the more willing you are to learn different skills, the better off you will be when it comes to career growth.

⦿ Work Setting

Masons usually work outdoors, but in contrast to the past when work slowed down in the winter months, new processes and materials allow more work to continue through variable weather conditions. Still, many shift to inside jobs during the colder months. Some restoration masons find themselves repairing fireplaces inside and therefore can continue working during inclement weather.

Success in the Real World

Matthew Gillard, Mason, Amesbury, Massachusetts

"I was disenfranchised with school," is how Matthew Gillard describes his life as a young student. He was frustrated and angry, too. Although his scores were quite high on IQ tests, Gillard had been put into a special education class starting in the fourth grade of his Amesbury, Massachusetts, elementary school. He blames it on all of the acting out he did after his parents divorced. Gillard felt like a failure, and he was miserable in the classroom. "I was much more creative with my hands," he adds.

By the time he got to high school, Gillard started working for his neighbor, who was a mason. Gillard would clean bricks and help out on jobs during the weekends and summers.

Although Gillard enjoyed math and woodshop classes, he had no intention of following his friends to college. He told his parents he was going to take a year off, but really he was just delaying having to tell them that he wasn't going the college route. At the end of the year, he told his mother that he really wanted to be a mason. He had enough of a taste to know it was something he wanted to pursue.

"If you want to do it, do it and be the best," Gillard's mother told him. She suggested that he call Richard Irons, the premier restoration mason in New England, and ask for a job. It took a few calls and some perseverance, but Irons told Gillard he could try out for a day. If Gillard did well, Irons said he'd be hired. That was in April 2001, and now Gillard is being groomed to take over the business when Irons retires.

For Gillard, masonry combines his love of math with his creativity, as well as his long-standing interest in history. He started working at just $10 an hour, but by the time he was twenty-three, he had bought his own house and was expecting to make close to $100,000 in 2008. "The sky is the limit," he says. But that's only for people who are willing to work hard, who are passionate and meticulous about their work. "We pride ourselves on being the best of the best in the industry."

He loves working with his hands, being outside, and the diversity of the jobs. Some days Gillard is designing brick walls, fireplaces, or patios. Other days he's laying brick or restoring 250-year-old fireplaces. "It's physical. I don't have to go to the gym," says the trim twenty-seven-year-old. "I feel healthy." The downside is the uncertainty of work and the possibility that the next job won't materialize. That can be unnerving, but that's why perfection and reputation are important.

Working on an old house with an antique fireplace that dates back to the 1700s gives Gillard an immense sense of pride. "I'll pick up a brick and I think of the last mason. He's dead and gone, and his work is still sitting here proudly." It's the fireplaces that are especially unique for him. "The fireplace is the center of the home," says Gillard. "It's nice to be part of that. It makes me so proud."

ⅢⅢ➡ Training and Certification

Most masons pick up their skills informally and on the job, while observing and learning from more experienced workers. Some receive initial training in vocational education schools, and others complete a formal apprenticeship. Individuals who learn by doing usually start out as basic helpers, laborers, or mason tenders. These workers carry materials, move or assemble scaffolds, and mix mortar. They also may learn restoration skills and cleaning or repointing techniques at the same time.

Apprenticeships for masons are often sponsored by local contractors, trade associations, or local unions. These programs usually require three years of on-the-job training and include classroom instruction in blueprint reading, mathematics, and layout work.

ⅢⅢ➡ The Numbers

There were 182,000 masonry jobs in 2006, according to the Bureau of Labor Statistics. About 24 percent of masons were self-employed and often worked on small jobs such as patios, walkways, and fireplaces. Jobs in this industry are expected to increase 10 percent between 2006 and 2016, which means more than 18,000 new openings. Employment should be especially steady for those with restoration skills who are capable of repairing many of the old brick buildings that have started to deteriorate. The demand for stonework in commercial lobbies is also growing.

The median hourly earnings of masons as of May 2006 were $20.66 and the highest 10 percent earned more than $32.43. Apprentices earn much less at first but can advance quickly.

MINING

Miners are currently in high demand, as shortages of skilled workers are reported around the country. "Probably finding and retaining the workforce is the number-one challenge we face, not only because of the demographics but because the workforce in the U.S. has changed so much," said Lee Chapman of Newmont Mining Corporation in Denver. "There is an enormous people shortage here," he said of the Nevada gold mines. "Technicians, craftsmen, and blue-collar skilled workers are scarce. Today, when we post a job we might get 10 applications and nobody standing at the door."

Mining has long had a reputation for being dirty and dangerous. The industry is in fact safer and more sophisticated than ever. Recent federal regulations have tightened security, and mining companies are working to ensure improved conditions at the mines. Another misconception about mining is that it all happens below ground, but much of mining is above ground in open pits, particularly the mining that takes place in the western United States.

⫸ The Work

The mining industry contains four main divisions, which are defined by the resources that are collected: oil and gas extraction, coal mining, metal ore mining, and nonmetallic mineral mining and quarrying. Products of the mining industry generate the majority of energy used in this country, from electricity in homes to fuel in vehicles. Uses of mined materials include coal, oil, and gas for energy; copper for wiring; gold for satellites and sophisticated electronic components; and stone and gravel for construction of roads and buildings. Other minerals are used as ingredients in medicines and household products.

In surface mining, miners typically operate huge machines that either remove the earth above the ore deposit, or dig and load the ore onto trucks. As the term suggests, surface mining does not require miners to work in underground tunnels and shafts. Workers at quarries have duties similar to those of surface miners. Using jackhammers and wedges, rock splitters remove pieces of stone from a rock mass. When it comes to oil drilling, companies select a site on which to install a derrick and begin extraction. This is often attempted off-shore, along the floor of the ocean.

We typically think of people having to burrow underground when we think of coal miners, but, as I just mentioned, many coal miners work at surface mines and never go into a tunnel. Coal is a fossil fuel that is used primarily for electric power generation and in the production of steel. Underground mining is necessary when the coal deposit lies deep below the surface of the earth.

Metal ore mining is the extraction of gold, silver, iron, copper, lead, and zinc. A massive amount of rock must often be extracted from the ground to obtain a useable amount of these metals. Similar to coal, these metals may be mined underground or on the surface.

Employment in the mining industry has been affected significantly by new technology and more sophisticated mining techniques that increase productivity. Most mining machines and control rooms are now automated or at least computer-controlled, requiring fewer human operators. Many mines also use other sophisticated technology such as lasers and robotics, which further increases work efficiency.

⯈ Work Setting

Work environments vary depending on what is being mined and where a mine is located. Working conditions in mines and quarries can be unusual and sometimes dangerous. Surface mining is much less hazardous. Physical strength and stamina are necessary for all of these jobs. Workers in surface mines, quarries, and wells are subject to rugged outdoor work in all kinds of weather and climates. Some surface mines and quarries shut down in the winter because snow and ice covering the mine site make work too difficult. Because they are largely automated, oil and gas sites typically operate year-round regardless of weather conditions. Offshore drilling sites may be evacuated in the event of serious hurricanes or storms.

Underground mines are damp and dark, and some can be very hot and noisy. At times, several inches of water may cover tunnel floors, which may only be lit by a miner's headlamp. Workers in mines with very low roofs may have to work on their hands and knees or while lying down in confined spaces. Needless to say, this is tough work.

⯈ Training and Certification

There are few formal education requirements for miners, but a lot of experience is needed before people are expected, or even permitted, to perform some of the advanced jobs. Most miners start off as helpers and learn on the job. Some formal training programs are available and are seen as more important now than they were in the past. These programs are growing in popularity as the sophistication of equipment is increasing. Technology is changing mining, and miners must adjust to the new techniques and machines. Some employers prefer to hire people who have had vocational training in high school or have attended postsecondary programs or technical schools. These programs and schools are typically found in mining regions.

The Federal Mine Safety and Health Act of 1977 mandates that each U.S. mine have an approved worker-training program in health and safety issues. In addition to new miner training, each miner must also receive at least eight hours of safety training each year, and miners assigned to new jobs must receive safety training relating to their new position.

As workers gain more experience, they can advance to higher-paying jobs requiring greater skill. Miners with significant experience or special training can become mine safety, health, and compliance officers, whose duties include mine safety inspection. Mining engineers were often miners at one time, although engineer is a professional position for which a bachelor's degree is required. It's always an option down the road.

⠿➡ The Numbers

There were approximately 619,000 jobs in the United States mining industry as of 2006. Average earnings were significantly higher than for other industries. For example, in 2006 miners earned $21.40 an hour in oil and gas extraction, $22.08 an hour in coal mining, $22.39 an hour in metal ore mining, and $18.74 an hour in nonmetallic minerals mining.

Employment in mining is expected to decrease. That said, employment in nonmetallic minerals mining should increase some because of continued demand for crushed stone, sand, and gravel used in construction. Environmental concerns, accompanied by strict regulations, have had a major impact on this industry. Restrictions on drilling in environmentally sensitive areas are also expected to limit mining, both onshore and offshore. Mining jobs are heavily concentrated in the parts of the country where large resource deposits exist, such as Kentucky, Pennsylvania, and West Virginia. Metal mining is more prevalent in the West and Southwest, particularly in Arizona, Nevada, and Montana. Surprisingly, about 80 percent of mining establishments employ fewer than twenty people, so these are mostly small operations.

Because workers in the mining industry are older than average, some companies may lose large numbers of their workforce. Employment opportunities will be best for those with previous experience and for those with technical skills.

PLUMBER, PIPE LAYER, AND PIPE FITTER

Plumbing has been around since ancient civilizations, when Romans and Greeks luxuriated in baths and delivered water through aqueducts. They needed potable water, and potable water is what they figured out how to get—and that was the start of plumbing systems as we know them. Plumbers now connect our homes, businesses, factories, heating systems, and more to water sources. While more advanced materials and technologies are used, the general concept hasn't changed much in thousands of years.

Modern plumbing involves more than clogged drains and leaking faucets, but for most of us that's what we think of first. Plumbers are responsible for steam heat systems, pipelines that carry waste and water, and piping natural gas.

⏵ The Work

Plumbers, pipe layers, and steamfitters install, maintain, and repair complex residential and commercial pipe systems. Some of these systems move water to and from municipal water treatment plants. Others dispose of waste, provide gas to stoves and furnaces, or provide for heating and cooling needs. Pipe systems in factories or power plants carry steam that powers huge turbines.

Although pipe laying, plumbing, pipe fitting, and steam fitting are often considered a single trade, workers generally specialize in one area. Pipe layers lay clay, concrete, plastic, or cast-iron pipe for drains, sewers, water mains, and oil or gas lines. Plumbers install and repair the water, waste disposal, drainage, and gas systems in homes and commercial or industrial buildings. Plumbers also install plumbing fixtures—think bathtubs, sinks, and toilets—as well as appliances such as dishwashers and water heaters. Pipe fitters install and repair both high- and low-pressure pipe systems used in manufacturing, the generation of electricity, and the heating and cooling of buildings. They also install automatic controls that are increasingly used to regulate these various systems. Some pipe fitters specialize in only one type of system. For example, steamfitters install pipe systems that move liquids or gases under high pressure, and sprinkler fitters install automatic fire sprinkler systems.

While working on construction projects, plumbers are often involved in the design process, collaborating with carpenters or electricians to plan out where pipes and fixtures fit into a building's blueprint. Their knowledge of codes is essential to the success of a project, and they should have a basic understanding of other trades.

⣿➡ Work Setting

Pipe fitters and steamfitters most often work in industrial settings or power plants. Plumbers work in commercial and residential settings where water and septic systems need to be installed and maintained. Pipe layers work outdoors, sometime in remote areas, as they build the pipelines that connect sources of oil, gas, and chemicals with their customers. All of these jobs can be physically demanding and require strength to carry pipes, other material, and equipment.

Success in the Real World

Louis Levesque, plumber, Kapuskasing, Ontario

Computers may have taken over many industries, but when it comes to plumbing Louis Levesque says actual plumbers, not machines, are required to do the work. "Computers can't really take over the plumbing world," says this forty-two-year-old, who has been working in the industry since he graduated high school. Levesque went to trade school and put in about 9,200 hours over five years to complete his apprenticeship. He has been working in northern Ontario since, and he is now part owner of GT Plumbing & Heating in Kapuskasing, Ontario.

Although Levesque spent most of his career in the field, he is now largely responsible for customer service and billing. It's something he really enjoys, particularly when it comes to dealing with the people. "There is a lot of work, and the money is great." When it comes to being in the field, Levesque says people have to be willing to get dirty. In rural areas such as his, the work is more predictable and high-rise buildings are a rarity. He said the benefit of an apprenticeship or even a job in an urban area is that the job is constantly different. Training programs will often provide one week of work in different specialties, and there is more diversity in what you're expected to know and be able to do.

But with five partners and twenty-seven employees, Levesque has constantly had challenges even though he isn't in a large city. And he points out that there is work year-round. He adds that union jobs continue to pay the best and are comparable to any other skilled trade. "There is really big potential," says Levesque. "And there will always be work in plumbing."

⮕ Training and Certification

Pipe layers, plumbers, pipe fitters, and steamfitters can enter the industry in a variety of ways. Most residential and industrial plumbers get their training in career and technical schools or from on-the-job training. Pipe layers, plumbers, pipe fitters, and steamfitters who do commercial work are usually trained through formal apprenticeship programs. Postsecondary courses in shop, plumbing, general mathematics, and drafting are all considered good preparation for this field.

Apprenticeship programs generally provide the most comprehensive training available for these jobs and are usually offered through unions or contractors. These programs are typically four or five years of paid, on-the-job training and at least 144 hours of related classroom instruction for each of those years. As apprentices gain experience, they learn how to work with various types of material and how to install different pipe systems and plumbing fixtures.

States typically require plumbers to be licensed. Requirements vary, but most localities require workers to have several years of experience and to pass an examination that tests their knowledge of general procedures and local plumbing codes.

⭬ The Numbers

There were 569,000 plumbers and pipe layers in the United States in 2006. About 55 percent were working on new construction, repair, or modernization, and about 12 percent were self-employed. These are among the highest-paid workers in the construction trade, with median salaries at $20.56 an hour. The highest 10 percent earn more than $34.79.

Employment in the United States for this sector is expected to grow by 10 percent between 2006 and 2016, which means close to 57,000 new jobs. Job opportunities are expected to be very good, especially for workers with welding experience. Demand for plumbers will stem from new construction and building renovation. Bath remodeling, in particular, is expected to remain popular and create opportunities for residential plumbers. Some employers report difficulty finding workers with the right qualifications, and many people are expected to retire from the trade between now and 2016.

ROOFER

Although many roofers have worked in general construction or continue to do so, roofing is a specialty in which contractors have their own expertise and employees. Like cars, roofs are here to stay, so even if new construction isn't booming, roofers will be needed to repair, replace, and maintain existing roofs. Roofers must be familiar with various materials—from asphalt and gravel to rubber and thermoplastics. Environmentally friendly roofs and sustainable roofing—even those with actual greenery incorporated—are something roofers will likely encounter more often in the future as well.

⮕ The Work

Roofing can be strenuous work and requires heavy lifting and working outdoors in all kinds of weather. Although roofers tend to schedule construction around nicer weather, repairs must be made during all types of storms or rain. Roofers must take safety seriously to prevent falling from high roofs or slipping during inclement weather. Roofers are typically the ones responsible for making absolute certain that a roof is watertight.

⮕ Work Setting

As the name implies, roofers are up on roofs almost all of the time they are working. Sometimes low roofs or flat roofs can provide a break from the more dangerous slanted roofs. Roofers can expect to spend most of their time outdoors. They should be comfortable with climbing and with moderate heights.

⮕ Training and Certification

Most roofers learn informally and by working for experienced roofers or contractors. Classes and safety courses are offered in some areas. A three-year roofing apprenticeship is another common way of getting into the field, and these are typically offered through roofing unions.

⮕ The Numbers

In 2006, there were approximately 156,000 roofing jobs in the United States. Most roofers work for roofing contractors, and about 20 percent of all roofers are self-employed. Faster-than-average job growth is expected between now and 2016, largely because of high turnover. It is expected that the industry will grow by about 14 percent in the United States, which would account for more than 21,000 new jobs. Median hourly wages for roofers in 2006 were $15.51, and the highest 10 percent earned more than $26.79.

SUBWAY, RAILROAD, AND STREETCAR OPERATOR

Working on trains is one of the coolest ways to see our country's landscape, but it can take you away from home for long stretches of time. Operating municipal subways and streetcars is an exciting way to interact with a lot of people on a daily basis while providing a crucial role in the community. Public transportation sure is getting quite a bit of attention, as gas prices rise and people are looking for alternative ways to get where they want to go. Thanks to this, railroad operators and subway drivers will play an even more crucial role in our society in the next decade.

ⅢⅢ➡ The Work

Rail transportation workers are employed by freight, passenger, and urban transit (better known as the subway). Freight trains transport billions of tons of goods to destinations within the United States and to ports to be shipped abroad. Passenger railroads deliver millions of passengers and commuters to destinations throughout the country. Rail transportation workers not only work on trains, but also in rail yards where the maintenance of cars and engines takes place.

Jobs vary quite a bit within this industry. For example, locomotive engineers operate large trains and carry cargo or passengers between stations. Most engineers run diesel-electric locomotives. Engineers must have a thorough knowledge of their routes and must be constantly aware of the condition and components of their train. Railroad conductors coordinate all activities of freight or passenger train crews, including scheduling and overseeing cargo. There are also railroad brake operators and yardmasters.

In contrast to other rail transportation workers, subway and streetcar operators generally work for public transit authorities. Subway operators control trains that transport passengers through cities and their suburbs. Increasingly, the train's speed and the amount of time spent at each station are controlled by computers and not by the operator. That said, humans must still be on alert in case of breakdowns or emergencies. Streetcar drivers tend to operate electric-powered streetcars or trolleys. Rail transportation workers should have good hearing, eyesight, hand-eye coordination, and mechanical aptitude. Physical stamina is required for most rail transportation jobs.

ⅢⅢ➤ Work Setting

Trains run constantly, which means that rail transportation employees work nights, weekends, and holidays to keep trains moving every day, all day. Freight trains are often dispatched at the will of a customer, which could mean working odd hours or on the weekends, but those who work on passenger trains tend to have regularly scheduled shifts. And I think it goes without saying that the appearance, temperature, and accommodations of passenger trains are far better than those on freight trains. Rail yard workers spend most of their time outdoors, work regardless of weather conditions, and may have physically strenuous duties.

⠀⟩ Training and Certification

Rail workers start out in a variety of positions to gain experience needed for more demanding assignments. They generally begin training to become a conductor and could continue to advance to the position of engineer. Much of the training occurs through a rail company's internal program and tends to require that applicants have at least a high school diploma or GED. Most rail transportation workers complete formal classroom and hands-on training before beginning work.

Most subway and streetcar operators actually start out as bus drivers and work their way up through the system. New operators must complete training programs and demonstrate an ability to troubleshoot problems and malfunctions as well as take charge during an emergency situation.

Train engineers must be federally licensed to operate freight and passenger trains. Some ongoing training is necessary to maintain these licenses.

⠀⟩ The Numbers

Employment in most railroad transportation occupations is not expected to change much through 2016, but that said, opportunities should be good for qualified applicants. Most of these openings are expected because of retiring workers. Also, demand for railroad freight service will grow as the need to transport goods increases. Railroads will also benefit from congested highways as commuters shift their habits and rely more on public transportation.

As of May 2006, median hourly earnings in this industry included $27.88 for rail engineers, $26.70 for conductors, and $23.55 for subway operators.

WASTE AND WATER TREATMENT PLANT OPERATOR

We all know clean water is essential for everyday life, but we don't usually think about how it gets that way before reaching our homes, schools, and offices. Water is pumped from wells, rivers, streams, and reservoirs to treatment plants, where it is treated and distributed to customers. Plant operators control equipment and processes that remove or destroy harmful materials, chemicals, and microorganisms from the water. Operators also control pumps, valves, and other equipment that move the water or wastewater through the various treatment processes. Most water treatment operators work in government or private water and sewage plants. Because of a large number of upcoming retirements and the difficulty of filling these positions, job opportunities should be quite good in the coming years.

⮕ The Work

Water treatment plant and system operators treat water so that it is safe to drink. Wastewater treatment plant and system operators remove harmful pollutants from domestic and industrial liquid waste so that it is safe to return to the environment.

In this vein, plant operators need mechanical aptitude and the ability to solve problems intuitively. They must have the ability to apply data to formulas that determine treatment requirements, flow levels, and concentration levels. Some basic familiarity with computers is also necessary, as operators typically use them to record data. Some plants also use computer-controlled equipment and instruments.

Operators read, interpret, and adjust meters and gauges to make sure that plant equipment and processes are working properly. Occasionally, operators must work during emergencies and under intense pressure. A heavy rainstorm, for example, may cause large amounts of wastewater to flow into sewers, exceeding a plant's treatment capacity.

Depending on the size of the plant, an operator may be responsible for all equipment, as often is the case with a smaller plant. In larger operations, he or she would likely oversee just one area.

Water quality standards are largely set by the Safe Drinking Water Act, which specifies standards for drinking water, and the Clean Water Act, which regulates pollutants that are discharged. Plant operators must be familiar with these guidelines as well as any local ones that exist.

⟫ Work Setting

Plant and system operators work both inside and out and may be exposed to noise from machinery and to unpleasant odors. Working as an operator can be physically demanding and is sometimes done in unclean locations. In this industry, you must pay close attention to safety procedures because of the presence of hazardous or unsanitary conditions.

⟫ Training and Certification

Employers usually hire high school graduates who are trained on the job and later become licensed. The completion of an associate's degree or a one-year certificate program in water quality and wastewater treatment technology is beneficial, especially since technology is increasing the complexity of the plants' operation and the equipment used. Most of these programs are offered by trade associations.

Many water control agencies offer courses to improve operator skills and knowledge. Operators must pass an examination certifying that they are capable of overseeing water treatment operations. Mandatory certification is implemented at the state level, and the licensing requirements vary widely among the states.

Plant superintendents typically need postsecondary training in water and wastewater treatment and significant experience as a plant operator. Education requirements are increasing as more complex treatment plants are built to meet drinking water and pollution standards. Superintendents of large plants often need at least a bachelor's degree in engineering or science.

ⅢⅢ➡ The Numbers

Water treatment plant and system operators held about 111,000 jobs in 2006, with almost 80 percent of them in local governments. Employment in this industry is expected to grow by 14 percent (or more than 15,000 jobs) between 2006 and 2016. Job opportunities should be excellent because of a large number of retirements. Job opportunities tend to be better in urban areas.

The median annual salary for the industry was $36,070 as of May 2006, and the highest 10 percent were earning more than $55,120.

WELDING

There has never been a better time to go into welding. At least that's what the folks at the American Welding Society (AWS) say. AWS expects half of the nation's welders to retire in the next several years, and many of the welding unions around the country are having trouble recruiting. Some are finding it so difficult that they've resorted to importing welders from other states while even offering signing bonuses as incentives.

Opportunities in welding are quite varied—from underwater welding to jobs on skyscrapers or in manufacturing plants. Many welders will tell you that they are really artists at the core, passionate about sculpting and creating. All of them say you have to be comfortable or get comfortable with the extreme heat required to do this job.

Success in the Real World

Dwayne "Cactus" Jones, welder, Grand Saline, Texas

"I had teaching shoved down my throat." For Dwayne "Cactus" Jones, a welder in eastern Texas, school and education were everything. His mother, a high school teacher, and his father, a principal, expected that their son would go to college. It was just a given. So, when Jones told his parents that he was planning to go to ironworking school, the news did not go over well. "I made tremendous waves," says Jones. He says his parents didn't talk to him for a few years and that they still seem peeved by his decision, even though he's almost fifty and incredibly successful. "I was the shame of the neighborhood."

Jones says he definitely felt like an outsider when he was watching his friends go off to college. His parents told him to move out, and his father predicted he'd fail at whatever he set out to do since he wouldn't have college degree. While crushed, Jones also saw this as a challenge. "I have a terrible ego and a tremendous amount of pride." Jones was determined to prove his father wrong. In 1980, he joined the ironworkers union in Houston and has been building ever since. "I love doing it," he says, even after nearly thirty years. He still drives by buildings in Houston and points up to the top or along the sides and says, "Hey, I built that."

Jones obviously has a knack for welding. He has his own company and is now in the business of building oil rigs. When he talks about his financial success, Jones puts it succinctly when he says, "I can afford whatever I want." That even includes a Mercedes he bought for his wife as a birthday gift. But when it comes to describing the ideal welder, Jones says it's tough. "You've either got it or you don't." He says that for those who have the talent and enjoy welding—which does require precision, patience, and a steady hand—unions are the way to go. Jones reminds anyone who asks that you have to work "very hard" and you can't mind being out in the cold or the heat. "If you're willing to put the time in, the sky is the limit."

Ⅲ➡ The Work

Because welders are needed in construction, manufacturing, and other industries, employers have a constant need for skilled workers. What exactly is welding? It's the most common way of permanently joining metal parts. In this process, heat as high as 800 degrees is applied to metal pieces, melting and fusing them to form a permanent bond. Because of its strength, welding is used in shipbuilding, automobile manufacturing, and aerospace construction. Skyscrapers are welded. Cars contain hundreds of welds. Your bed was probably welded, as were some of the tools in your basement.

Welders should have good eyesight, hand-eye coordination, and manual dexterity. They should be able to concentrate on detailed work for long periods of time and be able to work in awkward positions. In addition, welders must increasingly be willing to receive training. There are over eighty different welding processes that a welder can use. Some are performed manually while others are semiautomatic and require a welder to use machinery to complete a task. Skilled welding, soldering, and brazing workers generally use drawings or specifications to complete their work. Highly skilled welders often are trained to work with a wide variety of materials, such as titanium, aluminum, or plastics, in addition to steel.

⮕ Work Setting

Welders are often exposed to a number of hazards, the most obvious being the high heat. They wear safety shoes, goggles, and hoods with protective lenses. Welders and cutters may work outdoors, often in inclement weather, or inside, sometimes in studios or indoor job sites. They may also be required to lift heavy objects.

> " It's a shock for a lot of folks that you have to study and read and use math. This is quite a sophisticated science. There are always new metals, processes, and techniques. It's a challenge to keep up with the changes. "
>
> —*Connie Christopher,*
> *welding instructor, on welding*

⮕ Training and Certification

Several trade unions have programs that allow newcomers to obtain the training necessary to work as a welder while being paid in the process. These apprenticeships sometimes culminate in an associate's degree and are beneficial for future employment opportunities. Some welding positions require general certifications in welding or certification in specific skills. Although some employers provide training, most prefer to hire workers who already have experience or formal training. The welding unions are a significant source of training and apprenticeships.

⫸ The Numbers

There were about 462,000 jobs in welding in 2006, about two-thirds of which were in the manufacturing industry. Both a retiring workforce and growth in the oil and gas industries are expected to create excellent opportunities for welders. As we've mentioned, welding schools and industry experts report that skilled welders have little difficulty finding work. The median earnings for the industry were $15.10 an hour as of May 2006, with the top 10 percent earning more than $22.50.

Blue Collar in ACTION

Building More Than Ships in Newport News

The coasts of the United States used to be lined with shipbuilding towns and yards. One of the few that has remained a steadfast and imposing presence is the Northrop Grumman Shipyard in Newport News, Virginia. Better known for years as Newport News Shipbuilding, the yard has been constructing military ships since it launched its first vessel in 1891. Today, the company is the sole designer and builder of nuclear-powered aircraft carriers and only one of two yards in the entire nation that builds nuclear submarines.

Connected to the shipyard is one of the most impressive and productive training programs in the United States. The Apprenticeship School was founded in 1919 and trains participants in eighteen different trades through its four- and five-year-long programs to become part of Northrop Grumman's shipbuilding workforce. The apprenticeships train participants to be successful in shipbuilding careers while also providing rigorous academic courses. "We build three types of ships here; craftsmanship, scholarship, and leadership," says Robert Leber, the school's education and workforce director. The program is popular and competitive, so much so that recently Leber received three thousand applicants for just three hundred positions.

The school is unique in that it trains students for the trades, but it's simultaneously set up much like a typical college campus, with extracurricular activities, Division III sports teams, and a supportive, close-knit community. If students meet academic and grade requirements, they graduate from the program with an associate's degree. Even if they don't receive the degree, graduates are highly employable with exceptional technical skills and are still eligible to work in the shipyard, building warships, aircraft carriers, and submarines.

"These are not Tonka trucks," says Leber. "When you go home at night, you can honestly say you helped protect the country with the product you're building." A majority of the graduates of the Apprentice School go straight to the Northrop Grumman shipyard, and five years after graduation Leber says approximately 80 percent of the former apprentices are still working there.

Leber says training is more essential now than ever for getting into the trades. The willingness to be trained is a quality he looks for in applicants. You have to show up with a good attitude, Leber notes, and a willingness to learn and be instructed by others. He points to growth in new industries, such as solar panel installation, as sectors where jobs are expected to be plentiful, but will require significant skills. Not only do installers need to have electronic and technical abilities, but also they have to communicate with a property owner about how to operate the new systems. These jobs will require physical strength as well. "It's not going to take a college degree," he says, "but we need quality training after high school."

That's what you get at the Apprentice School, where Leber says students can challenge themselves while becoming master welders, electricians, or machinists and become integral to one of the most cutting-edge operations in the country.

Check out the Apprentice School at www.apprenticeschool.com.

Chapter 4

This Is Women's Work, Too

W omen make the best welders. At least that's what Dave Barton says. Barton, who is the senior welding engineer at Lincoln Electric in Cleveland, Ohio, says women tend to have exceptional hand-eye coordination, a crucial skill in welding. "They're very good," Barton says of females who weld. "That is, as long as they get over the fear factor." For many women—and men, too—the high heat used to weld can be daunting. "It's the eye-hand coordination that separates women from men." Dexterity is key, and Barton says women are naturally detail-oriented.

Connie Christopher agrees. "There is the eye for detail and such a patience requirement," both of which she says are female strong suits. Christopher fell into welding as a young Navy wife who was desperate to make some money. In 1973, she went to Electric Boat in Groton, Connecticut, and applied for a clerical position. There weren't any available, but she was told that there was a welding position open. "I'll take it," she said and then asked, "What's welding?" Coincidentally, Christopher had found her passion. "Once that shield went down I had a world of solitude. I fell in love with it." She's been welding since and went from working on submarines in Connecticut to railroads in Oregon. Now she teaches welding at Portland Community College.

Christopher says there were few female welders when she started in the industry, but she is slowly seeing more joining. There is always at least one female student in her classes, and recently she had six, something she thinks of as a sign that things are moving in the right direction. With massive welding shortages anticipated in the next decade, Christopher said there will be incredible opportunities for women. "Some places it's really accepted, and others there's a real gender bias," she says of how women are received differently depending on the area of the country. But overall, she thinks it's an incredible field for women.

When Christopher was working in Connecticut, she felt accepted as a woman in a male-dominated field. She was one of the lucky ones who didn't feel singled out for being a woman; she wasn't discriminated against and managed to have incredible male mentors. But when she moved to Oregon in 1979 to work for a shipbuilding company that had recruited her, she was confronted with a completely different attitude. When she walked onto the welding floor at her new job, she was told she couldn't take the test that was required to place her and others in an appropriate position according to their skill level. "If

" I am the only woman you will ever meet who legally gets paid to check shorts. "

—*Veronica Rose, master electrician from Long Island*

you weighed in at three hundred pounds I might think about hiring you," the supervisor said. "But I'm not going to have you distracting my welders."

We're used to seeing women behind desks in corporate offices, in boardrooms, or working as doctors and computer engineers. We've come a long way and think it's quite normal to find a female architect or accountant. Women have been working for decades on Wall Street and in marketing positions at large companies. But women haven't come quite as far in the skilled trades. They haven't made the same strides, and the stigma of being a woman in the trades still lingers. We find it an odd sight—and indeed it is highly unusual—to see a female plumber, auto mechanic, or trucker. I tend to crane my neck when I see a woman on a construction site, just to be sure I saw what I think I saw.

"Our first obstacle is image," says Ellen Voie, president and founder of Women in Trucking. "Women don't know they can do this job." With 20,000 truckers, Voie says it's an excellent time for women to consider this as a career. Most trucking equipment relies on hydraulics or other automatic mechanisms, which means heavy lifting is rarely necessary. Women are often hesitant to enter the skilled trades, and many wonder whether they can handle the work or will be welcome. But the trades have become incredible opportunities for females, even if they are still in the minority.

The trucking industry hasn't entirely adjusted to its female workforce, and Voie points out that many amenities across the country need improving. Some truck stops still don't have designated showers for women, and many of the on-site convenience stores don't carry women's toiletries. But her organization is working to improve these facilities as well as the perception that trucking is just for men. For people who enjoy driving and traveling, trucking can be a great career.

Companies often have training programs from three to six weeks long, after which new drivers are on the road with their first hauls. After just six weeks of training, Voie said first-time truckers can often start off with a $40,000 salary.

Did You KNOW?

THE NUMBERS DON'T LIE

In the United States, 24 percent of architects are women. Twenty-four percent of all computer programmers are women, and 21 percent of chemical engineers are female. But just 15 percent of all taxi drivers and chauffeurs are women. Thirteen percent of all police and patrol officers are women, and of all the cabinetmakers out there, just 6 percent are women. Of water and liquid waste facility operators, 6.2 percent are women and just 3.6 percent of all drywall installers are women. Of carpenters, only 1.9 percent are female, and 0.4 percent of all ironworkers are female.

When Linda Howard was ready to give up on being a nursing assistant, she went into trucking. She said many of her patients weighed more than 250 pounds and she simply couldn't lift them anymore. At forty-four, she was exhausted and achy every day after her ten-hour shifts. Her partner Cherie Ahlvers had lost her job, and the two women decided to find something they could do together. One of Howard's friends had long been telling her she should go into trucking. So both Howard and Ahlvers decided to give it a try and went to trucking school. Three years later they drive a dedicated route together, meaning they go from their home in Fernley, Nevada, which is outside Reno, to

Orlando, Florida, each week. They spend about five days on the road and are typically home Sundays and Mondays.

"I love it," says Howard. She loves the freedom, the driving, the open road, and seeing parts of America along the way. She enjoys not having a boss looking over her shoulder. "You need to love driving," she says. "You're basically queen of the road." Howard says she's never faced any problems for being a female trucker, and she generally finds that other drivers are welcoming toward the duo. On their down time, of which Howard says there really isn't much, she surfs the web and Ahlvers either watches movies or reads. Since they are both musicians, they tried to bring their instruments along for the long rides, but when Ahlvers began to teach herself saxophone in the small cab of the truck, Howard decided it was time to ban live music.

Howard says they were each making $40,000 to $50,000 their first year driving and have never had so much money. It's allowed the women to buy a house of their own and have plenty left over. "I know people who have spent $40,000 on college and don't make this much when they get out." But Howard warns that this is definitely not for everyone. To anyone thinking about getting into trucking, Howard suggests getting on a truck first just for a test run. Going along for a ride or two should give you a sense of whether this is something you could do, she says. "This lifestyle is an acquired taste." You are in small quarters, you don't have a private shower at your disposal and instead must rely on the truck stop facilities, plus the endless driving can get tiring.

Although women entered the workforce, and specifically the blue-collar workforce, in droves during World War II, many were sent home once the men returned from overseas. They were only welcome when the men weren't around and the women were desperately needed. These women had been enticed by the posters of Rosie the Riveter, a female riveter who was shown with muscles and brawn. Along with a "We Can Do It" slogan, women were encouraged to believe in and test their abilities. But once the men were back from war and back on the scene, most of the women were expected to take their place back in the home. But these women demonstrated that females can in fact work in factories, they can build equipment and machinery, and they can work blue-collar jobs. And that's not all. They showed that they are very good at it, too.

A record 68 million women are employed in the United States right now, but not many are in the trades. Thirty-nine percent are in management or professional jobs while 34 percent are in sales or office jobs and 20 percent are in service jobs. Just 6 percent are in production, transportation, and material moving, and 1 percent—or 680,000—work in construction or maintenance. Okay, that sounds like a lot of people and a lot of positions. And yes, in some ways that's a ton of jobs for women. But when you think about it compared to the number of men, it's really appalling.

Success in the Real World

Nancy Schoonover Hanlan, heavy equipment operator, Canton, Ohio

Nancy Schoonover Hanlan grew up the youngest of four girls, walking the line between being a tomboy and someone who was taught to act like a lady and wear frilly lace socks to church on Sundays. Hanlan, who was raised in Ohio, had always wanted to be a veterinarian but knew the money it would take to go through school was too much for her parents. She didn't know about grants and loans and instead opted for a local technical school where she earned a civil engineering degree. Hanlan joined the International Union of Operating Engineers, which is best known for training heavy equipment operators. Her father was a union member, and she had worked on cranes with him while growing up. It was something she enjoyed, and she knew she could make good money doing the work.

That was in the late 1970s, and Hanlan was just one of eight girls in her class. But she loved the work and spent eighteen years in the field, operating backhoes, paving machines, 824 compactors, and more. "It's something different every day," she says, adding that being outside and often working on a different team is what she appreciates most about the job. Nearly fifty at the time of this writing, Hanlan now works in the office of a construction company in Canton, Ohio.

She would highly recommend heavy machine operating to women. Thanks to hydraulics and other advances, the work isn't as physically demanding as it sounds. "Everything used to have monstrous levers," she says, but today's sophisticated equipment requires less heavy lifting than ever before. And Hanlan strongly recommends unions to women for their no-cost apprenticeship programs. She sees many women who enter the field in their twenties or thirties. "A gal that has children? She is able to provide for them this way."

In Canada, each province has impressively started funding initiatives to attract more women to the skilled trades, and the measures are working. Women in Skilled Trades is one such program and is offered through local colleges. This initiative works to help more women get into blue-collar careers while also addressing the skills shortages that exist. Slowly but surely, more women are joining blue-collar sectors, and approximately 1 million women work in the skilled trades. The data is different for each province, but in Newfoundland and Labrador, the number of women registering for the trades is up 35 percent since 2004. Keep in mind that Canada's population is smaller than that of the United States, hovering around 33 million. But still, as in the United States, there are huge gaps between the numbers of men and women working in these fields.

Women in Canada have been registering for apprenticeships in increasing numbers, though. According to the Canadian Council on Learning, the number of women enrolling increased threefold between 1991 and 2003. By 2003, women made up 10 percent of all apprentices, up from a mere 4 percent in 1991.

Back in the 1980s, when Lori Johnson walked through the halls of her automotive technology school, a few people continually called her nasty names. Some of the men decided she had come to meet a husband. Others just derided her for being a woman in a man's world. But after a while, people got over it. Then when she got her first job working on cars at a Cherry Hill, New Jersey, Honda dealership, she would see small lines of people being brought through the shop. They were being led as if on a museum tour and she soon realized that they were there to take a peek at the female under the hood. "It was almost like a circus," she says. "I was an exhibit."

Things have changed, and Johnson laughs about most of it now. She says that despite some of the obstacles, blue-collar careers offer incredible opportunities for women. Not only are these jobs an excellent way to put food on the table and care for your family, but they are also rewarding, challenging, and potentially lucrative. Male-only work just doesn't exist anymore. There are female heavy equipment operators, construction workers, and welders. We definitely don't see as many women in these careers as we should. Female loggers make up 1.7 percent of the industry, whereas 2.6 percent of electricians are women and 7.5 percent of painters are female. Approximately 1.2 percent of all pipe layers and plumbers are women. Of airline mechanics, 4.5 percent are women, and 2.8 percent of workers in auto mechanics and body shop repair are women.

Success in the Real World

Robyn Bush, ironworker, Bolingbrook, Illinois

You can be a feminine ironworker. Just ask Robyn Bush, who is pretty, petite, and the first female ironworker in her Local #444 in Joliet, Illinois, a suburb of Chicago. Her male coworkers will sometimes say, "You throw like a chick," when she tosses something their way. "I am a chick," she reminds them. Bush, thirty-four, has always been a tomboy, but she has her feminine side, too. She wants more women to know that wearing lipstick or carrying a purse is not forbidden just because you're in the trades. "I found my passion," says Bush, of landing with the ironworkers. She's been at it for about two years, following stints at Home Depot and some time working as a furniture upholsterer.

When she initially went to trade school for carpentry, Bush was told to go work in upholstering instead. But she wanted something more thrilling, more invigorating. That's exactly what she's found in ironworking. "It's man's best-kept secret," says Bush, who lives in Bolingbrook, Illinois, with her husband and two children. Bush had to get over her fear of heights pretty quickly, which she did, but not without coaching herself through some sticky moments. She would remind herself of what Simba, the newborn lion, from *The Lion King* says: "I laugh in the face of danger." That's exactly what Bush does each day that she is on a scaffolding or several stories off the ground. "My career empowers me," she says. "Whatever you believe is what you can do."

Tracy Warren-Burke has a business degree and co-owns Burke's Custom Metal Works, Inc. in Rollo Bay, Prince Edward Island, with her husband, who is a Red Seal welder. Warren-Burke says it has taken her years to get male customers to understand that she can assist them and answer questions regarding their sheet metal products and services. Although Warren-Burke doesn't have any women working for her company, she says women are often perfectly suited for the trades, especially when it comes to industries such as welding that require a certain amount of precision and patience.

"This is a male-dominated industry," says Warren-Burke. But she also points out that with each passing generation things change dramatically. A female in the skilled trades would have seemed bizarre thirty years ago. Not so anymore, and Warren-Burke says people are changing their expectations and stereotypes. "It will be even easier for the next generation."

We've got a long way to go. The unions are certainly helping in some ways. They are more receptive to women in the trades than in the past, and in some areas they are actively working to recruit females. In 2005, two dozen construction unions in New York City agreed to reserve 10 percent of their apprenticeships or openings for women. The initiative was started under Mayor Michael Bloomberg's Commission on Construction Opportunity, and the goal is supposed to be reached in 2010. Society in general is becoming more receptive to women in the trades, and many great organizations are working to help women find their way into the blue-collar workforce. We tell you more about those organizations later in this chapter.

While women should be prepared for the possibility of getting grief from a coworker or boss for being a female, there is much support out there. Organizations are tackling tough issues such as harassment and salary inequality. The path is clearer and easier for females than it's ever been. More important, these are industries that women enjoy, feel passionate about, and want to be in. Just like men, women find out that it's simply thrilling to build, bust down, create, and shape each and every day.

Women in nontraditional jobs (jobs in which you don't typically find women) pay better than those jobs that are considered more traditional for women. The sheer fact these jobs are thought of as male positions makes them more attractive to some women. In other words, for some women, it's a challenge of sorts to take on a career that would surprise people. Best of all, these careers provide self-esteem.

"A lot of parents don't realize these are skilled trades and that they're in very high demand," says Terri Burgess Sandu, interim director of Hard Hatted Women, a Cleveland-based organization. "We're changing the way we think about the skilled trades and getting girls to think about fields that are nontraditional for women." Burgess Sandu says there is certainly an image problem out there, but by educating women, more teachers, and parents, she hopes some of these perceptions can be changed. "We have to get women to realize these are great careers," she adds. "You are not the wrong gender." Hard Hatted Women offers a ten-week program through which women work on math skills and blueprint reading, and are introduced to using a variety of tools, all in preparation for joining a trade.

"When I saw a man sandblasting, I said, 'I want to do that.'" Karen Kreig had worked a variety of jobs and as a military brat she was used to bouncing around, so for a while switching jobs didn't bother her too much. But then she knew she ultimately wanted a pension, and she thought she'd like to stick with one thing. Kreig, who lives in Antelope, California, joined a labor union almost twenty-five years ago and has been learning one skill after the next ever since. Now fifty-six, she runs jackhammers, sandblasts, and lays concrete.

"You have to come out here ready to work," she says. And as a woman, "You have to get dirtier than them," she says referring to men. Kreig says she's never gotten much attitude, but partially that's because she's tough and isn't afraid to show it. She has thick skin, and she doesn't mind working hard or getting calloused hands or dirty jeans. "I knew I was entering a man's world and I had to prove myself." Kreig says she feels so much pride knowing that she's built bridges that take people to work every day or laid foundations for beautiful buildings.

Independence—gaining it and having it—is a strong theme for women who go into blue-collar work. A study published in 2002, based on interviews with eleven women who were interested in nontraditional careers, found that these women were seeking independence, had recently become independent (from a controlling husband, for example), or were seeking freedom in their jobs. Mary Sullivan, assistant dean for the School of Natural Resources at Pennsylvania College of Technology, was looking to identify the reasons women choose to go into blue-collar jobs. Many of the women were self-described tomboys or people who don't mind getting dirty. Others had predominantly played with boys while growing up or were surrounded by brothers and therefore used to grittier experiences.

Sylvia Keller, tool and die maker, Bradford, Ontario

When she was about to graduate high school, Sylvia Keller knew that she wanted to go into the skilled trades. While many of her friends were going off to universities, she decided she wanted to do something with her hands. "At least I'll be learning and not going to a university and coming out with nothing but debt," she thought at the time. Keller took a tool and die class and decided that was her industry. Really, her decision came out of her guidance counselor at trade school telling her that tool and die making would be too difficult for her and that she should consider something else, an industry perhaps that was less male dominated. Instead of changing her mind, Keller took it as a challenge and has been in the tool and die world ever since.

Tool and die makers are some of the most highly skilled tradespeople. Making tools, dies, and other precision equipment requires much training and dedication. Keller says she was given little encouragement or guidance when she started doing this work eleven years ago. But she's created a specialty for herself and has enjoyed the hard work.

Keller bought a house at age twenty-six and has watched many of her university-educated friends struggle to find high-paying jobs. In a good year, with overtime, Keller has made more than $90,000. Sharpening tools, machining, maintenance of dies, and the building of dies is all part of what Keller does on any given day. And she's constantly troubleshooting. "I like it," she adds.

After more than a decade in this industry, though, Keller is considering whether she would like to try a different trade. She's considering something in water maintenance or treatment. Whether she makes the switch or not, Keller says there are many skilled trades that overlap, and taking on a new challenge within a new industry is often possible. "I think it's the greatest thing to pick a skilled trade and just go do it."

This is just one study and one look at the reasons for women going into the trades. I know many women who start apprenticeships, join unions, or get into the trades because they are looking for a jump on life. Janice Layne from Chicago Women in Trades says many women come to her organization for assistance in getting into a trade once they've overcome other hardships. Sometimes it's a failed relationship or a less than stellar job record. Chicago Women in Trades prepares women through training and advocacy for trade jobs. Layne, a case manager with the organization, says some women are simply heading down this path because it's something they've always wanted to do.

Layne says her group also prepares women for challenges they may face in the workforce because of being female. It can be tough for women, she says, but at the same time the majority of employers and coworkers are quite supportive. "We're not trying to make it out like it's the big ol' bogeyman," she says, but still, Chicago Women and Trades helps women to prepare for the worst. Some women just want to be able to talk about their fears even if none of them ever come true.

A fourteen-week program offered by Chicago Women in Trades, similar to others across the country, provides a basic, hands-on introduction to some of the trades, teaches women about unions, and prepares participants to enter various careers. At Nontraditional Employment for Women (NEW) in New York City, women apply to a six-week program that introduces them to several trades and helps them into unions or apprenticeships. Many of the women are on their second careers; some are trying to jump-start their work life. Basic information, such as how to carry heavy materials, a primer on unions, and essential math training, is part of NEW's program.

Amy Peterson, president of NEW, said women tend to be particularly excited to get into the skilled trades. NEW trained 450 women in 2008, and the program has more than doubled in just three years. "The trades haven't come as far as some of the other careers like doctors and lawyers and even engineers," says Peterson. She said society still doesn't think of the trades as a natural place for women. But as the unions struggle to maintain and even increase membership, Peterson points out that women and minorities are more widely embraced. "A lot of women have always wanted to work with their hands," says NEW's president. Her organization introduces them to carpentry, painting, and electrical work. "The six weeks makes them aware of the opportunities. This isn't simple. It's a career." Of the women who start in the program, approximately 75 percent graduate and are on their way to a job.

> " The unions are struggling somewhat, so they are much more welcoming to women and minorities. "
>
> —Amy Peterson, president, Nontraditional Employment for Women

Without a program to guide her, Donna Curtin always knew in her gut what she wanted to do. As a child, Curtin would spend hours playing with toy trucks, not dolls. People always ask her why, and she says she really can't articulate it. "It's like asking someone why they like chocolate ice cream. You can't explain it. You just do." But in high school Curtin wasn't allowed to take shop classes because of her gender. Because she also enjoyed drawing, Curtin wasn't entirely devastated and instead focused on her other skills and ended up graduating from State University of New York, Binghamton, with a degree in studio art and psychology. She worked for years in graphic design, but all the while she was repairing and rebuilding her own cars. She would go to auctions and buy various vehicles to fix up. She had never taken an automotive class, but she was determined to teach herself how to repair cars. She checked out dozens of library books and poured through each one, trying to memorize every detail. She would practice on her own cars, rebuilding engines, making repairs, and painting the exteriors.

After years of pining to be around cars full-time, Curtin decided to open her own auto body shop. It took her five years, and she said she faced some discrimination from lenders, contractors, and locals in the town of Cicero, New York, where her shop is located. "Being female in this business doesn't sit well with a lot of guys," she says. But that said, her three technicians are men, and each one of them came from great jobs to work in her shop. She knows she treats them well, and she cares about them and their families. "It took a long time until I did find a crew who could deal with a woman as their boss." But Curtin was determined, and in the end she couldn't be happier. "I'm in heaven when I hear tools buzzing."

Johnson, the auto mechanic who was a novelty in the 1980s when she was getting started, sees the blue-collar world as far more open and accepting of women than it once was. She grew up in Michigan, her father and grandfather worked for General Motors, and her other grandfather ran a gas station. Her parents weren't thrilled when she opted to go to automotive technical school, but she knew she wanted to do something with her hands and she didn't want to sit at a desk all day.

As for being a female mechanic, Johnson says it's an excellent field for women. "It's a lifetime skill that you can always fall back on for a job," she says. Plus, Johnson points out that the money can be great.

"It's a career you will have for life. We're always going to drive cars, and they will always need to be repaired." And for Johnson, working as a mechanic has incredible benefits. "It's like solving a puzzle every day," she says. "Every day is a new day. Every day is problem solving." But she admits that she thinks women must still work hard—and maybe harder than men—to prove themselves.

Johnson took her love of repairing cars and her desire to help women navigate the car world and in 2006 opened Ladies Start Your Engines. She runs courses through this Philadelphia-based business to familiarize women with their own cars, and to educate women on car repair needs and terminology. She teaches her students, women only, how to change a tire, what to look for under a hood, and how to navigate the repair shop. Johnson wanted to help female drivers and repair shop customers feel more comfortable advocating for themselves and talking about their own cars. And for Johnson, she's combined a new-found love of teaching with a passion for car mechanics.

Becoming an entrepreneur has opened her eyes to the many possibilities and avenues available through the trades. "I never would have thought I'd be doing this," she says. But for Johnson it was about following a passion and sticking with something until she mastered it, and then the rest flowed from there. She says no one should think that they will be in the same position twenty years from now. Where you start off is just that: a starting point. And where you go from there, that's up to you.

Organizations Focused on Women

The apprenticeships and trainings specific to the industries we talked about in Chapter 3 are listed in the back of this book. Below we have laid out some of the organizations that are specifically dedicated to helping women succeed in the skilled trades. We have not included every single one, but rather taken a sampling to give readers an idea of the support and opportunities that are available to women. Don't worry if you don't see one near where you live. Do some research, ask your guidance counselor, or go online to find an organization near you.

A Commitment to Training and Employment for Women. This Toronto-based organization is a network of agencies that offers training and education opportunities for women in nontraditional fields. Through its extensive site, women can search for training opportunities in Ontario and find helpful resources and networking opportunities: www.actew.org.

Association for Women in Aviation Maintenance. This nonprofit was formed to advocate for women in the aviation maintenance field. While there are many resources for female pilots, this particular group focuses on the maintenance workers and provides networking opportunities and education. The group works to increase public awareness about the aviation maintenance sector: www.awam.org or (386) 424-5780.

Chicago Women in Trades. Through a fourteen-week program, this organization works with women to prepare them for the trades. Applicants must test into the program and are part of discussions on workplace harassment while also being exposed to what it means to be in the skilled trades: www.chicagowomenintrades.org or (312) 942-1444.

Coalition of Labor Union Women. This nonpartisan organization within the union movement is open exclusively to women members. The mission of CLUW is to unify female union members and focus on common goals and concerns. The organization promotes legislation, recruits women who are not currently part of unions, and works to involve more women in the political process. Ongoing education is also part of the mission of the CLUW, which has more than seventy-five chapters around the country: www.cluw.org or (202) 508-6969.

Hard Hatted Women. This Cleveland-based group offers preapprenticeship programs for women who are considering a career in the trades. HHW offers a ten-week program that introduces participants to carpentry, plumbing, electrical, and sheet metal work. The group helps to prepare women both mentally and physically for skilled trade jobs, while empowering them to achieve economic independence and workplace equality: www.hardhattedwomen.org or (216) 861-6500.

National Association of Women in Construction. Founded in 1953 to bring together women working in the construction industry, NAWIC has nearly 180 chapters around the world. The organization works to educate young girls and women and to provide resources and training for those looking to get into construction. NAWIC includes construction company owners and managers as well as those who work in the field: www.nawic.org or (800) 552-3506.

National Association for Women in Masonry. This is a fairly new organization that was formed to address the needs of women in the mason industry. The association is looking to create a community for women to discuss challenges, generate interest in the field, and promote the value of masonry through education: www.nawmonline.net.

National Institute for Women in Trades, Technology & Science. This institute provides women with the tools and training to enter male-dominated careers. Working within white-collar and blue-collar industries, IWITTS operates nationally to educate and train employers as well as women. Demonstration projects, online community building, and retention strategies are part of the mission. The institute offers an extensive website with resources for women in the trades: www.iwitts.com or (510) 749-0200.

Nontraditional Employment for Women. This New York City–based organization focuses on training, advocacy, and education for women looking to get into the trades. Through a six-week program, NEW familiarizes women with blue-collar industries. Participants learn about unions, benefits, workplace safety, and discrimination. They also learn basic skills such as painting techniques and how to properly carry heavy equipment. According to president Amy Peterson, most of the women working construction in New York City completed one of NEW's programs: www.new-nyc.org or (212) 627-6252.

Oregon Tradeswomen. This Portland, Oregon–based group provides education, mentoring, and programs for women who are considering a career in the trades. The group also provides assistance to women who need guidance with workplace issues. The organization sponsors support groups throughout Oregon to connect tradeswomen to each other. Oregon Tradeswomen offers extensive job resources as well as information about area unions: www.tradeswomen.net or (503) 335-8200.

Sisters in the Building Trades. The mission of this organization is to expand the network of women who are entering the construction workforce and to promote the field by offering beneficial career options. Mentoring, support, and recruitment are part of the mission. Located in the Seattle area, Sisters in the Building Trades is also a resource for apprenticeships and training: www.sistersinthebuildingtrades.org or (206) 618-6715.

Tradeswomen, Inc. This Oakland, California–based group was started in 1979 to support women in the trades. Now the organization creates opportunities for tradeswomen to support each other and learn from one another. The organization recruits women into the trades, promotes the role of women in these industries, and provides a resource for jobs, apprenticeships, and training: www.tradeswomen.org or (510) 891-8775.

Tradeswomen Now and Tomorrow. This national coalition of organizations advocates on behalf of women in the trades. The group works to achieve economic equality for women while promoting policies and legislative plans. TNT is a clearinghouse for sharing programming initiatives and offers women a resource for jobs, workplace issues, unions, and professional growth: www.tradeswomennow.org.

Vermont Works for Women. Based near Burlington, Vermont, this group works with women and girls to explore and pursue nontraditional careers. The organization hosts training and education programs that expose women to carpentry, painting, law enforcement, and more: www.nnetw.org or (800) 639-1472.

Washington Women in Trades. This Seattle-based organization works to improve women's economic equity through training and success in highly skilled careers in the construction, manufacturing, and transportation sectors. The group has built extensive networks of women in these industries while also educating women about nontraditional careers and the opportunities that exist in the trades. WWIT also offers resources for jobs and career training: www.wawomenin trades.com or (206) 903-9508.

Wider Opportunities for Women. Working across the country, WOW has trained and educated women while advocating for their access to well-paid work opportunities. This group works to help women and families attain economic independence through technical and nontraditional jobs. WOW works with women through programs that focus on literacy, technical and trade skills, the welfare-to-work transition, and career development: www.wowonline.org or (202) 464-1596.

Women Building Futures. This organization works to improve the lives of women through job training and preparedness. One of the group's programs is Fixit Chicks, a series of workshops that trains women in fields such as carpentry, plumbing, and electrical work: www.women-buildingfutures.com or (780) 452-1200 and www.fixitchicks.ca.

Women in Trades and Technology National Network. WITT is a Canada-based advocacy group that promotes the recruitment, training, and retention of women in the trades across the country. WITT offers many resources for women and has local offices throughout Canada: www.wittnn.com or (800) 895-WITT.

Women in Trucking. Devoted to female truckers, this organization's mission is to encourage more women to enter the trucking industry. The group promotes women to major companies and works on behalf of women to advocate for comfortable, equitable workplace environments. This organization works to reduce the obstacles women face in the field and serves as an all-around resource and community for women in the industry: www.womenintrucking.org or (888) 464-9482.

Women Unlimited. This small organization works with women in Maine to provide an introduction to the trades, training, and hands-on experience so as to expose participants to the construction industry. This is an excellent resource for connecting with other tradeswomen in the area: www.womenunlimited.org or (800) 281-5259.

Did You KNOW? In 1951, Lillian Baumbach Jacobs became the first woman to earn a master's license in plumbing. She was twenty-one at the time and living in the Washington, D.C., area, where she was working at her family's plumbing business, Baumbach Plumbers of Arlington, Virginia. Growing up, she routinely tagged along with her father, also a plumber, while he was making service calls.

Chapter 5

Green-Collar America
How Blue Collar Is Going Green

When Carolyn Coquillette gets to work each day, she can't imagine a place she'd rather be. "I have broken hybrids all around me," she says, referring to her repair shop Luscious Garage in San Francisco. "I'm pretty much in heaven." Although Coquillette has a habit of taking public transportation to work, she is passionate about hybrid cars, loves repairing them and working on them, and enjoys the instant gratification of being able to take something broken and pass it back to its owner once it's fixed. Plus, she gets to feel great about doing her part to help the environment.

After getting her undergraduate degree, Coquillette was working at a nonprofit organization, but on the side she wanted to be able to fix her own car. She figured that with a $120,000 education under her belt she

" Enthusiasm and passion, in many cases, trump rote learning."

—*David Hedlin,*
owner of Hedlin Farms,
Mount Vernon, Washington

should at least be able to do that on her own. So she signed up for a car mechanic class and enjoyed the work so much that she decided to trade in her job to become an auto technician. In 2007 she opened Luscious Garage, which she runs with one other female technician.

HYBRID MANIA

According to Hybridcar.com, 9,500 hybrids were sold in the United States in 2000, 88,000 were sold in 2004, and by the end of 2005, there were 212,000 hybrid cars on the road. By 2006, there were a whopping 254,545 new hybrids registered in the United States. The second highest sales month ever for hybrids was March 2008 when 38,214 cars were sold. The sales began to decline though throughout the rest of the year as the economy started to suffer.

Like others who have opted to work in green industries, Coquillette is expecting the alternative-fuel craze to drive hybrid sales. In turn, those hybrids will need routine maintenance and repairs. Coquillette says her shop is not only participating in this green movement by servicing hybrids but she is also offering cutting-edge technology as well as environmentally conscious products. "People are inspired by what we do."

America's big car companies have taken major steps toward manufacturing hybrids, plug-ins, and other alternative-fuel vehicles in massive quantities. In September 2008, General Motors, Ford, and Chrysler received a $25 billion loan from the federal government to refurbish their factories and auto plants to start producing these alternative-fuel and fuel-efficient vehicles. With these new factories come jobs. But not the kind that your grandfather had. I've said this before, but your grandfather's generation would barely recognize the car manufacturing plants of today.

Coquillette says the industry is responding to environmental demands and the need to reconfigure energy use. "We have very sophisticated automobiles on the road," adds Coquillette, explaining that when she lifts up the hood of a hybrid she's confronted with a whole world of technology and computerized equipment. "It's not mundane." And doing work that has a positive impact is what people in all green jobs say is one of the most appealing aspects of their careers. "It's really inspiring," says Coquillette of what she does.

Many of the green sector jobs are in the most obvious places. For almost every sector you can find a green job equivalent. Construction is beginning to see the prevalence of green construction, which uses recycled material or materials that haven't been treated with chemicals and paints that are not damaging to the environment. Bicycle repair shops are naturally green (especially if they operate their building in a green way) for the service they provide to commuters who are opting for two wheels instead of four. There are jobs for people weatherizing buildings, constructing wind turbines, farming, building responsibly, and offering sustainable landscaping services. Residential and commercial cleaning businesses can also find ways to prosper as clients begin to demand nontoxic cleaning products and services. You can apply this green stamp to just about every aspect of life, every industry, and every job.

A recent report by Duke University's Center on Globalization, Governance & Competitiveness looked at five popular technologies that reduce carbon emissions, including LED lighting, high-performance windows, auxiliary power units designed for long-haul trucks, solar power, and a specialized soil system that is used to treat hog waste. Although these may seem like obscure examples, the study set out to show the nearly endless ways in which green energy and green consciousness would be part of the next generation for the American workforce. In each of these sectors is the need for manufacturing, shipping, labor, and everything else that goes into creating, selling, and sustaining a product or industry. The study showed that the states most likely to benefit from the green revolution include Arizona, Pennsylvania, Ohio, Indiana, North Carolina, New Mexico, Nevada, and California. All of these attempts to cure, curb, and realize climate solutions will result in jobs.

Many cities across the country are adopting their own green economic plans, which include ways of not only becoming more green but also igniting a local green economy. The Apollo Alliance identifies ten areas in which changes can be made. The group in turn suggests that jobs will be created as a result, perhaps has many as 8 million of them.

1. **Promote hybrid cars.** You've heard about this one.
2. **Invest in more efficient factories.** Energy-saving systems can be installed to make factories more efficient and more responsible. Overhauling them requires workers.
3. **Encourage green building.** Offer incentives to contractors, builders, and owners who are willing to build energy-efficient homes and municipal buildings.
4. **Increase use of energy-efficient appliances.** Increase investments

in factories in North America while working to improve and
market energy-efficient appliances.

5. **Modernize electrical infrastructure.** Using the local workforce,
   overhaul the electrical grid system and employ new environmentally friendly technologies.

6. **Expand renewable energy development.** Promote solar and
   wind power while establishing clear goals for renewable energy
   and independence.

7. **Improve transportation.** Increase clean public transportation
   choices by upgrading rail and subway systems.

8. **Invest in smart urban growth.** Revitalize urban centers to
   promote vibrant cities and good jobs, while upgrading
   deteriorating infrastructure.

9. **Plan for a hydrogen future.** Invest in long-term research and
   development of hydrogen fuel cell technology.

10. **Preserve regulatory protections.** Ensure that regulation pro-
    motes and demands energy efficiencies and system reliability
    that protects the environment and people.

The green economy has simply exploded, and really it's only started.
Being green no longer means just shopping for expensive organic produce or driving hybrid cars. Like it or not, we're all thinking about how
much waste we create, how much energy we burn and fuel we use, and
how we can conserve or adjust our impact on the environment. There
has been a surge in interest in renewable energy, including wind, solar,
geothermal, and biomass power. It sounds complicated, but this is no
longer an issue left to the academics or the environmentalist groups.
It's even started to permeate pop culture. In the summer of 2008, Planet
Green, cable television's first twenty-four-hour eco network, was

launched. The 2008 James Bond film *Quantum of Solace* featured an eco-resort in Bolivia, and the very popular movie *Wall-E* starred a solar-powered trash compacting robot.

We have become addicted to foreign oil and use about 25 percent of the world's available oil in our country alone. As a nation, the United States is searching for the means to become energy independent and to clean up its act in an effort to stop the environmental crisis. This is everyone's problem, and green-collar workers are going to be the driving force behind fixing what is broken. It's clear that the younger generations will be most impacted by the destruction we've already done and by the efforts we're undertaking now to change our ways. Anyone at any age can go green or simply work a green job, and after talking to dozens of people in the green sector it's clear that environmental concerns are becoming a dominant force behind corporations, municipalities, and individuals. There are a lot of jobs to be had and money to be made in the green economy.

Think GREEN

Green jobs are in many familiar fields, and the ones that receive the most attention are in the energy and energy-efficient sectors. The big ones include:

- Retrofitting buildings for increased energy efficiency
- Expanding mass transit and freight rail
- Constructing efficient electrical grid systems
- Wind Power
- Solar Power
- Biofuels

—List based on projections by the Center for American Progress

So what exactly is a green-collar job? Green-collar jobs combine blue-collar jobs with environmentally focused work, and they are cropping up in every sector. Green-collar America is going to be mostly populated by the blue-collar worker, not the white-collar academic. "The green economy is not just a place where affluent people can spend money. It is fast becoming a place where ordinary people can earn money," writes Van Jones in his book *The Green Collar Economy*. Jones is an activist who advocates for green-collar jobs offering a way out of poverty for much of the American population. He is the president of Green for All, an organization that works to engage all sectors of society in the green revolution.

Some of these green jobs require specialized understanding or training while others are just familiar jobs being used in a different way. Green-collar jobs are available to people who already have blue-collar skills. These aren't jobs that typically require years of new training either. For example, if you want to work on hybrids, you still go to automotive school but would specialize in these alternative-fuel cars rather than, say, brake systems. Plumbers will find themselves installing low-flow toilets or showerheads rather than wasteful appliances. Jobs will be created from the construction of wind farms and green buildings, but they will be jobs that are largely similar to the ones you read about in Chapter 3. If you want to work with your hands and work in a blue-collar sector, but you're also conscious about wanting to feel good about your impact on the environment, then these green jobs are for you.

Wind turbines and wind farms are being built all across the country, solar energy is growing exponentially, homes and commercial buildings are being weatherized, and the auto world is changing. People want their heating systems replaced with fuel- and energy-efficient ones and businesses are starting to rethink their energy consumption. And that's just the beginning. This isn't just about saving polar bears. Really, even if you don't care about all of the environmental issues (although you should), you won't have much choice pretty soon. The United States is working to increase sustainable resources, renewable energy, and alternative fuels. That means we're trying to figure out other ways to power our lives. That's where hybrid cars, wind farms, and energy-conserving appliances come into the picture.

The American Solar Energy Society estimates that there are currently 8.5 million jobs in the United States in renewable energy or energy-efficient industries. This number is expected to grow to as many as 40 million by 2030. That's a ton more jobs and incredible opportunities that are being created by wind power, nuclear energy, green landscaping practices, weatherizing efforts, solar energy, and more. What's most incredible is that some green industries are already reporting workforce shortages. In September 2008 it was estimated that 60 percent of wind turbines were behind on maintenance because there weren't enough trained employees to do the work. The National Renewable Energy Lab has found that there is already a shortage of skilled workers in the green economy. These green industries are taking off faster than the skilled workers can keep up. Job openings, job opportunities, and the room for growth are enormous.

Different facts and figures are tossed around concerning just how many people this green revolution will impact. According to one report, an investment of $100 billion in clean energy technologies will create 2 million new jobs. This study, published by the Political Economy Research Institute, concluded that a good majority of the jobs would be created within sectors that already exist. Pipe fitters, welders, steel workers, and electricians will be able to take their skills and experience and transfer them to this world of green jobs. These opportunities are expected to be created through retrofitting buildings to improve energy efficiency, expanding mass transit and freight trains, building new electrical grid systems, and through wind or solar power. A study released in 2007 by the Renewable Energy Policy Project estimated that an additional 93,000 new manufacturing jobs would be created just for the production of solar power equipment.

While citizens and communities have long detested nuclear plants, this form of energy is one of the cleanest, most environmentally responsible ways to go. Europe is already using significant amounts of nuclear energy, and the United States is about to see its rebirth. In southern Texas, new plants are in the works and scheduled to be built sometime in 2010. Believe it or not, these facilities are already anticipating a shortage of workers. NRG Energy, which is building two new facilities, started recruiting workers nearly two years in advance. They plan to train these employees, have them work in other locations around the country, and then relocate them to Texas once the plants are up and running. All this effort is happening because it's nearly impossible to find a skilled workforce to hire and run nuclear power operations. Once they've completed training, NRG Energy's employees will start out with salaries between $65,000 and $75,000.

In the southeastern part of the United States, the utility Southern Co. estimates that energy facilities are currently short staffed by as many as 20,000 workers. That number is expected to increase to at least 40,000 by 2011. While only a fraction—about 1 percent—of our country's electricity comes from wind farms, this amount could increase to 20 percent by 2030, according to the Department of Energy. An estimated $1 trillion will be spent to get to this point. Included in these forecasts is the creation of an untold number of jobs. Wall Street continues to invest in wind power, which is still considered a frontier for investors.

The whole industry is expected to grow by as much as $65 billion by 2015. Once a foreign concept, these wind farms are cropping up everywhere from the middle of fields in the Midwest to the ocean along the New England coast.

Where am I going with all of this? I'm trying to draw you a picture—one that includes tons of different opportunities and industries all working toward common green goals. Some of the partners in this green revolution are truly amazing. The United Steel Workers Union and the Sierra Club, one of the country's largest environmental groups, have even teamed up to form the Blue Green Alliance. This collaboration is meant to raise awareness about green jobs while also confronting the issues facing corporations, small businesses, and individual workers.

"I think a lot of people have a misconception about labor and the environmental movement," says David Foster, executive director of the Blue-Green Alliance. Foster points out that the unions have long taken environmental issues seriously, especially when it comes to worker safety and health. Now these same unions are branching out into other directions while looking at ways to create jobs that will have a direct and positive impact on the environment, and they are finding ways to engage youth about how to become a part of these blue-collar jobs that are going green.

When you're looking for a job, ask about an employer's green practices. Sometimes it isn't obvious and you may need to probe to find out. Ask what they're doing to recycle, conserve, or reduce their carbon footprint. You may never know unless you ask.

Foster says the future is in solar energy, alternative fuels, and green construction. These fields are hot now and are going to stay hot for a long while. Foster says these industries "are the great creators of the twenty-first century." From solar installation to working at a hybrid manufacturing plant, he predicts, "This is where the jobs of the future will come from." Foster says it has been hard to get young adults to focus on green-collar jobs. Still, he's confident that enough do actually care and are activists in their own small way when it comes to helping the planet.

Foster explains these opportunities to younger workers in a simple way. "It's a blue-collar job with a green purpose." All that really means is that you could be putting together wind turbines rather than gas-guzzling Hummers. A carpenter could be working for an environmentally conscious contractor rather than one who is wasteful and uses toxic material. An electrician could install solar panels because she feels excited to participate in this green revolution. "It's not about making you do something you're not familiar with," says Foster. "It's about taking something you are familiar with and taking it to a new level." This is what the future will look like in every industry, he says. "You always have a more secure job when you are employed in the industries of the future rather than the past."

In 2007, the U.S. federal government passed the Green Jobs Act, which provides $120 million each year to begin training workers for jobs in the clean energy sector. These are secure jobs, jobs that are going to be around for decades and simply can't be outsourced. You can't send your house overseas to be weatherized, you can't ship your car to Japan to have it converted to a hybrid, and you're not about to ship your garage to another country to have solar panels installed. These jobs are staying right here in your own communities. They pay well, they are exciting, and you can feel really good about doing them.

State and local officials all over the United States are taking major steps to reform energy consumption. Many are mandating that their own towns rely on renewable energy. In Massachusetts, the Green Jobs Act became law in August 2008 and provides $68 million to green job initiatives. The act also mandated that the state's greenhouse gases be reduced by 80 percent by 2050. Many other states and municipalities are adopting similar measures, which means that drastic changes in energy have to happen. Alternative energy is no longer a hypothetical idea that is being tossed around as an option, but rather one that is being implemented right now.

Chicago is one city that has already made great strides toward being green. The city has planted more than 250,000 trees and has installed solar panels on some of the city's biggest tourist attractions and gems, such as the Field Museum and Art Institute. The Conference of Mayors, which includes mayors from across the country, has long been urging leaders to adopt the 2030 Challenge, which is aimed at reducing carbon emissions and pollution while cleaning up the air through green buildings, energy efficiency, and alternative fuels. The challenge also suggests such measures as using incentives to get more people to buy and drive plug-in hybrid cars.

Phoenix, Arizona, is patiently waiting for green jobs galore. In 2008, the Greater Phoenix Economic Council reported that there were eleven solar companies that had been to the region to scout for new manufacturing locations. The council estimated that the potential incoming companies represent approximately 4,800 jobs and $5.5 billion in investments.

Carlos Pete, solar panel installer, Hercules, California

Carlos Pete's job has literally changed his life, and it's helping to change the lives of others, too. Pete works as a solar panel installer. He used to work in the asphalt and paving business, and he was never particularly excited to go to work. But when he joined a program called Solar Richmond in Richmond, California, that trains workers in solar installation (run through RichmondBUILD), Pete started to get really excited about his job. "I feel like I've found my niche," says the thirty-year-old father of four, who lives in Hercules, California.

Pete now works at SolarCity, which is based in Foster City, California. He actually wears a green-collared uniform and spends his days installing panels that allow customers to harness solar energy. Pete's found a job that he enjoys doing and one that he feels really good about. "It makes so much more sense to be using solar energy," he says.

Pete installs panels on commercial buildings and recently completed a job at a huge rice farm. "I know down the road it will help my kids' kids to breathe better air." Pete is a convert, constantly talking to anyone who will listen about the benefits of solar power. He'd like to see more industrial buildings, hospitals, and schools use solar. "We have an indepletable resource in the sun. Why isn't our country doing more?" While working construction, Pete says he was frustrated to know that it could take him decades to become a foreman, but he sees more growth potential in the solar industry. "The sky is the limit."

In Victoria, British Columbia, the Canadian Centre for Environmental Education offers an opportunity to study green-related subjects and attain a certificate in environmental practice. The areas of concentration include environmental assessments, policy and legislation, pollution prevention, waste management systems, sampling and analytical work, strategic partnerships, environmental management systems, environmental education and training, natural resources planning, and communication and public awareness. Initiatives and programs such as these demonstrate the need for more educated, more informed people who are committed to green jobs and committed to turning all industries into green ones. In September 2008, it was estimated that there were 530,000 jobs in Canada related to the environment, according to the Calgary-based Environmental Career Organization of Canada. This same group estimates that green jobs will grow by 8.8 percent in the next five years.

Efforts and initiatives are happening on the corporate and municipal levels that are driving jobs and new opportunities for America's future workforce. The federal government is offering incentives to corporations by encouraging the construction of wind farms. Companies can receive up to a ten-year tax credit on income generated by wind power. Tax credits are offered to individual consumers as well who add solar panels or energy-efficient windows, for example. I'm telling you all of this so you can understand what is happening out there and to explain that all of these initiatives ultimately translate to more jobs.

Even if you didn't intend to get into the green-collar sector, there is ultimately great satisfaction knowing that you've made a contribution and are doing something worthwhile and helpful. Another benefit to these jobs is that they are plentiful, the industries are growing, and the opportunities are enormous. Getting in on the early stages is always an exciting thing. As Foster from Blue Green Alliance says, we don't have to be afraid of the future and of the unknown. We have to remember that these jobs are largely familiar to us. So many of these opportunities involve something we already know, such as electrical work, construction, manufacturing, or welding.

Brad Boggess used to have a job certifying homes for Energy Star, basically evaluating them to see if they could be dubbed *green*. But he watched as people built these environmental friendly homes and then stuffed them with less than environmentally friendly furniture. That's what gave him the idea for Sustainabuilt, his own small company that builds cabinetry from recycled wood. He builds some furniture as well, but cabinets are his specialty for now.

He says the furniture and construction industries are still largely relying on wood that has been treated with chemicals or hasn't been harvested in a responsible way. Boggess uses sustainable wood, such as bamboo, and all recyclable material at his shop in Garden City, Idaho. Most cabinet shops still use traditional lacquers and glues that have formaldehyde, but Boggess is working to buck that trend.

He says an apprenticeship is the best way to get started, and then on-the-job training teaches newcomers about the sustainable movements, the alternatives to chemicals, and how to find sustainable wood. "This is going to be how things are normally," says Boggess of the green movement. "Sustainable products are going to be the future." He says it's an exciting time to get into the green industry. "Start now and get into it," is Boggess's advice to young adults. "Getting into a company early will benefit you greatly in the future." Boggess is an example of someone who has taken a familiar skilled trade and turned it into a green job. With some additional research or job shadowing, you can take carpentry and construction to the next level by becoming a green builder.

Two other obviously green sectors are organic farming and sustainable fishing. Very few people are fishing the old-fashioned, harmless way. Very few individuals and small companies are taking the time to fish with nets or lines and not drag. But it's still an option. Farm-raised fish are typically grown in man-made environments that are heavily government regulated. Truly natural fishing, done without destroying bycatch (unwanted fish and other animals caught in fishing gear meant for other species) and the bottom of the ocean floor, is becoming more and more rare. But there is a push by fishers who want to make their livelihood in a responsible way. Some environmentalists are truly scared that the world's fish populations will soon be depleted if we don't change our ways. If you're interested in fishing, be sure to do your homework about the fishing companies that are hiring. Ask about their practices and educate yourself about how you can do your part to fish sustainably.

Success in the Real World

Kurt Martin, lobsterman, Orleans, Massachusetts

Kurt Martin was always fascinated by lobster traps. He just loved climbing on them and studying them when he was a kid. He would poke his hands through the ropes, imagining how the lobsters were caught. "I always really liked catching stuff," says Martin, who is close to forty now. He grew up on Cape Cod, so he was always around the water. When Martin was thirteen, he got ten of his own traps and set them near his hometown of Orleans, Massachusetts. When he graduated from high school in 1986 he knew what he wanted to do. "I told my Dad, 'I'll go fishing until I can't make anything, and then I'll go do something else.'"

Twenty years later he's still fishing, and for most of the year he's after lobsters. Martin has worked his way up from those ten original lobster traps to eight hundred, and he has one of 1,100 lobster permits in the state. But he won't say how many pounds he catches every season, since Martin says that's basically asking him his salary. But he will say that he makes a good living, good enough to spend a few weeks on vacation in the winter.

Nothing is more symbolic of summer in New England than fresh boiled lobsters. Although populations were once threatened and diminishing, the irresistible bottom crawlers are back in abundance. But Martin has been on boats where dragging has turned up so much dead fish and so much bycatch that it made him uncomfortable. "It was just stupid," he said of how much he's seen thrown overboard for the seagulls. He decided to become more environmentally sensitive.

Martin started fishing using an ancient technique. In the spring, before lobster season, he spends about eight weeks fishing with weirs, which are nets that the Romans used to catch fish. It's a passive, harmless way of hauling fish. Everything that is caught in weirs is alive and can be gently tossed back to sea if it's underweight or unappealing. He typically catches squid, mackerel, and sea bass this way. "There is no better way to catch fish," he says. But it's a slow and tough way to do so. It's hard to compete with big companies, and it's physically demanding work. Still, he says it's important to him to catch fish responsibly. He suspects that weir fishing won't be around forever since there is currently only one other operation in all of Massachusetts using weirs.

When it comes to his main business, Martin says lobstering is not particularly destructive either and offers a sustainable way to get seafood. The traps are dropped and pulled up without disturbing the ocean floor and without dragging nets that end up catching everything else along the way. Martin loves the idea of passing on his passion for fishing, and he'd love to see more young adults get into the general trade of fishing. But it's hard work, and he's not sure that many teens are cut out for the job.

Plus, he says, a financial aspect to the business can be particularly tricky for some. You make all of your money in one season, and you have to know how to manage that and make it last through the whole year. It can be tempting to spend everything that was made during a profitable month, when in reality you have to save for the off-season. Martin suggests that anyone thinking seriously about fishing should take some business courses to understand better how to manage a small company and personal finances.

Martin actually enjoys the challenge of saving from a good month and having to be accountable for that paycheck at the end of the week. "It's the challenge of making a living" that excites him. "It's totally up to me. There is no check waiting at the end of the week," he says. But beyond the money, Martin loves what he does. "There is tremendous freedom with being on the water. There is nothing given to you and there are no guarantees."

What about farming? Well, we've all heard about the state of farming in this country. More farms have gone out of business than at any other time in our nation's history. More massive crop companies are taking over, and the small farmer is indeed getting squeezed out. But that said, there are small, independent farming communities—many of them organic—cropping up all over the country. If you have an interest in this, you can make it happen. As of 2007, there were approximately 13,000 certified organic producers in the United States, according to the Organic Farming Research Foundation. The growth in the number of organic farms has increased steadily, and the entire organic industry has grown by about 20 percent in the past ten years. This is a good sign for farmers. We are all more aware of what we're eating, where our food is coming from, and how it's grown. In 2005, retail sales of organic food was close to $12.8 billion.

Did You KNOW?

In 1985, musicians Willie Nelson, Neil Young, and John Mellencamp organized the first Farm Aid concert in an effort to raise money to help keep families on their farms. Since then, the organization has raised more than $30 million for the cause. Farm Aid provides grants to farms, while enhancing farming resources and offering farmers help with understanding financing, planning, and regulations. More information can be found at www.farmaid.org.

Success in the Real World

David Hedlin, farmer, Mount Vernon, Washington

For David Hedlin and his wife, Serena Campbell, sustainable farming has always been important. Their thoughtful, deliberate approaches to crops, irrigation, pesticides, runoff, and soil maintenance are just second nature at Hedlin Farms. Hedlin is a third-generation farmer on the same land his Dutch grandfather purchased in 1904 in the Mount Vernon, Washington, area. Half of his 400 acres is certified organic, but when it comes to the other half Hedlin says it's still farmed in a responsible, sustainable manner. "We're using practices my grandfather used," he adds.

Much of what is grown at Hedlin Farms is grown for seeds. Cabbage, beet, and spinach seeds are harvested to then be used to plant crops all over the country. "I like the challenge and independence of farming," says Hedlin. "I truly feel privileged to be able to farm here. It's hard work, though." Hedlin says he's also always loved being in nature, interacting with the various elements. He says he gets an incredible sense of satisfaction when harvesting cabbage seeds since he knows that a mere one pound of seeds will grow 35,000 heads of cabbage. "It's fun to know that you are a part of that. That's what floats my boat."

Hedlin knows that he's a bit of a dying breed and farming families are splintering as younger generations head away from the fields to find other careers. Still, there are some who never grew up on a farm who are interested in getting started. Although he agrees that it's a lot easier to inherit your father's or grandfather's farm, Hedlin says there are still many ways into the industry without that connection. "I know farmers who started cold." He works with a program that sets up newer, aspiring farmers with those who are ready to retire and don't have someone waiting to take over their operation. No matter what, Hedlin says that, to get into farming and ultimately be successful, "you have to have the passion and the desire."

For anyone interested in farming, Hedlin suggests simply getting involved in a farming community, through working at a fertilizer company or grain company for example, so you have a handle on at least one aspect of the industry. Hedlin worked for a food processor after high school and before he decided to follow his family into farming.

Being a responsible steward is of utmost importance to Hedlin. While he says the official designation of *organic* is important, it's also crucial that people do right by the land. Some farmers can't afford to be certified organic, and others are more stringent than regulations require but they still haven't received the certification. More important, Hedlin says if you're interested in working at a farm and want to be comfortable with their practices, just ask. There is no special formula for determining whether a farm is sustainable or the practices responsible since the needs vary throughout the country depending on the region. "You need to find a fit with the people and the practices you're comfortable with," he adds.

The modern farmer must juggle a variety of concerns, including government regulations, waning interest in farms, pesticides and insect infestations, weather, and new techniques. But Hedlin finds these challenges to be invigorating, and to anyone who is overwhelmed by the issues facing farmers, he says, "Rather than be afraid of the complexity, embrace it." It's tough with farms going out of business though. "Every day that we keep our lands unpaved, more people see the value," says Hedlin. That's why he's optimistic that the family farm—his and others around the country—will continue for another 100 years.

Remember the nearly one hundred thousand new jobs estimated to be created by the solar power industry? A few of those individuals have landed with Blake Jones, who is the president and cofounder of Namaste Solar Electric Company. His Boulder, Colorado–based solar installation company started out small, but now he can barely keep up with customer demands. "It's growing like crazy," says Jones of the entire solar industry. "There is amazing growth potential." As more states mandate solar energy as a resource, the more the industry will grow. "Solar and renewables are going to be the most exciting energy."

When it comes to hiring his own workforce, Jones says he's typically looking for carpenters or electricians. The next best thing is someone who just has a real passion for solar or for getting into a green job. Until recently, most training for solar installation has happened on the job because there have been few, if any, formal programs. As the industry has grown, a few training programs have cropped up around the country, and Jones expects there will be many more in the next five to ten years. A few community colleges are offering courses and workshops, which he thinks are very beneficial for someone considering this career path. No matter how you get there, once you're in the business, Jones says, "The sky is the limit." From where he sits, Jones says the green revolution is just beginning.

Think GREEN

Even Oil Men Are Thinking Green

Oil tycoon and billionaire T. Boone Pickens has made his money drilling, but recognizing the crisis facing America, Pickens has been lobbying Washington and the country to join him in advocating for an energy plan that focuses on wind power. He has plans under way to create the largest wind farm in the world in West Texas. On his website, Pickens explains his motivation as follows: "America is in a hole and it's getting deeper every day. We import 70 percent of our oil at a cost of several hundred billion a year. I've been an oil man all my life, but this is one emergency we can't drill our way out of."

Chapter 6

We're Not Alone
Initiatives Working to Make the Blue-Collar Workforce Stronger

With workforce shortages and struggling vocational programs, I'm sure you're wondering if anyone else is out there trying to improve the economic climate. Yes, there are others, so the good news is that we are not alone. There are hundreds of companies, organizations, work programs, and initiatives that will really impress you. They impress me, and they make me feel optimistic that we are going to see changes in the attitudes and opportunities for young adults looking to get into the blue-collar workforce.

This chapter introduces you to some of the programs that are working for you and for the industries that are struggling to find workers. These initiatives are working to make the blue-collar landscape better. They are working to put pride back into blue-collar jobs.

We can't possibly tell you about all of them, but highlighting several can give you a sense of what is being done and where you may be able to find support or inspiration along the way.

Although vocational and technical education is hard to find in some schools and some towns have closed down their automotive classes or woodworking units, the career and technical education (CTE) curriculum is alive and well in this country. It needs to get better, that's for sure, but as you'll learn in this chapter, a lot of amazing programs and initiatives are promoting the trades and making a blue-collar career more accessible and attainable for people who are interested.

Half the battle is having people hear about these great careers. As Janet Bray has said, "You change perceptions with information." Bray, the executive director of the American Association for Career and Technical Education (ACTE), says her group is working hard to educate the public and parents about these opportunities. Bray says CTE classes around the country are already training students for jobs that don't yet exist. In other words, this field is ahead of the curve, anticipating the future, and ultimately working in your favor. Yes, some schools have cut their classes, but other parts of the country see CTE as a necessary part of education and of the health of our workforce. I'm confident that we'll start to see even more focus and attention given to these training programs.

There are currently 1,200 community colleges offering CTE, and 400 that are purely technical in nature. Bray says that there are even waiting lists at some of the CTE schools around the country. "CTE is the solution to a lot of the problems in the education system," she says. "We're working to meet the needs of every student, and every student has different needs." This type of approach is going to benefit students and ultimately blue-collar industries. Although vocational student enrollment has dropped slightly (by about 2 percent) since the 1990s, there are still more than 4 million students in vocational or technical programs. Basically, half of all high school students are involved in vocational programs on some level, as are one-third of all college students.

Blue Collar in ACTION

Keeping Cape Cod's Fishers Afloat

Remember the sustainable fishers who are being eaten alive by the big conglomerate fishing companies? Well, the Cape Cod Fisheries Trust has been established to buy up some of the most expensive fishing permits along Cape Cod (some go for as much $250,000) and then lease them back at an affordable fee to smaller fishermen and women who pledge to fish in a sustainable manner. The trust is looking to raise $10 million to keep about 150 permits out of the hands of the major companies that are taking over fishing. As fishers start to retire, their permits are worth hundreds of thousands of dollars, a fee that few young, small operations can afford. But by selling these permits to the trust, the trust can in turn lease them back to the smaller fishers.

Thanks to a major law called the Carl D. Perkins Vocational and Technical Education Act of 1998, a substantial amount of annual funding from the federal government is supporting CTE curriculum around the country. The Perkins Act helps to improve these technical courses and opportunities. The system isn't perfect, but headway is indeed being made.

Initiatives all over the country are working to connect people like you with the workforce and with the trades. Since we can't name all of them, you'll have to do some of the legwork on your own. Ask your guidance counselor for some direction, or call your nearby state university and community college, because these institutions are often affiliated with workforce initiatives. For example, the Center for Workforce Development connected with Maricopa Community College in Phoenix, Arizona, runs a massive annual job expo and a skilled trades fair and continually offers courses and partnerships between the communities and the future workforce. The center connects businesses that are short on workers with the community colleges and training programs that can supply the necessary and trained individuals.

The state of Delaware has set up a unique fund to better assist employers and further train employees when necessary, particularly at times when skills shortages hit hardest. The fund assists Delaware businesses by offering customized training programs that will help to further train or retain their employees. And in New York—where the number of students taking vocational classes plummeted from 41 percent in 1992 to 25 percent in 2001—efforts are under way to build up those programs once again. At Burgard Vocational High School in Buffalo, for example, a $30 million renovation was undertaken to add state-of-the-art equipment and facilities for CTE courses. Educators around the country are starting to see, not only the value in these classes, but also the need. We're desperate for skilled tradespeople, and the programs are starting to respond to the call for trained workers.

CONNECTING FARMERS

The national Farm Transition Network helps connect new farmers with retiring ones who are hoping to be able to turn over their land to the next generation. Financial arrangements are made for the sales of the farms, but the program is helping to ensure that farming continues on some of the great land across the country. Rather than having farms shuttered, the organization works to match aspiring farmers with veterans of the industry. The network has branches and partners throughout the country. More information, including links to these other partners, can be found at www.farmtransition.org.

Consider the following initiatives for training the future blue-collar workforce:

The Automotive Youth Educational Systems (AYES). We talked about this group in Chapter 3 for the training and certification they provide in auto mechanics. AYES is a nonprofit that works to connect automotive manufacturers with young men and women. This remarkable program started in 1996 and has been matching kids with cars ever since. AYES has partnered with more than 350 schools across the country. To find an AYES center near you or to learn more about the program, go to www.ayes.org.

Careers in Trades. This is the most comprehensive site for Canadian residents—including parents, teachers, and students—who are looking for more information about a blue-collar career. Careers in Trades offers resources to students seeking apprenticeships as well as businesses that are working to integrate the youngest members of the workforce into their operations. There are also informative and helpful employer profiles available. See www.careersintrades.ca.

Career Clusters. Have you heard of career clusters? Developed by the U.S. Department of Education, these clusters of study are designed to help introduce each student to the field in which he or she is most interested. The following are the sixteen career clusters that have been adopted in schools around the country. They aren't all perfectly paired, but the idea is to get students on the path toward what most interests them:

1. Agriculture, Food & Natural Resources
2. Architecture & Construction
3. Arts, A/V Technology & Communications
4. Business Management & Administration
5. Education & Training
6. Finance
7. Government & Public Administration
8. Health Science
9. Hospitality & Tourism
10. Human Services
11. Information Technology
12. Law, Public Safety, Corrections & Security
13. Manufacturing
14. Marketing, Sales & Service
15. Science, Technology, Engineering & Mathematics
16. Transportation, Distribution & Logistics

Traditional vocational education used to offer narrowly focused training. But that's not what employers are looking for today, even in a tool-and-die factory or construction firm. As you know by now, employers are looking for more well-rounded individuals who have a good handle on math and English. These career clusters were developed to assist students to more successfully transition from high school to postsecondary training or jobs. States currently have the option of adopting these clusters as a way of organizing curriculum at schools. The initiative is another example of trying to include all students in learning while broadening opportunities and topics so as to engage more individuals.

Home Builders Institute. This is the workforce development branch of the National Association of Home Builders. The group works to advance education and training programs that will serve the needs of the housing industry. HBI provides training and job placement and promotes the building industry as an attractive career. There are also student-run HBI chapters around the country. More information can be found at www.hbi.org.

Independent Learning Centre. Funded by the Canadian Ministry of Education, this initiative offers extensive courses and training in the skilled trades. It is an excellent resource for apprenticeships, and the CareerMATTERS program provides guidance and resources for post-secondary training and certifications. More can be found at www.ilc.org.

Learning for Life. This incredible organization offers an opportunity for businesses to partner with students to give youth the opportunity to explore the skilled trades. One of the programs, dubbed Exploring, is a mini-introduction to what it's like to be a carpenter, painter, plumber, or construction worker. This how-to initiative pairs interested youth with businesses and organizations to provide participants with early training in auto repair, farming, carpentry, forestry, plumbing, and more. The program helps to foster learning, partnerships, and skills development. Through Exploring's website you can search for opportunities in your area. More information can be found at www.learningforlife.org/exploring/skilledtrades.

National Center for the American Workforce. This organization is the workforce arm of the National Association of Manufacturers (NAM) and was created in January 2008 to specifically address the growing workforce shortages and shortages among skilled workers. The center is looking to expand its pool of potential workers, improve training, increase awareness of careers in manufacturing, and work with community colleges to enhance postsecondary education in the trades. More information can be found through NAM at www.nam.org.

RichmondBUILD. This preapprenticeship program is based in Richmond, a violent and struggling city in northern California. RichmondBUILD is a ten-week program that offers participants an opportunity to learn a trade and includes training in safety, CPR, power tools, framing, drywall, basic electrical, roofing, scaffolding, basic plumbing, and more. Some of the participants have struggled to hold a job or have been involved with violence in the past. Others are just interested in learning a new trade. The program even has its own solar component, which trains participants in solar installation. Run by the city of Richmond, the program started in May 2007, and since then the folks at RichmondBUILD estimate that they have a 90 percent placement rate with an average hourly wage of $18.33.

Skills2Compete. This initiative works to combat the notion that the only way to succeed is through college, while ensuring that our country's workforce is prepared and trained for job demands. Skills2Compete recognizes that today's blue-collar workforce must be highly trained to succeed. The initiative works to ensure that postsecondary training is available and that individuals have access to the necessary skills. More information can be found at www.skills2compete.org.

SkillsUSA. This national partnership between teachers and students (in high school and college) works to enhance preparation for careers in technical, skilled, and service occupations. The business community supports many of the programs, which prepare students for entering the workforce with the beginning knowledge, understanding, and skills required to succeed. More than 300,000 students join SkillsUSA each year. For more information, check out www.skillsusa.org.

Tradability.ca. A collaboration between the community and Ontario's government, Tradability.ca offers an extensive network of resources including apprenticeships and information about the skilled trades, options that are available, detailed job descriptions, and training requirements. More information can be found at Tradability.ca.

The Workforce Alliance (TWA). This national coalition of community organizations, colleges, unions, and businesses advocates for policies and practices that invest in the skills of the American workforce. TWA works to improve job training, expand access to such training, and encourage local initiatives. TWA has been focused on improving the skilled workforce to meet the demands of the twenty-first century, while lobbying Congress and providing improved resources to individuals. To learn more, check out www.work forcealliance.org.

Plenty more great organizations, programs, and initiatives are out there, but hopefully this gives you a sense of the kind of work that is happening. It's important to find out what is happening in your region of the country, too. Your public library, high school library, guidance counselor, and area trade associations are good places to find information. Even your local chamber of commerce may be able to direct you to some programs or organizations. People are generally excited to link youth with opportunities, so don't be afraid to ask. You have to put in some work if you expect to get something out of this. Thanks to these organizations and others, I think the future truly looks promising.

Blue Collar in ACTION

Using Tools to Bring Math to Life

"When you learn differently, you feel like there is something wrong with you," says Perry Wilson. He knows firsthand since he never really learned in a traditional way. Wilson couldn't do math, had trouble reading complete sentences, had dyslexia and other learning disabilities, and struggled through elementary school.

"As a child the education system just convinced me that I was stupid." Wilson's teachers in Kentucky, where he grew up, weren't much help. "They gave me so many Fs I just said, 'Okay, you're right, I'm stupid.'" He even failed the fifth grade. After that, Wilson's father took him out in the backyard, and the two built a tree house together. "My family rallied behind me when I was down." Decades later, when his best friend's son was struggling with third-grade math, Wilson took the young boy outside and they built a tree house. Wilson saw that it was a way to deal with anger, low self-esteem, and overwhelming frustration.

What Wilson had learned from his own experiences was that when he stopped taking math and started applying it, he could do it and he even enjoyed it. In fact, he was quite good at it. But it took Wilson the rest of his adult life to deal with the anger that had built up from being a child who was told that he was dumb. Wilson went to college on a basketball scholarship but only lasted a semester. When he finally took up carpentry, he said that's when it all clicked. He loved the numbers, the creative aspect, and the opportunity to build. "You're making something, and you look back at the end of the day and you can see where four bedrooms are going to be." Wilson says he started using significant math and did just fine.

In 1987, he realized there were so many children suffering through school, many with severe learning disabilities. He wanted to bring math to them in a useable, practical way—one that was exciting, too. That's what led Wilson to start If I Had A Hammer, an organization that teaches carpentry and math in a hands-on manner. If I Had A Hammer is now in 100 cities and has worked with 500,000 students. The program encourages creativity in children as they learn applied mathematics. To learn more about Wilson's organization, check out www.ifihadahammer.com.

Chapter 7

The Blue-Collar Savings Plan

Who do you think has a better standard of living, a plumber or a doctor? That's the question economics professor Laurence Kotlikoff asks in his book *Spend 'til the End*, and he was admittedly a bit surprised with the answer. Kotlikoff, a professor at Boston University, and his coauthor Scott Burns argue that depending on the circumstances, it just may be the plumber who ends up with the better standard of living.

Why? A lot of it starts with the cost of college and the loans you need to pay for such an education. "For a lot of people it doesn't pay to go to college," Kotlikoff says. "It may not pay if you don't make the median earnings." Kotlikoff says college has been oversold, what with the exorbitant loans and the interest rates attached to them. "It's a questionable investment to be borrowing that much money at a high interest rate."

Kotlikoff says the college route makes even less sense "if you haven't been a stellar student." If you make it through the four years and end up being stuck at an annual income of $50,000 a year for the rest of your life, Kotlikoff argues that your loan repayment will weigh you down. The plumber, free of college debt, has an opportunity to save or even spend on vacations, meals out, or new home appliances.

Plus, when it comes to the skilled trades and blue-collar jobs, Kotlikoff points out that "some of these jobs can extend beyond retirement." That's not typical with white-collar workers, though. Usually when you retire from an executive job or a sales position, or from being a company manager, that's it. "There aren't many people who work as a banker until they're seventy. If you want to, you may be able to be a plumber until you're seventy," says Kotlikoff.

In his book, Kotlikoff compares these two hypothetical people—the plumber and doctor—and after college loans, medical school loans, interest, malpractice insurance, and a higher tax rate, the example illustrates a point worth considering. "[College] has been oversold," says Kotlikoff. "Everyone is focused on education as the panacea without strong support for that." Kotlikoff says that when it comes to standard of living, the bottom line is that "whether you went to college matters, but it matters less than you think."

All that said, it's still important to invest in your future. Training is key to getting into the blue-collar workforce today, and it's crucial for moving up the ladder. You may need to spend some money before you can start making money. In other words, even though you may not be planning to finance a college degree you will likely need to pay to get trained. Few things are totally free, including the training and certifications needed for many blue-collar careers. You may be able to pay cash, you may have parents who are willing to help you out, you might have a savings plan, and, yes, you may have to take out a loan.

We're not planning to give you actual personal financial advice or tell you where to invest your money or how to get a loan. But we can try to help you think about the financial aspects involved in going blue collar. There may be a training program you have your eye on, an associate's degree that will get you where you want to go, or even enrollment costs for that cost-free apprenticeship. If you're going to go out on your own, you'll need to be able to fund your start-up.

While the unions usually cover the actual costs associated with their apprenticeships, it's possible that you'll need certain books or work clothes. You may have to buy basic supplies such as notebooks, if there is classroom training. Small expenses add up—as does the gas to get to and from your training—so it's a good idea to find out in advance just how much money you're going to need for all of the related expenses.

Loans are available for students interested in going into trade school. I know I've been pretty critical of college loans, especially the kinds that send thousands of students and their parents into long-term debt. But what we're talking about here are programs that have much more manageable fees and tuition attached. These programs will not cost you $30,000 a year for four years the way some private colleges will, but rather you may have to pay $5,000 for a license or a certification. Think about what you want to do, how badly you want it, how serious you are, and remember that you have to invest in your own future. That $5,000 to learn to drive a truck, for example, may seem like a ton of cash, but in the end it may be your ticket to a good career as a truck driver. More important, you'll have earned that money back in no time at all. I call that a smart investment.

Brian Greenberg works with families who are saving for college, many of whom are looking to sock away (or borrow) more than $100,000 to pay for their son or daughter to attend a private college or university. When it comes to saving for a trade school, Greenberg, an accountant with Brian C. Greenberg & Associates in Marlton, New Jersey, says basic principles of saving apply, only on a far smaller scale. Allocating a bit from each paycheck until you reach your goal is the first step toward saving. "There is nothing special or exotic about saving for a blue-collar career," he says.

But he points out that paying for a trade school is a whole lot less money than a four-year college tuition bill. And when it comes to the payoff, he says borrowing or spending savings of $5,000 to $8,000 could be an excellent investment. Greenberg says a young adult who is borrowing or saving for an $8,000 auto mechanic degree could be earning $40,000 their first year on the job. "That's a great investment. It's a nice deal."

Greenberg knows that for some families the $5,000 can be taxing, but he still suggests loans as one way of financing something that could get you into a great paying job. "More people should look at that rather than just going off to college." Although the money is significant for some, he says you can typically earn it all back in a relatively short amount of time. "The nut is a lot smaller than if you were saving $100,000 for college. You can go through a lot less hoops."

Talking Money with Mom and Dad

If you're heading off to a training program or apprenticeship, you may not have enough to go out on your own. Will you be living at home until you've saved? Lay down the ground rules with your parents or your family. It's important to make some decisions so that there are no misunderstandings. Maybe you'll live at home for the first year until you can pay rent on your own place. Perhaps your parents are even willing to front you some of the money they would have been spending on college. Also, if you're living at home, set a time line. How long do expect to live there? Until you've completed an apprenticeship? One year from the start of your first job? Two years from the end of high school? No matter what the length of time, it's a good idea to have an agreement upfront.

Maybe you're entirely on your own. Make a budget. Map out how much you need for the basics, like food, rent, and utilities. Are you working for a boss, or are you running your own one-person business? You need to think about advertising costs, gas, and other small fees. Don't get caught spending too much on your weekend fun, and don't forget to save. Just because you won't have college loans doesn't mean you couldn't end up in debt quite quickly.

When it comes to figuring out what you may need to save for and what you may need to spend to get yourself on the right track, we've outlined a few areas below. Each one of you will have a different set of circumstances and obstacles. You'll likely be coming from different family and financial situations. No one situation will be the same, but this list should help you start thinking.

Fees. Find out whether you will encounter fees to register, apply for, or enroll in any of the programs you're considering. Ask unions that cover apprenticeship costs if you are responsible for any of the extras, such as books or materials fees. Know the tuition fees associated with training programs. When it comes to certification costs, be sure you know how much you are expected to pay up front and whether you will need to apply for a license (which could mean an additional cost).

Room and board. Will you be living away from home? If you are living at home, will your parents expect you to contribute some money on a monthly basis for food? You may have to start paying car insurance, health insurance, or phone bills. These things add up.

It's important to have a conversation with your parents about what kinds of expenses you'll have once you've graduated from high school. Often parents want to see you demonstrate that you are responsible and that you are taking your decisions seriously. Maybe they will offer to contribute a portion toward healthcare, or auto insurance, or food costs. Maybe they'll cover everything, in which case you should have a plan for saving your money. Talk to them, so there is no misunderstanding, and think about asking them to split some of the costs with you. Maybe they are even willing to loan you some of the money that it takes to get the license you need to be on your way to earning a living.

Loans. Federal Financial Aid (or FAFSA) is the best place to start. More information and applications can be found at www.fafsa.edu.gov. This is one of the most common ways of applying for financial aid. Check out the Department of Education website as well for other links and resources at www.edu.gov. Your guidance counselor should be able to suggest loan options and may even have ideas about local scholarships or grants that are available. Use your guidance counselor and even your school or town librarians as resources. There are some private loan programs that have been set up specifically for trade schools and for community colleges. The websites mentioned above can direct you as can www.collegescholarships.org.

As for financial aid and applying for money, you should know that there are two main ways of paying for tuition costs. The first is grants and scholarships, money that you generally won't have to pay back. And then there are loans, which you must pay back but these could offer you an opportunity to take courses or earn certifications. I know I've talked about how much money people owe on college loans, but becoming certified or trained for many blue-collar jobs is no longer a luxury; it's a necessity. Perhaps you know of a course that will make you much more attractive to employers. Take it. If you're choosing wisely, the payoff should come soon after you start working. Just do your homework, figure out exactly what you need, rather than just signing up for classes you may never use and loans that will be hard to pay back.

My final piece of advice: if you're looking to save money or borrow money to finance your blue-collar training, spend less. Spend less on clothes, on food, on your car, and on entertainment. I know, I don't need to lecture you about this. I've told my kids this over and over, but you have to make some sacrifices. If you're trying to save to get some training so that you can get the job you want, now is the time to skimp on spending and make a budget. You can reward yourself with a vacation, a night out, a new jacket, or a new tool once you've completed your training and are on your way to earning. But for now, spend less.

Did You KNOW?

DO THE MATH

Looking for a way to save? At www.finaid.org you can calculate just how much you need to save to get to your goal. This handy online calculator will factor in how much you have in the bank, interest rates, and more. This is an easy way to set up goals, plus the site offers many resources dedicated to helping you save, invest, and plan for education-related expenses.

Chapter 8

Moving Up in the Blue-Collar World

W hen Veronica Rose joined the electrical union in 1978 she had no idea she would one day open her own commercial and industrial electrical company on Long Island. But she tells people who are anxious to run a business and be their own boss that these things take time. Rose worked in the industry for ten years before she even thought about opening her own shop, which she ultimately did in 1993. Looking back, she says she's glad she waited until she was ready and had the experience before going out on her own.

You have to have clients, you must build a reputation, and you have to have some financial padding to get started. I know we all want instant gratification. Most of us don't want to be told to wait our turn. And yes, it's important to reach for the stars. But you have to be responsible and you have to have a plan. Just because you don't own a business after your third year of working for a plumbing company doesn't mean there is something wrong. If this is a goal of yours, you have to work toward it. Set small goals to get to your larger goals and figure out exactly what you need—the capital, the skills, and the clients—before you can go out on your own. If you start your business too soon and without enough planning, and especially without enough expertise, you can count on having a rough time.

So what happens after you land your first job or have that license you were working toward? Now what? Are you already thinking about advancement? Do you want to be your own boss? Are you really prepared for that? You don't have to accept the weekly paycheck for life if you have other ideas in your head. If you want to run the show or simply branch out on your own, that's a great thing. But making the leap too soon and without preparation can be disastrous. Likewise, staying in the same job for too long can be frustrating and even unproductive. It's all about finding the right balance.

"The fine line is working for someone and working toward funding your own business," says Blair Glenn, the arborist from California. He long wanted to run his own business but knew that spending many years working for an expert would ultimately benefit him immensely. Glenn says a business background can be helpful, and taking a few business courses is something he recommends, though he adds that you certainly don't need a degree in business to be a success.

If you're working through a union, the promotions, pay increases, and job title changes are often clearly defined through specific guidelines. If you're working at a smaller company, it may be worth it to sit down with your boss and talk about your mutual goals and ideas about growth. Maybe they only have room for one manager and you want to be in that position. Perhaps you've already figured out that you are going to train with one company and then move to the next. Even if you never own your own business, you want to have a sense of your goals, where you want to go, and how you plan to climb the ladder. Thinking ahead is important, but so is gaining experience and learning your trade inside and out.

We should always be challenging ourselves, wanting more, growing and learning. If you want to master skills and need additional certificates, figure out how much it will cost and how you're going to pay for the extra credentials. Maybe your employer would be willing to share or even cover the expense of more training, since ultimately your advanced skills will benefit your boss. Be prepared to talk to your employer about bonuses, benefits, or profit sharing. Some companies—especially some of the green ones—are offering profit sharing. And know your limits. If you've been on the job for three weeks, that's not a good time to ask for a promotion. Learn your job, master your craft, and think about how you can grow.

Maybe you're not looking to start a business because that's simply not what you're after. Many people don't want that hassle and know they would not enjoy it. Others aren't cut out to manage a company and would prefer to grow from within a business owned by someone else. Growing from within is another incredibly exciting and lucrative way of getting to the top of the ladder. But you still need goals and you're probably going to need training, especially if you are hoping to advance. You just have to decide which steps are required to get you where you want to go. Then, focus on how you can do the job 110 percent better than the next guy. How do you plan to get recognized? Do you want to demonstrate that you are loyal and dependable, as well as a master at the trade? Adopting these traits early on will pay off in a big way down the road.

As you gain experience and learn a trade, you'll want to get noticed and recognized by your boss or supervisor. You don't have to be pushy about it, but letting the boss know that you're excelling or a top-notch worker is a good thing. A few tips for doing so:

1. **Stay upbeat.** You don't need to complain or gripe just because you weren't recognized or thanked. Sometimes supervisors really aren't aware of the nitty-gritty that you're doing. Work isn't supposed to be fun or perfect every single day, so don't complain if things don't go your way on occasion.

2. **Keep a list.** It's a good idea to jot down your accomplishments from week to week so that you can keep track of what you've achieved, problems you've solved, a crisis that was averted, or a compliment received from a customer.

3. **Talk to your boss.** Set up a time to meet with your boss or supervisor on a regular basis or ask that you be given a review every six months. Show that you want feedback and that you want the opportunity to talk about your own successes.

Do You Need a Resume?

Not everyone expects to see a resume when interviewing or hiring. But a resume is a chance for you to make a great first impression. You don't have to have graduated from college to have one, and you don't need to have had ten amazing jobs either. It's just an opportunity to put onto paper all the things you want to be able to tell a potential employer. Although resumes are thought of as something more often used in the white-collar world, they are becoming more necessary for blue-collar jobs. The more skilled and advanced the job is, the better off you are if you have a resume.

As resume writing expert Steven Provenzano says, it's a great piece of paper for everyone to have since a resume should ultimately list all of your accomplishments and skills. Provenzano—who has written six books about job hunting and resume writing and one on blue-collar resumes—says a resume allows you to spit out all of the information you want to share and hand it to a potential employer. You can't really expect someone to remember every last thing about you once you leave a job interview. So, that piece of paper serves as a resource for the employer. Really, it can't hurt, and it doesn't take long to put together a good-looking, informative resume.

"It allows you to represent yourself in the light you want," says Provenzano, who is in favor of each resume containing a short personal statement or objective. "Employers want to know who they are hiring." Provenzano says a lot of people do try to get by without a resume, but as all of the industries move toward requiring more skills and more training, the resume is going to become a more popular tool as well.

Provenzano suggests picking out key words that work for your industry. You have to match your resume to the job you're applying for. If you have carpentry and masonry skills but are applying for a mason job, you want to be sure to highlight your top-notch masonry skills and mention your carpentry ones as an extra added bonus. Be sure you know what an employer is looking for, which skills they value most, or which licenses, certificates, or experiences they are after. Provenzano says the best way to get a job—in an office or on a work site—is still through word of mouth. But a resume can help to remind a potential boss of all of your skills once you're no longer standing there to remind him or her of your credentials.

We've included a sample resume format here so you can take a crack at writing your own. Your guidance counselors should be able to help you further polish your resume. Monster.com, the massive job board, also has an entire section devoted to building a resume that contains tons of tips and suggestions for how to make yours stand out from others. But be sure to sell yourself. You'll see from our sample that there is a place for you to include your job objective right at the top. You should mention your passion and your drive, and don't be afraid to throw in your own personality. The resume doesn't have to be a formal or stuffy thing. You want to jump off the page and stand out from the other job applicants. I'm not suggesting that you say stupid things, but let an employer know how much you want the job or what it is that makes you tick.

Sample Resume

Here is a sample resume format to get you started.

YOUR NAME HERE
Your address, telephone numbers, and e-mail go here.

JOB TITLE SOUGHT: If applying for a specific, advertised job, list it here. Otherwise, briefly note the general job you are looking for, such as heavy equipment operator.

JOB OBJECTIVE: Sell yourself here. Explain your passion, your drive, and what you are looking for in a job. This is your opportunity to grab the attention of a potential employer. Take the time to write a few sentences about yourself, mention your unique skills or interests, and outline your career goals here.

JOB ACCOMPLISHMENTS: Separately list your job experience, with a brief description of each position. Be sure to mention skills, responsibilities, or accomplishments that would be relevant to the position for which you are applying.

• Job title
• Name of organization, address, telephone number
• Dates of employment
• Accomplishments/responsibilities

EDUCATION: List education completion (starting with high school if you do not have a college degree)

• School, degree, or certificate (if applicable), dates of enrollment, major and minor (if applicable)
• Postsecondary training, completed coursework, dates of enrollment

CERTIFICATIONS AND LICENSES: List any you have, including dates received.

ADDITIONAL SKILLS: List any skills that were not covered above, such as mastery of carpentry, excellent interpersonal skills, or computer proficiency.

AWARDS/HONORS: If you have them, don't be shy about sharing.

REFERENCES: If you wish to include these, list three professional references. Teachers are a great option, but always check with the individuals before you list their names.

Going Out on Your Own?

If you're really ready to open your own shop and run your own business, you'll see that there are many things to think about first. There are also a ton of books and online resources worth checking out that are focused on starting new businesses. Even if you're not there yet, it's a good idea to keep these in mind as you think about your plans for the future. Some of these may seem daunting, but as you move up, gain experience, earn money, and master skills, many of these elements will be much less intimidating and may even seem exciting.

1. **Build experience.** This is what you need to sustain your business. You've got to know what you're doing, and you have to know your trade or craft inside and out.

2. **Build a team.** You have to know who is working for you, and you have to know how to recruit and hire the people you want on your team. Their personalities and attitudes need to be compatible with yours, so decide what skills you are looking for.

3. **Business plan.** I can't stress this enough. If you don't have a business plan, you're more likely to fail. This will help set goals, track income, monitor expenses, and predict where you are going. It will help down the road to determine whether it's the right time to expand your business or cut back in certain areas.

4. **Money, money, money.** Having money to start your business is crucial, having income is crucial, and having enough to cover your salaries, expenses, equipment, licenses, rentals, and leases is of utmost importance. Don't go out on your own until you know the money is there.

5. **Marketing.** Have you thought about how you will be marketing your company? Maybe you'll sponsor a local event or participate in a

sports tournament. Will you give a free demonstration or workshop at the local high school? This is all marketing.

6. **Licenses and permits.** Depending on your trade, you may need a lot of these permits or only a few. Find out what you need so that you know how much you have to spend and so that you understand the application process. Be sure you know how many licenses you need so you don't run into trouble down the road.

7. **Equipment.** Are you planning to lease, rent, or buy your equipment? You have to be sure you have what you need, and you must have a plan for repairing and maintaining your equipment. Once a customer, big or small, hires you, you have to be able to deliver your service, so be sure to have the necessary tools and equipment.

8. **Location.** Have you decided whether you need a prominent location to set up shop or just a large location to store equipment? Think about demand and where in the country or in your state or even your county the need is the greatest. You should place yourself strategically so as to get the most out of your operation. Naturally, locations cost money, too, whether you're renting or buying, so keep this in mind.

Mostly, what I hope you will take away from this chapter is that you can reach for the moon but you have to do it when the time is right and only after some planning. More than anything, this isn't about doing one job or one task for the rest of your life. This is not about having the same entry-level job for the next ten years. This is not about pushing that lawn mower forever. But it is about the fact that knowing the best way to mow the lawn is essential if you want to run a landscaping business. Learning from the bottom up is actually a great way to invest in your future, and climbing up that ladder is ultimately going to bring you more challenges, more fulfillment, and more financial stability.

Chapter 9

The Rest of My Story

I'm going to let you in on a bit more of what I was really going through while starting up my business. Hopefully you'll see that no matter what you're feeling like on the inside and no matter how badly things are stacked against you, you just have to keep going. I hit a really rough patch after my first wife left and I ended up moving back home to my parents' house. It was April 7, 1983, at 6:45 PM when I was holding my son Anthony in one arm and reaching up with the other to knock on my parents' door. "Hi, Mom. I'm home." That was tough. I was there for eighteen months. Anthony went to day care at my aunt's house, and I went to work. Fortunately, my parents were willing to help and they loved Anthony and helped me raise him. There were many days when I felt like it was just Anthony and me against the world. At one point I was working three jobs and I was pretty poor. But I kept going.

I was also drinking too much. I told you I had a drinking problem, and it became a serious one. I was an alcoholic. The good news is that I've been sober since 1990. But before I get to that part of the story, I have to back up to tell you about when I started my business in the winter of 1981. I asked my dad if he would help me out. "Buy me a truck and I'll build a business," I said to him. He agreed, but not without warning. "I'm not a bank, Joey. You'd better make money." I've told you that I like challenges, right? I was excited to start earning a good living. I wanted to make my parents proud, but mostly I just wanted to prove that I could support myself. By the spring of 1982 I had thirty customers, and I was on my way to success.

I worked alone for nearly ten years. During the busiest times, especially when fall came around, I would hire a part-time crew to help pick up leaves. Things were going well with my business, and then in March 1986 I met my wife Dawn when we went on a blind date. Anthony was just five at the time, and Dawn had her four-year-old son, John Mark. We hit it off, so much so that after dating for only a month and a half we were already talking about buying a house and moving in together. Dawn's mother helped us to buy our first house, and we were married in June 1988.

I was in love, my business was growing, and I should have been happy. But my anger was raging and my drinking was bad. I would drink just to calm down and try to feel better about myself. It wasn't working. I don't know how Dawn put up with me. At first, she did, and then she got wise and decided she couldn't take it anymore. Our marriage was crumbling, the booze was coming between us, and she wanted out. We split up, and I was even more miserable. Through my drinking I kept working very hard. I channeled a huge amount of my anger and frustration with the world into my business. I could get sweaty and dirty and be physical all day long. I loved that. I still do. I needed it.

In 1990 I quit drinking. I showed up at my first Alcoholics Anonymous meeting, and really the rest is history. I'm not saying it's been easy, but that was the start of a whole new part of my life. There were days when I had to walk in circles to keep myself from popping open a can of beer. It can be all-consuming, at least for a while. But I had my last drink in September 1990 and owe a lot of my recovery to the men (yup, they were men) who put their arms around me and told me I could do it. I drank from age fifteen to thirty-one, and then, I'm proud to say, I stopped.

What I got back was something incredible. Dawn and I had divorced in November 1990, but two years later we got back together. We had been passing our son Joey back and forth, since we shared custody, and we still loved each other. My drinking was no longer going to come between us, and we decided to give things another try, so we were back together again as a family. It was a wonderful thing. I like to say that Dawn and I dated for another nine years before tying the knot yet again. Whatever you call it, we got married, for a second time, while standing next to the Christmas tree in 1999. We bought a house in Holliston, just outside Boston where we still live. Life was good.

But I got whacked again by something that sent me reeling. Dawn and I were expecting our second child together and our fourth between us. Our little girl Heather was born prematurely in January 2000 at just twenty-seven weeks old. On top of that, Heather had a rare heart defect. Even our amazing doctors at Children's Hospital in Boston knew little about her condition. They did everything they could, we did everything we could, and we stayed with her each night, hoping she would make it through. But on February 24, a Wednesday, at 9:45 in the morning, Heather passed away, at just six weeks old.

I thought I had been through enough. I thought all had gone wrong that could. I didn't think I'd get dealt a hand like this. It was too much. Some days I would just sob, unable to think about anything but my little baby girl. The doctors told Dawn and me that the way to get over our heartbreak was to have another child—when we were ready, of course. We'll never get over the loss of Heather, but we did have another baby. Madison was born in November 2002 and has kept us on our toes since. Here I am, close to fifty years old, and I have a little girl in my house who tries to tell me what to do and huffs away each time she doesn't get her way. She melts my heart, she's opened my eyes in new ways, and yes, she can make me nuts. But mostly she's brought laughter back into our home. Madison was exactly what Dawn and I needed to get back on track.

So, that's my story. Why am I telling you all of this? What does this have to do with this book, with being blue collar and proud of it? Because when I say that you can work hard, or you can work even harder and I tell you to stop complaining, I mean it. I've been there. Really, through alcoholism, through divorce, through loss, through loneliness, through a bankruptcy, and through the joys of raising a family and the thrills of running a business I've been there. I hear people say, "It's hard" or "I can't," and all I can think is, *Yes, it's hard. Life is hard.* And some days you feel like life might break you. But guess what? You don't have much of a choice. You have to get back up and get going again. Don't get me wrong. I'm not flying high every day. Every day isn't perfect. I have my ups and downs. I still have my bad days and my anger still builds until I think I'm going to explode, when I think about my baby Heather, or remember disturbing things from my childhood. Still, I know that we each have to keep going, through the rotten and the wonderful. It's the only way to succeed.

I've read books before and thought, *Ha, easy for this guy to say. He has no idea how hard it is.* Maybe you got to this point in the book and were thinking, *Well, this guy just doesn't understand. I bet he had it easy.* I wanted you to know that's not the case. I'm not whining or complaining but just telling you that you can't let your own problems, your own catastrophes, or your own heartaches stand in the way of becoming a success.

So how did I go from all of that to working on this book and starting my website? By the spring of 2003 I was so tired of dealing with my son's high school teachers. Joey was never very good at school even though he's smart. He reminds me a lot of myself. He's got my personality and my inability to sit still, and he absolutely loves working with his hands. But his teachers were telling me that he had to go to college. "He just has to, Mr. LaMacchia. It's the only way for him to get a good job." That's what they would say to me. They wouldn't even have a conversation with me about why college may not be for everyone. And they wouldn't even listen when all I wanted to say was that if my son could barely get through high school, I didn't think he would do very well in college. I had been through all of this just a few years earlier with my oldest son Anthony.

I heard about other people who were dealing with the same thing, and meanwhile Joey felt like there wasn't any support for him as the kid who wasn't planning to apply to college. No one would hear me out when I tried to explain that while I understood college was good for some, it wasn't for everyone. That's when I decided to start my website, BlueCollarandProudofIt.com. And that's when I realized there are tons of people out there who are being directed to college, and who are feeling isolated or stupid for not wanting to go. I've always wanted the site to be for people like Joey, and the hundreds of thousands of other people out there to see that they're not alone. I want parents to know that they haven't failed if their kid is interested in a trade or wants to a join a union apprenticeship. And I want people to see that there are awesome, respectable blue-collar jobs out there.

My son Anthony didn't go to college either, and he and I both struggled to explain that to teachers. Anthony worked with me for a few years after high school, but then decided he wanted to work as a real estate broker. I tease him because he goes to work in a suit and he gives me grief for being disorganized. But Anthony is happy, and he really enjoys what he's doing. I'm so proud of how far he has come, how hard he works, and how honest he is in business. Joey got his truck license a few years ago and has been working for me since 2004.

I just turned fifty years old, and I have thirteen employees, nine trucks, an asphalt business, a masonry division, and a booming land-scaping company. Since 2001, I've grossed a minimum of $1.5 million annually and am working toward higher numbers all the time. I just want parents and teachers and kids, especially, to see that going blue collar is not the kiss of death. I'm a pretty happy guy. I'm a successful businessman, and I have a trade that has become my expertise. I've learned from the bottom up, and I'm good at what I do. Who could argue that this isn't a good life? It *is* a good life. I go on wonderful vaca-tions with my family, have a granddaughter I enjoy, children I love, and a wonderful community. No one can take that away from me just because I don't have a college degree.

In the summertime, I often go to barbecues with my neighbors, and I notice that many of them are wearing Harvard and Yale T-shirts. I thought they were bragging at first, sort of shoving it in everyone's face that they were better or more educated. But you know what? It's just that they're proud of where they went to school. And they should be. To me their shirts sort of say, "White collar

their accomplishments on their shirts. Tha

on my shirt, too. Only my shirt says, "Blu

built this country." Isn't that okay? I think i

bery and the fear and recognize that even

college name on it, you can be respected a.... ....

could see t

holdin

get

part of the community and the workforce. When I'm at these barbecues, eating the same chicken and potato salad, standing in a backyard that looks like my backyard, I think about how, in the end, we all got to the same place. Only we did it in different ways. It takes pride and it takes self-esteem and it takes a ton of hard work, no matter who you are.

A severe case of ADHD broke my early childhood. There were school and family frustrations I dealt with almost every day. I've had anger beyond belief. I've had zero self-worth. I mean *zero*. I was always wondering, *What is wrong with me? Why am I so bad? Why don't I understand this?* But you just keep going, keep running, and for me, keep creating and telling my story. I started to wonder, *How many Joes are out there?* We'll never know for sure, but my guess is that there are a lot. And I bet there are even more people out there who aren't like me but they understand something I've just talked about in this book. They get it. They feel it. They're relieved someone understands them, and they're excited by what they're reading.

I was at an intersection recently, sitting in traffic, watching a father who was holding his four-year-old son in his arms. The kid was practically foaming at the mouth watching a man with a jackhammer digging in the street. You've probably seen this before: the kid who can't stop staring at the dump truck, the backhoe, or the crane. Kids are so excited when they come across construction sites. This little boy reminded me of a lion watching a wildebeest on the Serengeti. You

he kid squirming to break free and get closer, but his dad was
g him back, for safety reasons of course. And then, as these kids
older, they lose that lust. They lose it because of the messages they
are getting about the white-collar world. It's as if there are these magi-
cal blinking lights of college, of the Internet, of Wall Street just sucking
them in, guaranteeing them huge incomes. They forget that there are
people who first have to build those buildings and create those roads to
get you to work every day.

Still, there seems to be a natural craving in all of us. Some of us follow
it, others don't. But don't you think we should all have the option? And let's
face it; we have to spread around the jobs. We can't all be plumbers, and
we can't all be bankers. We need all of these jobs to make the world work.
We need the accountants, and we need the auto mechanics. But some days
I like to say that we need these blue-collar jobs even more. The appoint-
ment with your accountant can wait a day or a week, but if you have a
leak in your water tank you need a plumber immediately.

I think there should be blue-collar summer camp, just like there is
science camp and soccer camp. Why not? This stuff is exciting. Maybe
when that four-year-old gets a little older he would enjoy blue-collar
camp. And you know what? It won't kill you if you like it. It's not poi-
son. Even if you ended up becoming a scientist, what's wrong with having spent a summer session building and sawing or drilling? All those
soccer camp kids aren't professional athletes, but most of them had a
blast. We should let more kids play with tools, try to hammer, get a little
dirty, and feel what it's like to create something out of nothing.

As you've seen from this book, there are incredible jobs in the skilled
trades. Working in these industries is exciting, it's productive, it can be
lucrative, it's often good for your heart and your health, and it's an awesome option if you're dreading the cubicle. I do think we have a ways

to go, a ways to go to change the attitudes people have about the trades, but I think we're going to turn this around. I think we're going to get people to wake up and appreciate what we do and why we choose to work with our hands.

With people like Janet Bray from the Association for Career and Technical Education (ACTE), apprenticeship programs throughout the country, green-collar jobs opening up all kinds of opportunities, and guidance counselors who are willing to share a book like this with their students, we'll get back on track. Gene Bottoms, the senior vice president of the Southern Regional Education Board (SREB), is confident that we're already moving in the right direction. "There is a revitalized emphasis on career-tech in this country," he says. Bottoms works to improve education and work preparedness through various SREB initiatives. Although Bottoms recognizes that it's been a struggle to get people to pay attention to the importance of these programs, he says it is slowly happening. In many states, Bottoms points out, there are full-time technical high schools that have waiting lists. One reason, he says, is the sheer need for trained workers. "The largest number of jobs do require certification or an associate's degree."

All I'm really asking is that the trades be presented as an option. It's not for everyone, just like college isn't for everyone. But it should be out there, showcased as an exciting, responsible career choice. The way we have career day at school—when lawyers, accountants, and teachers talk about their professions—we, too, should have a skilled trades day to introduce students and young adults to these incredible opportunities. Then we can let them choose what interests them, what fits with their personality, and what gets them excited.

I started this book by explaining that this is a choice. You don't go into the blue-collar trades because there is nothing else to do or because you're lazy or because you're looking for an excuse not to go to college. People choose to do one of these jobs because it fits them, because they enjoy the work, and because they are well suited to it. Just the way a short baseball player is more suited to being a catcher and the tall lanky athlete is more suited to speed swimming, these jobs fit different personalities and talents.

The National Geographic Channel's *World's Toughest Fixes* just reinforces how much our culture is starting to pay attention to these jobs. We now have TV programs, educators, and communities looking at these jobs, these people, and these trades in a new way. We're shining the spotlight on the people who repair and build our country. I don't care whether it happens through this book, my website, a show on television, or because of workforce shortages, but we need to get people to pay attention to the importance of blue-collar work, of skilled trades, and of the growing green industries that are opening up a host of possibilities. I just hope that, whether you are a parent, a student, a teacher, or a friend, you will have a new understanding and appreciation of the blue-collar options out there. I hope you will see the value, the necessity, and the wonder in these blue-collar jobs, in these skilled trades, and in your son or daughter who has taken an interest in one of these careers. My hope is that people will, once and for all, understand why I say I'm blue collar and proud of it. We built America, we'll continue to build and fix this great country, and we can all be proud of that.

Chapter 10

Wait! I Have More Questions

I'm a Student and I Want to Know . . .

Q: I'm worried that my friends will think I'm taking the easy way out if I don't go to college.

A: You will be taking the easy way out if you don't have a plan or focus and if you aren't willing to work hard. Your college-bound buddies will also be taking the easy way out if they don't buckle down, study hard, and plan their career paths. Going to college doesn't mean that you will be working hard, and taking a blue-collar job does not mean that you will have it easy. We each have to decide for ourselves, no matter which career path we take, if we are going to try to slide by or if we are going to do the absolute best we can. I suggest working very hard and giving it all you've got. That's not the easy way out. But just remember, we're all different. We all wear different clothes, play different sports, and listen to different music. And we won't all like the same jobs. But we should all have goals and work hard to meet them.

Q: I'm tired of being asked, "What college are you going to?" People look at me like I'm crazy when I tell them I'm not going. What am I supposed to say to explain it?

A: Hopefully you have a plan for what you are going to do, and if you don't, you need to sit down and figure one out. That's what this book is supposed to help with. Narrow down your interests and figure out a direction. Do you want to go into electrical work? A green sector? Manufacturing? Decide how you're going to get a job or training. Only then will you be able to offer up an explanation when asked about what you're doing after high school. And even if no one was asking, you should have this plan anyway. You can always alter your plan or change your plan entirely, but being focused and having a goal to work toward are key components to success. And just think, your blue-collar job won't be shipped overseas. You can't outsource the repairs on your car or the installation of those solar panels.

Q: I started college a few years ago, but I'm miserable. I've always wanted to go into the trades. I enjoyed woodworking and would like to be a carpenter, but I have two years of school, lots of debt, and I feel trapped.

A: If you know woodworking and carpentry are for you, then follow your dreams. If you're not quite sure, take some time off from school and get an apprenticeship, or find a job with the best carpenter in your area, even on Saturdays. If this turns out to indeed be where you want to focus your time, you'll have to start paying back your loans. But there is no sense in continuing to accumulate school loans if you don't think you'll use that education. You may need to invest in tools and training. Plus, a starting salary in your new career could mean a tight budget at first. There is no sense in racking up more school loans. If you're following your passions, feel good about what you're doing, and have a sense of accomplishment, that's the real deal.

Q: **I really like the idea of pursuing a blue-collar career, but I don't know which one I'd be good at and I've never taken a shop class or a woodworking class. Where do I start?**

A: If you still have the time and the opportunity, take as many CTE classes as possible. If you think something interests you—woodworking or auto mechanics, for example—take a course. If you've finished high school or your school doesn't offer this, then get a job working in one or more of the trades that interest you. Perhaps you can spend your summer working two different jobs, or try one out on Saturdays so you can test the waters. Or bang on doors, make some phone calls, and find out if someone in your area is looking for an apprentice or helper. Explain that you're interested in learning more about their trade and that you want to experience it firsthand. You may not get lucky from your first phone call, but keep trying. And if all else fails, check out your local community college or continuing education center to see if you can take a single course in welding or plumbing.

Q: **My parents are insisting that I go to college and won't hear me out when I try to explain how much I don't want to go. I've tried to get them to understand that I have an interest in the trades and want to go that route. Help.**

A: It's your life, so dig in your heels. While your parents may mean well in that they want you to be happy and successful, perhaps they think the only way to get there is through college. Have you tried explaining that going to college is so unappealing that you likely won't do well anyway? Have you told them that you may cost them more than it's worth because you don't see yourself finishing? Often kids go to college, and they or their parents accumulate loans and then they still decide to learn a trade, which often means investing more money in that training or certification. If you know what you're interested in, find out some of the numbers and show them to your parents. What are your job prospects, and how much money might you be making? The Bureau of Labor Statistics (www.bls.gov) can help you nail down some of these figures. But explain again that this is about your life and your happiness and that you're not looking for a cop-out and not looking for handouts from Mom and Dad.

Q: My parents have offered to pay for college but they won't help me pay for trade school. Is this fair?

A: Well, it may not be fair, but if that's what is on the table, you have to make a decision. If you do not want to go to a four-year college but you have a plan with regard to trade school, then look into grants, scholarships, and student loans to help cover your costs. Unions often pay for training; other times, employers take care of these costs, so be sure to investigate all options before signing up at a private trade school. That said, you could also try explaining to your parents that this is something that is just as important to you as college is to other people. Explain that you don't want to waste their money. And explain what you want to do with the trade school training. You might even be able to strike a deal; tell your parents that you will reimburse them for the expense of the trade school if you don't put it to use within six months of receiving the certificate. This is almost a trial-and-error system. If it works, then they've made a great investment. You can also go to the Bureau of Labor Statistics (www.bls.gov) where you can find a ton of information on salaries and job growth for every industry. Show your parents the numbers, show them what you can make your first year or your fifth year, and talk to them about the actual dollars. This may help a lot when they see that you'll be making a real living and aren't just planning to take the easy way out. Remember, too, there are many people in college who are paying their own way. If you want something bad enough, you'll figure out a way to get it.

Q: I've always had the impression that going into one of the trades means being in a dangerous job. Is this true?

A: That's a completely legitimate fear since it's true that there are many more potential hazards in a physical job than in a desk job. You're more likely to get hurt operating heavy equipment, building bridges, or driving a truck cross-country than you are standing at the photocopy machine. That said, common sense and awareness are key. The law is also on your side. Employers are required to comply with strict, federally regulated safety codes of conduct. You do need to be properly trained in certain fields and jobs, but that's why there are licensing boards to help ensure safety and standards. These jobs are generally very safe, but of course building skyscrapers has risks and welding with extreme heat means you could get burned. But that won't happen if you're safe, if you follow rules, and if you know what you're doing. You could also get into a car accident on the way to work, but that would never stop you from showing up each day, right?

Q: What if I change my mind and decide that I do actually want a college degree? Will I have blown my chances at getting one?

A: No way. People go back to college when they are in their sixties. And if in five years or fifteen years you find that you want the degree, you can always go back to school. In fact, some of the people you met in this book went back years if not decades after high school. But the ones who did typically found that they knew exactly why they were going and were looking to specifically enhance and broaden their already established careers. Some of the industries we've talked about in this book have various options for advancement, and some of the more advanced jobs require a degree. For example, degrees come in handy for advanced careers in forestry, botany, and electrical engineering. Some careers may even benefit from degrees in business.

I'm a Parent and I Want to Know . . .

Q: My son is very smart, but he insists that he wants to become an auto mechanic. I think he'll be wasting his brain.

A: If he's passionate about being an auto mechanic, you should be excited that he wants to follow his dreams. Plus, I know of way too many people who wear suits to work and sit behind a desk and don't use much of their brain at all. Auto mechanics are highly skilled and are required to solve more problems in a day than most of us solve in a week or a month. Don't forget that we all use our brains differently and not only between 9:00 and 5:00. I'm a landscaper who is running a business, pushing lawn mowers, overseeing employees, and interacting with customers all day long. At night I enjoy watching business shows, and I read the *Wall Street Journal* every morning. I'm using my brain on the job and off the job. Encourage your son to follow his passion, to challenge himself to be the best possible mechanic (if you're really nice about it, maybe he'll fix your car once in a while), and then encourage him to exercise his brain in other ways while not working. This is something not enough of us do in our free time. And remember, your son's self-esteem is tied to his happiness, so if he is actually going to be happy working as an auto mechanic, bets are that his self-esteem will be high, too. What more could a parent want?

Q: I'm concerned that my son is not going to be able to support himself if he doesn't go to college. I know people with college educations make more money.

A: It is true that people with bachelor's degrees make, on average, more money than those who don't. But think about the averages. Factored into the lower pay scale are people who work at minimum wage for their whole lives. I'm not saying that there is anything wrong with this. But when you compare that with the hedge fund manager who is making a few million dollars a year there is just no way to compare. Instead, think about how well a prepared, trained, responsible, hardworking individual in any field can do. If you push your son into a high-paying field that he doesn't want to be in, chances are he's going to fail at it anyway. And if he doesn't fail he's likely going to be miserable. Let him head off into something he loves where he will be happier working harder and doing all that he can to get ahead. Chances are it will work out. And remember there are many, many people with bachelor's degrees who are working in jobs that have nothing to do with their degrees. There are also people who have bachelor's degrees who aren't happy and aren't making a great living. Remember, too, many of these blue-collar jobs cannot be outsourced. You don't call India when you have a leak under your sink, and you can't have your car shipped overseas when it needs a new part. That point alone offers some additional job security and peace of mind.

Q: Should I pay for my daughter's training or certification since she isn't willing to go to college?

A: If you were willing and able to pay for college or help pay for college, why wouldn't you do the same with regard to technical training? We all know that some kids go to college, party too much, rarely go to class, and waste their parents' money. This isn't acceptable, nor would it be if your daughter took advantage of your paying for her postsecondary training. But if she is committed and you are able, why not stick to your same commitment whether she is going to a university or a technical school? Maybe you could offer to pay for a portion, if you're afraid she won't take her responsibility seriously, and see where it goes from there. Only you know your child and her level of responsibility and your ability to afford something like that. But don't let the name of the school change your commitment to her education and training.

Q: I'm willing to pay for college for my daughter and won't need any loans. I just want her to get the degree, and then if she still wants to go into the trades, that's fine.

A: I would ask you first: do you want that for your daughter, or do you want that for you? Granted, it's a whole lot simpler in some parts of the country to just say, "Yup," when asked if your daughter is going to college. You don't have to explain the alternative. You don't have to make excuses or convince others that what she is doing is okay. But think about whether the degree will ultimately help your daughter. Your daughter's self-esteem is of utmost importance as well. If she's going to hate it, be miserable, and not work at school, she very well may end up feeling bad about herself and feeling like she's let you down as well. Think about why you are focused on the degree. If it's something that you want (and she does not), then it isn't going to help your daughter. And good for you for supporting what your daughter wants to do ultimately. And since you sound very generous, consider investing the money, because chances are your daughter is going to need some training or schooling down the line, and perhaps you'll be willing to help with that when the time comes.

Q: Our high school doesn't offer vocational training, and I would like my children to be exposed to those courses. I know that one of my sons would benefit from going into the trades, if not at least getting some real exposure to some of these fields. What can I do?

A: Look around. Your county or district may have access to a regional career and technical education (CTE) school where your kids can take some classes. Ask your school principal or guidance counselor about this. Getting a summer job or a job on the weekends can help your children test the waters without making lifelong commitments. It's also possible that your local community college offers courses for high schoolers. And if your son is set on a particular career, suggest to him that he try to hook up with someone in your town who might act as a mentor and teach him the ropes. Don't give up if your school doesn't offer much. There are definitely other ways.

Q: My daughter would like to apply to an apprenticeship program and has thought seriously about becoming an electrician or an ironworker. I'm just concerned that she could face a lot of discrimination. Aren't these fields for men? Is there something that is better suited for women?

A: It's true that there are more men than women in the trades. That is slowly changing, and employers are waking up to the fact that women can do this work just as well as men. Discrimination hasn't disappeared, that's for sure. But industries do understand that they need to recruit women. Some of these sectors are desperate for workers, and they are thrilled to have women apply. The unions are particularly open and welcoming to women. These industries are changing. Apprenticeship programs encourage women to apply, and unions provide an excellent community and support network for females. This is women's work, too. The jobs in the trades are family-sustaining, exciting, and full of growth potential.

I'm a Guidance Counselor and I Want to Know . . .

Q: The students I work with are afraid of being considered failures for not going to college. How can we change this perception?

A: Ask your students if they think the people who built their house, their cars, and their schools are failures. What about the ones who built that TV they spend too much time watching? Sometimes kids have a certain image in their heads. You can help change that image by reminding them of all the ways that blue-collar workers affect their life each and every day. Remind them of the pride and the skill it takes to build roads, bridges, and skyscrapers. Hardworking, dedicated individuals are not failures. As parents, teachers, and guidance counselors, we need to talk with more respect about the trades and about blue-collar jobs. These are respectable, honorable jobs that take a lot of hard work and brainpower. Some require training and certificates. We are craftspeople and masters of our industries. Builders talk about the overwhelming feeling when they complete a house; building a house is about creating a shelter and a sanctuary for other humans. Welding is a form of art, as is landscaping. These are all pursuits that should make us very proud of one another.

Q: I have a student who would like to go into fishing but there aren't many opportunities in our area. What should I suggest?

A: Relocation is necessary for some jobs, particularly ones such as logging or fishing, but that can be a drastic step. If you have a student who is really convinced that he wants to work in fishing and lives in Nebraska, I would suggest that he find the nearest fishing community and inquire about summer jobs. Perhaps he has relatives who live near the coast where he could hunker down for a few weeks in the summer to get some seasonal work and, more important, exposure to the industry. And then let your student know that if he or she is confident enough to give it a go, move. Many people do. Tell all of your students to seek out their passions.

Q: I support my students choosing their own path, but they are routinely telling me that they don't want to be labeled as "stupid" for not going to college.

A: Well, how stupid can you be if you can build a home or a car? College degrees do not make us smart, and they don't make us rich. It's not that easy! Being stupid is choosing to follow someone else's dreams rather than your own. Being stupid means not working hard in life and not focusing on your own goals and being the best you can be. Remind all of your students that they have to be smart about their decisions and about what they choose to do. It's stupid to go off to college without any direction or reason, all while accumulating debt. Likewise, it's stupid to leave high school with no plan and no idea of what you're going to do next. Your students don't have to know what they want to do with the rest of their lives. But a smart student will have the next year mapped out and will have a plan of sorts. Remember the skilled trades—plumbing, carpentry, auto mechanics, electrical work—are necessary, vital jobs. Anyone taking a job in these industries should be proud of her or his decision. Plus, your students will have a mobile job or skill that can go anywhere. When you've got a trade, you've got it made.

Q: I want to be able to offer industry expert advice and mentoring to some of the students at my school. How would I go about doing this?

A: There are so many great partnerships between schools and trades and business communities happening all over the country. It may take some legwork on your part, but choose a few industries—plumbing, electrical, and carpentry, for example—and contact the best or largest company or your area industry association to find out if they would be willing to come in and talk to students about job opportunities. Perhaps they would be willing to give an overview of the trade in which they specialize. Then take it a step further and work on setting up internships or work programs with some of these companies. Many companies are desperate for skilled workers, and many are thrilled to have the opportunity to train young employees their own way. You'll probably find that there are tradespeople very excited to share their craft or their skills and talk about their own opportunities with a younger generation. This is a nice way to set up a mentoring program as well.

Q: **Some of my students are concerned about getting stuck in a trade. What if they end up not liking it after a few months or even a few years?**

A: It's ridiculous to expect that every student would choose a career at sixteen or seventeen or eighteen years old and never change their focus. The most important thing is to start off with some goals. Those goals can change, and you can remind your students that it's okay to be indecisive about the rest of your life, but it's important to be decisive about the next few months and the willingness to work hard. Changing specialties or jobs or industries is quite common, especially for someone who is just starting out. Many of the skills throughout the trades are interchangeable. Remind your students that, when they are starting out, merely being part of a job site or a team will be beneficial in the future. Having carpentry skills when you really want to be an electrician is useful. And having some experience working construction is always helpful if you're thinking about going into masonry, for example.

Chapter 11

Your Guide to Schools, Apprenticeships, and Postsecondary Trainings Across the Country

As promised, this chapter offers an extensive listing of apprenticeships and trainings as well as unions, associations, and organizations that can assist with launching your blue-collar career. We don't cover every industry, nor is every single postsecondary training opportunity listed for each career. We started with the industries that we talked about in Chapter 3, and we've tried to include information on apprenticeships or certification opportunities in each state, though we don't always hit every single one. We've also tried to stick with those programs that are either recommended or accredited by the industry. That doesn't mean there aren't other great programs out there, perhaps through your local community college or even university. We've tried to do a lot of the work for you, but you'll still have to put in some time and effort. Your local library and the Internet are great resources as well.

We relied on Career Voyages (www.careervoyages.gov), a partnership between the U.S. Departments of Education and Labor, which is an extensive career guide. The National Center for Construction Education and Research (www.nccer.org), which boasts an incredible database of trade unions and contractor associations in many industries, was another resource for this chapter. Another helpful resource is www. nationalcontractors.com, which provides an overview of state-by-state licensing requirements for many blue-collar fields. There are many private, in-house programs that you may find through contractors, companies, and schools. We haven't included those since it would be nearly impossible to locate and list them all. We also looked to trade organizations that maintain guides for training programs around the country.

While this list was current and accurate at the time of publication, information changes rapidly and programs are routinely altered, added, or eliminated. Check with your nearest apprenticeship, union, or association for the most up-to-date information.

Automotive Service and Repair Technicians

While there are many different routes to take to become an employed auto mechanic or service technician, the National Automotive Technicians Education Foundation (NATEF) and National Institute for Automotive Service Excellence (ASE) offer outstanding and popular certification programs. Many community colleges can prepare you for a career in automotive service or body work, and many manufacturers and dealerships offer their own specialized programs.

Manufacturer-Specific Programs

Most car manufacturers have programs that give future or prospective employees manufacturer-specific training:

BMW—Service Technician Education Program (STEP)
www.bmwstep.com

GM—Automotive Service Educational Program (ASEP)
www.gmasepbsep.com

Honda—Professional Automotive Career Training (PACT)
www.hondacareers.com

Porsche—Porsche Technology Apprenticeship Program (PTAP)
www.uti.edu/Automotive/ManufacturerPrograms/Porsche/tabid/86/Default.aspx

Toyota—T-Ten
www.toyota.com/about/tten

Chrysler—College Automotive Program (CAP)
www.chryslercap.com

Ford—Automotive Student Service Educational Training (ASSET)
www.fordasset.com

Other Resources

Automotive Careers Today (www.autocareerstoday.net/training) has a searchable, nationwide database of community colleges, technical and vocational schools, and manufacturers that offer automotive training programs.

NATEF and ASE Certified Training Centers

Updated information can be found at www.natef.org.
(If a training center offers manufacturer-specific training it is noted below.)

Alabama

Allen Thornton Career and Technical Center
7275 Hwy. 72
Killen, AL 35645
(256) 757-2101
www.lcschools.org
Programs: Collision Repair and Refinish

Autauga County Technology Center
1301 Upper Kingston Rd.
Prattville, AL 36067
(334) 361-0258
www.autaugacountyschool.org
Programs: Automobile, Collision Repair and Refinish

Bell-Brown Area Vocational Center
PO Box 1380
Livingston, AL 35470
(205) 652-9469
Programs: Automobile

Bevill State Community College
101 S. State St.
Sumiton, AL 35148
(205) 648-3271
Programs: Collision Repair and Refinish

Bibb County Career Tech Center
17191 Hwy. 5
West Blocton, AL 35184
(205) 938-7434
Programs: Automobile, Collision Repair and Refinish

Bishop State Community College
Carver Campus
414 Stanton St.
Mobile, AL 36617
(251) 662-5386
Programs: Collision Repair and Refinish

Blount County Center of Technology
61500 U.S. Hwy. 231
Cleveland, AL 35049
(205) 625-3424
Programs: Automobile, Collision Repair and Refinish

Calhoun County Career Technical Center
1200 Church Ave. SE
Jacksonville, AL 36265

(256) 741-4619
Programs: Automobile, Collision Repair and Refinish

Chambers County Career Technical Center
502 AVC Dr. SE
LaFayette, AL 36862
(334) 864-8863
Programs: Automobile

Cherokee County Career and Tech Center
600 Bay Springs Rd.
Centre, AL 35960
(256) 927-8579
Programs: Automobile

Cleburne County Career Technical School
11200 Hwy. 46
Heflin, AL 36264
(256) 748-2961
www.cleburnecareertech.net/
Programs: Automobile

Cleburne County Career Technical School
11200 Hwy. 46
Heflin, AL 36264
(256) 748-2961
www.cleburnecareertech.net/
Programs: Collision Repair and Refinish

Coosa County Science and Technology Center
Route 2, Box 52
Rockford, AL 35136
(256) 377-4678
Programs: Automobile

Cullman Area Career Center
17640 Hwy. 31 N.
Cullman, AL 35058
(256) 734-7740
www.ccboe.org
Programs: Collision Repair and Refinish, Automobile

Dallas County AVC
1306 Roosevelt Ave.
Selma, AL 36701
(334) 872-2814
Programs: Automobile

Dekalb County Technology Center
429 Main St. E.
Rainsville, AL 35986

(256) 638-3070
Programs: Automobile, Collision Repair and Refinish

Dothan Technology Center
3165 Reeves St.
Dothan, AL 36303
(334) 794-1436
Programs: Automobile

Earnest Pruett Center of Technology
29490 U.S. Hwy. 72
Hollywood, AL 35752
(256) 574-6079
Programs: Collision Repair and Refinish

Eden Career Center
45 County Road 33
Ashville, AL 35953
(205) 594-4122
Programs: Collision Repair and Refinish

Etowah County Career Technical Center
105 Burke Ave. SE
Attalla, AL 35954
(256) 538-8948
www.ecboe.org/careertech
Programs: Automobile, Collision Repair and Refinish

Franklin County Career/Technical Center
85 Jail Springs Rd.
Russellville, AL 35653
(256) 332-2127
franklincoctc.com
Programs: Collision Repair and Refinish

G.C. Wallace Community College
Toyota T-TEN
1141 Wallace Dr.
Dothan, AL 36303
(334) 556-2253
www.wallace.edu/
Programs: Automobile

Houston County Career and Technology Center
801 8th Ave.
PO Drawer 3005
Ashford, AL 36312
(334) 899-3308
Programs: Automobile

J.F. Drake State Technical College
3421 Meridian St. North

Huntsville, AL 35811
(256) 551-3143
Programs: Automobile

**L.B.W. Community College-
MacArthur Campus**
1708 North Main St.
Opp, AL 36467
(334) 493-3573
www.lbwcc.edu/cms/page.aspx
Programs: Automobile

**Lawrence County Center of
Technology**
179 College St.
Moulton, AL 35650
(256) 905-2425
Programs: Automobile

Lawson State Community College
Ford ASSET
GM ASEP
Toyota T-TEN
1100 9th Ave. SW
Bessemer, AL 35022
(205) 929-3483
www.ls.cc.al.us
Programs: Medium/Heavy Truck

**Limestone County Career
Technical Center**
505 East Sanderfer Rd.
Athens, AL 35611
(256) 233-6463
Programs: Automobile, Collision Repair
and Refinish

Madison County Career Academy
1275 Jordan Rd.
Huntsville, AL 35811
(256) 852-2170
Programs: Collision Repair and Refinish

Marengo County Technical Center
2450 East Coast Ave.
Linden, AL 36748
(334) 295-4237
Programs: Automobile

**Muscle Shoals Center for
Technology**
3200 South Wilson Dam Hwy.
Muscle Shoals, AL 35661
(256) 389-2660
Programs: Collision Repair and Refinish

**North Baldwin Center for
Technology**

505 West Hurricane Rd.
Bay Minette, AL 36507
(251) 937-6751
www.nbctschool.com
Programs: Automobile

**Shades Valley Technical
Academy**
5191 Pine Whispers Dr.
Birmingham, AL 35210
(205) 379-2176
Programs: Collision Repair and Refinish

**Shelby County School of
Technology**
701 Hwy. 70
Columbiana, AL 35051
(205) 682-6650
Programs: Automobile, Collision Repair
and Refinish

Alaska

**Alaska Vocational Technical
Center**
809 Second Ave.
PO Box 889
Seward, AK 99664
(907) 224-6155
www.avtec.edu
Programs: Automobile

University of Alaska
Ford ASSET, GM ASEP
3211 Providence Dr., ADT 207
Anchorage, AK 99508
(907) 786-1485
Programs: Medium/Heavy Truck,
Automobile

University of Alaska Southeast
11120 Glacier Hwy.
Juneau, AK 99801
(907) 796-6126
www.uas.alaska.edu/automotive
Programs: Automobile

Arizona

Arizona Western College
2020 S. Ave. 8E
PO Box 929
Yuma, AZ 85366
(928) 344-7569
www.azwestern.edu
Programs: Automobile

GateWay Community College
108 North 40th St.
Phoenix, AZ 85034
(602) 286-8629
www.gatewaycc.edu
Programs: Automobile

Glendale Community College
Ford ASSET, Chrysler CAP
GM ASEP
6000 West Olive Ave.
Glendale, AZ 85302
(623) 845-3950
Programs: Automobile

Northland Pioneer College
102 First Ave.
Holbrook, AZ 86025
(928) 532-6839
Programs: Automobile

Pima Community College
1255 North Stone Ave.
Receiving Dept. COS 110
Tucson, AZ 85709
(520) 206-7194
www.pima.edu
Programs: Automobile

Universal Technical Institute
10695 W. Pierce St.
Avondale, AZ 85323
(623) 445-9452
Programs: Automobile

Arkansas

Area Vo-Tech Center
2203 S. Knoxville Ave.
Russellville, AR 72802
Programs: Automobile

**Arkansas State University Tech
Center**
33500 Hwy. 63 East
Marked Tree, AR 72365
(870) 358-2117
www.asutc.org
Programs: Automobile

Arkansas State University-Searcy
1800 East Moore Ave.
Searcy, AR 72143
(501) 207-4024
www.asub.edu
Programs: Automobile, Collision Repair
and Refinish

Arkansas Tech University Ozark Campus
1700 Helberg Ln.
Ozark, AR 72949
(50l) 667-2117
Programs: Automobile

Black River Technical College
1410 Hwy. 304 E
Pocahontas, AR 72455
(870) 248-4000
www.blackrivertech.org
Programs: Automobile

Conway Area Career Center
2300 Prince St.
Conway, AR 72034
(501) 450-4888
www.conwayschools.org
Programs: Collision Repair and Refinish

Cossatot Community College of the University of Arkansas
183 Hwy. 399
De Queen, AR 71832
Programs: Automobile

Crowley's Ridge Technical Institute
1620 New Castle Rd
Forrest City, AR 72335
(870) 633-5411
www.crti.tec.ar.us
Programs: Automobile

Jonesboro Area Technical Center
1727 South Main St.
Jonesboro, AR 72401
(870) 933-5891
Programs: Collision Repair and Refinish

Metropolitan Career and Technical Center
7701 Scott Hamilton Dr.
Little Rock, AR 72209
(501) 447-1200
Programs: Collision Repair and Refinish

North Arkansas College
1515 Pioneer Dr.
Harrison, AR 72601
(870) 391-3372
www.northark.edu
Programs: Collision Repair and Refinish

North Central Career Center
402 Oak St.
Leslie, AR 72645
(870) 447-2691

Programs: Automobile, Collision Repair and Refinish

Northwest Arkansas Community College
Regional Technology Center
2350 Old Farmington Rd.
Fayetteville, AR 72701
(479) 444-3058
www.rtc.nwacc.edu
Programs: Collision Repair and Refinish

Northwest Technical Institute
709 South Old Missouri Rd.
Springdale, AR 72764
www.nti.tec.ar.us
Programs: Automobile

Ozarka Technical College
218 College Dr.
Melbourne, AR 72556
(870) 368-7371
www.ozarka.edu
Programs: Automobile

River Valley Technical Center
1905 Poor Farm Rd.
Morrilton, AR 72110
(501) 354-9475
Programs: Automobile, Collision Repair and Refinish

Saline County Career Center
3199 S. Reynolds Rd.
Bauxite, AR 72011
(501) 602-2420
Programs: Automobile

U.A.M. College of Technology–McGehee
PO Box 747
1609 East Ash
McGehee, AR 71654
Programs: Automobile

University of Arkansas–Fort Smith
5210 Grand Ave.
Fort Smith, AR 72903
(479) 788-7703
Programs: Automobile

California

Abram Friedman Occupational Center
1646 S. Olive St.

Los Angeles, CA 90015
(213) 765-2400
afoc.adultinstruction.org
Programs: Automobile

American River College
4700 College Oak Dr.
Sacramento, CA 95841
(916) 484-8671
www.arc.losrios.edu/~autoteach
Programs: Automobile

Bakersfield College
1801 Panorama Dr.
Bakersfield, CA 93305
(661) 395-4574
Programs: Automobile

Butte College
GM ASEP
3536 Butte Campus Dr.
Oroville, CA 95965
(530) 895-2448
www.butte.edu/instruction/aut
Programs: Automobile

Cerritos Community College
Chrysler CAP
GM ASEP
Ford ASSET
11110 Alondra Blvd.
Norwalk, CA 90650
(562) 860-2451
www.cerritos.edu
Programs: Automobile

Chabot College
25555 Hesperian Blvd.
Hayward, CA 94545
(510) 723-6652
www.chabotcollege.edu
Programs: Automobile

Citrus Community College
1000 West Foothill Blvd.
Glendora, CA 91741
(626) 914-8738
www.citrus-auto.com
Programs: Automobile

College of Alameda
1148 Holly St.
Alameda, CA 94502
(510) 748-2309
Programs: Automobile

College of the Redwoods
7351 Tompkins Hill Rd
Eureka, CA 95501
(707) 476-4345
Programs: Automobile

Columbia College
11600 Columbia College Dr.
Sonora, CA 95370
(209) 588-5200
Programs: Automobile

Crawford Educational Complex
4191 Colts Way
San Diego, CA 92115
(858) 496-1855
www.sandi.net
Programs: Automobile

Cuyamaca College
Ford ASSET
GM ASEP
900 Rancho San Diego Pkwy.
El Cajon, CA 92019
(619) 660-4334
www.cuyamaca.edu
Programs: Automobile

Cypress College
9200 Valley View St.
Cypress, CA 90630
(714) 484-7250
www.cypresscollege.edu
Programs: Automobile, Collision Repair
and Refinish

De Anza College
21250 Stevens Creek Blvd.
Cupertino, CA 95014
(408) 864-8527
www.autotech.deanza.fhda.edu
Programs: Automobile

East Los Angeles College
1301 Avenida Cesar Chavez
Monterey Park, CA 91754
(323) 265-8726
Programs: Automobile

Evergreen Valley College
3095 Yerba Buena Rd.
San Jose, CA 95135
(408) 274-7900
Programs: Automobile

**Forty Niner Regional
Occupational Program**

360 Nevada St.
Auburn, CA 95603
Programs: Automobile

Fresno City College
GM ASEP
1101 East University Ave.
Fresno, CA 93741
(559) 442-4600
www.fresnocitycollege.edu
Programs: Automobile

Fullerton College
321 East Chapman Ave.
Fullerton, CA 92832
(714) 992-7246
www.full.coll.edu
Programs: Automobile

Long Beach City College
1305 East Pacific Coast Hwy.
Long Beach, CA 90806
Programs: Automobile and
Alternative Fuels

Long Beach Job Corps Center
1903 Santa Fe Ave.
Long Beach, CA 90810
(562) 983-1777
www.longbeach.jobcorps.gov
Programs: Automobile

Merced College
3600 "M" St.
Merced, CA 95348
(209) 386-6677
Programs: Automobile

**Mt. San Jacinto Community
College**
Honda PACT
1499 N. State St.
San Jacinto, CA 92583
(951) 487-6752
www.msjc.edu
Programs: Automobile

Oxnard College
4000 South Rose Ave.
Oxnard, CA 93033
(805) 986-5800
Programs: Automobile

Pasadena City College
1570 East Colorado Blvd.
Pasadena, CA 91106
(626) 585-7685
Programs: Automobile

Pierce College
6201 Winnetka Ave.
Woodland Hills, CA 91371
(818) 710-2975
Programs: Automobile

Rio Hondo College
Honda PACT
3600 Workman Mill Rd.
Whittier, CA 90601
(562) 692-0921
www.riohondo.edu/tech/auto
Programs: Automobile and
Alternative Fuels

Riverside Community College
GM ASEP
Ford ASSET
Toyota T-Ten
4800 Magnolia Ave.
Riverside, CA 92506
(951) 222-8348
Programs: Automobile

San Diego Miramar College
Toyota T-Ten
10440 Black Mountain Rd.
San Diego, CA 92126
(619) 388-7673
Programs: Automobile

San Joaquin Delta College
GM ASEP
5151 Pacific Ave.
Stockton, CA 95207
(209) 954-5233
Programs: Automobile

Santa Barbara City College
721 Cliff Dr.
Santa Barbara, CA 93109
(805) 965-0581
www.sbcc.edu/automotive
Programs: Automobile

Shasta College
11555 Old Oregon Tr.
Redding, CA 96049
Contact: Raleigh Ross, (530)
225-4903
Programs: Automobile

Shasta-Trinity ROP
4659 Eastside Rd.
Redding, CA 96001
Programs: Automobile

Skyline College
Toyota T-Ten
3300 College Dr.
San Bruno, CA 94066
(650) 738-4410
www.skylinecollege.edu/
automotive
Programs: Automobile

Southern California Regional Occupational Center
2300 Crenshaw Blvd.
Torrance, CA 90501
(310) 224-4218
Programs: Automobile

Universal Technical Institute
9494 Haven Ave.
Rancho Cucamonga, CA 91730
(623) 445-9452
Programs: Automobile

Valley View ROP
13135 Nason St.
Moreno Valley, CA 92555
(901) 485-5720
Programs: Automobile

Ventura College
4900 Loma Vista Rd.
Ventura, CA 93003
(805) 388-5480
Programs: Automobile

Victor Valley Community College
18422 Bear Valley Rd.
Victorville, CA 92307
(760) 245-4271
www.vvc.edu
Programs: Automobile

Wyo Tech
980 Riverside Pkwy.
W. Sacramento, CA 95605
(916) 376-8888
Programs: Automobile

Wyo Tech—Fremont Campus
420 Whitney Pl.
Fremont, CA 94539
Programs: Automobile

Wyo Tech—Long Beach
2161 Technology Pl.
Long Beach, CA 90810
(562) 437-0501
www.nitschools.com
Programs: Automobile

Yuba College
2088 North Beale Rd.
Marysville, CA 95901
(530) 741-6921
Programs: Automobile

Colorado

Aims Community College
4911 W. 20th St.
Greeley, CO 80634
(970) 339-6308
Programs: Collision Repair and Refinish

Arapahoe Community College
Chrysler CAP
5900 S. Santa Fe
Littleton, CO 80160
(303) 797-5846
www.arapahoe.edu
Programs: Automobile

Arapahoe Community College
GM ASEP
2500 West College Dr.
Littleton, CO 80160
(303) 797-5846
www.arapahoe.edu
Programs: Automobile

Boulder Technical Education Center
6600 East Arapahoe Rd.
Boulder, CO 80303
(303) 447-5220
Programs: Collision Repair and Refinish

Emily Griffith Opportunity School
1250 Welton St.
Denver, CO 80204
(720) 423-4836
www.egos-school.com
Programs: Collision Repair and Refinish

Front Range Community College
3645 West 112th Ave.
Westminster, CO 80031
(303) 404-5381
www.frontrange.edu
Programs: Automobile

Lincoln College of Technology
460 South Lipan St.
Denver, CO 80223
(303) 722-5724
www.lincolncollegeof

technology.com
Programs: Medium/Heavy Truck

Lincoln College of Technology
460 South Lipan St.
Denver, CO 80223
(303) 722-5724
www.dadc.com
Programs: Automobile

Morgan Community College
920 Barlow Rd.
Fort Morgan, CO 80701
(970) 542-3220
www.morgancc.edu
Programs: Automobile, Collision Repair and Refinish

Northeastern Junior College
100 College Ave.
Sterling, CO 80751
(970) 521-6694
www.njc.edu/autotech/home.html
Programs: Automobile

Pikes Peak Community College
5675 S. Academy Blvd.
Box C16
Colorado Springs, CO 80906
(719) 502-3142
Programs: Automobile

San Juan Basin Technical College
33057 Hwy. 160
PO Box 970
Mancos, CO 81328
(970) 565-8457
www.sanjuanbasintechschool.
org/automotive.htm
Programs: Automobile

Warren Technical Center
13300 West 2nd Pl.
Lakewood, CO 80228
(303) 982-8573
www.warrentech.org
Programs: Collision Repair and Refinish

Western Colorado Community College
2508 Blichmann Ave.
Grand Junction, CO 81505
(970) 255-2612
Programs: Automobile

Westwood College of Technology
7350 N. Broadway

Denver, CO 80221
(303) 426-7000
www.westwood.edu
Programs: Automobile

Connecticut

Baran Institute of Technology–Windsor
97 Newberry Rd.
East Windsor, CT 06088
(860) 627-4300
www.baraninstitute.com
Programs: Automobile

Gateway Community Technical College
GM ASEP
Toyota T-Ten
88 Bassett Rd.
North Haven, CT 06473
(203) 285-2334
Programs: Automobile, Alternative Fuels

Porter and Chester Institute
221 West Main St.
Lakeview Center
Branford, CT 06405
(203) 315-1060
www.ctschoolofelectronics.com
Programs: Automobile

Delaware

Delaware Technical and Community College
400 Stanton-Christiana Road
  Stanton Campus
Newark, DE 19713
(302) 453-3016
Programs: Automobile

Delaware Technical and Community College
Route 18
PO Box 610
Georgetown, DE 19947
(302) 855-5920
Programs: Automobile

District of Columbia
The Excel Institute
2851 V Street NE
Washington, DC 20018
(202) 387-1550
www.theexcelinstitute.org
Programs: Automobile

Florida

Atlantic Technical Center
Toyota T-Ten
4700 Coconut Creek Pkwy.
Coconut Creek, FL 33063
(754) 321-5169
www.atlantictechcenter.com
Programs: Automobile, Collision Repair and Refinish

Bowers/Whitley Career Center
13609 N. 22nd St.
Tampa, FL 33613
Programs: Automobile

Bradford-Union Area Career Tech Center
609 N. Orange St.
Starke, FL 32091
(904) 966-6763
Programs: Medium/Heavy Truck

Brevard Community College
1519 Clearlake Rd.
Cocoa Campus
Cocoa, FL 32922
Programs: Automobile

Brewster Tech Center
Ford ASSET
2222 N. Tampa St.
Tampa, FL 33602
(813) 276-5448
Programs: Automobile

Broward Community College
GM ASEP
7451 Riviera Blvd.
Miramar, FL 33023
www.broward.edu/auto
Programs: Automobile

Chipola College
3094 Indian Cir.
Marianna, FL 32446
(850) 718-2306
www.chipola.edu
Programs: Automobile

Common Campus OATC
1976 Lewis Turner Blvd.
Ft. Walton Beach, FL 32547
(850) 833-3500
Programs: Automobile

Crestview Vocational Technical Center
1250 N. Ferdon Blvd.
Crestview, FL 32536
(850) 689-7177
Programs: Automobile

D.A. Dorsey Educational Center
7100 NW 17 Ave.
Miami, FL 33147
(305) 693-2490
www.dadorsey.dadeschools.net
Programs: Automobile

Daytona Beach Community College
1770 Technology Blvd.
Advanced Technology Center
Daytona Beach, FL 32117
(386) 506-3612
www.dbcc.edu
Programs: Collision Repair and Refinish

Erwin Technical Center
2010 E. Hillsborough Ave.
Tampa, FL 33610
(813) 231-1800
Programs: Automobile

Florida Community College
GM ASEP
501 West State St.
Jacksonville, FL 32202
(904) 633-8334
www.fccj.edu/campuses/
  downtown/atc/index.html
Programs: Automobile

George Stone Vocational Center
2400 Longleaf Dr.
Pensacola, FL 32526
Contact: James Nevels, (850)
  941-6200
Programs: Automobile

Hialeah Senior High/Adult Center
251 E. 47th St.
Hialeah, FL 33013
(305) 882-1500
www.hhs.dadeschools.net
Programs: Automobile

Indian River Community College
3209 Virginia Ave.
Fort Pierce, FL 34981
(772) 462-7747
www.ircc.edu
Programs: Automobile

Lee County High Tech Center
3800 Michigan Ave. Central
Campus
Auto Service Technology
Fort Myers, FL 33916
(239) 334-4544
Programs: Automobile

**Lindsey Hopkins Technical
Education Center**
750 NW 20th St.
Miami, FL 33127
(305) 324-6070
www.lindsey.dadeschools.net
Programs: Automobile

**Miami Jackson Senior
High/Adult Center**
1751 NW 36th St.
Miami, FL 33142
(305) 634-2621
www.dadeschools.jackson.net
Programs: Automobile

Miami Lakes Educational Ctr.
5780 NW 158th St.
Miami Lakes, FL 33014
(305) 557-1100
Programs: Automobile, Medium/Heavy
Truck, Collision Repair and Refinish

Miami Northwestern Senior High
1100 NW 71st St.
Miami, FL 33150
(305) 836-0991
www.northwestern.
  dadeschools.net/
Programs: Automobile

Miami Senior High/Adult Center
2450 SW 1st St.
Miami, FL 33135
(305) 649-9800
www.mhs.dadeschools.net
Programs: Automobile

Mid-Florida Technical Institute
2900 West Oak Ridge Rd.
Bldg. 500
Orlando, FL 32809
(407) 251-6000
www.mft.ocps.net
Programs: Medium/Heavy Truck,
Collision Repair and Refinish

Palm Beach Community College
4200 Congress Ave.

Lake Worth, FL 33461
(561) 868-3542
www.pbcc.edu/AutoService.xml
Programs: Automobile

Parkway Academy @ BCC
7451 Riviera Blvd.
Miramar, FL 33023
(954) 961-2911
www.parkwaycharter.org
Programs: Automobile

Pensacola Junior College
1000 College Blvd.
Pensacola, FL 32504
Programs: Automobile

**Robert Morgan Educational
Center**
Honda PACT
18180 SW 122nd Ave.
Miami, FL 33177
(305) 253-9920
www.dadeschools.net
Programs: Automobile

Santa Fe Community College
3000 NW 83rd St.
Gainesville, FL 32608
(352) 395-5250
www.inst.sfcc.edu/~intech/auto
Programs: Automobile

Seminole Community College
Ford ASSET
GM ASEP
100 Weldon Blvd.
Sanford, FL 32773
(407) 328-2412
www.scc-fl.edu/automotive/astp
Programs: Automobile

Sheridan Technical Center
Chrysler CAP
Ford ASSET
5400 Sheridan St.
Hollywood, FL 33021
(754) 321-5549
www.sheridantechnical.com
Programs: Collision Repair and Refinish

South County Career Center
2810 John Sherman Way
Ruskin, FL 33570
(813) 233-3335
www.sccc.mysdhc.org/
Programs: Automobile

**South Dade Senior High/Adult
Center**
28400 SW 167th Ave.
Homestead, FL 33030
(305) 247-4244
www.sdhs.dadeschools.net
Programs: Automobile

**South Florida Community
College**
600 West College Dr.
Avon Park, FL 33825
(863) 784-7144
www.sfcc.cc.fl.us
Programs: Automobile

South Technical Academy
1300 SW 30th Ave.
Boynton Beach, FL 33426
(561) 364-7973
Programs: Automobile

**Southwest Miami Senior
High/Adult Center**
8855 SW 50th Terr.
Miami, FL 33165
(305) 274-0181
sweagles.dadeschools.net
Programs: Automobile

**Suwannee-Hamilton
Technical Center**
415 SW Pinewood Dr.
Live Oak, FL 32064
(386) 364-2773
Programs: Automobile, Collision Repair
and Refinish

Taylor Technical Institute
3233 Hwy. 19 South
Perry, FL 32348
(850) 838-2545
www.taylortech.org
Programs: Automobile

Tom P. Haney Technical Center
3016 Hwy. 77
Panama City, FL 32405
(850) 747-5500
Programs: Automobile

Traviss Career Center
3225 Winter Lake Rd.
Lakeland, FL 33803
(863) 499-2718
Programs: Collision Repair and Refinish

Universal Technical Institute
2202 West-Taft Vineland Rd.
Orlando, FL 32837
(407) 240-2422
Programs: Automobile

Walton Career
Development Center
761 N. 20th St.
Defuniak Springs, FL 32433
(850) 892-1240
www.150.176.104.165/
Programs: Automobile

Washington County School
Program @ Dozier
General Service Tech
4111 South St.
Marianna, FL 32446
(850) 482-9181
Programs: Automobile

Washington Holmes
Technical Center
757 Hoyt St.
Chipley, FL 32428
(850) 638-1180
www.whtc.org
Programs: Automobile

Westside Tech Center @
Apopka High School
955 East Story Rd.
Winter Garden, FL 34787
(407) 905-5508
Programs: Automobile

Withlacoochee Technical Institute
1201 W. Main St.
Inverness, FL 34450
(352) 726-2430
www.wtionline.cc
Programs: Automobile

Georgia

Altamaha Technical College
1777 West Cherry St.
Jesup, GA 31545
(912) 427-5831
www.altamahatech.edu
Programs: Automobile

Athens Technical College
800 US Hwy. 29 North
Athens, GA 30601
(706) 355-5095

www.athenstech.edu
Programs: Automobile

Augusta Technical College
3200 Augusta Tech Dr.
Bldg. 700
Augusta, GA 30906
(706) 771-4110
Programs: Automobile

Central Georgia Technical College
54 Hwy. 22
West Satellite Campus
Milledgeville, GA 31061
(478) 445-2327
www.centralgatech.edu
Programs: Automobile

Chattahoochee Technical College
980 S. Cobb Dr. SE
Marietta, GA 30060
(770) 528-4425
www.chattcollege.com
Programs: Automobile

Columbus Technical College
928 Manchester Expwy.
Columbus, GA 31904
(706) 649-1894
Programs: Automobile

Coosa Valley Technical College
One Maurice Culberson Dr.
Rome, GA 30161
(706) 295-6999
Programs: Automobile

Dalton State College
650 College Dr.
Dalton, GA 30720
(706) 272-4434
Programs: Automobile

Gwinnett Technical College
Chrysler CAP
GM ASEP
Toyota T-Ten
5150 Sugarloaf Pkwy.
Lawrenceville, GA 30043
(678) 226-6259
Programs: Automobile

Heart of Georgia Technical College
560 Pinehill Rd.
Dublin, GA 31021
(478) 274-7867
Programs: Automobile

Middle Georgia Technical College
80 Cohen Walker Dr.
Warner Robins, GA 31088
(478) 988-6800
Programs: Automobile

Moultrie Technical College
361 Industrial Dr.
Moultrie, GA 31788
(229) 217-4154
www.moultrietech.edu
Programs: Automobile

North Georgia Technical College
1500 Hwy. 197 North
Clarkesville, GA 30523
(706) 754-7739
www.northgatech.edu
Programs: Collision Repair and Refinish

Okefenokee Technical College
1701 Carswell Ave.
Waycross, GA 31503
(912) 287-5825
www.okefenokeetech.org
Programs: Automobile, Collision Repair
and Refinish

Savannah Technical College
5717 White Bluff Rd.
Savannah, GA 31405
(912) 303-1761
Programs: Automobile

Southwest Georgia
Technical College
15689 US Hwy. 19 N.
Thomasville, GA 31792
(229) 225-5085
Programs: Automobile

Technical Education Center
of Carroll County
1075 Newnan Rd.
Carrollton, GA 30116
(770) 832-8380
www.tec.carrollcountyschools.com/
    Tech_Web/techhigh_main.htm
Programs: Automobile

Valdosta Technical College
4089 Val Tech Rd.
Valdosta, GA 31602
(229) 333-2115
Programs: Automobile

West Central Technical College
997 South Hwy. 16
Carrollton, GA 30117
(770) 836-4707
Programs: Automobile

West Georgia Technical College
303 Fort Dr.
Receiving/Business Office
LaGrange, GA 30240
(706) 845-4323
www.westgatech.edu
Programs: Automobile

Hawaii

Honolulu Community College
874 Dillingham Blvd.
Honolulu, HI 96817
(808) 845-9127
Programs: Collision Repair and Refinish

Leeward Community College
Ford ASSET
96-045 Ala Ike St.
Pearl City, HI 96782
(808) 455-0438
Programs: Automobile

Idaho

Boise State University
1910 University Dr.
Boise, ID 83725
(208) 426-1241
www.selland.boisestate.edu
Automobile, Medium/Heavy Truck

Canyon-Owyhee School Service Agency
20567 Whittier Dr.
Greenleaf, ID 83626
(208) 337-3406
www.casa-sitech.org
Programs: Automobile

College of Southern Idaho
GM ASEP
315 Falls Ave.
Twin Falls, ID 83303
(208) 732-6325
www.csi.edu
Programs: Automobile, Collision Repair and Refinish

Dennis Technical Education Center
8201 W. Victory
Boise, ID 83709
(208) 384-3116
www.boiseschools.org
Programs: Collision Repair and Refinish

Eastern Idaho Technical College
1600 South 25th East
Idaho Falls, ID 83404
(208) 524-3000
www.eitc.edu
Programs: Automobile, Medium/Heavy Truck

Lewis-Clark State College
500 8th Ave.
Lewiston, ID 83501
(208) 792-2302
Programs: Automobile

Meridian Professional Technical Center
1900 West Pine Ave.
Meridian, ID 83642
(208) 350-4173
www.meridianschools.org
Programs: Automobile

North Idaho College
1000 W. Garden Ave.
Coeur d'Alene, ID 83814
(208) 769-3461
Programs: Automobile

Illinois

Chicago Vocational Career Academy
2100 East 87th St.
Chicago, IL 60617
Programs: Medium/Heavy Truck

College of Lake County
19351 West Washington St.
Grayslake, IL 60030
(847) 543-2509
www.clcillinois.edu
Programs: Automobile

College of Lake County
19351 W. Washington St.
Grayslake, IL 60030
(847) 543-2509
Programs: Collision Repair and Refinish

Harry S. Truman College
1145 W. Wilson Ave.
Chicago, IL 60640
(773) 907-3984
www.trumancollege.cc
Programs: Automobile

Highland Community College
2998 W. Pearl City Rd
Freeport, IL 61032
(815) 599-3554
www.highland.edu
Programs: Automobile, Collision Repair and Refinish

Illinois Central College
GM ASEP
One College Dr.
East Peoria, IL 61635
(309) 694-5583
www.icc.edu
Programs: Automobile

Illinois Valley Community College
815 N. Orlando Smith Ave.
Oglesby, IL 61348
(815) 224-2720
www.ivcc.edu/automotive
Programs: Automobile

John A. Logan College
700 Logan College Rd.
Carterville, IL 62918
(618) 985-3741
www.jalc.edu
Programs: Automobile

Joliet Junior College
1215 Houbolt Rd.
Joliet, IL 60431
(815) 280-2554
www.jjc.edu
Programs: Automobile

Kishwaukee College
21193 Malta Rd.
Malta, IL 60150
www.kishwaukeecollege.edu
Programs: Automobile, Collision Repair and Refinish

Lake Land College
5001 Lake Land Blvd.
Mattoon, IL 61938
(217) 234-5286
www.lakelandcollege.edu
Programs: Automobile

Lewis and Clark Community College
5800 Godfrey Rd.
Godfrey, IL 62035
(618) 468-4910
www.lc.edu
Programs: Automobile

Lincoln Land Community College
5250 Shepherd Rd.
Springfield, IL 62794
(217) 786-2417
www.llcc.edu
Programs: Automobile

Moraine Valley Community College
Chrysler CAP
900 W. College Pkwy.
Palos Hills, IL 60465
(708) 974-5713
www.morainevalley.edu/
   automotive
Programs: Automobile

Morton College
3801 South Central Ave.
Cicero, IL 60804
(708) 656-8000
Programs: Automobile

Parkland College
Ford ASSET
2400 West Bradley Ave.
Champaign, IL 61821
(217) 351-2209
www.parkland.edu
Programs: Automobile

Prairie State College
202 South Halsted St.
Chicago Heights, IL 60411
(708) 709-3614
Programs: Automobile

Rend Lake College
468 North Ken Gray Pkwy.
Ina, IL 62846
(618) 437-5321
Programs: Automobile

Richland Community College
One College Park
Decatur, IL 62521
(217) 875-7211
Programs: Automobile

Rock Valley College
4151 Samuelson Rd.
Rockford, IL 61109
(815) 921-3007
Programs: Automobile

Shawnee Community College
8364 Shawnee College Rd.
Ullin, IL 62992
(618) 634-3200
www.shawneecc.edu
Programs: Automobile

Southeastern Illinois College
3575 College Rd.
Harrisburg, IL 62946
(866) 338-2742
Programs: Medium/Heavy Truck

Southern Illinois University Carbondale
Mail Code 6895
SIUC Auto Tech
Carbondale, IL 62901
(618) 453-4024
www.siucautomotive.com
Programs: Automobile

Technology Center of DuPage
301 South Swift Rd.
Addison, IL 60101
(630) 691-7601
www.tcdupage.org
Programs: Collision Repair and Refinish

Triton College
GM ASEP
2000 Fifth Ave.
River Grove, IL 60171
(708) 456-0300
www.triton.edu
Programs: Automobile

Universal Technical Institute
601 Regency Dr.
Glendale Heights, IL 60139
(623) 445-9452
Programs: Medium/Heavy Truck, Automobile

Waubonsee Community College
Route 47 at Waubonsee Dr.
Receiving
Sugar Grove, IL 60554
(630) 466-2331
www.waubonsee.edu
Programs: Automobile

Indiana

Blue River Career Programs
801 St. Joseph St.
Shelbyville, IN 46176
(317) 392-4191
www.brcp.net
Programs: Automobile, Collision Repair and Refinish

Central Nine Career Center
1999 U.S. 31 South
Greenwood, IN 46143
(317) 888-4401
Programs: Medium/Heavy Truck

Four County Area Vocational Cooperative
221 Angling Rd.
Kendallville, IN 46755
Programs: Automobile

Hinds Career Center
1105 North 19th St.
Elwood, IN 46036
(317) 416-9727
www.hindscareercenter.org
Programs: Automobile

Hoosier Hills Career Center
3070 Prow Rd.
Bloomington, IN 47404
(812) 330-7730
Programs: Collision Repair and Refinish

Ivy Tech Community College– Evansville
3501 First Ave.
Evansville, IN 47710
(812) 422-0296
Programs: Automobile

Ivy Tech Community College– Lafayette
3101 S. Creasy Lane
Lafayette, IN 47905
(765) 269-5155
www.laf.ivytech.edu
Programs: Automobile

Ivy Tech Community College– Richmond
2325 Chester Blvd.
Richmond, IN 47374
(765) 966-2656
Programs: Automobile

Ivy Tech Community College
* Sellersburg
8204 Hwy. 311
Sellersburg, IN 47172
(812) 246-3301
Programs: Automobile

* South Bend
220 Dean Johnson Blvd.
South Bend, IN 46601
(574) 289-7001
Programs: Automobile

* Terre Haute
8000 South Education Dr.
Terre Haute, IN 47802
(812) 298-2372
Programs: Automobile, Collision Repair
and Refinish

Ivy Tech Community College
of Indiana
GM ASEP
Toyota T-Ten
1331 E. Washington St.
Indianapolis, IN 46202
(317) 269-9273
www.ivytech.edu/indianapolis
Programs: Automobile

J. Everett Light Career Center
1901 East 86th St.
Indianapolis, IN 46240
(317) 259-5265
www.jelcc.com
Programs: Automobile

Lincoln Technical Institute
7225 Winton Dr. #128
Indianapolis, IN 46268
(317) 632-5553
www.lincolnedu.com/campus/
indianapolis-in
Programs: Automobile, Medium/
Heavy Truck

McKenzie Career Center
7250 East 75th St.
Indianapolis, IN 46256
(317) 576-6420
Programs: Collision Repair and Refinish

Porter County Area Career Center
1005 North Franklin St.
Valparaiso, IN 46383
(219) 531-3170
www.porterco.org/pcve
Programs: Automobile

SCILL
1300 Kloeckner Dr.
Knox, IN 46534
(574) 772-8001
Programs: Automobile

Southeastern Career Center
901 West U.S. 50
Versailles, IN 47042
(812) 689-5253
www.sccusa.org
Programs: Automobile, Collision Repair
and Refinish

Vincennes University
1002 North First St.
Vincennes, IN 47591
Programs: Automobile

Iowa

Des Moines Area
Community College
Chrysler CAP
GM ASEP
Ford ASSET
2006 South Ankeny Blvd.
Ankeny, IA 50023
Programs: Automobile

Hawkeye Community College
1501 East Orange Rd.
Waterloo, IA 50704
(319) 296-2320
Programs: Automobile

Indian Hills Community College
626 Indian Hills Dr.
Building 14
Ottumwa, IA 52501
(641) 683-5176
www.indianhills.edu
Programs: Medium/Heavy Truck,
Automobile

Iowa Central Community College
330 Ave. M
Fort Dodge, IA 50501
Programs: Automobile

Iowa Lakes Community College
3200 College Dr.
Emmetsburg, IA 50536
(712) 852-5215
Programs: Automobile

Iowa Western Community College
2700 College Rd.

Box 4-C
Council Bluffs, IA 51503
(712) 388-6806
www.iwcc.edu/programs/
departments/auto.asp
Programs: Automobile

Kirkwood Community College
Toyota T-Ten
6301 Kirkwood Blvd. SW
Cedar Rapids, IA 52406
(319) 398-5474
www.kirkwood.edu
Programs: Automobile

North Iowa Area
Community College
500 College Dr.
Mason City, IA 50401
(641) 422-4243
www.niacc.edu/industrial/
automotive.html
Programs: Automobile

Scott Community College
500 Belmont Rd.
Bettendorf, IA 52722
(563) 441-4228
www.faculty.eicc.edu/dhanan
Programs: Automobile

Southeastern Community College
1500 West Agency Rd.
West Burlington, IA 52655
Programs: Automobile, Collision Repair
and Refinish

Western Iowa Tech
Community College
4647 Stone Ave.
Building A
Sioux City, IA 51102
(712) 274-8733
www.witcc.com
Programs: Automobile

Kansas

Barton County
Community College
245 NE 30th Rd.
Great Bend, KS 67530
(620) 792-9336
www.bartonccc.edu/
autotechnology
Programs: Automobile

Butler County Community College
901 South Haverhill Rd.
Room 402
El Dorado, KS 67042
(316) 322-3283
www.butlercc.edu/auto_collision_
repair/index.cfm
Programs: Automobile, Collision Repair
and Refinish

**Coffeyville Community College–
Columbus Technical Campus**
509 West Elm
Columbus, KS 66725
www.coffeyville.edu
Programs: Automobile

Coffeyville Community College
600 Roosevelt
Coffeyville, KS 67337
(620) 252-7550
www.coffeyville.edu
Programs: Automobile

**Cowley County
Community College**
125 S. Second
Arkansas City, KS 67005
(620) 441-5219
Programs: Automobile

Flint Hills Technical College
3301 West 18th Ave.
Emporia, KS 66801
(620) 341-2300
Programs: Automobile

Garden City Community College
801 Campus Dr.
Garden City, KS 67846
Programs: Automobile

**Hutchinson Vocational
Technical Center**
1500 Plaza Way
Hutchinson, KS 67501
(620) 665-4526
www.usd308.com
Programs: Automobile

Kansas City Kansas ATS
2220 North 59th St.
Kansas City, KS 66104
(913) 627-4125
Programs: Automobile

**Northwest Kansas
Technical College**

1209 Harrison St.
PO Box 668
Goodland, KS 67735
(785) 890-2140
www.nwktc.org
Programs: Collision Repair and Refinish

Pittsburg State University
81701 S. Broadway
Pittsburg, KS 66762
(620) 235-4827
Programs: Automobile

Pratt Community College
348 NE State Road 61
Pratt, KS 67124
(620) 672-5641
www.prattcc.edu
Programs: Automobile

Salina Area Technical School
2562 Centennial Rd.
Salina, KS 67401
www.salinatech.com
Programs: Automobile, Medium/Heavy
Truck, Collision Repair and Refinish

**Southwest Kansas
Technical School**
2215 North Kansas
Liberal, KS 67905
(316) 626-3819
www.usd480.net/swkts
Programs: Automobile

Wichita Area Tech College
301 S. Grove
Wichita, KS 67211
(316) 677-9458
www.watc.edu
Programs: Automobile, Collision Repair
and Refinish

Kentucky

**Ashland Community and
Technical College**
4818 Roberts Dr.
Ashland, KY 41102
(606) 326-2475
Programs: Automobile

**Barren County Area
Technology Center**
491 Trojan Trail
Glasgow, KY 42141
(207) 651-2196
Programs: Automobile

**Big Sandy Community and
Technical College**
150 Industrial Park Rd.
Hager Hill, KY 41222
(606) 789-5690
Programs: Medium/Heavy Truck,
Automobile

**Bluegrass Community
Technical College**
164 Opportunity Way
Lexington, KY 40511
(859) 246-2400
www.bluegrass.kctcs.edu
Programs: Automobile, Collision Repair
and Refinish

Boone County ATC
3320 Cougar Path
Hebron, KY 41048
(859) 689-7045
Programs: Collision Repair and Refinish

**Boyd County Career and
Technical Education Center**
12300 Midland Trail
Ashland, KY 41102
(606) 928-7120
Programs: Automobile

**C.E. McCormick Area
Technology Center**
50 Orchard Lane
Alexandria, KY 41001
(859) 635-4101
Programs: Automobile, Collision Repair
and Refinish

**Casey County Area
Vocational School**
1723 E. Ky. 70
Liberty, KY 42539
(606) 787-6241
Programs: Automobile

**Clay County Area
Technology Center**
1097 N. Hwy. 11
Manchester, KY 40962
(606) 598-2194
Programs: Automobile, Collision Repair
and Refinish

Clinton County ATC
Route 4, Box 40
Albany, KY 42602
(606) 387-6448
Programs: Automobile

Elizabethtown Community and Technical College
620 College Street Rd.
Elizabethtown, KY 42701
(270) 706-8657
Programs: Medium/Heavy Truck, Automobile

Gateway Community and Technical College
Toyota T-Ten
1025 Amsterdam Rd.
Covington, KY 41011
(859) 442-1112
Programs: Automobile, Collision Repair and Refinish

Grayson County Technology Center
252 Schoolhouse Rd.
Leitchfield, KY 42754
(270) 259-3195
Programs: Automobile

Green County Area Technology Center
102 Carlisle Ave.
Greensburg, KY 42743
(502) 932-4263
Programs: Automobile

Hazard Community and Technical College
101 Vo-Tech Dr.
Hazard, KY 41701
(606) 435-6101
Programs: Automobile

James D. Patton Area Technology Center
3234 Turkeyfoot Rd.
Ft. Mitchell, KY 41017
(859) 341-2266
Programs: Automobile, Collision Repair and Refinish

Jefferson Community and Technical College
Toyota T-Ten
727 West Chestnut St.
Louisville, KY 40203
(502) 213-4169
Programs: Automobile

Ky Tech-Bell County AVEC
Route 7, Box 199A
Pineville, KY 40977
(606) 337-3094

Programs: Automobile, Collision Repair and Refinish

Ky Tech-Bowling Green Reg Tech
1845 Loop Dr.
Bowling Green, KY 42101
(270) 901-1028
Programs: Automobile, Collision Repair and Refinish

Ky Tech-Carroll County ATC
1704 Highland Ave.
Carrollton, KY 41008
(502) 732-4479
Programs: Automobile

Ky Tech-Clark County Center
650 Boone Ave.
Winchester, KY 40391
(859) 744-1250
Programs: Automobile

Ky Tech-Corbin Area Technology Center
1909 South Snyder Ave.
Corbin, KY 40701
(606) 528-5338
Programs: Automobile

Ky Tech-Garrard County Center
306 West Maple Ave.
Lancaster, KY 40444
(859) 792-2144
Programs: Automobile

Ky Tech-Harrison County ATC
327 Webster Ave.
Cynthiana, KY 41031
(606) 234-1656
Programs: Automobile

Ky Tech-Knott County ATC
1996 Highway 160 S
Hindman, KY 41822
(606) 785-5350
Programs: Automobile

Ky Tech-Marion County ATC
721 East Main St.
Lebanon, KY 40033
(270) 692-3155
Programs: Automobile

Ky Tech-Millard ATC
7925 Millard Highway
Pikeville, KY 41501
(606) 437-6059
Programs: Automobile

Lake Cumberland Area Technology Center
2330 Hwy. 127 South
Russell Springs, KY 42642
Programs: Automobile

Letcher County Area Technology Center
185 Circle Dr.
Whitesburg, KY 41858
(606) 633-5053
Programs: Medium/Heavy Truck

Mason County Area Technology Center
646 Kenton Station Rd.
Maysville, KY 41056
(606) 759-7101
Programs: Automobile, Collision Repair and Refinish

Montgomery County ATC
682 Woodford Dr.
Mt. Sterling, KY 40353
(859) 498-1103
Programs: Automobile

Morgan County ATC
PO Box 249, Hwy. 191
West Liberty, KY 41472
(606) 743-8455
Programs: Collision Repair and Refinish

Morgan County ATC
PO Box 249, Hwy. 191
West Liberty, KY 41472
(606) 743-8456
Programs: Automobile

Muhlenberg County ATC
201 Airport Rd.
Greenville, KY 42345
(502) 338-1271
Programs: Automobile

Ohio County Area Technology Center
1406 S. Main St.
Hartford, KY 42347
Programs: Automobile

Oldham County Technical School
1650 Colonels Dr.
PO Box 127
Buckner, KY 40010
(502) 222-0131
Programs: Automobile

Owensboro Community and Tech College–SE Campus
1901 Southeastern Pkwy.
Owensboro, KY 42303
(270) 686-4461
Programs: Automobile

Paducah Area Technology Center
2400 Adams St.
Paducah, KY 42003
Programs: Collision Repair and Refinish

Rockcastle ATC
955 West Main St.
Mt. Vernon, KY 40456
(606) 256-4346
Programs: Automobile

Shelby County Area Technology Center
230 Rocket Lane
Shelbyville, KY 40065
(502) 633-6554
Programs: Automobile

Somerset Community College, South
808 Monticello St.
Somerset, KY 42501
(606) 677-4049
www.somerset.kctcs.edu/dc_dit.html
Programs: Medium/Heavy Truck

Southeast KY Community College–Harlan Campus
164 Ballpark Rd.
Harlan, KY 40831
(606) 573-1506
Programs: Automobile

UAW/LETC-Advanced Auto Training Program
2302 U.S. Highway 60 East
Bldg. 606
Morganfield, KY 42437
(270) 389-5311
www.uawletc.com
Programs: Automobile

Wayne County Area Technology Center
150 Cardinal Way
Monticello, KY 42633
(606) 348-8424
Programs: Automobile

West Kentucky Community and Technical College
234 Pioneer Industrial Dr.
Mayfield, KY 42066
(270) 247-9633
Programs: Medium/Heavy Truck

West Kentucky Community and Technical College
4810 Alben Barkley Dr.
Paducah, KY 42002
Programs: Collision Repair and Refinish

Louisiana

Delgado Community College
GM ASEP
Ford ASSET
615 City Park Ave.
New Orleans, LA 70119
(504) 671-6192
www.dcc.edu
Programs: Automobile

L.E. Fletcher Technical Community College
310 St. Charles St.
Houma, LA 70360
(985) 857-3655
www.ftcc.edu
Programs: Automobile

LTC-Acadian Campus
1933 West Hutchinson Ave.
Crowley, LA 70526
(318) 788-7521
www.acadiancampus.net
Programs: Medium/Heavy Truck

LTC-Ascension Campus
9697 Airline Hwy.
Sorrento, LA 70778
(225) 675-5398
www.ascensioncampus.edu
Programs: Automobile

LTC-Avoyelles Campus
1630 Prison Rd.
Cottonport, LA 71327
(318) 876-2891
Programs: Medium/Heavy Truck

LTC-Baton Rouge
3250 N. Acadian Thruway East
Baton Rouge, LA 70805
(225) 359-9425
www.ltc.edu
Programs: Automobile

LTC-Delta-Ouachita Campus
609 Vocational Pkwy.
West Monroe, LA 71292
(318) 397-6100
www.ltc.edu/muCampus
Delta-Ouachita.html
Programs: Automobile

LTC-Evangeline Campus
600 S. Martin Luther King Jr. Dr.
St. Martinville, LA 70582
(337) 394-6466
www.ltc.edu
Programs: Collision Repair and Refinish

LTC-Folkes DCI Campus
3337 Hwy. 10 East
Jackson, LA 70748
(225) 634-1200
www.ltc.edu
Programs: Automobile

LTC-Gulf Area Campus
1115 Clover St.
Abbeville, LA 70510
(337) 893-4984
www.ltc.edu
Programs: Medium/Heavy Truck, Collision Repair and Refinish

LTC-Hammond Area Campus
Toyota T-TEN
111 Pride Dr.
Hammond, LA 70404
(985) 543-4120
www.ltc.edu
Programs: Automobile

LTC-Jefferson Campus
5200 Blair Dr.
Metairie, LA 70001
(504) 671-6731
www.ltc.edu
Programs: Automobile

LTC-Morgan Smith Campus
1230 North Main St.
Jennings, LA 70549
(337) 824-4811
www.ltc.edu
Programs: Automobile

LTC-Northwest Campus
814 Constable St.
Minden, LA 71055
(318) 371-3035
www.ltc.edu
Programs: Automobile

LTC-Rayburn Correctional Center
27268 Highway 21
Angie, Louisiana 70426
(985) 986-5000
www.ltc.edu
Programs: Automobile

LTC-Sabine Valley Campus
1255 Fisher Rd.
Many, LA 71449
(318) 256-4101
www.ltc.edu
Programs: Automobile

LTC-Shreveport-Bossier Campus
2010 North Market St.
Shreveport, LA 71107
(318) 676-7811
Programs: Medium/Heavy Truck

LTC-Sullivan Campus
1710 Sullivan Dr.
Bogalusa, LA 70427
(985) 732-6640
www.ltc.edu
Programs: Automobile, Medium/
Heavy Truck

LTC-T.H. Harris Campus
332 East South St.
Opelousas, LA 70570
(337) 224-0501
www.ltc.edu
Programs: Medium/Heavy Truck

LTC-Tallulah
132 Old Hwy. 65 South
Tallulah, LA 71284
(318) 574-4820
www.ltc.etu
Programs: Automobile

LTC-Young Memorial Campus
900 Youngs Rd.
Morgan City, LA 70380
(985) 380-2436
www.ltc.edu
Programs: Automobile

**Sowela Technical
Community College**
3820 Sen. J. Bennet
  Johnston Ave.
Lake Charles, LA 70615
(337) 491-2698
www.ltc.edu
Programs: Automobile

Maine

**Biddeford Regional Center of
Technology**
10 Maplewood Ave.
Biddeford, ME 04005
(207) 282-1501
www.biddschools.org
Programs: Automobile

Capital Area Technical Center
40 Pierce Dr.
Suite 1
Augusta, ME 04330
(207) 626-2475
Programs: Collision Repair and Refinish
Certification Expiration: 6/2009

**Central Maine
Community College**
Ford ASSET
1250 Turner St.
Auburn, ME 04210
(207) 755-5320
www.cmcc.edu
Programs: Automobile

Mid-Maine Technical Center
3 Brooklyn Ave.
Waterville, ME 04901
(207) 873-0102
www.mmtc.ws
Programs: Automobile

**Northern Maine Community
College**
33 Edgemont Dr.
Presque Isle, ME 04769
(270) 768-2763
www.nmcc.edu
Programs: Automobile, Collision Repair
and Refinish

**Northern Penobscot Tech
Region III**
35 West Broadway
Lincoln, ME 04457
(207) 794-3940
Programs: Automobile
Certification Expiration: 6/2009

Oxford Hills Technical School
256 Main St.
South Paris, ME 04281
(207) 743-7756
Programs: Automobile, Collision Repair
and Refinish

**Southern Maine
Community College**
2 Fort Rd.
South Portland, ME 04106
(207) 741-5851
www.smccme.edu
Programs: Automobile

**Washington County
Community College**
1 College Dr.
Calais, ME 04619
(207) 454-1065
Programs: Automobile

Maryland

Allegany College of Maryland
12401 Willowbrook Rd. SE
Cumberland, MD 21502
(301) 784-5150
Programs: Automobile

Caroline Career and Tech. Center
10855 Central Ave.
Ridgely, MD 21660
(410) 479-0100
Programs: Automobile

**Carroll County Career and
Tech. Center**
1229 Washington Rd.
Westminster, MD 21157
(410) 751-3669
www.ccpl.carr.org/ccps/ccctc/
  introduction.htm
Programs: Automobile, Collision Repair
and Refinish

**Cecil County School
of Technology**
900 North East Rd.
North East, MD 21901
(410) 996-6250
Programs: Automobile

**Center for Career and
Technical Education**
14211 McMullen Hwy. SW
Cresaptown, MD 21502
www.boe.allconet.org/ccte
Programs: Collision Repair and Refinish

**Center of Applied
Technology North**
800 Stevenson Rd.
Severn, MD 21144

(410) 969-3100
Programs: Medium/Heavy Truck, Automobile, Collision Repair and Refinish

**Center of Applied
Technology South**
211 Central Ave. E
Edgewater, MD 21037
(410) 956-5900
www.catsouth.org
Programs: Automobile, Collision Repair
and Refinish

**Community College of
Baltimore County**
Ford ASSET
GM ASEP
Toyota T-Ten
800 South Rolling Road
Catonsville Campus
Baltimore, MD 21228
(410) 455-4968
Programs: Automobile

**Dorchester County School
of Technology**
2465 Cambridge Beltway
Cambridge, MD 21613
(410) 228-3457
Programs: Automobile

Montgomery College
51 Mannakee St.
Rockville, MD 20850
Programs: Automobile

Worcester Career and Tech. Center
6268 Worcester Hwy.
Newark, MD 21841
Programs: Automobile

Massachusetts

**Benjamin Franklin Institute of
Technology**
41 Berkeley St.
Boston, MA 02116
(617) 423-4630
www.bfit.edu/
Programs: Automobile

**Bristol-Plymouth Regional
Technical School**
940 County St.
Taunton, MA 02780
www.bptech.org
Programs: Collision Repair and Refinish

**Franklin County
Technical School**
82 Industrial Blvd.
Turners Falls, MA 01376
(413) 863-9561
www.fcts.org
Programs: Collision Repair and Refinish

**Greater Lawrence
Technical School**
57 River Rd.
Andover, MA 01810
(978) 686-0194
Programs: Automobile, Collision Repair
and Refinish

**Lynn Vocational
Technical Institute**
80 Neptune Blvd.
Lynn, MA 01902
(781) 477-7420
www.lynnschools.org
Programs: Collision Repair and Refinish

**Massachusetts Bay
Community College**
Chrysler CAP
GM ASEP
Toyota T-Ten
250 Elliott St.
Ashland, MA 01721
(781) 239-3045
www.mbcc.mass.edu
Programs: Automobile

**Montachusett Regional
Vocational Technical School**
1050 Westminster St.
Fitchburg, MA 01420
(978) 345-9200
www.montytech.net
Programs: Collision Repair and Refinish

**Mount Wachusett
Community College**
444 Green St.
Gardner, MA 01440
(978) 630-9336
www.mwcc.mass.edu/pro-
 grams/
 autotech/index.htm
Programs: Automobile

Upper Cape RVTS
220 Sandwich Rd.
Bourne, MA 02532
(508) 759-7711

www.uppercapetech.com
Programs: Automobile, Collision Repair
and Refinish

Michigan

**Allegan County Area Technical
and Education Center**
2891 116th Ave.
Allegan, MI 49010
Programs: Automobile

Baker College of Cadillac
9600 E. 13th St.
Cadillac, MI 49601
(231) 876-3125
www.baker.edu
Programs: Automobile

**Baker College of Clinton
Township**
34401 Gratiot Ave.
Clinton Township, MI 48035
(586) 790-9726
www.baker.edu
Programs: Automobile

Baker College of Flint
1050 W. Bristol Rd.
Flint, MI 48507
(810) 766-4110
www.baker.edu
Programs: Automobile

Baker College of Owosso
1020 S. Washington St.
Owosso, MI 48867
(989) 729-3407
www.baker.edu
Programs: Automobile

Bay de Noc Community College
2001 North Lincoln Rd.
Escanaba, MI 49829
(906) 786-5802
www.baycollege.edu
Programs: Automobile

Bay-Arenac ISD Career Center
4155 Monitor Rd.
Bay City, MI 48706
(989) 686-4770
www.baisd.net
Programs: Automobile, Medium/Heavy
Truck, Collision Repair and Refinish

Branch Area Careers Center
366 Morse St.
Coldwater, MI 49036
(517) 279-5704
www.brancg-isd.org
Programs: Automobile

Branch Area Careers Center
366 Morse St.
Coldwater, MI 49036
(517) 279-5704
www.branch-isd.org
Programs: Medium/Heavy Truck,
Collision Repair and Refinish

Calhoun Area Career Center
475 East Roosevelt Ave.
Battle Creek, MI 49017
(269) 968-2271
www.calhounareatech.com
Programs: Medium/Heavy Truck,
Collision Repair and Refinish

Capital Area Career Center
611 N. Hagadorn Rd.
Mason, MI 48854
(517) 244-1343
Programs: Collision Repair and Refinish

Career Preparation Center
12200 Fifteen Mile Rd.
Sterling Heights, MI 48312
Programs: Collision Repair and Refinish

Careerline Tech Center
13663 Port Sheldon Rd.
Holland, MI 49424
(616) 738-8950
www.oaisd.org/ctc
Programs: Automobile, Collision Repair
and Refinish

Clare-Gladwin RESD
4041 East Mannsiding
Clare, MI 48617
(989) 386-9330
Programs: Automobile

COOR Career Tech Center
10775 North St. Helen Rd.
Roscommon, MI 48653
(989) 275-5000
Programs: Automobile

**Copper Country
Intermediate School**
809 Hecla St.
Hancock, MI 49930

(906) 482-4250
www.copperisd.org/
Programs: Automobile

Delta College
GM ASEP
1961 Delta Rd.
University Center, MI 48710
Programs: Automobile

**Delta Schoolcraft Career
Technical Center**
2525 Third Avenue S
Escanaba, MI 49829
Programs: Automobile

Delta-Schoolcraft ISD
100 North Cedar St.
Manistique, MI 49854
(906) 341-4300
Programs: Automobile

Dickinson-Iron Technical Center
300 North Blvd.
Kingsford, MI 49802
www.diisd.org
Programs: Automobile

Frederick V. Pankow Tech Center
24600 Pankow Blvd.
Clinton Township, MI 48036
(586) 783-6570
Programs: Collision Repair and Refinish

Ferris State University
708 Campus Drive
Auto Center 101
Big Rapids, MI 49307
(231) 591-5987
www.ferris.edu
Programs: Automobile, Medium/
Heavy Truck

GASC Technology Center
G-5081 Torrey Rd.
Flint, MI 48507
(810) 760-1444
www.gasctech.us
Programs: Medium/Heavy Truck

**Golightly Career and
Technical Center**
900 Dickerson St.
Detroit, MI 48215
(313) 822-8820
Programs: Collision Repair and Refinish

**Grand Rapids
Community College**
622 Godfrey SW
Grand Rapids, MI 49503
(616) 234-3825
www.grcc.edu/?automotive
Programs: Automobile

Henry Ford Community College
5101 Evergreen Rd.
Dearborn, MI 48128
(313) 845-6350
www.hfcc.edu
Programs: Automobile

Henry Ford Community College
Ford ASSET
5101 Evergreen Rd.
Dearborn, MI 48128
(313) 845-6350
www.hfcc.edu
Programs: Automobile

Hill Career Academy
5815 Wise Rd.
Lansing, MI 48911
(517) 755-4152
www.hometown.aol.com/
autohcat
Programs: Automobile

**IOSCO Regional Educational
Service Agency**
27 N. Rempert Rd.
Tawas City, MI 48763
(989) 362-3006
www.ioscoresa.net/
Programs: Automobile

Jackson Area Career Center
Toyota T-Ten
6800 Browns Lake Rd.
Jackson, MI 49201
(517) 990-6605
www.jcisd.org
Programs: Automobile, Collision Repair
and Refinish

Kent Career Technical Center
1655 East Beltline NE
Grand Rapids, MI 52501
(616) 364-8421
www.kentISD.org
Programs: Medium/Heavy Truck,
Collision Repair and Refinish

Kirtland Community College
10779 N. St. Helen Rd.
Roscommon, MI 48653
(989) 275-5000
www.kirtland.edu/academic/
aut.htm
Programs: Automobile

Lansing Community College
4100 W. Automotive Technology
Lansing, MI 48917
(517) 483-1387
www.lcc.edu/tech/AutoBody
Repair
Programs: Collision Repair and Refinish

Lenawee Vo-Tech Center
1372 N. Main St.
Adrian, MI 49221
Programs: Collision Repair and Refinish

Macomb Community College
GM ASEP
14500 East Twelve Mile Rd.
Warren, MI 48088
(586) 445-7290
www.macomb.edu
Programs: Automobile

**Mason-Lake Intermediate
School District**
3000 North Stiles Rd.
Scottville, MI 49454
(231) 845-6211
Programs: Automobile

Mecosta Osceola Career Center
15830 190th Ave.
Big Rapids, MI 49307
(231) 796-5805
www.moisd.org

**Mid Michigan
Community College**
1375 South Clare Ave.
Harrison, MI 48625
(517) 386-6642
www.midmich.edu
Programs: Automobile

Montcalm Area Career Center
1550 West Sidney Rd.
Sidney, MI 48885
(989) 328-6621
www.maisd.com
Programs: Automobile, Medium/Heavy
Truck, Collision Repair and Refinish

Mott Community College
1401 East Court Street Regional
Technology Center
Flint, MI 48503
(810) 232-7560
www.mcc.edu
Programs: Automobile

**Mt. Pleasant Area
Technical Center**
1155 South Elizabeth St.
Mt. Pleasant, MI 48858
(989) 775-2210
www.mpatc.com
Programs: Automobile

**Muskegon Area Career
Tech Center**
200 Harvey St.
Muskegon, MI 49442
Programs: Automobile, Collision Repair
and Refinish

**Newaygo County Career
Technical Center**
4645 West Career Pathway
Fremont, MI 49412
(231) 924-0380
Programs: Automobile

**Oakland School Technical
Center, SW Campus**
1000 Beck Rd.
Wixom, MI 48393
(248) 668-5640
Programs: Medium/Heavy Truck

**Oakland Schools Technical
Campus SE**
5055 Delemere Ave.
Royal Oak, MI 48073
(248) 288-4363
Programs: Collision Repair and Refinish

**Oakland Technical Center,
NW Campus**
8211 Big Lake Rd.
Clarkston, MI 48346
Programs: Automobile, Collision Repair
and Refinish

Regional Career Tech. Center
1520 South Congress
Ypsilanti, MI 48197
(734) 482-8485
www.ypsd.org
Programs: Collision Repair and Refinish

Sanilac Career Center
175 East Aitken Rd.
Peck, MI 48466
Programs: Automobile

Sault Area Career Center
1311 Bingham
Sault Ste. Marie, MI 49783
Programs: Automobile

**Southern Lakes Career
Technical Center**
2100 W. Thompson Rd.
Fenton, MI 48430
(810) 750-8398
Programs: Automobile

**St. Clair Technical
Education Center**
499 Range Rd.
Marysville, MI 48040
(810) 364-8990
Programs: Automobile, Collision Repair
and Refinish

St. Joseph Co. Career Tech Ed.
62445 Shimmel Rd.
Centreville, MI 49032
(269) 467-9945
Programs: Automobile

**Traverse Bay Area
Career-Tech Center**
880 Parsons Rd.
Traverse City, MI 49686
(231) 922-6290
Programs: Automobile, Collision Repair
and Refinish

Tuscola Technology Center
1401 Cleaver Rd.
Caro, MI 48723
(989) 673-5300
Programs: Medium/Heavy Truck

Van Buren Vo-Tech Center
250 South St.
Lawrence, MI 49064
(269) 674-8001
www.vbisd.org
Programs: Collision Repair and Refinish

Washtenaw Community College
4800 East Huron River Dr.
Ann Arbor, MI 48106
www.wccnet.edu
Programs: Automobile, Collision Repair
and Refinish

Wayne County Community
College District
21000 Northline Rd.
Taylor, MI 48180
(734) 374-3200
www.wcccd.edu
Programs: Automobile

Wexford-Missaukee Area Career
Tech Center
9901 E 13th St.
Cadillac, MI 49601
(231) 876-2200
www.wmaisd.org
Programs: Medium/Heavy Truck,
Automobile

William D. Ford Career
Technical Center
36455 Marquette St.
Westland, MI 48185
(734) 419-2140
www.wwcsd.net/fctc
Programs: Collision Repair and Refinish

Minnesota

Anoka Technical College
1355 West Hwy. 10
Anoka, MN 55303
(763) 576-4852
Programs: Automobile

Central Lakes College
501 College Dr.
Brainerd, MN 56401
(218) 855-8114
Programs: Automobile

Century College
3300 Century Ave. N
White Bear Lake, MN 55038
(651) 779-3429
www.century.edu
Programs: Automobile

Dakota County Technical College
GM ASEP
1300 145th Street E, CR 42
Rosemount, MN 55068
(651) 423-8232
www.dctc.edu
Programs: Automobile, Collision Repair
and Refinish

Dunwoody College of Technology
Chrysler CAP

818 Dunwoody Blvd.
Minneapolis, MN 55403
(612) 374-5800
Programs: Automobile, Collision Repair
and Refinish

Hennepin Technical College
Ford ASSET
9000 Brooklyn Blvd.
Brooklyn Park, MN 55445
(763) 488-2410
www.hennepintech.edu
Programs: Automobile, Medium/
Heavy Truck

Hibbing Community College
1515 East 25th St.
Hibbing, MN 55746
www.hibbing.edu
Programs: Automobile

Minnesota State College–
Southeast Tech
1250 Homer Rd.
Winona, MN 55987
(507) 453-2660
Programs: Collision Repair and Refinish

Minnesota State Community
and Technical College
1900 28th Ave. S
Moorhead, MN 56560
(218) 299-6548
www.minnesota.edu
Programs: Automobile

Minnesota State Community
and Technical College
900 Hwy. 34 E
Detroit Lakes, MN 56501
(218) 846-3790
www.minnesota.edu
Programs: Automobile

Minnesota West Community
and Technical College
401 West St.
Jackson, MN 56143
(507) 847-7948
www.mnwest.edu
Programs: Automobile

Northland Community and
Technical College
1101 Hwy. One E
Thief River Falls, MN 56701
(218) 681-0805

www.northlandcollege.edu
Programs: Automobile

Pine Technical College
900 4th Street SE
Pine City, MN 55063
(320) 629-5162
Programs: Automobile

Ridgewater College,
Willmar Campus
2101 15th Ave. NW
Willmar, MN 56201
(320) 231-2995
Programs: Automobile

South Central Technical College
1920 Lee Blvd.
North Mankato, MN 56003
(507) 389-7232
Programs: Automobile

St. Cloud Technical College
1540 Northway Dr.
St. Cloud, MN 56303
www.sctonline.com
Programs: Automobile, Collision Repair
and Refinish

Wright Technical Center
1400 Hwy. 25 N
Buffalo, MN 55313
(763) 684-2205
Programs: Automobile

Mississippi

Clinton Career Complex
715 Lakeview Dr.
Clinton, MS 39056
(601) 924-0247
www.clintonpublcschools.com
Programs: Automobile

East Mississippi
Community College
8731 South Frontage Rd.
Mayhew, MS 39753
(662) 243-1904
Programs: Automobile

Hinds Community College
501 Main St.
Raymond, MS 39154
(601) 857-3311
Programs: Automobile

**Mississippi Gulf Coast
Community College**
21500 B St.
West Harrison Center
Long Beach, MS 39560
Programs: Automobile, Collision Repair
and Refinish

**New Albany Union
Vocational Center**
203 Hwy. 15 N
New Albany, MS 38652
(662) 534-1810
www.newalbanyvocational
    center.com/
Programs: Automobile

**Northwest Mississippi
Community College**
Chrysler CAP
4975 Hwy. 51 N
Senatobia, MS 38668
(662) 562-3391
www.northwestms.edu/programs/
    2002-03/autotechnology.html
Programs: Automobile

Pearl River Community College
101 US Hwy. 11 N
Box 5014
Poplarville, MS 39466
www.prcc.edu
Programs: Automobile

Raymond Campus Career Center
14020 Hwy. 18
Raymond, MS 39154
(601) 857-5536
www.hindscc.edu
Programs: Automobile

**Tippah Career and
Technology Center**
2560 CR 501
Ripley, MS 38663
Programs: Automobile
Certification Expiration: 5/2010

Missouri

**Boonslick Technical
Education Center**
1694 W. Ashley Rd.
Boonville, MO 65233
(660) 882-5306
Programs: Automobile

**Cape Girardeau Career and
Tech Center**
1080 S. Silver Spring Rd.
Cape Girardeau, MO 63703
(573) 334-0826
www.capectc.org
Programs: Automobile

Carthage Technical Center
609 River St.
Carthage, MO 64836
(417) 359-7026
Programs: Automobile

Columbia Area Career Center
4203 South Providence Rd.
Columbia, MO 65203
(573) 214-3800
www.career-center.org
Programs: Automobile

Eldon Career Center
112 South Pine St.
Eldon, MO 65026
(573) 392-8060
Programs: Automobile

**Excelsior Springs Area
Career Center**
614 Tiger Dr.
Excelsior Springs, MO 64024
(816) 630-9240
Programs: Automobile

Four Rivers Career Center
1978 Image Dr.
Washington, MO 63090
(636) 239-7777
Programs: Collision Repair and Refinish

Grand River Technical School
1200 Fair St.
Chillicothe, MO 64601
(816) 646-3414
Programs: Collision Repair and Refinish

**Hannibal Career and
Technical Center**
4550 McMasters Ave.
Hannibal, MO 63401
(573) 221-4430
Programs: Automobile

**Herndon Career Center,
West Campus**
11501 East 350 Highway
Raytown, MO 64138
(816) 268-7140

www.herndoncareercenter.com
Programs: Automobile, Collision Repair
and Refinish

Hillyard Technical Center
3434 Faraon St.
St. Joseph, MO 64506
(816) 671-4170
www.hillyardtech.com
Programs: Automobile

**Lake Career and
Technical Center**
269 Dare Blvd.
Camdenton, MO 65486
(573) 346-9260
Programs: Automobile

Lamar Area Vo-Tech School
501 Maple St.
Lamar, MO 64759
(417) 682-3384
Programs: Automobile

**Lebanon Technology and
Career Center**
757 Brice St.
Lebanon, MO 65536
Programs: Automobile

Linn State Technical College
One Technology Dr.
Linn, MO 65051
(573) 897-5178
www.linnstate.edu
Programs: Automobile, Collision Repair
and Refinish

Longview Community College
GM ASEP
Ford ASSET
500 S.W. Longview Rd.
Lee's Summit, MO 64081
(816) 672-2061
Programs: Automobile

Moberly Area Tech Center
1623 Gratz Brown Rd.
Moberly, MO 65270
(660) 269-2690
Programs: Automobile, Collision Repair
and Refinish

Nichols Career Center
605 Union St.
Jefferson City, MO 65101
(573) 659-3119
Programs: Collision Repair and Refinish

Ozarks Tech. Community College
1001 E. Chestnut Expwy.
Springfield, MO 65801
(417) 447-8108
www.otc.edu
Programs: Medium/Heavy Truck,
Collision Repair and Refinish

Ranken Technical College
GM ASEP
Toyota T-TEN
4431 Finney Ave.
St. Louis, MO 63113
(314) 286-4861
www.ranken.edu
Programs: Automobile, Collision Repair
and Refinish

State Fair Community College
3201 West 16th St.
Sedalia, MO 65301
(660) 596-7243
www.sfccmo.edu
Programs: Automobile

UniTec Career Center
7163 Raider Rd.
Bonne Terre, MO 63628
(573) 358-3011
Programs: Automobile

Fort Peck Community College
1st Ave. and Yankton St.
Poplar, MT 59255
(406) 768-5476
www.fpcc.edu
Programs: Automobile

**Montana State University,
Billings**
3803 Central Avenue College
of Technology
Billings, MT 59102
(406) 247-3049
Programs: Medium/Heavy Truck

**Montana State University,
Billings**
3803 Central Ave College
of Technology
Billings, MT 59102
(406) 247-3043
www.msubillings.edu/cot/
programs/progautotech.htm
Programs: Automobile

**Montana State University,
Billings**
3803 Central Avenue College of
Technology
Billings, MT 59102
(406) 247-3042
Programs: Collision Repair and Refinish

**Montana State University,
Northern**
Toyota T-TEN
300 11th St. West
Havre, MT 59501
(406) 265-4179
Programs: Automobile

**Montana Tech-College of
Technology**
25 Basin Creek Rd.
Butte, MT 59701
(406) 496-3752
www.mtech.edu
Programs: Automobile

**University of Montana-Helena
College of Tech**
2300 Airport Rd.
Helena, MT 59601
(406) 444-6806
Programs: Automobile

Central Community College
East Highway #6, Box 1024
Hastings, NE 68930
(402) 461-2567
Programs: Automobile

Metropolitan Community College
North 30th St. and Fort St.
Omaha, NE 68111
(402) 738-4500
Programs: Collision Repair and Refinish

Northeast Community College
801 East Benjamin Ave.
Norfolk, NE 68701
Programs: Automobile

**Omaha Public Schools,
Career Center**
3230 Burt St.
Omaha, NE 68131
(402) 557-3700
www2.ops.org/center/
Programs: Automobile

**Southeast Community College,
Lincoln Campus**
8800 O St.
Lincoln, NE 68520
(402) 437-2640
www.southeast.edu
Programs: Automobile

Southeast Community College
Chrysler CAP
GM ASEP
Ford ASSET
600 State St.
Milford, NE 68405
(402) 761-8317
www.southeast.edu
Programs: Automobile, Medium/
Heavy Truck

**Western Nebraska
Community College**
1601 East 27th St.
Scottsbluff, NE 69361
(308) 635-6083
www.wncc.net
Programs: Automobile, Collision Repair
and Refinish

**Community College of
Southern Nevada**
GM ASEP
3200 East Cheyenne Ave.
North Las Vegas, NV 89030
(702) 651-4187
Programs: Automobile

**Truckee Meadows
Community College**
475 Edison Way
Reno, NV 89502
(775) 856-5312
Programs: Automobile

**Concord Regional Technology
Center—General Service Tech**
170 Warren St.
Concord, NH 03301
(603) 225-0800
Programs: Automobile

Manchester School of
Technology
530 S. Porter St.
Manchester, NH 03103
(603) 624-6490
www.mansd.org
Programs: Automobile

Mascenic Automotive
Career Center
175 Turnpike Rd.
New Ipswich, NH 03071
(603) 878-4585
Programs: Automobile

Mt. Washington Valley Career
and Tech Center
176 Main St.
Conway, NH 03818
www.mwvctc.com
Programs: Automobile

Nashua Community College
Honda PACT
505 Amherst St.
Nashua, NH 03061
(603) 882-6923
www.nashua.tec.nh.us
Programs: Automobile

New Hampshire Community
Technical College
2020 Riverside Dr.
Berlin, NH 03570
(603) 752-1113
Programs: Automobile

New Hampshire Community
Technical College
GM ASEP
Toyota T-Ten
277 Portsmouth Ave.
Stratham, NH 03885
(603) 772-1194
Programs: Automobile

Sugar River Valley RTC
243 N. Main St.
Newport, NH 03782
(603) 863-3759
Programs: Automobile

New Jersey

Brookdale Community College
GM ASEP
Toyota T-Ten

765 Newman Springs Rd.
Lincroft, NJ 07738
(732) 224-2747
Programs: Automobile

Burlington County Institute
of Technology
695 Woodlane Rd.
Westhampton, NJ 08060
(609) 267-4226
Programs: Automobile

Camden County College
GM ASEP
Toyota T-Ten
200 College Dr.
Blackwood, NJ 08012
(856) 227-7200
www.camdencc.edu/
    departments/auto-tech
Programs: Automobile

Camden County Technical
School
6008 Browning Rd.
Pennsauken, NJ 08109
(856) 663-1040
www.ccts.tec.nj.us
Programs: Automobile

Cape May County
Vocational School
188 Crest Haven Rd.
Cape May Court House, NJ
    08210
Programs: Automobile

Essex County Vocational School
620 West Passaic Ave.
West Caldwell, NJ 07006
(973) 395-8559
Programs: Automobile

Essex County Vocational School
91 West Market St.
Newark, NJ 07103
(973) 395-8555
www.essextech.org
Programs: Automobile

Gloucester County Institute
of Technology
Ford ASSET
1360 Tanyard Rd.
Sewell, NJ 08080
(856) 468-1445
Programs: Automobile

Hudson County School
of Technology
8511 Tonnelle Ave.
North Bergen, NJ 07047
(201) 295-4574
Programs: Automobile

Lincoln Technical Institute
2299 Vauxhall Rd.
Union, NJ 07083
(908) 964-7800
www.lincolntech.com
Programs: Automobile

Mercer County
Community College
Chrysler CAP
1200 Old Trenton Rd.
Trenton, NJ 08690
(609) 570-3776
www.mccc.edu/automotive
Programs: Automobile

Monmouth County
Vocational School
2 Swartzel Dr.
Middletown Campus
Middletown, NJ 07748
Programs: Automobile

Monmouth County
Vocational School
280 Atlantic Street
Keyport Campus
Keyport, NJ 07735
Programs: Automobile

Monmouth County
Vocational School
417 Middle Rd.
Hazlet Center
Hazlet, NJ 07730
(732) 671-0650
Programs: Automobile, Collision Repair
and Refinish

Passaic County
Technical Institute
45 Reinhardt Rd.
Wayne, NJ 07470
(973) 389-4287
Programs: Collision Repair and Refinish

Sussex County Vo-Tech School
105 North Church Rd.
Sparta, NJ 07871
(973) 383-6700
Programs: Medium/Heavy Truck

New Mexico

Eastern New Mexico University
52 University Blvd.
Roswell, NM 88201
(505) 624-7115
www.rosewell.enmu.edu
Programs: Automobile

New Mexico Junior College
GM ASEP
Ford ASSET
5317 Lovington Hwy.
Hobbs, NM 88240
(505) 492-2864
Programs: Automobile

San Juan College
Chrysler CAP
GM ASEP
Toyota T-Ten
4601 College Blvd.
Farmington, NM 87402
(505) 566-3388
www.sanjuancollege.edu/pages/
450.asp
Programs: Automobile

University of New Mexico
200 College Rd.
Gallup, NM 87301
(505) 863-7529
Programs: Automobile

New York

Alfred State College of Technology
2530 South Brooklyn Ave.
Wellsville, NY 14895
(607) 587-3118
www.alfredstate.edu
Programs: Medium/Heavy Truck, Automobile

Apex Technical School
635 Avenue of the Americas
New York, NY 10011
(212) 620-2863
www.apexschool.net
Programs: Automobile

Bronx Community College of CUNY
University Avenue West 181st St.
Bronx, NY 10453
(718) 289-5213
www.bcc.cuny.edu
Programs: Automobile

Burton Ramer Technical Career Center
179 County Route 64
Mexico, NY 13114
(315) 963-4246
www.oswegoboces.org/courses/
high_autobody.asp
Programs: Automobile, Collision Repair and Refinish

Capital Region BOCES
1015 Watervliet-Shaker Rd.
Albany, NY 12205
www.bocescareertech.org
Programs: Medium/Heavy Truck, Collision Repair and Refinish

Columbia-Greene Community College
Toyota T-Ten
4400 Route 23
Hudson, NY 12534
(518) 828-4181
Programs: Automobile

Delhi College of Technology
2 Main St.
Delhi, NY 13573
(607) 746-4144
www.delhi.edu/academics/
techdivision
Programs: Automobile

Erie 2-Chautauqua-Cattaraugus BOCES
8685 Erie Rd.
Willis H. Carrier Educational Center
Angola, NY 14006
www.e2ccb.org
Programs: Automobile

Erie Community College Vehicle Technical Training Center
Chrysler CAP
Ford ASSET
5885 Big Tree Rd.
Orchard Park, NY 14127
(716) 270-2630
www.ecc.edu
Programs: Automobile

F. Donald Myers Education Center
15 Henning Rd.
Saratoga Springs, NY 12866

(518) 581-3600
Programs: Automobile, Collision Repair and Refinish

Finger Lakes Technical and Career Center
3501 County Rd. #20
Stanley, NY 14561
(585) 526-6471
www.wflboces.org
Programs: Automobile

Genesee Valley BOCES
27 Lackawanna Ave.
Mount Morris, NY 14510
(585) 658-7811
www.gvboces.org/
Programs: Automobile

Harkness Career and Technical Center
99 Aero Dr.
Cheektowaga, NY 14225
(716) 632-6680
www.e1b.org
Programs: Automobile

HFM BOCES Career and Tech. Center
2755 State Hwy. 67
Johnstown, NY 12095
(518) 762-4298
Programs: Automobile

Hudson Valley Community College
Chrysler CAP
GM ASEP
80 Vandenburgh Ave.
Troy, NY 12180
(518) 629-7276
www.hvcc.edu
Programs: Automobile, Collision Repair and Refinish

Jefferson Lewis BOCES-Bohlen Center
20104 NYS Route 3
Watertown, NY 13601
www.boces.com
Programs: Automobile

LoGuidice Educational Center
9520 Fredonia-Stockton Rd.
Fredonia, NY 14063
(800) 344-9611
Programs: Automobile

Madison Oneida Boces
4937 Spring Rd.
Verona, NY 13478
(315) 361-5724
Programs: Automobile

Monroe Community College
GM ASEP
Toyota T-Ten
1000 East Henrietta Rd.
Rochester, NY 14623
(716) 292-3746
www.monroecc.edu/go/ATC
Programs: Automobile

Morrisville State College
Ford ASSET
80 Eaton St.
Morrisville, NY 13408
(315) 684-6222
www.morrisville.edu
Programs: Automobile

New York Automotive and Diesel Institute
178-18 Liberty Ave.
Jamaica, NY 11433
(718) 658-0006
Programs: Medium/Heavy Truck, Collision Repair and Refinish

Oneida County BOCES
4747 Middle Settlement Road
Occupational Education Building
New Hartford, NY 13413
(315) 793-8656
www.oneida-boces.org
Programs: Automobile

Orange-Ulster CTEC
53 Gibson Rd.
Goshen, NY 10916
(845) 291-0411
Programs: Automobile, Collision Repair and Refinish

Putnam/Northern Westchester BOCES
200 BOCES Dr.
Building A Receiving
Yorktown Heights, NY 10598
www.pnwboces.org
Programs: Automobile, Collision Repair and Refinish

Rockland BOCES
65 Parrott Road
Career Education Center

West Nyack, NY 10994
(845) 627-4700
www.rocklandboces.org
Programs: Collision Repair and Refinish

School of Cooperative Technical Education
321 East 96th St.
New York, NY 10128
www.co-optech.org
Programs: Automobile

Southern Adirondack Education Center
General Service Tech
1051 Dix Ave.
Hudson Falls, NY 12839
(518) 746-3456
www.wswheboces.org
Programs: Automobile

Suffolk County Community College
GM ASEP
Toyota T-Ten
535 College Rd.
Selden, NY 11787
(631) 451-4905
www.sunysuffolk..edu
Programs: Automobile

Tompkins-Seneca-Tioga BOCES
555 Warren Road
Building B, Powell
Ithaca, NY 14850
(607) 257-1555
www.tstboces.org
Programs: Automobile

Western Suffolk BOCES
152 Laurel Hill Rd.
Northport, NY 11768
(631) 261-3600
www.wsboces.org
Programs: Automobile

Wilson Technology Center
17 Westminster Ave.
Dix Hills, NY 11746
www.wsboces.org
Programs: Collision Repair and Refinish

North Carolina

Alamance Community College
1247 Jimmie Kerr Rd.
Graham, NC 27253

(336) 506-4282
Programs: Automobile

Asheville-Buncombe Technical Community College
340 Victoria Rd.
Asheville, NC 28801
(828) 254-1921
www.abtech.edu
Programs: Automobile

Beaufort County Community College
5337 US Hwy. 264 E
Washington, NC 27889
(252) 940-6247
www.beaufortccc.edu
Programs: Automobile

Blue Ridge Community College
180 West Campus Dr.
Flat Rock, NC 28731
www.blueridge.edu
Programs: Automobile

Caldwell Community College and Technical Institute
2855 Hickory Blvd.
Hudson, NC 28638
(828) 726-5272
www.cccti.edu
Programs: Automobile

Catawba Valley Community College
2550 Hwy. 70 SE
Hickory, NC 28602
(828) 327-7000
www.cvcc.edu
Programs: Automobile

Central Academy of Technology and Arts
600 Brewer Dr.
Monroe, NC 28110
(704) 296-3088
Programs: Automobile, Collision Repair and Refinish

Central Carolina Community College
1105 Kelly Dr.
Sanford, NC 27330
(919) 718-7303
Programs: Automobile

Central Piedmont
Community College
Chrysler CAP
GM ASEP
Toyota T-Ten
1325 East 7th St.
Charlotte, NC 28235
(704) 330-6659
www.cpcc.edu
Programs: Automobile

Craven Community College
800 College Ct.
New Bern, NC 28562
(252) 638-7347
Programs: Automobile

Davidson County
Community College
297 DCCC Rd.
Lexington, NC 27293
(336) 249-8186
www.davidsonccc.edu
Programs: Automobile

Fayetteville Technical
Community College
2201 Hull Rd.
Fayetteville, NC 28303
(910) 678-8260
www.faytechcc.edu
Programs: Automobile

Forsyth Technical
Community College
2100 Silas Creek Pkwy.
Winston-Salem, NC 27103
(336) 757-7279
www.forsythtech.edu
Programs: Automobile

Gaston College
201 Hwy. 321 S
Dallas, NC 28034
(704) 922-6388
Programs: Automobile

Guilford Technical
Community College
GM ASEP
Ford ASSET
601 High Point Rd.
Jamestown, NC 27282
(336) 334-4822
www.gtcc.edu/academic/trans
Programs: Automobile, Collision Repair
and Refinish, Medium/Heavy Truck

Lenoir Community College
231 NC Hwy. 58 S
Kinston, NC 28502
(252) 527-6223
www.lenoircc.edu
Programs: Automobile

Martin Community College
1161 Kehukee Park Rd.
Williamston, NC 27892
(252) 792-1521
Programs: Automobile

McDowell Technical
Community College
54 College Dr.
Marion, NC 28752
(828) 652-0656
Programs: Collision Repair and Refinish

Pinckney Academy
160 Pinckney Rd.
Carthage, NC 28327
(910) 690-7564
Programs: Automobile

Robeson County Career Center
1339 Hilly Branch Rd.
Lumberton, NC 28360
(910) 671-6095
Programs: Automobile

Rowan-Cabarrus
Community College
1333 Jake Alexander Blvd.
Salisbury, NC 28146
(704) 637-0760
ww.rowancabarrus.edu
Programs: Automobile

Sandhills Community College
3395 Airport Rd.
Pinehurst, NC 28374
(910) 695-3958
Programs: Automobile

Sellars-Gunn Education Center
612 Apple St.
Burlington, NC 27217
(336) 570-6130
Programs: Automobile

Universal Technical Institute
Nascar Technical Institute
220 Byers Creek Rd.
Mooresville, NC 28117
Programs: Automobile

Vance-Granville
Community College
PO Box 917
Henderson, NC 27536
(252) 492-2061
www.vgcc.edu
Programs: Automobile

Wake Technical
Community College
9101 Fayetteville Rd.
Receiving Dept
Raleigh, NC 27603
Programs: Automobile

Wayne Community College
GM ASEP
3000 Wayne Memorial Drive
Drawer Box 8002
Goldsboro, NC 27533
Programs: Automobile

Weaver Academy
300 S. Spring St.
Greensboro, NC 27401
(336) 370-2377
Programs: Automobile, Collision Repair
and Refinish

Wilkes Career Ed. Center
374 Lincoln Heights Rd.
Wilkesboro, NC 28697
(336) 667-3653
Programs: Automobile

Wilkes Community College
1328 South Collegiate Dr.
Wilkesboro, NC 28697
(336) 838-6284
www.wilkescc.edu

North Dakota
Bismarck State College
1500 Edwards Ave.
Bismarck, ND 58506
(701) 224-5594
www.bismarckstate.com
Programs: Automobile, Collision Repair
and Refinish

Bismarck Technical Center
1200 W. College Dr.
Bismarck, ND 58506
(701) 224-5405
www.bpsvotech.org
Programs: Automobile

James Valley Career and
Technology
910-12th Ave. NE
Jamestown, ND 58401
(701) 252-8841
Programs: Collision Repair and Refinish

Lake Region State College
1801 College Dr. N
Devils Lake, ND 58301
(701) 662-1558
www.lrsc.nodak.edu
Programs: Automobile

Missouri River
Correctional Center
3303 East Main Ave.
Bismarck, ND 58506
(701) 328-9683
Programs: Automobile

North Dakota State College
of Science
800 North 6th St.
Wahpeton, ND 58076
(701) 671-2656
www.ndscs.edu
Programs: Automobile

North Valley Career and
Technology Center
1540 School Rd.
Grafton, ND 58237
(701) 352-3705
Programs: Automobile

Quentin Burdick Job Corps
Center
1500 University Ave. W
Minot, ND 58703
(701) 857-9664
www.burdickjobcorps.com
Programs: Automobile

Southeast Region Career
and Tech. Center
2101 9th Street N
Wahpeton, ND 58075
(701) 671-2656
Programs: Automobile

United Tribes Technical College
3315 University Dr.
Bismarck, ND 58504
(701) 255-3285
Programs: Automobile

Williston State College
1410 University Ave.
Williston, ND 58801
(701) 774-4274
Programs: Automobile

Ohio

Apollo Career Center
3325 Shawnee Rd.
Lima, OH 45806
(419) 998-2951
Programs: Automobile, Collision Repair
and Refinish

Ashland County West Holmes
Career Center
1783 State Route 60
Ashland, OH 44805
(419) 289-3313
Programs: Automobile

Auburn Career Center
8140 Auburn Rd.
Concord Twp., OH 44077
(440) 358-8032
www.auburncc.org
Programs: Automobile, Collision Repair
and Refinish

Belmont Career Center
110 Fox-Shannon Place
St. Clairsville, OH 43950
(740) 695-9130
Programs: Automobile, Collision Repair
and Refinish

Buckeye Career Center
545 University Drive NE
New Philadelphia, OH 44663
(330) 339-2288
Programs: Automobile

Butler Tech
D. Russel Lee Career Center
3603 Hamilton Middletown Rd.
Hamilton, OH 45011
(513) 868-6300
www.butlertech.org
Programs: Automobile

Collins Career Center
11627 State Route 243
Chesapeake, OH 45619
(740) 867-8133
Programs: Automobile, Medium/Heavy
Truck, Collision Repair and Refinish

Columbus State
Community College
Ford ASSET
550 East Spring St.
Columbus, OH 43216
(614) 287-5408
www.cscc.edu/DOCS/AUTO/
index.htm
Programs: Automobile

C-TEC Career Center
150 Price Rd.
Newark, OH 43055
(740) 366-3351
Programs: Medium/Heavy Truck

Cuyahoga Community College
GM ASEP
11000 Pleasant Valley Rd.
Parma, OH 44130
(216) 987-5224
www.tri-c.edu
Programs: Automobile

Cuyahoga Valley Career Center
8001 Brecksville Rd.
Brecksville, OH 44141
(440) 746-8265
Programs: Collision Repair and Refinish

Diamond Oaks Career
Development Center
6375 Harrison Ave.
Cincinnati, OH 45247
(513) 612-3688
www.greatoaks.com/pages/
-4461-/
Programs: Collision Repair and Refinish

Ehove Career Center
316 West Mason Rd.
Milan, OH 44846
(419) 499-4663
Programs: Medium/Heavy Truck,
Collision Repair and Refinish

Four County Career Center
22-900 State Route #34
Archbold, OH 43502
(419) 267-3331
www.fourcounty.net
Programs: Automobile, Collision Repair
and Refinish

Jefferson County JVS
1509 County Highway 22A
Bloomingdale, OH 43910
(740) 264-5545
Programs: Collision Repair and Refinish

Knox County Career Center
306 Martinsburg Rd.
Mt. Vernon, OH 43050
(740) 397-5820
Programs: Automobile, Collision Repair
and Refinish

**Live Oaks Career
Development Center**
5956 Buckwheat Rd.
Milford, OH 45150
(513) 575-1900
www.greatoaks.com
Programs: Collision Repair and Refinish

Lorain County JVS
15181 State Route 58 S
Oberlin, OH 44074
(440) 774-1051
Programs: Medium/Heavy Truck,
Collision Repair and Refinish

Maplewood Career Center
7075 State Route 88
Ravenna, OH 44266
(330) 296-2892
Programs: Automobile, Collision Repair
and Refinish

Medina County Career Center
1101 W. Liberty St.
Medina, OH 44256
(330) 725-8461
Programs: Medium/Heavy Truck,
Automobile

**Miami Valley Career
Technology Center**
6800 Hoke Rd.
Clayton, OH 45315
(937) 854-6378
Programs: Collision Repair and Refinish,
Medium/Heavy Truck

**Mid-East Career and Tech.
Center–Buffalo Campus**
57090 Vocational Rd.
Senecaville, OH 43780
(740) 455-3111
www.adultcentereducation.org
Programs: Automobile, Medium/
Heavy Truck

Northwest Career Center
2960 Cranston Dr.
Dublin, OH 43017
(614) 365-5325
Programs: Collision Repair and Refinish

Ohio Technical College
1374 East 51st St.
Cleveland, OH 44103
(216) 881-1700
www.ohiotechnicalcollege.com
Programs: Automobile, Medium/Heavy
Truck, Collision Repair and Refinish

Penta Career Center
30095 Oregon Rd.
Perrysburg, OH 43551
(419) 661-6495
Programs: Collision Repair and Refinish

Pickaway-Ross CTC
895 Crouse Chapel Rd.
Chillicothe, OH 45601
(740) 642-2550
www.pickawayross.com
Programs: Automobile

**Pioneer Career and
Technology Center**
27 Ryan Rd.
Shelby, OH 44875
(419) 347-7744
Programs: Collision Repair and Refinish

Portage Lakes Career Center
4401 Shriver Rd.
Green, OH 44232
(330) 896-8227
Programs: Automobile

**Scarlet Oaks Career
Development Center**
Chrysler CAP
Ford ASSET
GM ASEP
Honda PACT
3254 East Kemper Rd.
Cincinnati, OH 45241
(513) 771-8810
www.greatoaks.com
Programs: Collision Repair and Refinish

Sinclair Community College
444 W. 3rd St.
Dayton, OH 45402
(937) 512-4502
www.sinclair.edu
Programs: Automobile

Southern Hills Career Center
9193 Hamer Rd.
Georgetown, OH 45121
(937) 378-6131
Programs: Automobile

Stark State College of Technology
GM ASEP
Toyota T-Ten
5600 Whipple Avenue NW
North Canton, OH 44720
(330) 494-6170
Programs: Automobile

Tolles Technical Center
7877 State Route 42 S
Plain City, OH 43064
(614) 873-4666
Programs: Automobile, Collision Repair
and Refinish

Tri Star Career Compact
715 E. Wayne St.
Celina, OH 45822
(419) 586-8300
Programs: Automobile

Tri-County Career Center
15676 State Route 691
Nelsonville, OH 45764
(740) 753-3511
Programs: Automobile

Tri-Rivers Career Center
2222 Marion-Mt. Gilead Rd.
Marion, OH 43302
(740) 389-4681
www.tririvers.com
Programs: Automobile

**Trumbull Career and
Technical Center**
528 Educational Hwy.
Warren, OH 44483
www.tctchome.com
Programs: Automobile, Collision Repair
and Refinish

University of Northwestern Ohio
Toyota T-Ten
1441 North Cable Rd.
Lima, OH 45805
(419) 998-3135
www.unoh.edu
Programs: Automobile, Medium/Heavy
Truck, and Alt. Fuels

Upper Valley JVS
8811 Career Dr.
Piqua, OH 45356
(937) 778-1980
Programs: Collision Repair and Refinish

Warren County Career Center
3525 N. State Route 48
Lebanon, OH 45066
(513) 932-5677
www.wccareercenter.com
Programs: Automobile

Washington State
Community College
710 Colegate Dr.
Marietta, OH 45750
(740) 374-8716
Programs: Automobile

Wayne County Career Center
518 West Prospect St.
Smithville, OH 44677
(330) 669-2134
Programs: Collision Repair and Refinish

West Shore CTPD
14100 Franklin Blvd.
Lakewood, OH 44107
(216) 529-4150
www.lakewoodcityschools.org
Programs: Automobile

Oklahoma

Autry Technology Center
1201 W. Willow
Enid, OK 73703
(580) 548-3310
www.autrytech.com
Programs: Medium/Heavy Truck

Byng School
500 S. New Bethel Blvd.
Ada, OK 74820
(580) 436-0791
Programs: Automobile

Caddo-Kiowa Vo-Tech Center
PO Box 190
North VoTech Rd.
Fort Cobb, OK 73038
(405) 643-5511
Programs: Automobile, Collision Repair
and Refinish

Canadian Valley AVTS
6505 East Hwy. 66
El Reno, OK 73036
(405) 262-2629
Programs: Medium/Heavy Truck,
Collision Repair and Refinish

Canadian Valley
Technology Center
1401 Michigan Ave.
Chickasha, OK 73018
(405) 222-7537
Programs: Automobile, Medium/Heavy
Truck, Collision Repair and Refinish

Francis Tuttle Technology Center-
Reno
7301 West Reno Rd.
Oklahoma City, OK 73078
(405) 717-4274
www.francistuttle.com
Programs: Automobile

Gordon Cooper
Technology Center
1 John C. Bruton Blvd.
Shawnee, OK 74804
(405) 273-7493
Programs: Automobile, Medium/Heavy
Truck, Collision Repair and Refinish

Great Plains AVTS
4500 West Lee Blvd.
Lawton, OK 73505
www.gptech.org/courses/ft/
Programs: Medium/Heavy Truck,
Collision Repair and Refinish

High Plains Technology Center
3921 34th St.
Woodward, OK 73801
(580) 571-6173
www.hptc.net
Programs: Automobile, Medium/
Heavy Truck

Indian Capital Technology Center
240 Vo-Tech Dr.
Tahlequah, OK 74465
(918) 456-2594
www.ictctech.com/Bill/Bill.htm
Programs: Automobile, Collision Repair
and Refinish

Jim E. Hamilton Vo-Tech
Skills Center
53468 Mineral Springs Rd.
Hodgen, OK 74939
Programs: Automobile

Kiamichi AVTS
810 Waldron Dr. Durant Campus
Durant, OK 74701
(580) 924-7081
Programs: Automobile

*
13739 SE 202nd Rd.
Talihina, OK 74571
Programs: Automobile

*
107 South 15th
Hugo, OK 74743
(580) 326-6491
Programs: Collision Repair and Refinish

*
1410 Old Military Rd.
Stigler, OK 74462
(918) 967-2801
www.kiamichi_stigler.tec.ok.us
Programs: Automobile

*
1509 S. McKenna
Poteau, OK 74953
(918) 647-4525
Programs: Automobile

Meridian Technology Center
1312 Sangre Rd.
Stillwater, OK 74074
(405) 377-3333
www.meridian-technology.com
Programs: Collision Repair and Refinish

Metro Tech–South Bryant
Campus
4901 South Bryant Ave.
Oklahoma City, OK 73129
(405) 605-2238
Programs: Collision Repair and Refinish

Mid-America Technology Center
PO Box H
I-35 and Hwy. 59 Interchange
Wayne, OK 73095
www.matech.org
Programs: Automobile, Collision Repair
and Refinish

Moore Norman
Technology Center
4701 12th Ave. NW
Norman, OK 73069
(405) 217-8247
Programs: Collision Repair and Refinish

Northeast Technology Center
19901 S. Hwy. 69
Afton, OK 74331
(918) 257-8324
Programs: Automobile, Collision Repair
and Refinish

* South Campus
PO Box 825
Pryor, OK 74362
(918) 825-5555
www.netechcenters.com
Programs: Automobile, Collision Repair
and Refinish

Northwest Technology Center
1801 South 11th St.
Alva, OK 73717
(580) 327-0344
Programs: Automobile, Collision Repair
and Refinish

Oklahoma City
Community College
GM ASEP
7777 South May Ave.
Automotive Technician
    Internship Program (ATIP)
Oklahoma City, OK 73159
(405) 682-1611
Programs: Automobile

Oklahoma State University
Chrysler CAP
GM ASEP
Toyota T-Ten
1801 East 4th St. Pro-Tech
Okmulgee, OK 74447
(918) 293-5390
www.osuokmulgee.edu/
    academics/automotive/
    pro-tech.php
Programs: Automobile, Collision Repair
and Refinish

Pioneer Technology Center
2101 North Ash
Ponca City, OK 74601
(580) 718-4281
Programs: Collision Repair and Refinish

Red River Technology Center
3300 West Bois D'Arc
Duncan, OK 73533
(580) 255-2903
Programs: Collision Repair and Refinish

Southern Oklahoma
Technology Center
2610 Sam Noble Pkwy.
Ardmore, OK 73401
(580) 223-2070
Programs: Medium/Heavy Truck,
Collision Repair and Refinish

Tri County Technology Center
6101 SE Nowata Rd.
Bartlesville, OK 74006
(918) 331-3288
www.tctc.org
Programs: Collision Repair and Refinish

Tulsa Technology Center,
Lemley Campus
3420 South Memorial Dr.
Tulsa, OK 74147
(918) 828-3037
www.tulsatech.com
Programs: Medium/Heavy Truck

Western Technology Center
621 Sooner Drive
PO Box 1469
Burns Flat, OK 73624
(580) 562-3181
www.wtc.tec.ok.us.br_repair.html
Programs: Collision Repair and Refinish

Oregon

Central Oregon
Community College
2600 NW College Way
Ponderosa 2
Bend, OR 97701
(503) 383-7701
Programs: Automobile

Chemeketa Community College
4000 Lancaster Dr. NE
Salem, OR 97309
(503) 399-6521
Programs: Automobile

Lane Community College
4000 E. 30th Ave.
Advanced Technology Division
Eugene, OR 97405
Programs: Automobile

Linn-Benton Community College
6500 Pacific Blvd. SW
Albany, OR 97321
(541) 917-4602
www.linnbenton.edu/auto
Programs: Automobile

Mt. Hood Community College
Chrysler CAP
Ford ASSET
Honda PACT
26000 SE Stark St.

Gresham, OR 97030
(503) 491-7111
www.mhcc.edu/pages/1204.asp
Programs: Automobile

Portland Community College
17705 NW Springville Rd.
Portland, OR 97229
(503) 614-7508
www.11spot.pcc.edu/~Autobod/
Programs: Medium/Heavy Truck,
Collision Repair and Refinish

Portland Community College
GM ASEP
1200 SW 49th Ave.
PO Box 19000
Portland, OR 97280
(503) 977-4173
Programs: Automobile

Rogue Community College
3345 Redwood Hwy.
Grants Pass, OR 97527
Programs: Automobile

Umpqua Community College
Toyota T-Ten
1140 Umpqua College Rd.
Roseburg, OR 97470
(541) 440-4652
www.umpqua.edu
Programs: Automobile

Pennsylvania

Automotive Training Center
114 Pickering Way
Exton, PA 19341
www.autotraining.edu
Programs: Automobile, Collision
Repair and Refinish

Automotive Training Center
@ Warminster
900 Johnsville Blvd.
Warminster, PA 18974
(215) 259-1900
Programs: Automobile, Collision Repair
and Refinish

Bedford County Technical Center
195 Pennknoll Rd.
Everett, PA 15537
(814) 623-2760
www.bedfordctc.org
Programs: Automobile

Berks Career and Tech Center, East Campus
3307 Friedensburg Rd.
Oley, PA 19547
(610) 374-4073
www.berkscareer.com
Programs: Medium/Heavy Truck, Collision Repair and Refinish

Berks Career and Tech Center, West Campus
1057 County Rd.
Leesport, PA 19533
(610) 374-4073
Programs: Automobile, Collision Repair and Refinish

Center for Arts and Tech, Brandywine
1635 East Lincoln Hwy.
Coatesville, PA 19320
(610) 384-1585
Programs: Automobile

Center for Arts and Technology
1580 Charlestown Rd.
Pickering Campus
Phoenixville, PA 19460
(610) 933-8877
www.cciu.org
Programs: Automobile

Clarion County Career Center
447 Career Rd.
Shippenville, PA 16254
(814) 226-4391
www.ccccntr.org
Programs: Automobile

Columbia-Montour AVTS
5050 Sweppenheiser Dr.
Bloomsburg, PA 17815
(570) 784-8040
Programs: Automobile, Collision Repair and Refinish

Community College of Allegheny County
Chrysler CAP
Ford ASSET
1000 McKee Rd.
Oakdale, PA 15071
(412) 269-4905
www.ccac.edu
Programs: Automobile

Community College of Allegheny County
GM ASEP
1000 McKee Rd.
Oakdale, PA 15071
(412) 788-7381
www.ccac.edu
Programs: Automobile

Crawford County AVTS
860 Thurston Rd.
Meadville, PA 16335
(814) 724-6024
Programs: Automobile

Cumberland-Perry AVTS
110 Old Willow Mill Rd.
Mechanicsburg, PA 17055
(717) 697-0354
www.cpauts.org
Programs: Medium/Heavy Truck

Delaware County Community College
85 N. Malin Rd.
Broomall, PA 19008
(610) 328-7714
www.dccc.edu/teched/
Programs: Automobile

Eastern Center for Arts and Technology
3075 Terwood Rd.
Willow Grove, PA 19090
(215) 784-4800
www.eastech.org
Programs: Collision Repair and Refinish

Franklin County CTC
2463 Loop Rd.
Chambersburg, PA 17201
(717) 263-9033
Programs: Automobile

Harrisburg Area Community College
GM ASEP
One HACC Dr.
Harrisburg, PA 17110
(717) 780-2651
www.hacc.edu
Programs: Automobile

Indiana County Technology Center
441 Hamill Rd.
Indiana, PA 15701

(724) 349-6700
www.ictc.ws
Programs: Automobile

Johnson College
3427 North Main Ave.
Scranton, PA 18508
(570) 702-8975
www.johnson.edu
Programs: Automobile

Lancaster County Career and Technology Center
1730 Hans Herr Dr.
PO Box 527
Willow Street, PA 17584
www.lcctc.org
Programs: Automobile, Medium/Heavy Truck, Collision Repair and Refinish

Lehigh Career and Technical Institute
4500 Education Park Dr.
Schnecksville, PA 18078
(610) 799-1396
www.lcti.org
Programs: Collision Repair and Refinish

Lycoming County Career and Tech. Center
293 Cemetery St.
Hughesville, PA 17737
(570) 584-2300
Programs: Automobile

Mercer County Career Center
776 Greenville Rd.
Mercer, PA 16137
(724) 662-3000
www.mccc.onlinecommunity.com
Programs: Automobile, Medium/Heavy Truck, Collision Repair and Refinish

Milton Hershey School
851 Spartan Lane
Hershey, PA 17033
(717) 520-2888
www.mhs-pa.org
Programs: Automobile

Monroe Career and Technical Institute
66 Laurel Lake Dr.
Bartonsville, PA 18321
Programs: Automobile

MTC Red Rock Job Corps
Route 487 N
Lopez, PA 18628
(570) 477-0300
Programs: Automobile

North Montco Technical
Career Center
1265 Sumneytown Pike
Lansdale, PA 19446
(215) 368-1177
Programs: Medium/Heavy Truck,
Collision Repair and Refinish

Northampton County Area
Community College
Chrysler CAP
GM ASEP
3835 Green Pond Rd.
Bethlehem, PA 18020
(610) 861-5327
www.northampton.edu
Programs: Automobile

Northern Tier Career Center
RR 1 Box 157A
Towanda, PA 18848
(570) 265-8111
Programs: Automobile

Parkway West AVTS
7101 Steubenville Pike
Oakdale, PA 15071
(412) 923-1772
www.parkwaywest.org
Programs: Collision Repair and Refinish

Pennsylvania College of
Technology
Ford ASSET
Toyota T-Ten
One College Ave.
Williamsport, PA 17701
(570) 326-3761
www.pct.edu
Programs: Automobile, Medium/Heavy
Truck, Collision Repair and Refinish

Rosedale Technical Institute
215 Beecham Dr., Suite 2
Pittsburgh, PA 15205
(412) 521-6200
www.rosedaletech.org
Programs: Automobile, Medium/
Heavy Truck

Schuylkill County AVTS,
South Center
15 Maple Ave.
Mar-Lin, PA 17951
(717) 874-1034
Programs: Automobile

Schuylkill Training and
Tech Center
101 Technology Dr.
Frackville, PA 17931
(570) 874-1034
www.stcenters.org
Programs: Automobile

Somerset County
Technology Center
281 Technology Dr.
Somerset, PA 15501
(814) 443-3651
Programs: Automobile

Steel Center Vo-Tech School
565 Lewis Run Rd.
Jefferson Hills, PA 15025
(412) 469-3200
www.scavts.tec.pa.us
Programs: Collision Repair and Refinish

Sun Area Career and
Technology Center
815 E. Market St.
21st Century Dr.
New Berlin, PA 17855
(570) 966-1031
Programs: Automobile, Medium/Heavy
Truck

Universal Technical Institute
750 Pennsylvania Dr.
Exton, PA 19341
Programs: Automobile, Medium/
Heavy Truck

Upper Bucks County AVTS
3115 Ridge Rd.
Perkasie, PA 18944
(215) 795-2911
Programs: Automobile, Collision Repair
and Refinish

Western Area CTC
688 Western Ave.
Canonsburg, PA 15317
(724) 746-2890
www.wactc.net
Programs: Collision Repair and Refinish

Western Center for
Technical Studies
77 Gratersford Rd.
Limerick, PA 19468
(610) 489-7272
www.westerncenter.org
Programs: Collision Repair and Refinish

WyoTech–Blairsville
500 Innovation Dr.
Blairsville, PA 15717
www.wyotech.com
Programs: Automobile, Collision Repair
and Refinish

York County School of
Technology
2179 S. Queen St.
York, PA 17402
(717) 741-0820
www.ycstech.org
Programs: Collision Repair and Refinish

York County School of
Technology
2179 S. Queen St.
York, PA 17402
(717) 741-2143
www.ycstech.org
Programs: Automobile

Rhode Island

Motoring Technical
Training Institute
54 Water St.
East Providence, RI 02914
(401) 494-4840
Programs: Automobile

New England Institute of
Technology
2500 Post Rd.
Warwick, RI 02886
(401) 739-5000
www.neit.edu
Programs: Automobile, Collision Repair
and Refinish

South Carolina

Anderson District 1 and 2
Career and Tech
702 Belton Highway
Williamston, SC 29697
(864) 847-4121
Programs: Automobile

Applied Technology Education Campus
874 Vocational Lane
Camden, SC 29020
(803) 425-8982
Programs: Automobile

Barnwell County Career Center
5214 Reynolds Rd.
Blackville, SC 29817
(803) 259-5512
Programs: Automobile

BJ Skelton Career Center
1400 Griffin Mill Rd.
Easley, SC 29640
(864) 855-8195
Programs: Automobile

Central Carolina Tech College
506 N. Guignard Dr.
Sumter, SC 29150
(803) 778-6674
www.cctech.edu
Programs: Automobile

Cope Area Career Center
6052 Slab Landing Rd.
Cope, SC 29038
(803) 534-7661
www.Orangeburg4.com
Programs: Automobile

Fairfield Career and Technology Center
1451 US Hwy. 321 N
Winnsboro, SC 29180
(803) 635-5506
Programs: Automobile

Florence-Darlington Technical College
2715 W. Lucas St., Hwy. 52
Florence, SC 29501
(843) 661-8188
www.fdtc.edu
Programs: Automobile

Greenville Technical College
506 S. Pleasantburg Dr.
Greenville, SC 29606
(864) 250-8451
www.greenvilletech.com/
academics/index.html
Programs: Automobile

Lee County Career and Technology Center

310 Roland St.
Bishopville, SC 29010
Programs: Automobile

Orangeburg Calhoun Technical College
3250 St. Matthews Rd.
Orangeburg, SC 29118
(803) 535-1304
www.octech.edu
Programs: Automobile

Piedmont Technical College
620 Emerald Road
Bldg. M, Rec. Dept.
Greenwood, SC 29646
(864) 941-8468
www.ptc.edu/department
_automotive/
Programs: Automobile

Spartanburg Community College
Ford ASSET
PO Box 4386 Business I-85
New Cut Rd.
Spartanburg, SC 29305
(864) 592-4727
www.stcsc.edu/FordAuto/
Programs: Automobile

Technology Center
3720 Magnolia St.
Orangeburg, SC 29118
(803) 536-4473
Programs: Collision Repair and Refinish

Trident Technical College
7000 Rivers Ave.
N. Charleston, SC 29406
www.tridenttech.org/automotive
Programs: Automobile

York Technical College
452 S. Anderson Rd.
Hwy. 21 By-Pass
Rock Hill, SC 29730
(803) 981-7073
www.yorktech.com/automotive
Programs: Automobile

South Dakota

Lake Area Technical Institute
230-11th St. NE
Watertown, SD 57201
www.lati.tec.sd.us/diesel2.htm
Programs: Medium/Heavy Truck

Southeast Technical Institute
2320 North Career Ave.
Sioux Falls, SD 57107
(605) 367-4888
www.southeasttech.edu
Programs: Automobile

Southeast Technical Institute
2320 North Career Ave.
Sioux Falls, SD 57107
(605) 367-7676
www.Southeasttech.com
Programs: Collision Repair and Refinish

Western Dakota Tech. School
800 Mickelson Dr.
Rapid City, SD 57703
(605) 718-2922
Programs: Automobile

Tennessee

Chattanooga State Technical Community College
4501 Amnicola Hwy.
Chattanooga, TN 37406
(423) 697-4780
www.Chattanoogastate.edu
Programs: Automobile, Medium/Heavy Truck, Collision Repair and Refinish

Greeneville County Center for Technology
1121 Hal Henard Rd.
Greeneville, TN 37743
Contact: James Wilds, (423) 639-0171
www.gcschools.net
Programs: Automobile

Nashville Auto-Diesel College
1524 Gallatin Rd.
Nashville, TN 37206
www.nadcedu.com
Programs: Automobile, Medium/Heavy Truck,Collision Repair and Refinish

Southwest Tennessee Community College
GM ASEP
5983 Macon Cove
Memphis, TN 38134
(901) 333-4152
Programs: Automobile

Tennessee Tech Center
at Athens
1635 Vo-Tech Dr.
Athens, TN 37371
(423) 744-2814
Programs: Automobile

Tennessee Tech Center
at Clarksville
3789 Guthrie Hwy.
Clarksville, TN 37040
Programs: Automobile

Tennessee Tech Center
at Covington
1600 Hwy. 51 S
Covington, TN 38019
(901) 475-2526
Programs: Automobile
Certification Expiration: 9/2009

Tennessee Tech Center
at Crossville
910 Miller Ave.
Crossville, TN 38555
(931) 484-7502
www.ttcc.edu
Programs: Automobile, Collision
Repair and Refinish

Tennessee Tech Center
at Dickson
740 Hwy. 46 S
Dickson, TN 37055
(615) 441-6220
www.ttcdickson.edu
Programs: Automobile

Tennessee Tech Center
at Harriman
1745 Harriman Hwy.
PO Box 1109
Harriman, TN 37748
(865) 882-6703
www.harriman.tec.tn.us/
Programs: Automobile, Medium/
Heavy Truck

Tennessee Tech Center
at Hohenwald
813 West Main St.
Hohenwald, TN 38462
(931) 796-5351
www.hohenwald.tec.tn.us
Programs: Automobile

Tennessee Tech Center
at Jacksboro
PO Box 419
Jacksboro, TN 37757
(423) 566-9629
www.ttcjacksboro.edu
Programs: Automobile

Tennessee Tech Center
at Jackson
2468 Technology Center Dr.
Jackson, TN 38301
(901) 424-0691
www.ttcjackson.edu
Programs: Automobile, Collision Repair
and Refinish

Tennessee Tech Center
at Knoxville
1100 Liberty St.
Knoxville, TN 37919
(865) 546-5567
www.knoxville.tec.tn.us
Programs: Automobile, Medium/Heavy
Truck, Collision Repair and Refinish

Tennessee Tech Center
at Livingston
740 High Tech Dr.
Livingston, TN 38570
(931) 403-3106
www.ttclivingston.edu
Programs: Automobile

Tennessee Tech Center
at McKenzie
16940 Highland Dr.
McKenzie, TN 38201
(731) 352-5364
Programs: Automobile

Tennessee Tech Center
at McMinnville
241 Vo-Tech Dr.
McMinnville, TN 37110
(931) 473-5587
Programs: Automobile

Tennessee Tech Center
at Memphis
550 Alabama Ave.
Memphis, TN 38105
www.memphis.tec.tn.us
Programs: Automobile

Tennessee Tech Center
at Morristown
821 West Louise Ave.
Morristown, TN 37813
(423) 586-5771
www.morristown.tec.tn.us
Programs: Automobile, Collision Repair
and Refinish

Tennessee Tech Center
at Murfreesboro
1303 Old Fort Pkwy.
Murfreesboro, TN 37129
(615) 898-8010
www.murfreesboro.tec.tn.us
Programs: Automobile

Tennessee Tech Center
at Nashville
GM ASEP
100 White Bridge Rd.
Nashville, TN 37209
(615) 425-5580
Programs: Automobile

Tennessee Tech Center at Paris
312 South Wilson St.
Paris, TN 38242
(731) 644-7365
www.paris.tec.tn.us
Programs: Collision Repair and Refinish

Tennessee Tech Center
at Shelbyville
1405 Madison St.
Shelbyville, TN 37160
(931) 685-5013
www.ttcshelbyville.edu
Programs: Collision Repair and Refinish

Tennessee Tech Center
at Whiteville
1685 Highway 64
Whiteville, TN 38075
(731) 254-8521
www.ttcwhiteville.edu
Programs: Automobile

Texas

Advanced Technology Center
3201 Ave. Q
Lubbock, TX 79411
(806) 766-1354
www.lubbockisd.org/atc
Programs: Collision Repair and Refinish

**Amarillo Area Center for
Advanced Learning**
1050 N. Forest St.
Amarillo, TX 79106
(806) 326-2800
www.amaisd.org/aacal/
  specialties.html
Programs: Automobile

Austin Community College
1020 Grove Blvd.
Riverside Campus Bldg. B
Austin, TX 78741
(512) 223-6099
www.austincc.edu
Programs: Automobile

Birdville Career Center
6010 Walker St.
Haltom City, TX 76117
(817) 547-5700
Programs: Automobile

Brookhaven College
GM ASEP
Ford ASSET
3939 Valley View Lane
Farmers Branch, TX 75244
(972) 860-4189
Programs: Automobile

**Capitol City Trade and
Technical School**
205 East Riverside Dr.
Austin, TX 78704
Programs: Automobile

Del Mar College
4101 Old Brownsville Rd.
Corpus Christi, TX 78404
Programs: Automobile

Eastfield College
3737 Motley Dr.
Mesquite, TX 75150
(972) 860-7128
www.efc.dcccd.edu
Programs: Automobile, Collision
Repair and Refinish

Gary Job Corps Center
2800 Airport Highway 21 East
  Bldg. 10, 302 Receiving Dept.
San Marcos, TX 78666
(512) 396-6718
Programs: Automobile

Houston Community College
4638 Airline Dr.
Houston, TX 77022
(713) 718-8100
www.hccs.cc.tx.us/necollege/
  AutoTech/INDEX.htm
Programs: Automobile

Hurst Euless Bedford ISD
1849 Central Dr., Bldg. E
Bedford, TX 76022
(817) 354-3541
www.hebisd.edu
Programs: Automobile, Collision Repair
and Refinish

**James Ratteree Career
Development Center**
2121 MacArthur Blvd.
Irving, TX 75060
(972) 313-4811
Programs: Collision Repair and Refinish

**Joe Calvillo Career and
Technology Education Complex**
3601 North Mile 5-1/2 West
Weslaco, TX 78596
www.wisd.us
Programs: Automobile

Kilgore College
1100 Broadway
Kilgore, TX 75662
(903) 983-8152
www.kilgore.edu
Programs: Automobile, Collision
Repair and Refinish

Lamar State College, Port Arthur
1500 Procter St.
Port Arthur, TX 77640
(409) 984-6422
Programs: Automobile

Laredo Community College
5500 South Zapata Highway
Laredo, TX 78046
(956) 721-5172
www.laredo.edu
Programs: Automobile

Lincoln Technical Institute
2915 Alouette Dr.
Grand Prairie, TX 75052
(972) 660-5701
www.lincolntech.com
Programs: Automobile, Medium/
Heavy Truck

Midland College
3200 W. Cuthbert
Midland, TX 79705
(432) 681-6344
Programs: Automobile

Miller Career and Tech Center
1734 Katyland Dr.
Katy, TX 77493
(281) 237-6337
Programs: Automobile

San Jacinto College
8060 Spencer Highway
Pasadena, TX 77505
(281) 476-1865
Programs: Automobile

San Jacinto College
GM ASEP
Ford ASSET
Honda PACT
Toyota T-Ten
8060 Spencer Highway
PO Box 2008
Pasadena, TX 77501
(281) 476-1865
www.sanjac.edu/autotech
Programs: Automobile

South Plains College, Levelland
1401 College Ave., Box 87
Levelland, TX 79336
(806) 894-9611
www.southplainscollege.edu/ast
Programs: Automobile

South Texas College
GM ASEP
3700 W. Military Hwy.
McAllen, TX 78503
(956) 872-2706
www.southtexascollege.edu/
  technology/auto.html
Programs: Automobile

St. Philip's College
GM ASEP
1801 Martin Luther King Dr.
San Antonio, TX 78203
(210) 531-3575
www.accd.edu/spc/auto
Programs: Automobile

Stuart Career Center
300 Y.M.C.A. Dr.
Baytown, TX 77521
Programs: Automobile

Texas State Technical College
300 Homer K. Taylor Dr.
Sweetwater, TX 79556
(325) 235-8209
Programs: Automobile

Texas State Technical College
Toyota T-Ten
3801 Campus Dr.
Waco, TX 76705
(254) 867-4855
www.waco.tstc.edu.aut
Programs: Automobile, Medium/
Heavy Truck

Texas State Technical College
200 Bolling Dr.
Waco, TX 76705
(254) 867-4854
www.waco.tstc.edu
Programs: Collision Repair and Refinish

Texas State Technical College
1902 North Loop 499
Central Receiving
Harlingen, TX 78550
(956) 364-4659
www.harlingen.tstc.edu
Programs: Automobile, Collision
Repair and Refinish

Tyler Junior College
1530 SSW Loop 323
Tyler, TX 75701
(903) 510-2153
www.tjc.edu
Programs: Automobile

Universal Technical Institute
721 Lockhaven Dr.
Houston, TX 77071
(602) 216-7613
Programs: Automobile, Medium/Heavy
Truck, Collision Repair and Refinish

Western Technical College
9624 Plaza Cir.
El Paso, TX 79927
(915) 760-8109
www.wtc-ep.edu/
Programs: Automobile

Utah

Bridgerland Applied
Technology Center
1301 North 600 West
Logan, UT 84321
(435) 753-6780
www.bridgerlandatc.org
Programs: Automobile, Collision Repair
and Refinish

College of Eastern Utah
451 East 400 North
Price, UT 84501
(435) 613-5221
Programs: Automobile

Dixie State College
225 South 700 East
St. George, UT 84770
(435) 652-7858
Programs: Automobile

Salt Lake Community College
9750 South 300 West
Sandy, UT 84070
(801) 957-4144
www.slcc.edu
Programs: Automobile

Salt Lake/Tooele ATC
1655 East 3300 South
Salt Lake City, UT 84106
(801) 493-8726
www.sltatc.org
Programs: Automobile

Snow College-Ephraim
150 East College Ave.
PO Box 1036
Ephraim, UT 84627
Programs: Automobile

Snow College-Richfield Campus
800 West 200 South
Richfield, UT 84701
(435) 893-2215
www.svatc.tec.ut.us/SVATC/PRO
GRAMS/Auottec1.htm
Programs: Automobile

UAW-LETC
20 West 1700 South
Clearfield, UT 84016
(801) 416-4437
www.uaw-letc.com
Programs: Medium/Heavy Truck, Automobile, Collision Repair and Refinish

Utah Valley State College
800 W. University Blvd.
Orem, UT 84058
(801) 863-7126
Programs: Automobile

Weber State University
Chrysler CAP
GM ASEP
Honda PACT
Toyota T-Ten
1504 University Cir.
Ogden, UT 84408
(801) 626-7183
www.weber.edu/automotive
Programs: Automobile

Vermont

Cold Hollow Career Center
184 Missisquoi St.
Enosburg Falls, VT 05450
(802) 933-4003
Programs: Automobile

North Country Career Center
209 Veterans Avenue
PO Box 705
Newport, VT 05855
(802) 334-7921
www.ncuhs.org
Programs: Automobile

Southwest Vermont
Regional Technical
321 Park St.
Bennington, VT 05201
(802) 447-0220
Programs: Automobile

Stafford Technical Center
8 Stratton Rd.
Rutland, VT 05701
(802) 770-1033
www.staffordonline.org
Programs: Automobile

Virginia

Advanced Technology Institute
5700 Southern Blvd.
Virginia Beach, VA 23462
(757) 490-1241
www.auto.edu
Programs: Automobile

Arlington Career Center
816 S. Walter Reed Dr.
Arlington, VA 22204
(703) 228-5800
Programs: Collision Repair and Refinish

Blue Ridge Community College
1 College Lane
Weyers Cave, VA 24486
(540) 234-9261
www.brcc.edu/auto
Programs: Automobile

**Botetourt Technical
Education Center**
253 Poor Farm Rd.
Fincastle, VA 24090
(540) 473-8216
Programs: Collision Repair and Refinish
Certification Expiration: 7/2009

Danville Community College
1008 South Main St.
Danville, VA 24541
(434) 797-8521
Programs: Automobile

Dickenson County Career Center
Route 1 Box 325
Clinchco, VA 24226
(276) 835-9384
Programs: Automobile, Collision Repair
and Refinish

Edison Academy
5801 Franconia Rd.
Alexandria, VA 22310
(703) 924-8111
www.fcps.edu/edisonacademy
Programs: Automobile

Germanna Community College
2130 Germanna Hwy.
Locust Grove, VA 22580
(540) 423-9841
Programs: Automobile

Giles County Technology Center
1827 Wenonah Ave
Pearisburg, VA 24134
(540) 921-1166
Programs: Automobile

Marshall Academy
7731 Leesburg Pike
Falls Church, VA 22043
www.fcps.edu/marshallacademy
Programs: Automobile

**Norfolk Technical and
Vocational Center**
1330 North Military Hwy.
Norfolk, VA 23502
(757) 441-5625
Programs: Collision Repair and Refinish

**Northern Virginia
Community College**
GM ASEP
3001 N. Beauregard St.
Alexandria, VA 22311
(703) 845-6523
www.nvcc.edu
Programs: Automobile

**Northern Virginia
Community College**
6901 Sudley Road
Manassas Campus
Manassas, VA 20109
(703) 257-6678
www.nvcc.edu/manassas/auto/
     index.htm
Programs: Automobile

Richmond Technical Center
2020 Westwood Ave.
Richmond, VA 23230
(804) 780-6237
Programs: Collision Repair and Refinish

Rowanty Technical Center
20000 Rowanty Rd.
Carson, VA 23830
(434) 246-5741
www.rowanty.com
Programs: Automobile

**Russell County Career and
Tech Center**
Box 849
Lebanon, VA 24266
(276) 889-6550
Programs: Automobile

**Southside, VA
Community College**
1041 West 10th St., Pickett
     Park
Blackstone, VA 23824
(434) 292-1608
www.southside.edu/classes/
     diesel
Programs: Medium/Heavy Truck

**Spotsylvania Career and
Technical Center**
6713 Smith Station Rd.
Spotsylvania, VA 22553
(540) 898-2655
Programs: Automobile

**Thomas Nelson
Community College**
99 Thomas Nelson Dr.
Hampton, VA 23670
(757) 825-2700
www.tncc.edu
Programs: Automobile

Tidewater Community College
Chrysler CAP
Toyota T-Ten
1428 Cedar Rd.
Chesapeake Campus
Chesapeake, VA 23322
(757) 822-5196
www.tcc.edu
Programs: Automobile

Tidewater Tech
5301 E. Princess Anne Rd.
Norfolk, VA 53502
(757) 628-3300
www.tidewatertechtrades.edu
Programs: Automobile

**Virginia Beach Tech. and
Career Center**
2925 North Landing Rd.
Virginia Beach, VA 23456
(757) 427-5300
www.vbschools.com
Programs: Collision Repair and Refinish

**William N. Neff Center for
Science and Technology**
255 Stanley St.
Abingdon, VA 24210
(276) 628-1870
Programs: Automobile, Collision Repair
and Refinish

Washington

Bates Technical College
2201 South 78th St.
Tacoma, WA 98409
(253) 680-7469
www.bates.ctc.edu
Programs: Automobile

Bellingham Technical College
3028 Lindbergh Ave.
Bellingham, WA 98225
(360) 752-7404
www.btc.ctc.edu
Programs: Medium/Heavy Truck,
Automobile

Centralia College
600 West Locust St.
Centralia, WA 98531
(360) 736-9391
www.centralia.ctc.edu
Programs: Medium/Heavy Truck

Clark College
Toyota T-Ten
1933 Fort Vancouver Way
Vancouver, WA 98663
(360) 992-2235
www.clark.edu
Programs: Automobile

Clark County Skills Center
12200 NE 28th St.
Vancouver, WA 98682
(360) 604-1050
www.cc-sc.com
Programs: Medium/Heavy Truck

Columbia Basin College
2600 North 20th Ave.
Pasco, WA 99301
(509) 547-0511
www.columbiabasin.edu/home/
    index.asp?page=760
Programs: Automobile

Green River Community College
12401 SE 320th St.
Auburn, WA 98092
(253) 833-9111
www.instruction.greenriver
    .edu/autobody
Programs: Collision Repair and Refinish

**Lake Washington
Technical College**
11605 132nd Avenue NE
Kirkland, WA 98034
Programs: Automobile

Lower Columbia College
1600 Maple St.
Longview, WA 98632
(360) 442-2725
www.lowercolumbia.edu
Programs: Automobile

Olympic College
1600 Chester Ave.
Bremerton, WA 98337
(360) 475-7340
Programs: Automobile

Perry Technical Institute
2011 West Washington Ave.
Yakima, WA 98903
Programs: Automobile

Renton Technical College
Ford ASSET
3000 NE 4th St.
Renton, WA 98056
(425) 235-2489
www.rtc.edu
Programs: Automobile, Collision Repair
and Refinish

Shoreline Community College
Chrysler CAP
GM ASEP
16101 Greenwood Avenue N
Seattle, WA 98133
(206) 546-4573
www.shoreline.edu/auto.html
Programs: Automobile

Shoreline Community College
Honda PACT
Toyota T-TEN
16101 Greenwood Avenue N
Seattle, WA 98133
(206) 546-4101
www.shoreline.edu/auto.html
Programs: Automobile

Skagit Valley College
2405 East College Way
Mount Vernon, WA 98273
(360) 416-7600
Programs: Automobile

**South Seattle Community
College**
6000 16th Ave. SW
Seattle, WA 98106
(206) 768-6832
www.sccd.ctc.edu/south/
    programs/autocoll.htm
Programs: Collision Repair and Refinish

Spokane Community College
Toyota T-Ten
1810 N. Greene St., MS 2180
Spokane, WA 99217

(509) 533-7100
www.scc.spokane.edu/
    automotive
Programs: Automobile

Walla Walla Community College
500 Tausick Way
Walla Walla, WA 99362
(509) 527-4569
Programs: Automobile, Medium/Heavy
Truck, Collision Repair and Refinish

Wenatchee Valley College
1300 Fifth St.
Wenatchee, WA 98801
(509) 682-6631
www.wvc.edu/directory/
    departments/autotech
Programs: Automobile

**West Sound Technical Skills
Center–General Service Tech**
101 National Avenue N
Bremerton, WA 98312
(360) 478-6948
www.wstsc.com
Programs: Automobile

West Virginia

**Academy of Careers and
Technology**
390 Stanaford Rd.
Beckley, WV 25801
(304) 256-4615
www.collision.wvact.net
Programs: Collision Repair and Refinish

**Carver Career and Technical
Education Center**
4799 Midland Dr.
Charleston, WV 25306
(304) 348-1965
Programs: Automobile, Collision Repair
and Refinish

Fred W. Eberle Technical Center
Route 5, Box 2
Buckhannon, WV 26201
(304) 472-1259
Programs: Medium/Heavy Truck

**Hampshire County Career
Training Center**
HC 63, Box 1980
Romney, WV 26757
Programs: Automobile

James Rumsey Technical
Institute
3274 Hedgesville Rd
Martinsburg, WV 25401
(304) 754-7925
Programs: Automobile

John D. Rockefeller IV
Career Center
95 Rockyside Rd.
New Cumberland, WV 26047
(304) 564-3337
www.jdrcc.hanc.tec.wv.us
Programs: Collision Repair and Refinish

Mercer County Technical
Education Center
1397 Stafford Dr.
Princeton, WV 24740
(304) 425-9551
Programs: Automobile

Monongalia County Technical
Education Center
1000 Mississippi St.
Morgantown, WV 26501
(304) 291-9240
Programs: Automobile

Nicholas County Career and
Technical Center
HC 59, Box 311, Milam Rd.
Craigsville, WV 26205
(304) 742-5416
Programs: Automobile

PRT Vocational Technical Center
PO Box 29, Route 2,
   Harmony Acres
St. Marys, WV 26170
(304) 684-2464
Programs: Automobile

Randolph County Vo-Tech Center
200 Kennedy Dr.
Elkins, WV 26241
(304) 636-9195
Programs: Collision Repair and Refinish

South Branch Vo-Tech Center
401 Pierpont St.
Petersburg, WV 26847
(304) 257-1331
Programs: Automobile

Tucker County Career Center
Route 3, Box 152
Hambleton, WV 26269

(304) 478-3111
Programs: Collision Repair and Refinish

United Technical Center
Route 3, Box 43-C
Clarksburg, WV 26301
(304) 624-3280
www.wvonline.com/utc
Programs: Automobile

Wyoming County Career
and Technical Center
HCR 72, Box 200
Pineville, WV 24874
(304) 732-8050
www.wcvtc.wyom.tec.wv.us
Programs: Medium/Heavy Truck

Wisconsin

Blackhawk Technical College
1740 Hwy. 14 W
Janesville, WI 53545
(608) 743-4470
Programs: Automobile

Chippewa Valley
Technical College
620 W. Clairemont Ave.
Eau Claire, WI 54701
(715) 855-7539
Programs: Automobile, Medium/Heavy
Truck, Collision Repair and Refinish

Fox Valley Technical College
GM ASEP
1825 N. Bluemount Dr.
Appleton, WI 54912
(920) 735-5750
www.fvtc.edu/tp2.asp?ID
   =Technical+Diplomas&pix=008
Programs: Automobile, Medium/Heavy
Truck, Collision Repair and Refinish

Gateway Technical College
4940 88th Ave.
Kenosha, WI 53144
(262) 564-3924
www.gtc.edu/pages/display.asp
   ?campus=AVIA&display
   =aviaweb
Programs: Automobile

Lakeshore Technical College
1290 North Ave.
Cleveland, WI 53015
(920) 693-1252

www.gotoltc.edu
Programs: Automobile, Collision Repair
and Refinish

Madison Area Technical College
3550 Anderson St.
Madison, WI 53704
(608) 246-6823
www.madison.tec.wi.us/matc/
   offerings/programs/pd/auto
   motive/default2.shtm
Programs: Automobile

Madison Area Technical College
3550 Anderson St.
Madison, WI 53704
(608) 246-6829
www.madison.tec.wi.us/matc/
   offerings/programs/pd/pd
   324121.shtm
Programs: AutomobileMedium/
Heavy Truck

Mid-State Technical College
500 32nd St. N
Wisconsin Rapids, WI 54494
Programs: Automobile

Milwaukee Area
Technical College
GM ASEP
Ford ASSET
6665 South Howell Ave.
Oak Creek, WI 53154
(414) 571-4773
www.matc.edu
Programs: Automobile

Moraine Park Technical
College District
235 North National Ave.
Fond du Lac, WI 54936
Programs: Automobile

Nicolet Area Technical College
PO Box 518, Co. Hwy. G
Rhinelander, WI 54501
Programs: Automobile

Northcentral Technical College
1000 West Campus Dr.
Wausau, WI 54401
(715) 675-3331
www.ntc.edu
Programs: Automobile

Northeast Wisconsin
Technical College
2740 West Mason St.
Green Bay, WI 54307
(920) 498-5664
www.nwtconline.com/
   Programs/AutoBody.htm
Programs: Automobile, Medium/Heavy
Truck, Collision Repair and Refinish

Southwest Wisconsin
Technical College
1800 Bronson Blvd.
Fennimore, WI 53809
(608) 822-2729
www.swtc.edu
Programs: Automobile

Waukesha County
Technical College
GM ASEP
2110 B. Peawaukee Rd.
Waukesha, WI 53188
(262) 691-5514
www.wctc.edu
Programs: Collision Repair and
Refinish

Waukesha County
Technical College
GM ASEP
Toyota T-Ten
800 Main St.
Pewaukee, WI 53072
(262) 691-5514
www.wctc.edu
Programs: Automobile

Western Technical College
304 Sixth Street N (C14)
   Industrial Technologies Division
La Crosse, WI 54602
www.westerntc.edu
Programs: Automobile

Wisconsin Indian Head
Technical College
600 North 21st St.
Superior, WI 54880
(715) 394-6677
Programs: Automobile
Certification Expiration: 5/2011

WITC Rice Lake
1900 College Dr.
Rice Lake, WI 54868
(715) 234-7082
Programs: Automobile

Wyoming

Laramie County
Community College
1400 East College Dr.
Cheyenne, WY 82007
(307) 778-5222
www.lccc.wy.edu
Programs: Automobile, Medium/
Heavy Truck

Western Wyoming
Community College
2500 College Dr. #444
Rock Springs, WY 82902
www.wwcc.cc.wy.us/
   xautomotive/
Programs: Automobile

WyoTech
4373 North 3rd St.
Laramie, WY 82072
(307) 742-3776
www.wyotech.com
Programs: Automobile, Medium/Heavy
Truck, Collision Repair and Refinish

Carpentry

I t is possible to get into carpentry through informal apprenticeships and on-the-job training, but formal training will improve your job prospects. The following is a list of training centers that offer carpentry certification and are accredited by the National Center for Construction Education and Research (NCCER). NCCER is an education foundation that develops highly regarded standardized craft training programs. The Associated Builders and Contractors (ABC), which has chapters throughout the country, is another resource and network for finding possible training opportunities.

Alabama

Construction Education Foundation of Alabama
6700 Oporto-Madrid Blvd.
Birmingham, AL 35206
(205) 956-0146
www.cefalabama.org

North Alabama Craft Training Foundation
152 Hollington Dr.
Huntsville, AL 35811
(256) 851-1566

Alaska

ABC of Alaska Inc.
360 West Benson Blvd.,
Suite 200
(907) 565-5600
www.abcalaska.org

Associated General Contractors of Alaska
8005 Schoon St.
Anchorage, AK 99518
(907) 561-5354
www.agcak.org

Council of Athabascan Tribal Governments
Yukon Flats Center-Fort Yukon
Fort Yukon, AK 99740
(907) 662-3612
www.catg.org

Northern Industrial Training LLC
6177 East Mountain Heather Way
Palmer, AK 99645-9505
(907) 557-6400
www.nitalaska.com

Vocational Training and Resource Center
3239 Hospital Dr.
Juneau, AK 99801-0000
(907) 463-7130
www.ccthita-vtrc.org

Arkansas

N/A

Arizona

Arizona Builders Alliance
1825 West Adams
Phoenix, AZ 85007
(602) 274-8222
www.azbuilders.org

Arizona Public Service
1611 South Main St.
Snowflake, AZ 85937
(928) 536-6232
www.aps.com

California

Calexico Community Action Council
2151 Rockwood Ave., Ste. 166
Calexico, CA 92231
(760) 357-6464
www.ccac-vtc.org

Center for Seabees and Facilities Engineering
3502 Goodspeed St., Ste. 1
Naval Base Ventura County, CA 93041
(805) 982-3615
www.npdc.navy.mil/csfe

Shasta Builder's Exchange Community Fund
2985 Innsbruck Dr.
Redding, CA 96003
(530) 222-1917
www.shastabe.com

Colorado

ABC Western Colorado Chapter
2754 Compass Dr., Ste. 305
Grand Junction, CO 81506
(970) 243-7950
www.wcoabc.org

Construction Industry Training Council of Colorado Inc.
646 Mariposa St.
Denver, CO 80204
(303) 893-1500

T and D Services
1143 Michael Cir.
Meeker, CO 81641
(970) 260-3415

Connecticut

Construction Education Center Inc.
2138 Silas Deane Hwy.,
Ste. 101
Rocky Hill, CT 06067
(860) 529-5886
www.thinkconstruction.org

Delaware

N/A

District of Columbia

N/A

Florida

ABC Florida Gulf Coast Chapter
2008 North Himes Ave.
Tampa, FL 33607
(813) 879-8064
www.abcflgulf.org

Builders Association of North Central Florida
2217 NW 66th Ct.
Gainesville, FL 32653
(352) 372-5649
www.bancf.com

Covington and Associates Inc.
532 Dr. Mary M. Bethune Blvd.
Daytona Beach, FL 32114
(386) 239-9755

The Southern Company
One Energy Place
Pensacola, FL 32503
(850) 444-6821

Georgia

CEFGA—Construction Education Foundation of Georgia
3585 Lawrenceville Suwanee Rd
Suwanee, GA 30024
(678) 889-4445
www.cefga.org

Hawaii

ABC Hawaii Chapter
80 Sand Island Access Rd.
#119
Honolulu, HI 96819
(808) 845-4887
www.abchawaii.org

Idaho

Construction Education Foundation of Idaho (CEFI) Inc.
1649 West Shoreline Dr.
Boise, ID 83702
(208) 344-2531
www.cefidaho.org

Illinois

Associated Builders and Contractors, Illinois Chapter Inc.
1691 Elmhurst Rd.
Elk Grove Village, IL 60007
(847) 709-2960
www.abcil.org

Choice Construction Services
665 Hillcrest Blvd.
Hoffman Estates, IL 60195
(847) 483-4056
www.ietc-dupageco.com/Choice
  ConstructionSer

Institute for Construction Education
2353 Federal Dr.
Decatur, IL 62526
(217) 877-7523
www.iceschool.org

Indiana

N/A

Iowa

ABC of Iowa
475 Alices Rd., Ste. A
Waukee, IA 50263
(515) 987-3790
www.abciowa.org

Kansas

ABC Heart of America Chapter
6950 Squibb Rd., Ste. 418
Mission, KS 66202
(913) 831-2221
www.abcksmo.org

Kentucky

Kentuckiana ABC
1810 Taylor Ave.
(502) 456-5200 or
  (800) 411-5848
www.kyanaabc.com

Western Kentucky Construction Association–AGC
2201 McCracken Blvd.
Paducah, KY 42001
(270) 744-6261
www.wkca.org

Louisiana

ABC Pelican Chapter
19251 Highland Rd.
Training Center A
Baton Rouge, LA 70809
(225) 752-0088
www.abcpelican.org

Advanced Safety and Training Management Inc.
500 Rue Chavaniac
Lafayette, LA 70508
(337) 839-0053
www.advancedsafetytraining.com

Associated Builders and Contractors–Bayou Chapter
101 Riverbend Dr.
St. Rose, LA 70087
(504) 468-3188
www.abcbayou.org

Maine

N/A

Maryland

ABC Metropolitan Washington
4061 Powder Mill Rd., Ste. 120
Calverton, MD 20705
(301) 595-9711
www.abcmetrowashington.org

Baltimore Metro Chapter ABC
1220-B East Joppa Rd.,
  Ste. 322
Towson, MD 21286
(410) 821-0351
www.abcbaltimore.org

Cumberland Valley Chapter ABC
530 North Locust St.
Hagerstown, MD 21740
(301) 739-1190
www.abccvc.com

Massachusetts

George W. Gould Construction Institute
200 Wheeler Rd.
Burlington, MA 01803
(781) 270-9990
www.gwgci.org

Michigan

ABC Incorporated Saginaw Valley Chapter
4520 East Ashman Rd., Ste. G
Midland, MI 48642
(989) 832-8879
www.abcsvac.org

Associated Builders and Contractors Inc.
Western Michigan Chapter
580 Cascade West Pkwy.
Grand Rapids, MI 49546
(616) 942-9960
www.abcwmc.org

Construction Education Trust
31800 Sherman Ave.
Madison Heights, MI 48071
(248) 298-3600
www.cet-tech.com

Tri-Counties Multi Trade Centers
1745 Hancock
Detroit, MI 48208
(313) 867-9330
www.tcmtc.com

Minnesota

Construction Education Foundation of Minnesota
10193 Crosstown Cir.
Eden Prairie, MN 55344
(952) 941-8693
www.mnabc.com

Mississippi

Mississippi Construction Education Foundation
290 Commerce Park Dr.
Ridgeland, MS 39157
(601) 605-2989
www.mcef.net

Missouri

N/A

Montana

Montana Contractors' Association
1717 11th Ave.
Helena, MT 59601
(406) 442-4162
www.mtagc.org

Nebraska

ABC Nebraska Cornhusker Chapter
2602 Harney St.
Omaha, NE 68131
(402) 344-4258
www.abcnebraska.org

Nevada

Nevada Center for Vocational Education and Research
1227 Kimmerling Rd.
Gardnerville, NV 89460
(775) 265-2818

ABC of Southern Nevada
5070 Arville St., Ste. 4
Las Vegas, NV 89118
(702) 227-0536
www.abclasvegas.org

ABC Sierra Nevada Chapter
240 South Rock Blvd., Ste. 121
Reno, NV 89502
(775) 358-7888
www.abcsierranv.org

New Hampshire

Associated Builders and Contractors of New Hampshire/ Vermont Chapter
58 Chenell Dr.
Concord, NH 03301
(603) 226-4789
www.abcnhvt.org

New Jersey

ABC New Jersey Chapter
720 King George Post Rd.
Fords, NJ 08863
(732) 661-1045
www.abcnjc.org

New Mexico

ABC New Mexico Chapter
3540 Pan American
  Freeway NE
Albuquerque, NM 87107
(505) 830-4222
www.abcnm.org

New Mexico Building Branch, AGC
1615 University Blvd., NE
Albuquerque, NM 87102
(505) 842-1462
www.agc-nm.org

New York

CTC of New York State
6369 Collamer Dr.
East Syracuse, NY 13057
(315) 463-7539
www.abcnys.org

North Carolina

Carolinas AGC Inc.
1100 Euclid Ave.
Charlotte, NC 28203

(704) 372-1450
www.cagc.org

North Dakota

AGC of North Dakota
422 North Second St.
Bismarck, ND 58501
(701) 223-2770
www.agcnd.org

Ohio

ABC Northern Ohio Chapter
9255 Market Pl. W
Broadview Heights, OH 44147
(440) 717-0389
www.nocabc.com

ABC Ohio Valley CEF
33 Greenwood Ln.
Springboro, OH 45066
(937) 704-0111
www.ovabc.org

Building Trades Institute, LLC
459 Orangepoint Dr.
Lewis Center, OH 43035
(740) 548-8091
www.buildingtradesinstitute.com

Construction Craft Academy
9760 Shepard Rd
Macedonia, OH 44056
(800) 442-0067
www.craftacademy.com

Oklahoma

AGC of Oklahoma–Building Chapter
605 NW 13th St., Ste. A
Oklahoma City, OK
  73103-2213
(405) 528-4605
www.agcok.com

AYUDA Assessment, Training, Consulting and OQ LLC
10612 Turkey Run Dr.
Edmond, OK 73025
(405) 844-8684
www.ayudallc.com

Oregon

AGC Oregon Columbia Chapter
8111 NE Holman St.
Portland, OR 97218
(503) 682-3363
www.agc-oregon.org

Pennsylvania

ABC Central, PA Chapter
898 North Eagle Valley Rd.
Milesburg, PA 16853
(814) 353-1999
www.abccentralpa.org

ABC Southeast, PA Chapter
430 West Germantown Pike
East Norriton, PA 19403
(610) 279-6666
www.abcsepa.org

ABC Western Pennsylvania Inc.
3500 Spring Garden Ave.
Pittsburgh, PA 15212
(412) 231-1446
www.abcwpa.org

Associated Builders and Contractors, Eastern PA
1036 North Godfrey St.
Allentown, PA 18109
(610) 821-6869
www.abceastpa.org

Keystone Chapter ABC
135 Shellyland Rd.
Manheim, PA 17545
(717) 653-8106
www.abckeystone.org

Rhode Island

ABContractors Rhode Island Chapter
400 Massasoit Ave., Ste. 108
East Providence, RI 02914
(401) 438-8446
www.abcri.org

South Carolina

N/A

South Dakota

N/A

Tennessee

ABC Mid-Tennessee Chapter
1604 Elm Hill Pike
Nashville, TN 37210
(615) 399-8323
www.abctennessee.com

**AGC of Tennessee–
Tri Cities Branch**
249 Neal Dr.
Blountville, TN 37617
(423) 323-7121
www.tnagc.org/TRI

Construction Education Partnership
Simpson St. and Island Dr.
Kingsport, TN 37660
(423) 578-2710

West Tennessee Chapter of ABC
1995 Nonconnah Blvd.
Memphis, TN 38132
(901) 794-9212
www.wtcabc.org

Texas

ABC of Greater Houston Inc.
3910 Kirby Dr., Ste. 131
Houston, TX 77098
(713) 523-6258
www.abchouston.org

ABC South Texas Chapter
10408 Gulfdale Rd.
San Antonio, TX 78216
(210) 342-1994
www.abcsouthtexas.org

ABC Southeast Texas
2700 North Twin City Hwy.
Nederland, TX 77627
(409) 724-7886
www.abcsetx.org

Central Texas ABC Chapter
3006 Longhorn Blvd., Ste. 104
Austin, TX 78758
(512) 719-5263
www.abccentraltexas.org

The Victor Group
801 High Ridge Dr.
Friendswood, TX 77546
(281) 850-8079
www.thevictorgroup.net

Saulsbury Industries D/B/A Construction Workforce Training Center
5308 Andrews Hwy.
Odessa, TX 79762
(432) 366-7676
www.cwtc-tx.com

Utah

N/A

Vermont

Vermont Construction Careers Council
148 State St.
Montpelier, VT 05602
(802) 223-2374
www.agcvt.org

Virginia

ABC Virginia
14120 Parke Long Ct., Ste. 111
Chantilly, VA 20151
(703) 968-6205
www.abcva.org

Washington

Construction Industry Training Council of Washington
1930-116th Ave. NE, Ste. 201
Bellevue, WA 98004
(425) 454-2482
www.citcwa.org

West Virginia

N/A

Wisconsin

Associated Training Services
Corp–WI
7190 Elder Ln.
Sun Prairie, WI 53590
(608) 837-2851 ext. 119
www.operator-school.com

ABC of Wisconsin Inc.
5330 Wall St.
Madison, WI 53718
(608) 244-6056
www.abcwi.org

Wyoming

Corinthian Colleges
1706 Bill Nye Ave.
Laramie, WY 82070
(307) 742-3530
www.cci.edu

Wyoming Contractors Association AGC
2220 North Bryan Stock Trail
Casper, WY 82601
(307) 237-4400
www.wcagc.org

Union Opportunities with United Brotherhood of Carpenters and Joiners of America

The national carpenters union offers a popular apprenticeship program, which usually lasts four years, and consists of classroom time as well as on-the-job training. You can find additional contact information for the UBC Locals at www.carpenters.org. At least one union office is listed for each state. Because of the sheer number of local offices, we've only listed regional offices for many areas of the country.

Alaska

Alaska Regional Council of
Carpenters 4059
401 Denali St. #100
Anchorage, AK 99501
(907) 274-2722
arcc4059@alaska.net

Alabama

Alabama Carpenters
Regional Council 4001
7970 Crestwood Blvd., Ste. B
Irondale, AL 35210
(205) 951-1569
acrcdm@attglobal.net

Arkansas

Arkansas Regional Council
of Carpenters 4004
1407 South Knoxville Ave.
Russellville, AR 72802
(479) 968-1724
arkregcouncil@cox-internet.com

Arizona

Phoenix Local Union #408
(Arizona)
4547 West McDowell Rd.
Phoenix, AZ 85035
(602) 484-0444
www.azcarpenterslocal408.com

California

South West Regional Council
of Carpenters 4008
533 South Fremont Ave.,
10th Flr.
Los Angeles, CA 90071-1706
(213) 385-1457

Northern California Regional
Council 4140
448 Hegenberger Rd.
Oakland, CA 94621-1418
(510) 568-4788
www.norcalcarpenters.org

Colorado

Denver Local Union #1068
5155 East 39th Ave.
Denver, CO 80207
(303) 355-8774

Connecticut

New London Local Union #1302
171 Thames St.
Groton, CT 06340
(860) 449-0891
hammer@local1302.com
www.local1302.com

Delaware

Wilmington Local Union #626
PO Box 151
New Castle, DE 19720
(302) 328-9439

Florida

Central/North Florida Regional Council 4032
7402 North 56th Street #840
Tampa, FL 33617
(813) 987-2333

South Florida Carpenters Regional Council 4154
295 West 79th Pl.
Hialeah, FL 33014
(305) 557-6100
sfcrc@worldnet.att.net
www.southfloridacarpentersrc.net

Georgia

Southeastern Carpenters Regional Council 4043
3710 Executive Center Dr.,
Ste. A
Augusta, GA 30907
(706) 854-8777

Hawaii

**Honolulu Local Union #745
(Hawaii)**
1311 Houghtailing St.
Honolulu, HI 96817-2412
(808) 847-5761

Iowa

Des Moines Local Union #106
3851 Delaware Ave.
Des Moines, IA 50313
(515) 262-8079

Idaho

Boise Local Union #635
875 West McGregor Ct., Ste. 160
Boise, ID 83705
(208) 336-9243

Illinois

Heartland Regional Council of Carpenters 4274
201 East 3rd St.
Sterling, IL 61081-3611
(815) 626-2177
ottawa@essex1.com
www.heartlandcouncil.org

Chicago and Northeast Illinois District Council 4275
12 East Erie St.
Chicago, IL 60611
(312) 787-3076
www.carpentersunion.org

Mid-Central Ill. District Council 4281
#1 Kalmia Way
Springfield, IL 62702
(217) 744-1831
www.illinoiscarpenters.com

Indiana

Indiana Regional Council of Carpenters 4014
2635 Madison Ave.
Indianapolis, IN 46225
(317) 783-1391

Kansas

Wichita Local Union #201
1215 Carey Ln.
Wichita, KS 67217
(316) 522-8911

Kentucky

Louisville Local Union #1031 (Kentucky)
3934 Dixie Hwy., Ste. #410
Louisville, KY 40216
(502) 447-0420
www.ksdcc.org

Louisiana

Louisiana/Mississippi Carpenters Regional Council 4034
1615 East Judge Perez,
Ste. 502
Chalmette, LA 70043
(504) 276-7171
lmcrc@lmcrc.com
www.lmcrc.com

Maine

Vermont/Maine/New Hampshire Local Union #1996
60 Industrial Dr.
Augusta, ME 04330-9302
(207) 621-8160
ubc1996@midmaine.com
www.home.sprynet.com/~lu1996

Maryland

Mid-Atlantic Regional Council 4067
5701 Silver Hill Rd.
Forestville, MD 20747
(301) 735-6660

Massachusetts

New England Regional Council 4064
803 Summer St., 4th Fl.
South Boston, MA 02127
(617) 268-3400
NERC@necarpenters.org
www.necarpenters.org

Michigan

**Michigan Regional
Council 4085**
3800 Woodward Ave., Ste.
 1200
Detroit, MI 48201
(313) 832-3887
info@hammer9.com
www.hammer9.com

Minnesota

**Lakes and Plains Regional
Council 4020**
700 Olive St
St Paul, MN 55101
(651) 646-7207

Missouri

**Kansas City and Vicinity
District Council 4088**
625 West 39th Street, Ste. 201
Kansas City, MO 64111
(816) 931-3414
www.carpenters-kc.org

**St. Louis Missouri District
Council 4089**
1401 Hampton Ave.
St. Louis, MO 63139-3199
(314) 644-4800
www.carpdc.org

Mississippi

**Louisiana/Mississippi Carpenters
Regional Council 4034**
1615 East Judge Perez,
 Ste. 502
Chalmette, LA 70043
(504) 276-7171
lmcrc@lmcrc.com
www.lmcrc.com

Montana

Butte Local Union #112
PO Box 3412/156 West Granite
Butte, MT 59701
(406) 782-8542
local112@in-tch.com

Nebraska

Omaha Local Union #444
9615 Ida St.
Omaha, NE 68122
(402) 345-3558
carpenters444@earthlink.net

Nevada

**Southwest Regional Council-
Southern Nevada Branch 24008**
501 North Lamb Blvd., 2nd Fl.
Las Vegas, NV 89110
(702) 531-1800
mfurmanswrc@earthlink.net

**Southwest Regional Council–
Northern Nevada Branch 34008**
1150 Terminal Way
Reno, NV 89502
(702) 323-5786

New Hampshire

Portsmouth Local Union #3073
PO Box 2059
Portsmouth, NH 03801
(207) 439-4281

New Jersey

**New Jersey Regional
Council 4018**
91 Fieldcrest Eastern Ave
Edison, NJ 08837
(732) 417-9229
CAP_DIST@msn.com

New Mexico

**Mountain West Regional Council
of Carpenters 4031**
1021 Cardenas Dr. NE
Albuquerque, NM 87110
(505) 256-3396

New York

**New York City and Vicinity
District Council 4112**
395 Hudson St.
New York, NY 10014
(212) 366-7500
info@nycdistrictcouncil.com
www.nycdistrictcouncil.com

**Empire State Regional
Council 4304**
270 Motor Pkwy.
Hauppauge, NY 11788
(631) 952-0808

North Carolina

Morrisville Local Union #2003
412 Redpath Dr.
Garner, NC 27529
(919) 773-0943

North Dakota

Fargo Local Union #1176
3002 1st Ave. N
Fargo, ND 58102-3098
(701) 235-4981
local1176@hotmail.com
www.mncarpenter.org

Ohio

**Ohio and Vicinity Regional
Council of Carpenters 4046**
3615 Chester Ave.
Cleveland, OH 44114
(216) 391-2828
www.ovrcc.com

Oklahoma

Tulsa Local Union #943
5476 South 108th E Ave.
Tulsa, OK 74146-5817
(918) 628-0410
carp943@hotmail.com

Oregon

**Western District Council LPI
Portland 4144**
12788 SE Stark St.
Portland, OR 97233
(503) 228-0235
www.wciw.org

Pennsylvania

Greater Pennsylvania Regional
Council 4025
495 Mansfield Ave.
Pittsburgh, PA 15205
(412) 922-6200
www.greaterpacarpenters.org

Metropolitan Regional Council of
Philadelphia and Vicinity 4148
1803 Spring Garden St.
Philadelphia, PA 19130-3916
(215) 569-1634
www.philacarpenter.org

Rhode Island

Providence Local Union #94
14 Jefferson Park Rd.
Warwick, RI 02888
(401) 467-7070

South Carolina

Columbia Local Union #1778
7420 North Main St.
Columbia, SC 29203
(803) 754-9170
LU1778@bellsouth.net

South Dakota

N/A

Tennessee

Tennessee Carpenters Regional
Council 4036

2544 Elm Hill Pike
Nashville, TN 37214
(615) 884-4484
www.tncarpenters.com

Texas

Texas Carpenters and Millwrights
Reg Council 4161
5364 Fredericksburg Rd., Ste.
 130
San Antonio, TX 78229
(210) 366-4133
TSDCCTEXAS@aol.com

Utah

Salt Lake City Local Union #184
8149 South Welby Park Dr.
West Jordan, UT 84088
(801) 280-0292
local184@msn.com

Vermont

N/A

Virginia

Carpenters East Coast Industrial
Council 4166
PO Box 190
Marion, VA 24354
(276) 783-7065
cecic@adelphia.net
www.cecic.org

Washington

Pacific Northwestern Regional
Council of Carpenters 4240
25120 Pacific Hwy. S, Ste. 200
Kent, WA 98032
(253) 945-8800
www.carpenterspnwrc.org

West Virginia

Charleston Local Union #1207
1812 Garfield Ave.
Parkersburg, WV 26101
(304) 342-4321

Wisconsin

Midwestern Council of Industrial
Workers 4021
404 North Main St. #103
Oshkosh, WI 54901
(920) 426-2700
www.mciw.org

Northern Wisconsin Regional
Council of Carpenters 4183
N2216 Bodde Rd.
Kaukauna, WI 54130-9740
(920) 996-2300
www.NWRCC.ORG

Wyoming

Cheyenne Local Union #469
PO Box 65
Cheyenne, WY 82003
(307) 632-3250

Community Colleges with Carpentry Programs

Alabama

Bishop State
Community College
351 North Broad St.
Mobile, AL 36603
(251) 690-6416
www.bishop.edu

Gadsden State
Community College
1001 George Wallace Dr.
Gadsden, AL 35902
(256) 549-8200
www.gadsdenstate.edu

Trenholm State
Technical College
1225 Air Base Blvd.
Montgomery, AL 36108
(334) 420-4200
www.trenholmtech.cc.al.us

Jefferson Davis
Community College
220 Alco Dr.
Brewton, AL 36426
(251) 867-4832
www.jdcc.edu

J. F. Ingram State
Technical College
5375 Ingram Rd.
Deatsville, AL 36022
(334) 285-5177

John C. Calhoun State
Community College
6250 U.S. Highway 31 N
Tanner, AL 35671
(256) 306-2500
www.calhoun.edu

Lawson State Community
College–Birmingham Campus
3060 Wilson Rd. SW
Birmingham, AL 35221
(205) 925-2515
www.lawsonstate.edu

Northwest Shoals Community
College–Muscle Shoals
800 George Wallace Blvd.
Muscle Shoals, AL 35661
(256) 331-5200
www.nwscc.edu

Reid State Technical College
I-65 and Hwy. 83
Evergreen, AL 36401
(251) 578-1313
www.rstc.cc.al.us

Shelton State
Community College
9500 Old Greensboro Rd.
Tuscaloosa, AL 35405
(205) 391-2347
www.sheltonstate.edu

Alaska

Ilisagvik College
Narl Facility
Barrow, AK 99723
(907) 852-3333
www.ilisagvik.cc

Arkansas

Cossatot Community College
of the University of Arkansas
183 Hwy. 399
De Queen, AR 71832
(870) 584-4471
www.cccua.edu

National Park
Community College
101 College Dr.
Hot Springs, AR 71913
(501) 760-4222
www.npcc.edu

South Arkansas
Community College
300 South West Ave.
El Dorado, AR 71731
(870) 862-8131
www.southark.edu

California

American River College
4700 College Oak Dr.
Sacramento, CA 95841
(916) 484-8011
www.arc.losrios.edu/

Bakersfield College
1801 Panorama Dr.
Bakersfield, CA 93305
(661) 395-4011
www.bakersfieldcollege.edu/

Chabot College
25555 Hesperian Blvd.
Hayward, CA 94545
(510) 723-6600
www.chabotcollege.edu

Fullerton College
321 East Chapman Ave.
Fullerton, CA 92832
(714) 992-7000
www.fullcoll.edu

Hartnell College
156 Homestead Ave.
Salinas, CA 93901
(831) 755-6700
www.hartnell.edu

Laney College
900 Fallon St.
Oakland, CA 94607
(510) 834-5740
www.laney.peralta.edu

Long Beach City College
4901 East Carson St.
Long Beach, CA 90808
(562) 938-4111
www.lbcc.edu

Los Angeles Trade
Technical College
400 West Washington Blvd.
Los Angeles, CA 90015
(213) 763-7000
www.lattc.edu

Palomar College
1140 West Mission
San Marcos, CA 92069
(760) 744-1150
www.palomar.edu

Rio Hondo College
3600 Workman Mill Rd.
Whittier, CA 90601
(562) 692-0921
www.riohondo.edu

Colorado

N/A

Connecticut

N/A

Delaware

N/A

Florida

Brevard Community College
1519 Clearlake Rd.
Cocoa, FL 32922
(321) 632-1111
www.brevardcc.edu

Charlotte Technical Center
18150 Murdock Cir.
Port Charlotte, FL 33948
(941) 255-7500
www.charlottetechcenter.
ccps.k12.fl.us

D. G. Erwin Technical Center
2010 East Hillsborough Ave.
Tampa, FL 33610
(813) 231-1800
www.erwin.edu

First Coast Technical Institute
2980 Collins Ave.
Saint Augustine, FL 32084
(904) 824-4401
www.fcti.org

**Florida Community College
at Jacksonville**
501 West State St.
Jacksonville, FL 32202
(904) 632-3000
www.fccj.edu

George Stone Career Center
2400 Longleaf Dr.
Pensacola, FL 32526
(850) 941-6200
www.georgestonecenter.com

**Hillsborough
Community College**
39 Columbia Dr.
Tampa, FL 33606
(813) 253-7000
www.hccfl.edu

Indian River Community College
3209 Virginia Ave.
Fort Pierce, FL 34981
(772) 462-4722
www.ircc.edu

**Lee County High Tech Center
Central**
3800 Michigan Ave.
Fort Myers, FL 33916
(239) 334-4544
www.hightechcentral.org

Lively Technical Center
500 North Appleyard Dr.
Tallahassee, FL 32304
(850) 487-7555
www.livelytech.com

Manatee Technical Institute
5603 34th St. W
Bradenton, FL 34210
(941) 751-7900
www.manateetechnical
institute.org/

Mid Florida Tech
2900 West Oak Ridge Rd.
Orlando, FL 32809
(407) 855-5880
www.mft.ocps.net

**Okaloosa Applied
Technology Center**
1976 Lewis Turner Blvd.
Fort Walton Beach, FL 32547
(850) 833-3500
www.okaloosa.k12.fl.us/oatc

Palm Beach Community College
4200 Congress Ave.
Lake Worth, FL 33461
(561) 967-7222
www.pbcc.edu/

**Pinellas Technical
Education Center**
901 34th St. S.
Saint Petersburg, FL 33711
(727) 893-2500
www.myptec.org

**Radford M. Locklin
Technical Center**
5330 Berryhill Rd.
Milton, FL 32570
(850) 983-5700
www.santarosa.k12.fl.us/ltc/

Ridge Career Center
7700 State Rd. 544
Winter Haven, FL 33881
(863) 419-3060
www.polk-fl.net/ridge

**Saint Johns River
Community College**
5001 Saint Johns Ave.
Palatka, FL 32177
(386) 312-4200
www.sjrcc.edu

Santa Fe Community College
3000 NW 83rd St.
Gainesville, FL 32606

(352) 395-5000
www.sfcc.edu

**South Florida
Community College**
600 West College Dr.
Avon Park, FL 33825
(863) 453-6661
www.southflorida.edu

Taylor Technical Institute
3233 Hwy. 19 S
Perry, FL 32348
(850) 838-2545
www.taylortech.org

Tom P. Haney Technical Center
3016 Hwy. 77
Panama City, FL 32405
(850) 747-5500
www.bay.k12.fl.us

**Washington-Holmes
Technical Center**
757 Hoyt St.
Chipley, FL 32428
(850) 638-1180
www.whtc.us

Georgia

Albany Technical College
1704 South Slappey Blvd.
Albany, GA 31701
(229) 430-3500
www.albanytech.edu

Altamaha Technical College
1777 West Cherry St.
Jesup, GA 31545
(912) 427-5800
www.altamahatech.edu

Atlanta Technical College
1560 Metropolitan Pkwy. SW
Atlanta, GA 30310
(404) 225-4603
www.atlantatech.org/

Augusta Technical College
3200 Augusta Tech Dr.
Augusta, GA 30906
(706) 771-4000
www.augustatech.edu

Central Georgia
Technical College
3300 Macon Tech Dr.
Macon, GA 31206
(478) 757-3400
www.centralgatech.edu

Chattahoochee Technical College
980 South Cobb Dr.
Marietta, GA 30060
(770) 528-4545
www.chattcollege.com

Columbus Technical College
928 Manchester Expwy.
Columbus, GA 31904
(706) 649-1800
www.columbustech.org

Coosa Valley Technical College
One Maurice Culberson Dr.
Rome, GA 30161
(706) 295-6963
www.coosavalleytech.edu

Flint River Technical College
1533 Hwy. 19 S
Thomaston, GA 30286
(706) 646-6148
www.flintrivertech.edu

Griffin Technical College
501 Varsity Rd
Griffin, GA 30223
(770) 228-7348
www.griffintech.edu

Gwinnett Technical College
5150 Sugarloaf Pkwy.
Lawrenceville, GA 30043
(770) 962-7580
www.gwinnetttech.edu

Heart of Georgia Technical College
560 Pinehill Rd.
Dublin, GA 31021
(478) 275-6589
www.heartofgatech.edu

Moultrie Technical College
800 Veterans Pkwy. N
Moultrie, GA 31788
(229) 891-7000
www.moultrietech.edu

Ogeechee Technical College
One Joe Kennedy Blvd.
Statesboro, GA 30458
(912) 681-5500
www.ogeecheetech.edu

Okefenokee Technical College
1701 Carswell Ave
Waycross, GA 31503
(912) 287-6584
www.okefenokeetech.edu

Hawaii

Hawaii Community College
200 West Kawili St.
Hilo, HI 96720
(808) 974-7611
www.hawaii.hawaii.edu

Honolulu Community College
874 Dillingham Blvd.
Honolulu, HI 96817
(808) 845-9211
www.honolulu.hawaii.edu

Kauai Community College
3-1901 Kaumualii Hwy.
Lihue, HI 96766
(808) 245-8311
www.kauai.hawaii.edu

Idaho

North Idaho College
1000 West Garden Ave.
Coeur D'Alene, ID 83814
(208) 769-3300
www.nic.edu

Illinois

Black Hawk College
6600-34th Ave.
Moline, IL 61265
(309) 796-5000
www.bhc.edu

Carl Sandburg College
2400 Tom L. Wilson Blvd.
Galesburg, IL 61401
(309) 344-2518
www.sandburg.edu

City Colleges of Chicago–
Kennedy-King College
6800 South Wentworth Ave.
Chicago, IL 60621
(773) 602-5000
www.kennedyking.ccc.edu

John A. Logan College
700 Logan College Rd.
Carterville, IL 62918
(618) 985-3741
www.jalc.edu

Kaskaskia College
27210 College Rd.
Centralia, IL 62801
(618) 545-3000
www.kaskaskia.edu

Kishwaukee College
21193 Malta Rd.
Malta, IL 60150
(815) 825-2086
www.kishwaukeecollege.edu

Parkland College
2400 West Bradley Ave.
Champaign, IL 61821
(217) 351-2200
www.parkland.edu

Southeastern Illinois College
3575 College Rd.
Harrisburg, IL 62946
(618) 252-5400
www.sic.edu

Southwestern Illinois College
2500 Carlyle Ave.
Belleville, IL 62221
(618) 235-2700
www.swic.edu

Indiana

Ivy Tech Community College–
Central Indiana
50 West Fall Creek Parkway N. Dr.
Indianapolis, IN 46208
(317) 921-4800
www.ivytech.edu/indianapolis/

Ivy Tech Community College–
East Central
4301 South Cowan Rd., Box
3100

Muncie, IN 47302
(765) 289-2291
www.ivytech.edu/muncie

Ivy Tech Community College–Lafayette
3101 South Creasy Lane
Lafayette, IN 47905
(765) 269-5000
www.ivytech.edu/lafayette

Ivy Tech Community College–Northcentral
220 Dean Johnson Blvd.
South Bend, IN 46601
(574) 289-7001
www.ivytech.edu/southbend

Ivy Tech Community College–Southwest
3501 First Ave.
Evansville, IN 47710
(812) 426-2865
www.ivytech.edu/evansville

Ivy Tech Community College–Wabash Valley
7999 US Hwy. 41
Terre Haute, IN 47802
(812) 299-1121
www.ivytech.edu/terrehaute

Iowa

Des Moines Area Community College
2006 Ankeny Blvd.
Ankeny, IA 50023
(515) 964-6241
www.dmacc.edu

Iowa Central Community College
330 Ave. M
Fort Dodge, IA 50501
(515) 576-7201
www.iowacentral.edu

Iowa Lakes Community College
19 South 7th St.
Estherville, IA 51334
(712) 362-2601
www.iowalakes.edu

Kirkwood Community College
6301 Kirkwood Blvd. SW
Cedar Rapids, IA 52406
(319) 398-5411
www.kirkwood.edu

Northeast Iowa Community College–Calmar
1625 Hwy. 150
Calmar, IA 52132
(563) 562-3263
www.nicc.edu

North Iowa Area Community College
500 College Dr.
Mason City, IA 50401
(641) 423-1264
www.niacc.edu

Northwest Iowa Community College
603 West Park St.
Sheldon, IA 51201
(712) 324-5061
www.nwicc.edu

Southwestern Community College
1501 West Townline St.
Creston, IA 50801
(641) 782-7081
www.swcciowa.edu

Western Iowa Tech Community College
4647 Stone Ave.
Sioux City, IA 51102
(712) 274-6400
www.witcc.edu

Kansas

Coffeyville Community College
600 Roosevelt
Coffeyville, KS 67337
(620) 251-7700
www.coffeyville.edu

Flint Hills Technical College
3301 West 18th St.
Emporia, KS 66801
(620) 343-4600
www.fhtc.kansas.net

Hutchinson Community College
1300 North Plum St.
Hutchinson, KS 67501
(620) 665-3500
www.hutchcc.edu

Manhattan Area Technical College
3136 Dickens Ave.
Manhattan, KS 66503
(785) 587-2800
www.matc.net

Neosho County Community College
800 West 14th St.
Chanute, KS 66720
(620) 431-2820
www.neosho.edu

North Central Kansas Technical College
Hwy. 24
Beloit, KS 67420
(785) 738-2276
www.ncktc.edu

Northwest Kansas Technical College
1209 Harrison St.
Goodland, KS 67735
(785) 890-3641
www.nwktc.edu

Salina Area Technical School
2562 Centennial Rd.
Salina, KS 67401
(785) 309-3100
www.salinatech.com

Southwest Kansas Technical School
2215 North Kansas
Liberal, KS 67901
(620) 604-2900
www.usd480.net/swkts/main.html

Wichita Area Technical College
301 South Grove
Wichita, KS 67211
(316) 677-9400
www.watc.edu

Kentucky

Ashland Community and Technical College
1400 College Dr.
Ashland, KY 41101
(606) 326-2000
www.ashland.kctcs.edu/

Big Sandy Community and
Technical College
One Bert Combs Dr.
Prestonsburg, KY 41653
(606) 886-3863
www.bigsandy.kctcs.edu

Bluegrass Community and
Technical College
470 Cooper Dr.
Lexington, KY 40506
(859) 246-2400
www.bluegrass.kctcs.edu/

Bowling Green Technical College
1845 Loop Dr.
Bowling Green, KY 42101
(270) 901-1000
www.bowlinggreen.kctcs.edu

Elizabethtown Community
and Technical College
600 College Street Rd.
Elizabethtown, KY 42701
(270) 769-2371
www.elizabethtown.kctcs.edu

Hazard Community and
Technical College
One Community College Dr.
Hazard, KY 41701
(606) 436-5721
www.hazard.kctcs.edu

Jefferson Community and
Technical College
109 East Broadway
Louisville, KY 40202
(502) 213-4000
www.jefferson.kctcs.edu

Madisonville Community College
2000 College Dr.
Madisonville, KY 42431
(270) 821-2250
www.madcc.kctcs.edu

Maysville Community and
Technical College
1755 U.S. 68
Maysville, KY 41056
(606) 759-7141
www.maycc.kctcs.edu

Owensboro Community and
Technical College
4800 New Hartford Rd.

Owensboro, KY 42303
(270) 686-4400
www.octc.kctcs.edu

Somerset Community College
808 Monticello St.
Somerset, KY 42501
(877) 629-9722
www.somerset.kctcs.edu/

Southeast Kentucky Community
and Technical College
700 College Rd.
Cumberland, KY 40823
(606) 589-2145
www.southeast.kctcs.edu

West Kentucky Community and
Technical College
4810 Alben Barkley Dr.
Paducah, KY 42002
(270) 554-9200
www.westkentucky.kctcs.edu

Louisiana

Louisiana Technical College–
Folkes Campus
3337 Hwy. 10
Jackson, LA 70748
(225) 634-2636
www.ltc.edu/home.htm

Louisiana Technical College–
Huey P. Long Campus
304 South Jones St.
Winnfield, LA 71483
(318) 628-4342
www.ltc.edu

Louisiana Technical College–
Jumonville Memorial
605 Hospital Rd.
New Roads, LA 70760
(225) 638-8613
www.ltc.edu

Louisiana Technical College–
Lafourche Campus
1425 Tiger Dr.
Thibodaux, LA 70301
(985) 447-0924
www.ltc.edu

Louisiana Technical College–
Lamar Salter Campus
15014 Lake Charles Hwy.
Leesville, LA 71446
(337) 537-3135
www.ltc.edu

Louisiana Technical College–
Northwest Louisiana Campus
814 Constable St.
Minden, LA 71055
(318) 371-3035
www.ltc.edu

Louisiana Technical College–
Shreveport-Bossier Campus
2010 North Market St.
Shreveport, LA 71107
(318) 676-7811
www.ltc.edu

Louisiana Technical College–
Sullivan Campus
1710 Sullivan Dr.
Bogalusa, LA 70427
(985) 732-6640
www.ltc.edu

Louisiana Technical College–
Teche Area Campus
609 Ember Dr.
New Iberia, LA 70560
(337) 373-0011
www.techeareacampus.net

Louisiana Technical College–
West Jefferson Campus
475 Manhattan Blvd.
Harvey, LA 70058
(504) 361-6464
www.ltc.edu

Louisiana Technical College–
Young Memorial Campus
900 Youngs Rd.
Morgan City, LA 70380
(985) 380-2436
www.ltc.edu

Nunez Community College
3710 Paris Rd.
Chalmette, LA 70043
(504) 278-7497
www.nunez.edu

Maine

**Northern Maine
Community College**
33 Edgemont Dr.
Presque Isle, ME 04769
(207) 768-2700
www.nmcc.edu

**Southern Maine
Community College**
2 Fort Rd.
South Portland, ME 04106
(207) 741-5500
www.smccme.edu

Maryland

N/A

Massachusetts

North Bennet Street School
39 North Bennet St.
Boston, MA 02113
(617) 227-0155
www.nbss.org

Michigan

**Kalamazoo Valley
Community College**
6767 West O Ave.
Kalamazoo, MI 49003
(269) 488-4100
www.kvcc.edu

Kirtland Community College
10775 North Saint Helen Rd.
Roscommon, MI 48653
(989) 275-5000
www.kirtland.edu

Lansing Community College
419 North Capitol Ave.
Lansing, MI 48901
(517) 483-1957
www.lansing.cc.mi.us

Mott Community College
1401 East Court St.
Flint, MI 48503
(810) 762-0200
www.mcc.edu

Oakland Community College
2480 Opdyke Rd.
Bloomfield Hills, MI 48304
(248) 341-2000
www.oaklandcc.edu

Minnesota

Alexandria Technical College
1601 Jefferson St.
Alexandria, MN 56308
(320) 762-0221
www.alextech.edu

Hennepin Technical College
9000 Brooklyn Blvd.
Brooklyn Park, MN 55445
(952) 995-1300
www.hennepintech.edu

Lake Superior College
2101 Trinity Rd.
Duluth, MN 55811
(800) 432-2884
www.lsc.edu

Leech Lake Tribal College
6945 Littlewolf Rd. NW
Cass Lake, MN 56633
(218) 335-4200
www.lltc.org

**Mesabi Range Community and
Technical College**
1001 Chestnut St. W
Virginia, MN 55792
(218) 741-3095
www.mr.mnscu.edu

**Minneapolis Community and
Technical College**
1501 Hennepin Ave.
Minneapolis, MN 55403
(612) 659-6000
www.minneapolis.edu

**Minnesota State College–
Southeast Technical-Winona**
1250 Homer Rd.
Winona, MN 55987
(507) 453-2700
www.southeastmn.edu

**Minnesota State Community
and Technical College**
1414 College Way

Fergus Falls, MN 56537
(218) 736-1500
www.minnesota.edu

**Minnesota West Community and
Technical College**
1593 11th Ave.
Granite Falls, MN 56241
(320) 564-4511
www.mnwest.edu

**Northland Community and
Technical College**
1101 Hwy. #1 E
Thief River Falls, MN 56701
(218) 681-0701
www.northlandcollege.edu

Northwest Technical College
905 Grant Ave. SE
Bemidji, MN 56601
(218) 333-6600
www.ntcmn.edu

Ridgewater College
2101 15th Ave. NW
Willmar, MN 56201
(800) 722-1151
www.ridgewater.edu

Riverland Community College
1900 8th Ave. NW
Austin, MN 55912
(507) 433-0600
www.riverland.edu

**Rochester Community and
Technical College**
851 30th Ave. SE
Rochester, MN 55904
(507) 285-7210
www.rctc.edu

Saint Cloud Technical College
1540 Northway Dr.
Saint Cloud, MN 56303
(320) 308-5000
www.sctc.edu

**Saint Paul College—
A Community and
Technical College**
235 Marshall Ave.
Saint Paul, MN 55102
(651) 846-1600
www.saintpaul.edu

South Central College
1920 Lee Blvd.
North Mankato, MN 56003
(507) 389-7200
www.southcentral.edu

Mississippi

Coahoma Community College
3240 Friars Point Rd.
Clarksdale, MS 38614
(662) 627-2571
www.coahomacc.edu

East Central Community College
275 West Broad St.
Decatur, MS 39327
(601) 635-2111
www.eccc.edu

Hinds Community College
501 East Main St.
Raymond, MS 39154
(601) 857-5261
www.hindscc.edu

Meridian Community College
910 Hwy. 19 N
Meridian, MS 39307
(601) 483-8241
www.meridiancc.edu

Mississippi Gulf Coast Community College
51 Main St.
Perkinston, MS 39573
(601) 928-5211
www.mgccc.edu

Pearl River Community College
101 Hwy. 11 N
Poplarville, MS 39470
(601) 403-1000
www.prcc.edu

Southwest Mississippi Community College
College Dr.
Summit, MS 39666
(601) 276-2000
www.smcc.edu

Missouri

Hannibal Career and Technical Center
4550 Mcmasters Ave.
Hannibal, MO 63401
(573) 221-4430
www.hannibal.tec.mo.us

Hillyard Technical Center
3434 Faraon St.
Saint Joseph, MO 64506
(816) 671-4170
www.hillyardtech.com

Mineral Area College
5270 Flat River Rd.
Park Hills, MO 63601
(573) 431-4593
www.mineralarea.edu

Nichols Career Center
605 Union
Jefferson City, MO 65101
(573) 659-3100
www.jcps.k12.mo.us/
  education/school/school.php
  ?sectionid=707

North Central Missouri College
1301 Main St.
Trenton, MO 64683
(660) 359-3948
www.ncmissouri.edu

Rolla Technical Institute
1304 East 10th St.
Rolla, MO 65401
(573) 458-0150
www.rolla.k12.mo.us

St. Louis Community College–Florissant Valley
3400 Pershall Rd.
St. Louis, MO 63135
(314) 513-4200
www.stlcc.edu

St. Louis Community College–Forest Park
5600 Oakland Ave.
St. Louis, MO 63110
(314) 644-9100
www.stlcc.edu

Montana

Flathead Valley Community College
777 Grandview Dr.
Kalispell, MT 59901
(406) 756-3822
www.fvcc.edu

Nebraska

N/A

Nevada

N/A

New Hampshire

N/A

New Jersey

N/A

New Mexico

Central New Mexico Community College
525 Buena Vista SE
Albuquerque, NM 87106
(505) 224-3000
www.cnm.edu

Clovis Community College
417 Schepps Blvd.
Clovis, NM 88101
(505) 769-2811
www.clovis.edu

Luna Community College
Hot Springs Blvd.
Las Vegas, NM 87701
(505) 454-2500
www.luna.edu

Navajo Technical College
Lower Point Rd., SR 371
Crownpoint, NM 87313
(505) 786-4100
www.navajotech.edu

New Mexico State University–
Grants
1500 Third St.
Grants, NM 87020
(505) 287-7981
www.grants.nmsu.edu/

San Juan College
4601 College Blvd.
Farmington, NM 87402
(505) 326-3311
www.sanjuancollege.edu

North Carolina

Alamance Community College
1247 Jimmie Kerr Rd.
Graham, NC 27253
(336) 578-2002
www.alamance.cc.nc.us

Asheville-Buncombe Technical
Community College
340 Victoria Rd.
Asheville, NC 28801
(828) 254-1921
www.abtech.edu

Bladen Community College
7418 NC Hwy. 41 W
Dublin, NC 28332
(910) 879-5500
www.bladen.cc.nc.us

Blue Ridge Community College
180 West Campus Dr.
Flat Rock, NC 28731
(828) 694-1700
www.blueridge.edu

Cape Fear Community College
411 North Front St.
Wilmington, NC 28401
(910) 362-7000
www.cfcc.edu

Central Carolina
Community College
1105 Kelly Dr.
Sanford, NC 27330
(919) 775-5401
www.cccc.edu

Cleveland Community College
137 South Post Rd.
Shelby, NC 28152

(704) 484-4000
www.clevelandcommunity
  college.edu

College of the Albemarle
1208 N. Road St.
Elizabeth City, NC 27906
(252) 335-0821
www.albemarle.edu

Forsyth Technical
Community College
2100 Silas Creek Pkwy.
Winston-Salem, NC 27103
(336) 723-0371
www.forsythtech.edu

Guilford Technical
Community College
601 High Point Rd.
Jamestown, NC 27282
(336) 334-4822
www.gtcc.edu/

McDowell Technical
Community College
54 College Dr.
Marion, NC 28752
(828) 652-6021
www.mcdowelltech.edu

Pamlico Community College
5049 Hwy. 306 S
Grantsboro, NC 28529
(252) 249-1851
www.pamlicocc.edu

Piedmont Community College
1715 College Dr.
Roxboro, NC 27573
(336) 599-1181
www.piedmontcc.edu

Robeson Community College
5160 Fayetteville Rd
Lumberton, NC 28360
(910) 272-3700
www.robeson.cc.nc.us

South Piedmont
Community College
680 Highway 74 W
Polkton, NC 28135
(704) 272-7635
www.spcc.edu

Southwestern
Community College
447 College Dr.
Sylva, NC 28779
(828) 586-4091
www.southwesterncc.edu

Surry Community College
630 S. Main St.
Dobson, NC 27017
(336) 386-3204
www.surry.edu

Vance-Granville
Community College
PO Box 917, SR 1126
Henderson, NC 27536
(252) 492-2061
www.vgcc.edu

North Dakota

Bismarck State College
1500 Edwards Ave.
Bismarck, ND 58506
(701) 224-5400
www.bismarckstate.edu

Cankdeska Cikana
Community College
214 1st Ave.
Fort Totten, ND 58335
(701) 766-4415
www.littlehoop.edu

Ohio

N/A

Oklahoma

Autry Technology Center
1201 West Willow
Enid, OK 73703
(580) 242-2750
www.autrytech.com

Caddo Kiowa Technology Center
Career Tech Rd.
Fort Cobb, OK 73038
(405) 643-5511
www.caddokiowa.com

Eastern Oklahoma County
Tech. Center
4601 North Choctaw Rd.
Choctaw, OK 73020
(405) 390-9591
www.eoctech.org

Francis Tuttle Technology Center
12777 North Rockwell Ave.
Oklahoma City, OK 73142
(405) 717-4732
www.francistuttle.com

Gordon Cooper
Technology Center
1 John C. Bruton Blvd.
Shawnee, OK 74804
(405) 273-7493
www.gctech.org

Great Plains Technology Center
4500 West Lee Blvd.
Lawton, OK 73505
(580) 355-6371
www.gptech.org

High Plains Technology Center
3921 34th St.
Woodward, OK 73801
(580) 256-6618
www.hptc.net

Indian Capital
Technology Center–Muskogee
2403 North 41st St. E
Muskogee, OK 74403
(918) 687-6383
www.ictctech.com

Kiamichi Technology Center–
Mcalester
301 Kiamichi Dr.
Mcalester, OK 74501
(918) 465-2323
www.kiamichi
  -mcalester.tec.ok.us/

Kiamichi Technology Center–
Stigler
1410 Old Military Rd.
Stigler, OK 74462
(918) 465-2323
www.kiamichi-stigler.tec.ok.us

Kiamichi Technology Center–
Talihina
Hwy 63a and Vo-Tech Dr.
Talihina, OK 74571
(918) 465-2323
www.okktc.org

Meridian Technology Center
1312 South Sangre Rd
Stillwater, OK 74074
(405) 377-3333
www.meridian-technology.com

Metro Technology Centers
1900 Springlake Dr.
Oklahoma City, OK 73111
(405) 424-8324
www.metrotech.org

Tulsa Technology Center–
Lemley Campus
3420 South Memorial Dr.
Tulsa, OK 74145
(918) 828-1000
www.tulsatech.com

Oregon

Chemeketa Community College
4000 Lancaster Dr. NE
Salem, OR 97305
(503) 399-5000
www.chemeketa.edu

Pennsylvania

Community College of
Allegheny County
800 Allegheny Ave.
Pittsburgh, PA 15233
(412) 323-2323
www.ccac.edu

Delaware County
Community College
901 South Media Line Rd.
Media, PA 19063
(610) 359-5000
www.dccc.edu

Johnson College
3427 North Main Ave.
Scranton, PA 18508
(570) 342-6404
www.johnson.edu

Thaddeus Stevens College
of Technology
750 East King St.
Lancaster, PA 17602
(717) 299-7730
www.stevenscollege.edu

Rhode Island

N/A

South Carolina

Greenville Technical College
506 South Pleasantburg Dr.
Greenville, SC 29607
(864) 250-8111
www.greenvilletech.com

South Dakota

Lake Area Technical Institute
230 11th St. NE
Watertown, SD 57201
(605) 882-5284
www.lakeareatech.edu

Mitchell Technical Institute
821 North Capital St.
Mitchell, SD 57301
(605) 995-3023
www.mitchelltech.edu

Western Dakota
Technical Institute
800 Mickelson Dr.
Rapid City, SD 57703
(605) 394-4034
www.wdt.edu

Tennessee

N/A

Texas

Austin Community College
District
5930 Middle Fiskville Rd.
Austin, TX 78752
(512) 223-7000
www.austincc.edu

Coastal Bend College
3800 Charco Rd.
Beeville, TX 78102
(361) 358-2838
www.coastalbend.edu

McLennan Community College
1400 College Dr.
Waco, TX 76708
(254) 299-8000
www.mclennan.edu

Texarkana College
2500 North Robison Rd.
Texarkana, TX 75599
(903) 838-4541
www.texarkanacollege.edu

Utah

Mountainland Applied
Technology College
987 South Geneva Rd.
Orem, UT 84058
(801) 863-6282
www.mlatc.edu

Ogden-Weber Applied
Technology College
200 North Washington Blvd.
Ogden, UT 84404
(801) 627-8300
www.owatc.com

Salt Lake Community College
PO Box 30808
Salt Lake City, UT 84130
(801) 957-4333
www.slcc.edu

Uintah Basin Applied
Technology College
1100 East Lagoon St. 124-5
Roosevelt, UT 84066
(435) 722-4523
www.ubatc.edu

Vermont

N/A

Virginia

N/A

Washington

Bates Technical College
1101 South Yakima Ave.
Tacoma, WA 98405
(253) 680-7000
www.bates.ctc.edu/

Grays Harbor College
1620 Edward P. Smith Dr.
Aberdeen, WA 98520
(360) 532-9020
www.ghc.ctc.edu

Green River Community College
12401 SE 320th St.
Auburn, WA 98092
(253) 833-9111
www.greenriver.edu/

Seattle Community College–
Central Campus
1701 Broadway Ave.
Seattle, WA 98122
(206) 587-3800
www.seattlecentral.org

Spokane Community College
1810 North Greene St.
Spokane, WA 99217
(509) 533-8020
www.scc.spokane.edu

Walla Walla Community College
500 Tausick Way
Walla Walla, WA 99362
(509) 522-2500
www.wwcc.edu

Wenatchee Valley College
1300 Fifth St.
Wenatchee, WA 98801
(509) 682-6800
www.wvc.edu

West Virginia

N/A

Wisconsin

Blackhawk Technical College
6004 Prairie Rd.
Janesville, WI 53547
(608) 758-6900
www.blackhawk.edu

Chippewa Valley
Technical College
620 West Clairemont Ave.
Eau Claire, WI 54701
(715) 833-6200
www.cvtc.edu

College of Menominee Nation
N 172 Hwy. 47/55
Keshena, WI 54135
(715) 799-5600
www.menominee.edu

Fox Valley Technical College
1825 North Bluemound Dr.
Appleton, WI 54912
(920) 735-5600
www.fvtc.edu

Gateway Technical College
3520 30th Ave.
Kenosha, WI 53144
(262) 564-2200
www.gtc.edu

Lac Courte Oreilles Ojibwa
Community College
13466 West Trepania Rd.
Hayward, WI 54843
(715) 634-4790
www.lco.edu

Lakeshore Technical College
1290 North Ave.
Cleveland, WI 53015
(920) 693-1000
www.gotoltc.edu

Madison Area Technical College
3550 Anderson St.
Madison, WI 53704
(608) 246-6100
www.matcmadison.edu

Mid-State Technical College
500 32nd St. N
Wisconsin Rapids, WI 54494
(715) 422-5300
www.mstc.edu

Milwaukee Area
Technical College
700 West State St.
Milwaukee, WI 53233
(414) 297-6370
www.matc.edu

Moraine Park Technical College
235 North National Ave.
Fond Du Lac, WI 54936
(920) 922-8611
www.morainepark.edu

Nicolet Area Technical College
Hwy G South
Rhinelander, WI 54501
(715) 365-4410
www.nicoletcollege.edu

Southwest Wisconsin Technical
College
1800 Bronson Blvd.
Fennimore, WI 53809
(608) 822-3262
www.swtc.edu

Waukesha County Technical
College
800 Main St.
Pewaukee, WI 53072

(262) 691-5566
www.wctc.edu

Western Technical College
304 6th St. N
La Crosse, WI 54602
(608) 785-9200
www.westerntc.edu

Wyoming

N/A

Construction

Construction work includes a huge number of different job opportunities and possibilities. There are basic laborer jobs, and there are intense specialties within this industry, such as pile drivers or crane operators. Many apprenticeships provide you with introductory skills or even specialized skills in a particular sector. Many of the best apprenticeships are offered through the Laborers International Union of North America and the American General Contractors (AGC). Others may be found through independent contractors.

Resources
Associated General Contractors of America, www.agc.org
Laborers International Union of North America, www.liuna.org

Laborers—AGC Education and Training Sites
www.laborers-agc.org

Alabama

Alabama Laborers–
AGC Joint Training Facility
PO Box 303
Miracle Hills Rd.
Springville, AL 35146
(205) 467-6201

Alaska

Alaska Laborers Training
Trust Fund
13500 Old Seward Highway
Anchorage, AK 99515
(907) 345-3853

Arizona

Arizona Laborers' Training Fund
512 West Adams, Unit 3
Phoenix, AZ 85003
(602) 716-9601

Training Site
Arizona Laborers' Training Fund
5995 South Trekell Rd.
Casa Grande, AZ 85003
(520) 876-5555

Arkansas

South Central Laborers Training
and Apprenticeship Fund
9297 Hwy. 979
PO Box 376
Livonia, LA 70755
(225) 637-2311

California

Terence J. O'Sullivan Laborers
Training Center
1001 Westside Dr.
San Ramon, CA 94583-4098
(925) 828-2513
Apprentice Tel.:
(925) 556-0858

Laborers Training and Retraining
Trust Fund of Southern California
1385 West Sierra Madre Ave.
Azusa, CA 91702
(626) 610-1700

Colorado

Colorado Laborers' and
Contractors' Education
and Training Fund
10505 Havana St.
Brighton, CO 80601
(303) 287-3116

Connecticut

New England Laborers'
Training Trust Fund
Route 97 and Murdock Rd.
PO Box 77
Pomfret Center, CT 06259
(860) 974-1455

Delaware

LIUNA Local 199 Apprenticeship
532 South Claymont St.

Wilmington, DE 19801
(302) 654-0338
(302) 654-2880

District of Columbia

Francis L. Greenfield Laborers'
Training and Apprenticeship
Institute
4849A Lydell Rd.
Cheverly, MD 20781
(301) 772-8820
www.dclaborers.org

Florida

See Georgia

Georgia

Laborers' Southeast
Training Fund
1724 Roadhaven Dr.
Stone Mountain, GA 30083
(678) 937-1654

Georgia Satellites

Savannah River Laborers'
Training Center
2507 Mike Padgett Hwy.
Augusta, GA 30906
(706) 793-6363

Tennessee Laborers'
Training Center
10629 Dutchtown Rd.
Knoxville, TN 37932
(865) 671-3420

Hawaii

Hawaii Laborers' Apprenticeship
and Training Program
96-138 Farrington Hwy.
Pearl City, HI 96782
(808) 455-7979

Idaho

See Oregon

Illinois

Chicagoland Laborers Training
and Apprentice Center
PO Box 88658
1200 Old Gary Ave.
Carol Stream, IL 60188
(630) 653-0006
www.chicagolaborers.org

Illinois Laborers' and Contractors
Joint Apprenticeship and
Training Program
Rural Route 3, Box 138
Mt. Sterling, IL 62353
(217) 773-2741

Railroad Training and
Education Fund
2205 West Wabash Ave.,
Ste. 211
Springfield, IL 62704
(217) 787-2923

Indiana

Indiana Laborers' Training
Trust Fund
PO Box 758
Bedford, IN 47421
(812) 279-9751
www.indianalaborers.org

Iowa

Laborers Local 43 Training and
Education Fund
5000 J Street SW
Cedar Rapids, IA 52404
(319) 366-0859

Iowa Laborers' Education and
Training Fund
Jack G. Jones Training Center
5806 Meredith Dr., Ste. C
Des Moines, IA 50322
(515) 270-6965

Iowa Local 177
Laborers Local 177 Training
and Education Fund
2121 Delaware
Des Moines, IA 50317
(515) 265-2558

Kansas

Greater Kansas City Laborers'
Training Fund
8944 Kaw Dr.
Kansas City, KS 66111
(913) 441-6100

Construction Industry Laborers
Training Fund of Western
Missouri and Kansas
21201 South Mullen Rd.
Belton, MO 64012
(816) 331-6862

Kentucky

Kentucky Laborers' Joint
Apprenticeship and Training
Trust Fund
2000 U.S. Bypass South
Lawrenceburg, KY 40342
(502) 839-3155

Louisiana

South Central Laborers Training
and Apprenticeship Fund
9297 Hwy. 979
PO Box 376
Livonia, LA 70755
(225) 637-2311

Maine

See Massachusetts

Maryland

Laborers' District Council
Training Fund for Baltimore
and Vicinity
3200 Wilkens Ave.
Baltimore, MD 21229
(410) 525-1500

Massachusetts

New England Laborers'
Training Trust Fund
37 East St.
Hopkinton, MA 01748

(508) 544-9830
www.nelaborerstraining.com

New England Laborers'
Training Trust Fund
Route 97 and Murdock Rd.
PO Box 77
Pomfret Center, CT 06259
(860) 974-1455
www.nelaborerstraining.com

Michigan

Michigan Laborers' Training and
Apprenticeship Institute
11155 South Beardslee Rd.
Perry, MI 48872
(517) 625-4919
www.mltai.org
or
W-8008 South US 2
Iron Mountain, MI 49801
(906) 774-5703
or
Michigan Laborers' Training and
Apprenticeship Institute
5555 Cogswell
Wayne, MI 48184
(734) 729-7005

Minnesota

Construction Laborers'
Education, Training, and
Apprenticeship Fund of
Minnesota and
North Dakota
2350 Main St.
Lino Lakes, MN 55038
(651) 653-6710
www.mnndt.org
Apprentice Tel.:
   (651) 762-8235

Mississippi

South Central Laborers Training
and Apprenticeship Fund
9297 Hwy. 979
PO Box 376
Livonia, LA 70755
(225) 637-2311

Missouri

AGC Eastern Missouri Laborers'
Joint Training Fund
35 Opportunity Rd.
High Hill, MO 63350
(636) 585-1500
www.laborers-highhill.org

Western Missouri and Kansas
Construction Industry Laborers
   Training Fund of Western
   Missouri and Kansas
21201 South Mullen Rd.
Belton, MO 64012
(816) 331-6862

Montana

Laborers-AGC Training Program
for Montana
3100 Horseshoe Bend Rd.
Helena, MT 59602
(406) 442-9964

Nebraska

Contractors-Laborers Training
and Apprentice Fund
11000 North 72nd St.
Omaha, NE 68122
(402) 573-7878

Nevada

Northern Nevada Laborers–
AGC Training Center
570 Reactor Way
Reno, NV 89502
(775) 856-3660

Southern Nevada Laborers'
Training Trust Local #872
4211 East Bonanza Rd.
Las Vegas, NV 89110
(702) 452-9410

New Hampshire

See Massachusetts

New Jersey

New Jersey Building Laborers' Training and Apprenticeship Fund
31 Mott Ave.
Monroe Township, NJ 08831
(732) 521-0200

New Jersey Construction Craft Laborers' Apprenticeship Program
31 Mott Ave.
Monroe Township, NJ 08831
(732) 521-0200

Local #472 Safety, Education, and Training Trust Fund
378 County Rd.
Cliffwood, NJ 07721
(732) 583-6235

Local #172 Safety, Education, and Training Fund
1100 Black Horse Pike
Folsom, NJ 08037
(609) 567-1959

New Mexico

New Mexico Laborers' Training Trust Fund
1030 San Pedro NE
Albuquerque, NM 87110
(505) 265-2843

New York

Cement and Concrete Workers Education and Training Fund
29-18 35th Ave.
Long Island City, NY 11106
(718) 392-6970

Laborers' Local 147 Training Fund
4332 Katonah Ave.
Bronx, NY 10470
(718) 994-6664

Buffalo Laborers' Training Fund
1370 Seneca St.
Buffalo, NY 14210
(716) 825-0883

Laborers' Local 754 Welfare Fund
215 Old Nyack Turnpike
Chestnut Ridge, NY 10977
(845) 425-5073

Westchester Building and Construction Laborers' Local 235 Benefit Fund
41 Knollwood Rd.
Elmsford, NY 10523
(914) 592-3331

Pavers and Road Builders District Council Apprenticeship, Skill Improvement and Safety Fund
136-25 37th Ave.
Flushing, NY 11354
(718) 961-6964

Eastern New York Laborers' Training Center Inc.
666 Wemple Road
PO Box 100
Glenmont, NY 12077
(518) 426-0290

Westchester Heavy Construction Laborers' Education and Training Fund
LIUNA Local 60
140 Broadway
Hawthorne, NY 10532
(914) 769-2440

LIUNA Local 1298 Training Fund
1611 Locust Ave.
Bohemia, NY 11716
(631) 218-1376

General Building Laborers' Local #66 Training Fund
1600 Walt Whitman Rd.
Melville, NY 11747
(631) 454-2330

Laborers' Local #17 Training and Education Fund
451 Little Britain Rd.
Newburgh, NY 12550
(845) 562-1121

LIUNA Local 731 Training Center
34-11 35th Ave.
Astoria, NY 11106
(718) 752-9860

Laborer's-AGC
42-53 21st St.
Long Island City, NY 11101
(718) 383-6863

Laborers' Local 91 Educational and Training Fund
2556 Seneca Ave.
Niagara Falls, NY 14305-3246
(716) 297-4722

Local #1000 Training and Apprenticeship Fund
PO Box 128
Poughkeepsie, NY 12602
(845) 471-2470

Upstate New York Laborers' Education and Training Fund
PO Box 4069
8005 SR 104
Oswego, NY 13126
(315) 343-8553

North Carolina

Virginia and North Carolina Laborers' Training Trust Fund
1500 East Little Creek Rd., Ste. 307
Norfolk, VA 23518
(757) 962-6184

North Dakota

Construction Laborers' Education, Training, and Apprenticeship Fund of Minnesota and North Dakota
2350 Main St.
Lino Lakes, MN 55038
(651) 653-6710
www.mnndt.org
Apprentice Tel.: (651) 762-8235

Ohio

Ohio Laborers' Training and Upgrading Trust Fund
25721 Coshocton Rd.
Howard, OH 43028
(740) 599-7915
www.ohiolaborerstraining.com
or

Middletown Applied Remediation School (MARS)
5527 Hamilton-Middletown Rd.
Middletown, OH 45402
(513) 539-7133

Oklahoma

South Central Laborers Training and Apprenticeship Fund
9297 Hwy. 979
PO Box 376
Livonia, LA 70755
(225) 637-2311

Oregon

Oregon–Southern Idaho Laborers-Employers Training Trust Fund
6011 Marcus Harris Ave. NE
Adair Village
Corvallis, OR 97330
(541) 745-5513

Pennsylvania

Laborers' District Council of Eastern Pennsylvania Training Fund
6740 Allentown Blvd., Ste. 2
Harrisburg, PA 17112
(800) 478-0058
www.laborerseastpa.org

Laborers' District Council of Philadelphia Education and Training/Apprenticeship Fund
500 Lancaster Pike
Exton, PA 19341
(610) 524-0404
www.ldc-phila-vic.org

Western Pennsylvania Laborers' Education and Training Trust Fund
317 Deer Creek Rd.
Saxonburg, PA 16056
(800) 442-8868
(724) 352-2224
www.laborpa.org/trainingcenter

Rhode Island

See Massachusetts

South Carolina

Laborers' Southeast Training Fund
1724 Roadhaven Dr.
Stone Mountain, GA 30083
(678) 937-1654

South Dakota

Construction Laborers' Education, Training, and Apprenticeship Fund of Minnesota and North Dakota
2350 Main St.
Lino Lakes, MN 55038
(651) 653-6710
www.mnndt.org

Tennessee

Tennessee Laborers' Training Center
10629 Dutchtown Rd.
Knoxville, TN 37932
(865) 671-3420

Texas

South Central Laborers Training and Apprenticeship Fund
9297 Hwy. 979
PO Box 376
Livonia, LA 70755
(225) 637-2311

Utah

Northwest Laborers-Employers Training Trust Fund
5667 West Dannon Way
West Jordan, UT 84088
(801) 280-7195

Vermont

See Massachusetts

Virginia

Virginia-Williamsburg
Virginia and North Carolina Laborers' Training Trust Fund
1500 East Little Creek Rd., Ste. 307
Norfolk, VA 23518
(757) 962-6184

Virginia-Roanoke
Laborers' Union #980 Training Trust Fund
6145 Airport Rd.
Roanoke, VA 24019
(540) 366-3401

Washington

Northwest Laborers-Employers Training Trust Fund
27055 Ohio Ave.
Kingston, WA 98346
(800) 240-9112

West Virginia

West Virginia Laborers' Training Trust Fund
Turkey Foot Rd.
PO Box 6
Mineral Wells, WV 26150
(304) 489-9665
www.wvccl.org

Wisconsin

Wisconsin Laborers' Apprenticeship and Training Center
4633 LIUNA Way, Ste. 100
   (Apprentice)
Deforest, WI 53532
(608) 846-5764
(608) 846-5768
(800) 275-6939
www.wilaborers.org

Wyoming

Laborers Joint Apprenticeship and Training Trust for Wyoming
1021 West 23rd, Ste. B
Cheyenne, WY 82001
(307) 632-1510

Accredited Training Centers Approved by the National Center for Construction Education and Research (NCCER)

Alabama

N/A

Alaska

N/A

Arizona

Northern Arizona Vocational
Institute of Technology
1320 E Thornton Road
Show Low, AZ 85901
(928) 532-0269
www.navit.edu

Arkansas

Northern Industrial Training LLC
6177 East Mountain Heather
  Way
Palmer, AK 99645-9505
(907) 557-6400
www.nitalaska.com

Vocational Training and
Resource Center
3239 Hospital Dr.
Juneau, AK 99801-0000
(907) 463-7130
www.ccthita-vtrc.org

California

Welltech National Training Systems Inc.
2751 East El Presidio St.
Carson, CA 90810-1139
(310) 223-6062
www.welltechsafety.com

Colorado

ABC Western Colorado Chapter
2754 Compass Dr., Ste. 305
Grand Junction, CO 81506
(970) 243-7950
www.wcoabc.org

Connecticut

Construction Education
Center Inc.
2138 Silas Deane Hwy., Ste. 101
Rocky Hill, CT 06067
(860) 529-5886
www.thinkconstruction.org

Delaware

N/A

District of Columbia

N/A

Florida

N/A

Georgia

N/A

Hawaii

N/A

Idaho

N/A

Illinois

Associated Builders and
Contractors, Illinois Chapter Inc.
1691 Elmhurst Rd.
Elk Grove Village, IL 60007
(847) 709-2960
www.abcil.org

Choice Construction Services
665 Hillcrest Blvd.
Hoffman Estates, IL 60195
(847) 483-4056
www.ietc-dupageco.com/
  ChoiceConstructionSer

Indiana

N/A

Iowa

N/A

Kansas

ABC Heart of America Chapter
6950 Squibb Road, Suite 418
Mission, KS 66202
(913) 831-2221
www.abcksmo.org

Kentucky

N/A

Louisiana

N/A

Maine

Associated General Contractors
of Maine
188 Whitten Rd.

Augusta, ME 04332
(207) 622-4741
www.acm-inc.org

Maryland

Cumberland Valley Chapter ABC
530 North Locust St.
Hagerstown, MD 21740
(301) 739-1190
www.abccvc.com

Massachusetts

N/A

Michigan

Construction Education Trust
31800 Sherman Ave.
Madison Heights, MI 48071
(248) 298-3600
www.cet-tech.com

Minnesota

N/A

Mississippi

Mississippi Construction Education Foundation
290 Commerce Park Drive, Suite B
Ridgeland, MS 39157
(601) 605-2989
www.mcef.net

Missouri

N/A

Montana

N/A

Nebraska

N/A

Nevada

N/A

New Hampshire

N/A

New Jersey

ABC New Jersey Chapter
720 King George Post Rd., Suite 303
Fords, NJ 08863
(732) 661-1045
www.abcnjc.org

New Mexico

New Mexico Building Branch, AGC
1615 University Boulevard, NE
Albuquerque, NM 87102
(505) 842-1462
www.agc-nm.org

New York

CTC of New York State
6369 Collamer Dr.
East Syracuse, NY 13057
(315) 463-7539
www.abcnys.org

North Carolina

N/A

North Dakota

N/A

Ohio

Building Trades Institute, LLC
459 Orangepoint Dr., Suite F
Lewis Center, OH 43035
(740) 548-8091
www.buildingtradesinstitute.com

Construction Craft Academy
9760 Shepard Rd
Macedonia, OH 44056
(800) 442-0067
www.craftacademy.com

Oklahoma

N/A

Oregon

AGC Oregon Columbia Chapter
8111 NE Holman St
Portland, OR 97218
(503) 682-3363
www.agc-oregon.org

Pennsylvania

Associated Builders and Contractors, Eastern PA
1036 North Godfrey St.
Allentown, PA 18109
(610) 821-6869
www.abceastpa.org

Rhode Island

N/A

South Carolina

N/A

South Dakota

N/A

Tennessee

N/A

Texas

Saulsbury Industries D/B/A Construction Workforce Training Center
5308 Andrews Highway
Odessa, TX 79762
(432) 366-7676
www.cwtc-tx.com

TABACON Systems Inc.
4419 Roseland St.
Houston, TX 77006
(713) 522-0496
www.tabaconsystemsinc.com

The Victor Group
801 High Ridge Dr.
Friendswood, TX 77546
(281) 850-8079
www.thevictorgroup.net

Utah

N/A

Vermont

N/A

Virginia

N/A

Washington

N/A

West Virginia

N/A

Wisconsin

N/A

Wyoming

Wyoming Contractors
Association AGC
2220 North Bryan Stock Trail
Casper, WY 82601
(307) 237-4400
www.wcagc.org

Electrician

Most electricians attend an extensive apprenticeship program, either through a union or an independent contractor. Most states and many communities require electricians to be licensed, so the training is rarely optional. While becoming an apprentice usually requires some form of basic registration, becoming a journeyman or a master electrician typically requires passing a written exam and completion of a certain number of work hours. In Texas, for example, a journeyman electrician receives a license after 8,000 hours of on-the-job training under a master electrician and by passing a written exam.

Independent Public NCCER Accredited Training Centers

Alabama

Construction Education
Foundation of Alabama
6700 Oporto-Madrid Blvd.
Birmingham, AL 35206
(205) 956-0146
bmccain@cefalabama.org
www.cefalabama.org

Diversified Employment
Service Inc.
211-C Hwy. 43 S
Saraland, AL 36571
(251) 679-0018

North Alabama Craft Training
Foundation
152 Hollington Dr.
Huntsville, AL 35811
(256) 851-1566

Alaska

Associated Builders and
Contractors of Alaska Inc.
360 West Benson Blvd.,
Ste. 200
Anchorage, AK 99503
(907) 565-5600
www.abcalaska.org

Associated General Contractors of Alaska
8005 Schoon St.
Anchorage, AK 99518
(907) 561-5354
www.agcak.org

Council of Athabascan Tribal Governments
Yukon Flats Center-Fort Yukon
Fort Yukon, AK 99740
(907) 662-3612
www.catg.org

Northern Industrial Training LLC
6177 East Mountain Heather Way
Palmer, AK 99645-9505
(907) 557-6400
www.nitalaska.com

Arkansas

Arkansas Chapter AGC Inc.
523 East Capitol Ave.
Little Rock, AR 72202
(501) 376-6641
www.agcar.net

Arizona

Arizona Builders Alliance
1825 West Adams
Phoenix, AZ 85007
(602) 274-8222
www.azbuilders.org

Arizona Public Service
1611 South Main St.
Snowflake, AZ 85937
(928) 536-6232
www.aps.com

SouthWest Electrical Training Center
1717 East Van Buren
Phoenix, AZ 85006
(480) 659-2903
www.swetc.org

California

ABC Southern California Chapter
1400 North Kellogg Dr., Ste. A

Anaheim, CA 92807
(714) 779-3199
www.abcsocal.org

Calexico Community Action Council
2151 Rockwood Ave., Ste. 166
Calexico, CA 92231
(760) 357-6464

Center for Seabees and Facilities Engineering
3502 Goodspeed St., Ste. 1
Naval Base Ventura County, CA 93041
(805) 982-3615
www.npdc.navy.mil/csfe

Shasta Builder's Exchange Community Fund
2985 Innsbruck Dr.
Redding, CA 96003
(530) 222-1917
www.shastabe.com

Welltech National Training Systems Inc.
2751 East El Presidio St.
Carson, CA 90810-1139
(310) 223-6062
www.welltechsafety.com

Colorado

ABC Western Colorado Chapter
2754 Compass Dr., Ste. 305
Grand Junction, CO 81506
(970) 243-7950
www.wcoabc.org

Construction Industry Training Council of Colorado Inc.
646 Mariposa St.
Denver, CO 80204
(303) 893-1500

T and D Services
1143 Michael Cir.
Meeker, CO 81641
(970) 260-3415

Connecticut

Construction Education Center Inc.

2138 Silas Deane Hwy., Ste. 101
Rocky Hill, CT 06067
(860) 529-5886
www.thinkconstruction.org

Industrial Management and Training Institute Inc.
233 Mill St.
Waterbury, CT 06706
(203) 753-7910
www.imtiusa.com

Delaware

N/A

Florida

ABC Florida Gulf Coast Chapter
2008 North Himes Ave.
Tampa, FL 33607
(813) 879-8064
www.abcflgulf.org

Builders Association of North Central Florida
2217 NW 66th Ct.
Gainesville, FL 32653
(352) 372-5649
www.bancf.com

The Southern Company
One Energy Place
Pensacola, FL 32503
(850) 444-6821

Georgia

Construction Ed. Foundation of Georgia
3585 Lawrenceville Suwanee Rd
Suwanee, GA 30024
(678) 889-4445
www.cefga.org

Hawaii

ABC Hawaii Chapter
80 Sand Island Access Rd. #119
Honolulu, HI 96819
(808) 845-4887
www.abchawaii.org

Idaho

N/A

Illinois

ABC, Illinois Chapter Inc.
1691 Elmhurst Rd.
Elk Grove Village, IL 60007
(847) 709-2960
www.abcil.org

Choice Construction Services
665 Hillcrest Blvd.
Hoffman Estates, IL 60195
(847) 483-4056
www.ietc-dupageco.com/
ChoiceConstructionSer

Institute for Construction Education
2353 Federal Dr.
Decatur, IL 62526
(217) 877-7523
www.iceschool.org

Indiana

N/A

Iowa

ABC of Iowa
475 Alices Rd., Ste. A
Waukee, IA 50263
(515) 987-3790
www.abciowa.org

ECI of Iowa
1710 4th Ave. S
Clear Lake, IA 50428
(641) 357-2125
www.iowaworkforce.org/eci

Kansas

ABC Heart of America Chapter
6950 Squibb Rd., Ste. 418
Mission, KS 66202
(913) 831-2221
www.abcksmo.org

Kentucky

Kentucky Department of Corrections
2439 Lawrenceburg Rd.
Frankfort, KY 40602
(502) 564-4795 ext. 229
www.corrections.ky.gov/

Western Kentucky Construction Association–AGC
2201 McCracken Blvd.
Paducah, KY 42001
(270) 744-6261
www.wkca.org

Louisiana

ABC Pelican Chapter
19251 Highland Rd,
   Training Center A
Baton Rouge, LA 70809
(225) 752-0088
www.abcpelican.org

ABC Pelican Southwest Chapter
222 Walcot Rd.
Westlake, LA 70669
(337) 882-0204
www.abcpelicansw.net

ABC Bayou Chapter
101 Riverbend Dr.
St. Rose, LA 70087
(504) 468-3188
www.abcbayou.org

Maine

N/A

Maryland

ABC Metropolitan Washington
4061 Powder Mill Rd., Ste. 120
Calverton, MD 20705
(301) 595-9711
www.abcmetrowashington.org

Massachusetts

George W. Gould Construction Institute

200 Wheeler Rd.
Burlington, MA 01803
(781) 270-9990
www.gwgci.org

Baltimore Metro Chapter ABC
1220-B East Joppa Rd., Ste. 322
Towson, MD 21286
(410) 821-0351
www.abcbaltimore.org

Cumberland Valley Chapter ABC
530 North Locust St.
Hagerstown, MD 21740
(301) 739-1190
www.abccvc.com

Michigan

ABC Central Michigan Chapter
1501 Rensen St., Ste. C
Lansing, MI 48910
(517) 394-4481
www.abccmc.org

ABC Inc. Saginaw Valley Chapter
4520 East Ashman Rd., Ste. G
Midland, MI 48642
(989) 832-8879
www.abcsvac.org

Associated Builders and Contractors Inc. Western Michigan Chapter
580 Cascade West Pkwy.
Grand Rapids, MI 49546
(616) 942-9960
www.abcwmc.org

Construction Education Trust
31800 Sherman Ave.
Madison Heights, MI 48071
(248) 298-3600
www.cet-tech.com

Tri-Counties Multi Trade Centers
2200 Ewald Cir.
Detroit, MI 48238
(313) 867-9330
www.tcmtc.com

Minnesota

Construction Education Foundation of Minnesota

10193 Crosstown Cir.
Eden Prairie, MN 55344
(952) 941-8693
www.mnabc.com

Mississippi

Mississippi Construction Ed.
Foundation
290 Commerce Park Dr., Ste. B
Ridgeland, MS 39157
(601) 605-2989
www.mcef.net

Missouri

Vatterott Educational Centers Inc.
8580 Evans Ave., Ste. A
St. Louis, MO 63134
(314) 264-1806
www.vatterott-college.edu

Montana

N/A

Nebraska

ABC Nebraska Cornhusker
Chapter
2602 Harney St.
Omaha, NE 68131
(402) 344-4258
www.abcnebraska.org

Nevada

ABC of Southern Nevada
5070 Arville St., Ste. 4
Las Vegas, NV 89118
(702) 227-0536
www.abclasvegas.org

Associated Builders and
Contractors–Sierra Nevada
Chapter
240 South Rock Blvd., Ste. 121
Reno, NV 89502
(775) 358-7888
www.abcsierranv.org

Nevada Center for Vocational
Education and Research

1227 Kimmerling Rd.
Gardnerville, NV 89460
(775) 265-2818

New Hampshire

N/A

New Jersey

ABC New Jersey Chapter
720 King George Post Rd.,
Ste. 303
Fords, NJ 08863
(732) 661-1045
www.abcnjc.org

New Mexico

ABC New Mexico Chapter
3540 Pan American Freeway
NE, Ste. F
Albuquerque, NM 87107
(505) 830-4222
www.abcnm.org

New York

CTC of New York State
6369 Collamer Dr.
East Syracuse, NY 13057
(315) 463-7539
www.abcnys.org

North Carolina

ABC of the Carolinas Inc.
2101 Sardis Rd. N
Charlotte, NC 28227
(704) 367-1331
www.abccarolinas.org

Carolinas AGC Inc.
1100 Euclid Ave.
Charlotte, NC 28203
(704) 372-1450
bstricker@carolinasagc.org
www.cagc.org

North Dakota

N/A

Ohio

ABC Northern Ohio Chapter
9255 Market Pl. W
Broadview Heights, OH 44147
(440) 717-0389
www.nocabc.com

ABC Ohio Valley CEF
33 Greenwood Ln.
Springboro, OH 45066
(937) 704-0111
www.ovabc.org

Building Trades Institute, LLC
459 Orangepoint Dr., Ste. F
Lewis Center, OH 43035
(740) 548-8091
www.buildingtradesinstitute.com

Construction Craft Academy
9760 Shepard Rd.
Macedonia, OH 44056
(800) 442-0067
www.craftacademy.com

Oklahoma

ABC of Oklahoma
1915 North Yellowood Ave.
Broken Arrow, OK 74012
(918) 254-8707
www.abcofoklahoma.com

AGC of Oklahoma–
Building Chapter
605 NW 13th St., Ste. A
Oklahoma City, OK 73103-
2213
(405) 528-4605
www.agcok.com

AYUDA Assessment, Training,
Consulting and OQ LLC
10612 Turkey Run Dr.
Edmond, OK 73025
(405) 844-8684
www.ayudallc.com

Oregon

N/A

Pennsylvania

ABC Central, PA Chapter
898 North Eagle Valley Rd.
Milesburg, PA 16853
(814) 353-1999
www.abccentralpa.org

ABC Southeast, PA Chapter
430 West Germantown Pike
East Norriton, PA 19403
(610) 279-6666
www.abcsepa.org

ABC Western Pennsylvania Inc.
3500 Spring Garden Ave.
Pittsburgh, PA 15212
(412) 231-1446
www.abcwpa.org

ABC Eastern PA
1036 North Godfrey St.
Allentown, PA 18109
(610) 821-6869
www.abceastpa.org

Keystone Chapter ABC
135 Shellyland Rd.
Manheim, PA 17545
(717) 653-8106
www.abckeystone.org

Rhode Island

N/A

South Carolina

N/A

South Dakota

N/A

Tennessee

ABC Mid-Tennessee Chapter
1604 Elm Hill Pike
Nashville, TN 37210
(615) 399-8323

**Construction Education
Partnership**
Simpson St. and Island Dr.

Kingsport, TN 37660
(423) 578-2710

West Tennessee Chapter of ABC
1995 Nonconnah Blvd.
Memphis, TN 38132
(901) 794-9212
www.wtcabc.org

Texas

**ABC Merit Shop Training
Program Inc.**
7433 Leopard St.
Corpus Christi, TX 78409
(361) 289-1636
www.ctccb.org

ABC of Greater Houston Inc.
3910 Kirby Dr., Ste. 131
Houston, TX 77098
(713) 523-6258
www.abchouston.org

ABC South Texas Chapter
10408 Gulfdale Rd.
San Antonio, TX 78216
(210) 342-1994
www.abcsouthtexas.org

ABC Southeast Texas
2700 North Twin City Hwy.
Nederland, TX 77627
(409) 724-7886
www.abcsetx.org

ABC Texas Mid Coast CEF
116 Jason Plaza
Victoria, TX 77901
(361) 572-0299
www.abcvicotia.vbxhosting.org

Central Texas ABC Chapter
3006 Longhorn Blvd., Ste. 104
Austin, TX 78758
(512) 719-5263
www.abccentraltexas.org

**Saulsbury Industries D/B/A
Construction Workforce
Training Center**
5308 Andrews Hwy.
Odessa, TX 79762
(432) 366-7676
www.cwtc-tx.com

TABACON Systems Inc.

4419 Roseland St.
Houston, TX 77006
(713) 522-0496
www.tabaconsystemsinc.com

The Victor Group
801 High Ridge Dr.
Friendswood, TX 77546
(281) 850-8079
www.thevictorgroup.net

Utah

N/A

Vermont

N/A

Virginia

ABC Virginia
14120 Parke Long Ct., Ste. 111
Chantilly, VA 20151
(703) 968-6205
www.abcva.org

M. C. Dean Inc.
22461 Shaw Rd.
Dulles, VA 20166
(703) 802-6231
www.mcdean.com

Washington

**Construction Industry Training
Council of Washington**
1930 116th Ave. NE, Ste. 201
Bellevue, WA 98004
(425) 454-2482
www.citcwa.org

West Virginia

N/A

Wisconsin

ABC of Wisconsin Inc.
5330 Wall St.
Madison, WI 53718
(608) 244-6056
www.abcwi.org

Wyoming

Lifelong Learning Center
1013 West Cheyenne Dr., Ste. A
Evanston, WY 82930
(307) 789-5742
www.uintaeducation.org

Corinthian Colleges Inc.
1706 Bill Nye Ave.
Laramie, WY 82070
(307) 742-3530
www.cci.edu

**Wyoming Contractors
Association AGC**
2220 North Bryan Stock Trail
Casper, WY 82601
(307) 237-4400
www.wcagc.org

Union Training Centers

The National Joint Apprenticeship Training Committee (NJATC) is a partnership between the International Brotherhood of Electrical Workers (IBEW) and the National Electrical Contractors Association (NECA). Not all centers offer every type of training. Contact your nearest center for more detailed information on programs.

Alaska

Korn Feind Training Center
AJEATT
PO Box 60134
Fairbanks, AK 99706
(907) 479-4449
www.ajeatt.org

**Tom Cashen Training Center
(All Training)**
AJEATT
5800 B St.
Anchorage, AK 99518
(907) 337-9508
www.ajeatt.org

Alabama

Birmingham Electrical JATC
5000 East Lake Blvd.
Birmingham, AL 35217
(205) 849-5522
www.bejatc.org

Mobile Electricians JATC
2244 Halls Mill Rd.
Mobile, AL 36606
(251) 478-4918
www.ibewlocal505.org

Montgomery Electrical JATC
PO Box 3204
Montgomery, AL 36109
(334) 272-8830

North Alabama Electrical JATC
1805 East 17th St.
Sheffield, AL 35660
(256) 383-9507

Arkansas

El Dorado Electrical JATC
810 North Newton Ave.
El Dorado, AR 71730
(870) 863-9181

Fort Smith Electrical JATC
2914 Midland Blvd.
Fort Smith, AR 72904
(479) 783-1149
www.fort-smith
  -electrical-jatc.com

Jonesboro Electrical JATC
PO Box 577
2904 King St.
Jonesboro, AR 72403
(870) 932-2114

Little Rock Electrical JATC
7418 South University
Little Rock, AR 72209
(501) 565-0768

Arizona

Globe-Miami Electrical JATC
630 North Craycroft Rd.,
  Ste. 181
Tucson, AZ 85711
(520) 323-1622

Phoenix Electrical JATC
615 East Palo Verde Dr.
Phoenix, AZ 85012
(602) 263-8104
www.pejatc.org

Southwestern Line AJATC
815 East 12th St.
Building B
Lawrence, KS 66044
(785) 832-2578
www.swlcat.org

Tucson Electrical JATC
1665 East 18th, Ste. 107
Tucson, AZ 85719
(520) 690-4690

California

Alameda County Electrical JATC
3033 Alvarado St.
San Leandro, CA 94577
(510) 351-5282

California-Nevada Electrical AJATC
9846 Limonite Ave.
Riverside, CA 92507
(951) 685-8658
www.calnevjatc.org

Central Valley Electrical JATC
1925 Yosemite Blvd.
Modesto, CA 95354
(209) 579-5417

Contra Costa Co. Electrical JATC
1255 Muir Road
Martinez, CA 94553
(925) 372-7083
www.ibewlu302.com

Fresno Madera Kings and Tulare Counties JATC
5420 East Hedges Ave.
Fresno, CA 93727
(559) 251-5174
www.fresnojatc.org

Kern County Electrical JATC
401 19th St.
Bakersfield, CA 93301
(661) 324-0105
kcett@sbcglobal.net

Los Angeles County Electrical JATC
6023 South Garfield Drive
Commerce, CA 90040
(323) 221-5881
www.laett.com

Motion Picture Employers and IBEW No. 40
5643 Vineland Ave.
North Hollywood, CA 91601
(818) 762-4239

Northern CA Sound and Communication JATC
911 Bern Ct., Ste. 100
San Jose, CA 95112
(408) 453-2101

NW Line JATC
6162 Northeast 80th Ave.
Portland, OR 97218
(503) 253-8202
www.northwestlinejatc.org

Orange County Electrical JATC
717 South Lyon St.
Santa Ana, CA 92705
(714) 245-9988
www.ocett.org

Redwood Empire JATC
1700 Corby Ave., Ste. F
Santa Rosa, CA 95407
(707) 523-3837
www.rejatc.org

Riverside Area Electrical JAC
1855 Business Center Dr.
San Bernardino, CA 92408
(909) 890-1703

Sacramento Area JATC
2836 El Centro Rd.
Sacramento, CA 95833
(916) 646-6688
www.340jatc.org

San Bernardino Mono and Inyo Counties Electrical JATC
1855 Business Center Dr.
San Bernardino, CA 92408
(909) 890-1703

San Diego Electrical Training Trust
4675 Viewridge Ave., Ste. D
San Diego, CA 92123-1644
(858) 569-6322
www.positivelyelectric.org

San Francisco Joint Electrical Training Trust
4056 Mission St.
San Francisco, CA 94112
(415) 587-2053
www.sfelectricaltraining.com

San Joaquin and Calaveras Counties Electrical JATC
1531 El Pinal Dr.
Stockton, CA 95205
(209) 467-1012

San Luis Obispo County Electrical JATC
363 Edna Rd.
San Luis Obispo, CA 93401-7930
(805) 543-5693
www.ibew639.org

San Mateo County Electrical JATC
625 Industrial Rd.
San Carlos, CA 94070
(650) 591-5217

Santa Barbara Area Electrical JATC
100-A Thomas Rd.
Buellton, CA 93427
(805) 348-1200
www.cccneca.or

Santa Clara County Electrical JATC
908 Bern Ct.
San Jose, CA 95112
(408) 453-1022
www.ejatc332.org

Solano and Napa Counties Electrical JATC
720-A Technology Way
Napa, CA 94558
(707) 251-0315

Tri County Electrical JATC
10300 Merritt St.
Castroville, CA 95012
(831) 633-3063

Ventura County Electrical JATC
201 Bernoulli Cir., Unit A
Oxnard, CA 93030
(805) 604-1155
www.ibewlu952.org

Colorado

Colorado Springs Electrical
402 West Pikes Peak Ave.
Colorado Springs, CO 80905
(719) 473-1781

Denver Area Electrical JATC
5610 Logan St.
Denver, CO 80216
(303) 295-1903
www.djeatc68.com

Mountain States Line Constructors JATC
7001 South 900 E
Suite 240
Midvale, UT 84047-1718
(801) 562-2929
www.mslcat.org

Pueblo Electrical JATC
2901 Farabaugh Lane
Pueblo, CO 81005
(719) 566-8008

Western Colorado Electrical JATC
Cliford, CO 81520
(970) 523-7726

Connecticut

Hartford Electricians JATC
208 Murphy Rd.
Hartford, CT 06114-2107
(860) 525-5982
bchejatc@snet.net

Local Union 208 IBEW JATC
43 North Ave.
Norwalk, CT 06851
(203) 840-1010

Local Union 488 IBEW/JATC
501 Main St.
Route 25
Monroe, CT 06468
(203) 452-7679

Neca and Local Ninety
2 North Plains Industrial Rd.
Wallingford, CT 06492
(203) 265-3820
www.jatc90.org

Northeastern Ajatc
1513 Ben Franklin Hwy.
Douglasville, PA 19518
(610) 326-2860
www.neat1968.org

District of Columbia
American Line Builders
PO Box 370
Medway, OH 45341
(937) 849-4177
www.albat.org

Washington D.C. Joint Apprenticeship and Training
4371 Parliament Pl., Ste. A
Lanham, MD 20706
(301) 459-2900
www.washdcjatc.org

Delaware

IBEW Joint Apprenticeship and Training Trust
814 West Basin Rd.
New Castle, DE 19720
(302) 322-5089
www.ibew313.org/jatc.htm

Northeastern AJATC
1513 Ben Franklin Hwy.
Douglasville, PA 19518
(610) 326-2860
www.neat1968.org

Florida

Central Florida Electrical JATC
2738 North Forsyth Rd.
Winter Park, FL 32792
(407) 678-3733
www.cfelectricaljatc.org

Daytona Beach Electrical JATC
790 Commonwealth Blvd.
Port Orange, FL 32129
(386) 322-6236
www.ibew756.com

Florida East Coast Electrical JATC
201 Southeast 24th St.
Ft. Lauderdale, FL 33316
(954) 523-4400

Gainesville Electrical JATC
PO Box 5428
2420 Northeast 17th Terr.
Gainesville, FL 32627-5428
(352) 376-8375

Gulf Coast Electrical JATC
7830 North Palafox St.
Pensacola, FL 32534
(850) 477-8767

Jacksonville Electrical JATC
4951 Richard St.
Jacksonville, FL 32207
(904) 737-7533
www.jaxaet.org

Miami Electrical JATC
1601 Northwest 17th Ave.
Miami, FL 33125
(305) 324-7578

Tampa Area Electrical JATC
5625 Harney Rd.
Tampa, FL 33610
(813) 621-3002
www.tampajatc.org

Georgia

Albany Electrical JATC
PO Box 916
Albany, GA 31702
(229) 436-2417

Atlanta Electrical JATC
540 Central Ave. SW
Atlanta, GA 30312
(404) 523-5400
www.aejatc.org

CSRA Electrical JATC
1248 Reynolds St.
Augusta, GA 30901
(706) 722-4100

LU 779 IBEW
PO Box 1361
Columbus, GA 31902
(706) 322-8217

Macon Electrical JATC
1046 Patterson St.
Macon, GA 31204
(478) 743-7017

Savannah Electrical JATC
1526 Dean Forest
Savannah, GA 31408
www.ibew508.com

SELCAT Trust Fund
PO Box 2004
Newnan, GA 30264
(678) 423-1338
www.selcat.com

Hawaii

Hawaii Electricians JATC
1935 HAU St., Room 301
Honolulu, HI 96819
(808) 847-0629

Idaho

Eastern Idaho Electrical JATC
PO Box 4887
540 Pershing Ave.
Pocatello, ID 83205
(208) 232-4300
www.eijatc.org

**Southwestern Idaho
Electrical JATC**
121 East 34th St.
Boise, ID 83714-6502
(208) 384-0538
www.swidjatc.org

Illinois

Bloomington Electrical JATC
2407 Beich Rd., Ste. B
Bloomington, IL 61704-0854
(309) 829-9819
www.bnjatc.org

Champaign-Urbana JATC
3301 Boardwalk Dr.
Champaign, IL 61822
(217) 352-3704

Chicago Electrical JATC
6201 West 115th St.
Alsip, IL 60803
(708) 389-1340
www.intechonline.org

**Danville NECA-IBEW
Electrical JATC**
1290 Michigan Ave.
Danville, IL 61834
(217) 304-4335

Dupage County Electrical JATC
28600 Belle Visa Pkwy.,
　Ste. 1500
Warrenville, IL 60555
(630) 393-1701
www.ibew701.org

ECA/IBEW Local 193 JATC
3150 Wide Track Dr.
Springfield, IL 62703
(217) 544-3479

Electricians Joint Apprenticeship
IBEW 649
4051 Humbert Rd.
Alton, IL 62002
(618) 466-3411

IBEW JATC Local 176
1110 Northeast Frontage Rd.
Joliet, IL 60431
(815) 741-2758
jatc@ibewlocal176.org

IBEW LU 117 NECA JATC
765 Munshaw Ln.
Crystal Lake, IL 60014
(847) 854-7200

Lake County JATC
31290 North U.S. Hwy. 45,
　Unit A
Libertyville, IL 60048
(847) 566-2200
www.lakecountyjatc.org

NECA-IBEW Local 146
3390 North Woordford St.
Decatur, IL 62526
(217) 875-3041

**NECA-IBEW Local Union 461
JATC**
591 Sullivan Rd., Ste. 200
Aurora, IL 60506
(630) 897-0461

Northern Illinois Electrical JATC
619 Southrock Dr.
Rockford, IL 61102
(815) 969-8484
jatc364@jatc364.net

Peoria Electrical JATC
707 Northeast Jefferson Ave.
Peoria, IL 61603
(309) 673-6900

Quad City Electrical JATC
1700 52nd Ave., Ste. C
Moline, IL 61265
(309) 762-3270
www.qcejatc.org

**SO. IL DIV CH NECA-IBEW LU
702 JATC**
106 North Monroe St.
West Frankfort, IL 62896
(618) 937-3311

Southwestern Illinois JATC
2000B Mall St.
Collinsville, IL 62234
(618) 343-1954
www.309jatc.org

Indiana

**Electrical JATC of Northern
Indiana**
301 East 8th St.
Michigan City, IN 46360
(219) 879-1090

Evansville Electrical JATC
1321 Edgar St.
Evansville, IN 47710
(812) 422-3343
www.evvjatc.org

Fort Wayne Electrical JATC
138 Chambeau Rd.
Fort Wayne, IN 46805
(219) 483-6257

Indianapolis Electrical JATC
1751 South Lawndale Ave.
Indianapolis, IN 46241
(317) 270-5282
union@iejatac.org
www.iejatc.org

Lafayette Electrical JATC
PO Box 5015
2953 South Creasy Ln.
Lafayette, IN 47903
(765) 449-4300
www.lejatc.com

Lake County Electricians' JATAC
2515 169th St.
Hammond, IN 46323
(219) 845-3454
www.ibew697.org

Marion Kokomo JATC
PO Box 2796
Kokomo, IN 46904
(765) 457-5371

Muncie Electrical JATC
4601 South Meeker Ave.
Muncie, IN 47302
(765) 287-9841

South Bend and Vicinity Electrical JATC
56365 Peppermint Rd.
South Bend, IN 46619
(574) 233-1721
www.jatc153.com

Terre Haute Electrical JATC
950 Ohio St.
Terre Haute, IN 47807
(812) 235-7541

Iowa

Cedar Rapids Electrical JATC
2300 Johnson Ave. NW
Cedar Rapids, IA 52404
(319) 654-9238

Dubuque Electrical JATC
1948 Northwest 92nd Ct.
Clive, IA 50325
(800) 572-6191
www.iowajatc.org

Missouri Valley Line Constructors JATC
1707 North 14th St.
Indianola, IA 50125
(515) 971-6468
www.movalleyjatc.org

Sioux City Electrical JATC
1948 Northwest 92nd Ct.
Clive, IA 50325
(515) 224-4349
www.iowajatc.org

Southeast Iowa JATC
1205 North Central Ave.
Burlington, IA 52601
(319) 753-1165

Waterloo Electrical JATC
1948 Northwest 92nd Ct.
Clive, IA 50325
(800) 572-6191
www.iowajatc.org

Kansas

Hutchinson Electrical JATC
427 North Main
Hutchinson, KS 67501
(620) 663-3431

Southwestern Line AJATC
815 East 12th St.
Building B
Lawrence, KS 66044
(785) 832-2578
office@swlcat.org
www.swlcat.org

Topeka Electrical JATC
PO Box 750901
1620 Northwest Gage, Ste. B
Topeka, KS 66675
(785) 232-5154
jatc@ibew226.kscoxmail.com
www.topekaelectricaljatc.com

Wichita Electrical JATC 810
West 13th St. N
Wichita, KS 67203-3406
(316) 264-9231
tnaylor@wejatc.org
www.wejatc.org

Kentucky

Louisville Electrical JATC
4315 Preston Hwy., Ste. 100
Louisville, KY 40213
(502) 581-9210
swillinghurst@loujatc.com

Owensboro Electrical JATC Trust
2911 West Parrish Ave.
Owensboro, KY 42301
(270) 684-3058

Paducah JATC
PO Box 3085
Paducah, KY 42002-3085
(270) 575-9646
padelectjatc@yahoo.com

Louisiana

Alexandria Electrical JATC
6703 Masonic Dr.
Alexandria, LA 71301
(318) 443-5811
www.ibew576.org

Baton Rouge Area Electrical JATC
13456 Jefferson Hwy.
Baton Rouge, LA 70817
(225) 752-4861
brejatc@aol.com

Bogal U.S.A. Electrical JATC
501 Commerce Point
New Orleans, LA 70123
(504) 733-9370

Lake Charles Electrical JATC
PO Box 18072
Lake Charles, LA 70616-8072
(337) 433-7277
carlosjatclu861@hotmail.com

Monroe Electrical JATC
PO Box 2333
Monroe, LA 71207
(318) 387-4411

New Orleans Electrical JATC
3200 Ridgelake Dr., Ste. 301
Metairie, LA 70002-4930
(504) 835-9899
mjb@noejatc.org
www.noejatc.org

Shreveport Area Electrical JATC
1013B Gould Dr.
Bossier City, LA 71111
(318) 746-6180
elecjatc@bellsouth.net

Maine

Augusta Electrical JATC
176 Main St.
Fairfield, ME 04937
(207) 453-0135
www.ibew1253.org/jatc.htm

Portland Electrical JATC
PO Box 1289
238 Goddard Road
Lewiston, ME 04240
(207) 786-9770
jatc567@yahoo.com
www.ibew567.com

Maryland

Baltimore Electrical JATC
2699 West Patapsco Ave.
Baltimore, MD 21230

(410) 247-3313
jatcneca@connext.net

Western Maryland JATC
307 East Offutt St.
PO Box 122
Cumberland, MD 21502
(301) 724-5282
wmjatc@hereintown.net

Massachusetts

Boston Electrical JATC
194 Freeport St.
Dorchester, MA 02122
(617) 436-0980

Brockton Electricians JATC
111 Rhode Island Rd.
Lakeville, MA 02347
(508) 947-8555

Northeastern AJATC
1513 Ben Franklin Hwy.
Douglasville, PA 19518
(610) 326-2860
neatapps@aol.com
www.neat1968.org

Springfield JATC
185 Industry Ave.
Springfield, MA 01104
(413) 737-2253

Worcester Electricians JATC
51 Union St.
Worcester, MA 01608
(508) 753-8635
www.ibewlocal96.org/node/9

Michigan

Ann Arbor Electrical JATC
13400 Luick Dr.
Ann Arbor, MI 48118
(734) 475-1180

Battle Creek Electrical JATC
1375 West Michigan Ave.
Battle Creek, MI 49017
(269) 660-0004
bcejatc@yahoo.com

Bay City JATC
1206 West Thomas
Bay City, MI 48706

(989) 686-4890
www.ibew692.org

Detroit JATC
2277 East 11 Mile Rd., Ste. 1
Warren, MI 48092
(586) 751-6600
www.ibewlocal58.org

Escanaba JATC
2205 North 19th St.
Escanaba, MI 49829
(906) 786-4600

Flint Electrical JATC
5209 Exchange Dr.
Flint, MI 48507
(810) 720-0583
flintjatc@sbcglobal.net

IBEW Local 219/Iron Mountain Electrical JATC
205 East Flesheim St.
Iron Mountain, MI 49801
(906) 779-1505
ibew219@bresmanlinknet

Kalamazoo Electrical JATC
1473 North 30th St.
Galesburg, MI 49053
(269) 382-1762

Lansing Electrical JATC
5708 Corner Stone Dr.
PO Box 40010, MC 4102W
Lansing, MI 48901
(517) 483-9688
www.lejatc.org

Marquette JATC
119 South Front St.
Marquette, MI 49855
(906) 226-7497

Saginaw Electrical JATC
7303 Gratiot Rd.
Saginaw, MI 48609
(989) 781-1079
sagejatc@charterinternet.com

Traverse City Electrical JATC
3912 Blair Townhall Rd. W
Traverse City, MI 49684
(231) 943-4193
tcjatc@charterinternet.com

West Michigan Electrical JATC

140 North 64th Ave.
Coopersville, MI 49404
(616) 837-7149 ext. 6
wmjatc@aol.com

Minnesota

IBEW/NECA Twin Ports Arrowhead Electrical JATC
802 Garfield Ave., Ste. 102
Duluth, MN 55802
(218) 722-8115
dul_irjatc@charterinternet.com

Iron Range Electrical JATC
802 Garfield Ave., Ste. 102
Duluth, MN 55802
(218) 722-8115

Minneapolis Electrical JATC
13100 Frankfort Pkwy.
St. Michael, MN 55376
(763) 497-0072
www.mplsjatc.org

South Central Minnesota JATC
1914 South Broadway
Rochester, MN 55904
(507) 529-7721
aspast@aol.com

St. Paul Area Electrical JATC
1330 Conway St., Ste. 150
St. Paul, MN 55106
(651) 776-4239
www.ibew110.org

Mississippi

Corinth Tupelo, MS JATC
PO Box 1027
105 North Madison St.
Corinth, MS 38835
(662) 286-2897

IBEW/JATC Local Union 903
2417 32nd St.
PO Drawer L
Gulfport, MS 39502
(228) 861-9881

Jackson JATC
PO Box 7624
Jackson, MS 39284
(601) 372-4650

Meridian Area Electricians JATC
PO Box 964
Meridian, MS 39302
(601) 483-0486

Missouri

Jefferson City Electrical JATC
209 Flora Dr.
Jefferson City, MO 65101
(573) 635-2145
www.jatc257@earthlink.net

Joplin JATC
3302 South Main
Joplin, MO 64804
(417) 624-2499

Kansas City Electrical JATC
303 East 103rd Terr.
Kansas City, MO 64114
(816) 942-3242
www.kcjatc124.org/index.html

Local 350 JATC
PO Box 2223
St. Louis, MO 63109
(314) 644-3030

Missouri Valley Line Constructors
JATC
1707 North 14th St.
Indianola, IA 50125
(515) 971-6468
www.movalleyjatc.org

Springfield, MO and Vicinity
Electricians JATC
2902 East Division
Springfield, MO 65803
(417) 866-1030

St. Joseph Electrical JATC
742 South 6th St.
St. Joseph, MO 64501
(816) 232-8090
545jatc@sbcglobal.net

St. Louis Electricians JATC
2300 Hampton Ave., Ste. A
St. Louis, MO 63139
(314) 644-3587
www.stlejatc.org

Montana

IBEW LU 233
2616 Bozeman Ave.
Helena, MT 59601
(406) 449-7173

IBEW LU 768
2616 Bozeman Ave.
Helena, MT 59601
(406) 449-7173

Montana Electrical JATC
2616 Bozeman Ave.
PO Box 4177
Helena, MT 59604
(406) 449-7173

Mountain States Line Constructors JATC
7001 South 900 E, Ste. 240
Midvale, UT 84047-1718
(801) 562-2929
www.mslcat.org

Nebraska

Lincoln Electrical JATC
6200 South 14th St.
Lincoln, NE 68512
(402) 423-4497

Omaha Electrical JATC
8960 L St., Ste. 200
Omaha, NE 68127
(402) 331-3103
www.electriciansjatc.org

Nevada

California-Nevada Electrical
AJATC
9846 Limonite Ave.
Riverside, CA 92507
(951) 685-8658
www.calnevjatc.org

Electrical JATC For Southern
Nevada
620 Legion Way
Las Vegas, NV 89110
(702) 459-7949

Northern Nevada Electrical JATC
4635 Longley Lane, Suite 108

Reno, NV 89502
(775) 358-4301

New Hampshire

IBEW LU 490 JATC
48 Airport Rd.
Concord, NH 03301
(603) 226-3964

New Jersey

Asbury Park Area Electrical JATC
PO Box 1256
Wall, NJ 07719
(732) 681-7111

IBEW Local Union 269 JATC
676 Whitehead Rd.
Trenton, NJ 08648
(609) 394-1337

JATC LU 351 South Jersey NECA
1837 Northeast Blvd.
Vineland, NJ 08360
(856) 696-2333

Jersey City Electrical JATC
65 West Century Rd.
Paramus, NJ 07652
(201) 265-7273
www.ibewlocal164.com

Local 456 IBEW JATC
1295 Livingston Ave.
North Brunswick, NJ 08902
(732) 246-2122

Paterson Electrical JATC
50 Parsippany Rd.
PO Box 5355
Parsippany, NJ 07054
(973) 428-2848
www.ibewlocal102.org

New Mexico

New Mexico Electrical JATC
4501 Montbel Loop NE
Albuquerque, NM 87107
(505) 341-4444
www.nmjatc.org

New York

Central New York Electrical JATC
4566 Waterhouse Rd.
Clay, NY 13041
(315) 546-0221
www.cnyjatc.org

EJATC of Watertown, NY
25001 Water St.
Watertown, NY 13601
(315) 782-1675
www.ibew910.org

IBEW Local 106 JATC
322 James Ave.
Jamestown, NY 14701
(716) 484-9445

Ithaca, NY Electrical JATC
701 West State St.
Ithaca, NY 18450
(607) 272-2809

JAC Joint Industry Board of
Electric Industry
158-11 Harry Van Arsdale Jr.
  Dr.
Flushing, NY 11365
(718) 591-2000

JATC Electrical Industry of
Nassau and Suffolk County
370 Motor Pkwy.
Hauppauge, NY 11788
(631) 434-3939
www.lijatc.org

Local 139 IBEW JATC
508 College Ave.
Elmira, NY 14901
(607) 732-1237

Local 325 JATC
24 Emma St.
Binghamton, NY 13905
(607) 729-6171

Local 363 IBEW JATC
67 Commerce Dr. S
Harriman, NY 10926
(845) 783-3600
www.ibewlu363.com

Local 41 IBEW JATC
South 3546 California Rd.
Orchard Park, NY 14127

(716) 662-6111
www.ibewlocal41.org

Niagara County Electrical JATC
8803 Niagara Falls Blvd.
Niagara Falls, NY 14304
(716) 297-3650

Rochester Electrical JATC
470 West Metro Park, Ste. B
Rochester, NY 14623
(716) 235-5050

Tri-City LU 236 Electrical JATC
428 Old Niskayuna Rd.
Latham, NY 12110
(518) 785-5167
www.tricityjatc.org

Westchester Fairfield JEATC
200 Bloomingdale Rd.
White Plains, NY 10605
(914) 946-0472
www.wfjatc.com

North Carolina

Carolinas Electrical JATC
PO Box 820
Hampstead, NC 28443
(910) 270-8570

Carolinas Electrical JATC-342
454 East Monmouth St.
Winston-Salem, NC 27127
(336) 721-2506

Charlotte Electrical JATC
4324 Barringer Dr.
Charlotte, NC 28217
(704) 523-7001

Local 238 IBEW JATC
45 Sardis Rd.
Asheville, NC 28806-9545
(828) 665-2198

Raleigh-Durham Electrical JATC
PO Box 13551
Research Triangle Park, NC 27709
(919) 596-6931

North Dakota

Dakotas and Western MN
Areawide JATC
2901 1st Ave. N
Fargo, ND 58102-3001
(701) 293-1300
www.dakotasjatc.org

Dakotas Electrical JATC
2901 1st Ave. N
Fargo, ND 58102-1817
(701) 293-1300

Ohio

Akron Area Electrical JATC
2650 South Main St., Ste. 100
Akron, OH 44319
(330) 644-4286

American Line Builders
PO Box 370
Medway, OH 45341
(937) 849-4177
www.albat.org

Butler Warren County
Electrical JATC
4300 Millikin Rd.
Hamilton, OH 45011
(513) 863-6115
www.ibew648.org

Canton Electrical JATC
2333 Nave Rd. SE
Massillon, OH 44646
(330) 830-6446
www.cantonjatc.org

Cincinnati Ohio Area
Electricians JATC
5179 Fishwick Dr.
Cincinnati, OH 45216
(513) 281-6924
www.electricaltc.org

Cleveland Electrical JATC
Valley View, OH 44125
(216) 573-0400
www.cejatc.org

Columbus Electrical JATC
947 Goodale Blvd.
Columbus, OH 43212
(614) 463-5282
www.electricaltrades.org

Dayton Ohio Area Electrical JATC
6550 Poe Ave.
Dayton, OH 45414-2527
(937) 264-2052
www.daytonohiojatc.org

Lake Ashtabula and Geauga
Electrical JATC
8376 Munson Rd.
Mentor, OH 44060
(440) 255-3028

Lima Area Electrical JATC
1975 North West St.
Lima, OH 45801
(419) 229-2774
www.ibewlu32.com

Lorain County Electrical JATC
105 Cooper Foster Park Rd. W
Lorain, OH 44053
(440) 233-7156

Mahoning-Trumbull
Electrical JATC
8166 Market St., Ste. D
Youngstown, OH 44512
(330) 965-0578
www.mtjatc.org

Mansfield Area Electrical JATC
PO Box 2831
Mansfield, OH 44906
(419) 526-6330

Marietta Electrical JATC
50 Sandhill Rd.
Reno, OH 45773-8002
(740) 373-5054

Newark Electrical JATC
5805 Frazeysburg Rd.
Nashport, OH 43830
(740) 454-2304

Portsmouth Electrical JATC
411 South West St.
Piketon, OH 45661
(740) 289-3208

Steubenville Electrical JATC
626 North 4th St.
Steubenville, OH 43952
(740) 282-7572

Toledo Electrical JATC
803 Lime City Road

Rossford, OH 43460
(419) 666-8088
www.tejatc.org

Warren Electrical JATC
2430 Parkman Rd. NW
Warren, OH 44485
(330) 394-3606
www.warrenjatc.org

Oklahoma

Ponca City Electrical JATC
112 Northeast 50th St.
Oklahoma City, OK 73105
(405) 848-8621

Tulsa Electricians JATC
PO Box 50158
Tulsa, OK 74150
(918) 592-2929

Western Oklahoma
Electrical JATC
PO Box 96245
1700 Southeast 15th St.
Oklahoma City, OK
   73143-6245
(405) 672-7600

Oregon

Central Electrical JATC
33309 Highway 99 E
Tangent, OR 97389
(541) 917-6199
www.cjatc.org

Crater Lake Electrical JATC
4864 Airway Dr.
Central Point, OR 97502
(541) 773-5888
www.clejatc.clearwire.net

NECA IBEW Electrical JATC
16021 Northeast Airport Way
Portland, OR 97230
(503) 262-9991
www.nietc.org

NW Line JATC
6162 Northeast 80th Ave.
Portland, OR 97218
(503) 253-8202
www.northwestlinejatc.org

Pacific Inside Electrical JATC
3427 Ash St.
North Bend, OR 97459
(541) 756-6997

Pennsylvania

Apprentice Training for the
Electrical Industry
2150 South 3rd St.
Philadelphia, PA 19148
(215) 567-6405

Chester Electrical JATC
3729 Chichester Ave.
Boothwyn, PA 19061-3135
(610) 494-2820

Harrisburg Electrical JATC
1501 Revere St.
Harrisburg, PA 17104
(717) 232-7093

Local 375 IBEW JATC
1201 West Liberty St.
Allentown, PA 18102-3135
(610) 432-9762

Local 380 IBEW JATC
4020 Cross Keys Rd.
Collegeville, PA 19426
(610) 489-6399

Local 56 IBEW EETF
185 Pennbriar Dr.
Erie, PA 16509
(814) 825-5505

Local 607 IBEW Shamokin JATC
150 South Market St.
Shamokin, PA 17872
(570) 648-9831

Local 743 IBEW and NECA
Penn-Del-Jersey Chapter
20 Morgan Dr.
Reading, PA 19608
(610) 777-3150

Northeastern AJATC
1513 Ben Franklin Hwy.
Douglasville, PA 19518
(610) 326-2860
www.neat1968.org

Pittsburgh Electrical JATC
5 Hot Metal St., Ste. 100

Pittsburgh, PA 15203-2356
(412) 432-1145

Scranton Electricians JATC
431 Wyoming Ave.
Scranton, PA 18503
(570) 344-3953
www.ibew81.com

Western Central Pennsylvania Electricians JATC
Edwin D. Hill Complex
217 Sasafrass Ln.
Beaver, PA 15009
(724) 775-6920

Wilkes-Barre Electrical JATC
1269 San Souci Pkwy.
Wilkes Barre, PA 18706
(570) 823-4028

Williamsport Electrical JATC
500 Jordan Ave.
Montoursville, PA 17754
(570) 368-8984
www.ibewlocalunion812.org

York Electricians JATC
300 Hudson St.
York, PA 17403
(717) 843-8368

Rhode Island

Local 99 IBEW JATC
22 Amflex Dr.
Cranston, RI 02921
(401) 946-9908

South Carolina

Charleston Area Electrical JATC
3345 Seiberling Rd.
Charleston Heights, SC 29418
(843) 554-1080

South Dakota

Dakota Electrical JATC
9221/2 East St. Patrick St.
Rapid City, SD 57701
(605) 343-0954

Missouri Valley Line Constructors JATC

1707 North 14th St.
Indianola, IA 50125
(515) 971-6468
www.movalleyjatc.org

Sioux Falls Electrical JATC
3509 South Norton
Sioux Falls, SD 57501
(605) 343-0370

Tennesseee

Chattanooga Electrical JATC
3924 Volunteer Dr.
Chattanooga, TN 37416
(423) 894-9053
www.chattanoogaelectricaljatc.com

Knoxville Electrical JATC
3211 Regal Dr., Ste. D
Alcoa, TN 37701
(865) 379-6214

Local 1925 IBEW
402 Jackson St.
Martin, TN 38237
(731) 587-3457

Memphis Electrical JATC
703 South Greer, Building A
Memphis, TN 38111
(901) 452-4492

Nashville Electrical JATC
310 Fesslers Lane
Nashville, TN 37210
(615) 242-9950
www.nejatc.org

Oak Ridge Electrical JATC
PO Box 4968
Oak Ridge, TN 37831-4968
(865) 483-9955

Tri-Cities Area JATC
PO Box 388
Blountville, TN 37617
(423) 323-5411

Texas

Austin Electrical JATC
4000 Caven Rd.
Austin, TX 78744
(512) 389-3024

www.ibew520.org/page/page/1058543.htm

Beaumont Electrical JATC
PO Box 1323
707 Helena Ave.
Nederland, TX 77627
(409) 717-3102

East Texas Electrical JATC
2914 East Marshall Ave.
Lonview, TX 75601
(903) 753-7646

El Paso Electricians JATC
6967 Commerce Ave.
El Paso, TX 79915
(915) 872-9927
www.epjatc.com

Galveston Electrical JATC
6227 Avenue J
Galveston, TX 77551
(409) 744-0424

Houston Electrical JATC
108 Covern St.
Houston, TX 77061
(713) 649-2739
www.houstonjatc.com

Local 898 IBEW JATC
909 Caddo St.
San Angelo, TX 76901
(915) 655-1401

North Texas Electrical JATC
680 West Tarrant Road
Grand Prairie, TX 75050
(972) 266-8383
www.ntejatc.org

South Texas Electrical JATC
2503 Blanco Rd.
San Antonio, TX 78212
(210) 225-8900

Texarkana Electrical JATC
PO Box 490
Nash, TX 75569
(903) 838-8531

Texas Gulf Coast Electrical JATC
1901 North Port
Corpus Christi, TX 78401
(361) 884-8414
www.ccjatc.com

Tyler Joint Apprenticeship Committee
200 North John Ave.
Tyler, TX 75702
(903) 595-0294

Waco Electricians Area Wide JATC
1813 Orchard Lane
Waco, TX 76705
(254) 754-3121

West Texas Electrical JATC
PO Box 245
200 South Fannin
Amarillo, TX 79105
(806) 372-1581

Wichita Falls Electrical JATC
6111 Jacksboro Hwy.
Wichita Falls, TX 76302
(940) 322-1661

Utah

Mountain States Line Constructors JATC
7001 South 900 East
Midvale, UT 84047-1718
(801) 562-2929
www.mslcat.org

Utah Electrical JATC
3400 West 2100 South
Salt Lake City, UT 84119
(801) 975-1945
www.uejatc.org

Vermont

Vermont Electrical JATC
3 Gregory Dr.
South Burlington, VT 05403
(802) 878-3468

Virginia

Hampton Roads Electrical JATC
552 Industrial Park Dr.
Newport News, VA 23608
(757) 875-1744

Richmond Electricians JATC
11255 Air Park Rd.
Ashland, VA 23005-3436

(804) 353-2655
www.rjatc.org

Roanoke Area Electrical JATC
PO Box 982
Roanoke, VA 24005
(540) 982-0688

Tidewater Electrical Industry
828 Providence Rd., Ste. A
Chesapeake, VA 23225
(757) 480-2812

Washington

Cowlitz Wahkiakum Electrical JATC
1145 Commerce Ave.
PO Box 1076
Longview, WA 98632
(360) 425-3550

Inland Empire Electrical Training Trust
3210 East Ferry Ave.
Spokane, WA 99202
(509) 534-0922

LU 112 NECA Electrical JATC
8340 West Gage Blvd.
Kennewick, WA 99336
(509) 783-0589
www.jatc112.org

Northwest Washington Electrical Industry JATC
306 Anderson Rd.
Mt. Vernon, WA 98273
(360) 428-5080
www.nwejatc.org

NW Line JATC
6162 Northeast 80th Ave.
Portland, OR 97218
(503) 253-8202
www.northwestlinejatc.org

Puget Sound Electrical JATC
550 Southwest 7th St.
Renton, WA 98055-2917
(425) 228-1777
www.psejatc.org

Southwest Washington Electrical JATC
3001 South 36th St., Ste. A
Tacoma, WA 98409
(253) 475-2922

www.swwaejatc.org

West Virginia

Charleston Electrical JATC
810 Indiana Ave.
Charleston, WV 25302
(304) 345-5166

Clarksburg Electrical JATC
1001 North 12th St.
Clarksburg, WV 26301
(304) 622-0151

Huntington Electrical JATC
1850 Madison Ave.
Huntington, WV 25704
(304) 429-3841

Parkersburg Electrical JATC
1847 7th St.
Parkersburg, WV 26101
(304) 485-7412

Wheeling Electrical JATC
82 Burkham Ct.
Wheeling, WV 26003
(304) 242-3870
www.wjatc.org

Wisconsin

Appleton/Oshkosh Area Electrical JATC

Eau Claire Area Electrical JATC

Madison Area Electrical JATC

Northeast WI Area Electrical JATC

Racine Area Electrical JATC

Southcentral, WI Area Electrical JATC

WI River Valley Area Electrical JATC
2730 Dairy Dr.
Suite 102
Madison, WI 53718
(608) 221-3321
www.wijatc.org

Local 127 IBEW JATC
3030 39th Ave.
Kenosha, WI 53144
(262) 654-0912

Milwaukee Electrical JATC
3303 South 103rd St.
Milwaukee, WI 53227
(262) 543-9060
www.mejatc.com

Missouri Valley Line
Constructors JATC
1707 North 14th St.

Indianola, IA 50125
(515) 971-6468
www.movalleyjatc.org

Wyoming

Wyoming Electrical JATC
2080 North Skyview Dr.

Casper, WY 82601
(307) 234-8311
www.wyojatc.org

Community Colleges and Technical Schools for Electrical Training

Some states do not have colleges offering specific training in the electrical craft but may have a program in "Electrical, Electronic, and Communications Engineering Technology," for example. For states with fewer than ten electrician programs, we've included those technology programs as well.

Alabama

Bevill State Community College
101 State St.
Sumiton, AL 35148
(205) 648-3271
www.bscc.edu

Bishop State Community College
351 North Broad St.
Mobile, AL 36603
(251) 690-6416
www.bishop.edu

Gadsden State
Community College
1001 George Wallace Dr.
Gadsden, AL 35902
(256) 549-8200
www.gadsdenstate.edu

George C. Wallace
Community College–Dothan
1141 Wallace Dr.
Dothan, AL 36303

(334) 983-3521
www.wallace.edu

George C. Wallace State Community College–Selma
3000 Earl Goodwin Pkwy.
Selma, AL 36703
(334) 876-9227
www.wccs.edu

Trenholm State
Technical College
1225 Air Base Blvd.
Montgomery, AL 36108
(334) 420-4200
www.trenholmtech.cc.al.us

Jefferson Davis
Community College
220 Alco Dr.
Brewton, AL 36426
(251) 867-4832
www.jdcc.edu

J. F. Drake State
Technical College

3421 Meridian St. N
Huntsville, AL 35811
(256) 539-8161
www.drakestate.edu

J. F. Ingram State
Technical College
5375 Ingram Rd.
Deatsville, AL 36022
(334) 285-5177

John C. Calhoun State
Community College
6250 US Hwy. 31 N
Tanner, AL 35671
(256) 306-2500
www.calhoun.edu

Lawson State Community
College–Birmingham Campus
3060 Wilson Rd SW
Birmingham, AL 35221
(205) 925-2515
www.lawsonstate.edu

Lurleen B. Wallace
Community College
1000 Dannelly Blvd.
Andalusia, AL 36420
(334) 222-6591
www.lbwcc.edu

Northwest Shoals Community
College–Muscle Shoals
800 George Wallace Blvd.
Muscle Shoals, AL 35661
(256) 331-5200
www.nwscc.edu

Shelton State
Community College
9500 Old Greensboro Rd.
Tuscaloosa, AL 35405
(205) 391-2347
www.sheltonstate.edu

Alaska

Ilisagvik College
Barrow, AK 99723
(907) 852-3333
www.ilisagvik.cc

Arizona

Cochise College
4190 West Hwy. 80
Douglas, AZ 85607
(520) 364-7943
www.cochise.edu

Gateway Community College
108 North 40th St.
Phoenix, AZ 85034
(602) 392-5000
www.gwc.maricopa.edu

Mohave Community College
1971 Jagerson Ave.
Kingman, AZ 86409
(928) 757-4331
www.mohave.edu

Northland Pioneer College
103 North First Ave.
Holbrook, AZ 86025
(928) 524-7600
www.npc.edu

Central Arizona College
8470 North Overfield Rd.

Coolidge, AZ 85228
(520) 494-5444
www.centralaz.edu

Glendale Community College
6000 West Olive Ave.
Glendale, AZ 85302
(623) 845-3000
www.gc.maricopa.edu

Mesa Community College
1833 West Southern Ave.
Mesa, AZ 85202
(602) 461-7000
www.mc.maricopa.edu

Pima Community College
2202 West Anklam Rd.
Tucson, AZ 85709
(520) 206-4500
www.pima.edu

Arkansas

Cossatot Community College
183 Hwy. 399
De Queen, AR 71832
(870) 584-4471
www.cccua.edu

Ouachita Technical College
One College Cir.
Malvern, AR 72104
(501) 337-5000
www.otcweb.edu

Arkansas State University–Beebe
1000 Iowa St.
Beebe, AR 72012
(501) 882-3600
www.asub.edu

Arkansas State University–
Mountain Home
1600 South College St.
Mountain Home, AR 72653
(870) 508-6100
www.asumh.edu

East Arkansas
Community College
1700 Newcastle Rd.
Forrest City, AR 72335
(870) 633-4480
www.eacc.edu

National Park
Community College
101 College Dr.
Hot Springs, AR 71913
(501) 760-4222
www.npcc.edu

North Arkansas College
1515 Pioneer Dr.
Harrison, AR 72601
(870) 391-3200
www.northark.edu

Northwest Arkansas
Community College
One College Dr.
Bentonville, AR 72712
(479) 636-9222
www.nwacc.edu

Southern Arkansas
University Tech
100 Carr Rd.
Camden, AR 71701
(870) 574-4500
www.sautech.edu

California

Allan Hancock College
800 South College Dr.
Santa Maria, CA 93454
(805) 922-6966
www.hancockcollege.edu/

American River College
4700 College Oak Dr.
Sacramento, CA 95841
(916) 484-8011
www.arc.losrios.edu/

Antelope Valley College
3041 West Ave. K
Lancaster, CA 93536
(661) 722-6300
www.avc.edu

Bakersfield College
1801 Panorama Dr.
Bakersfield, CA 93305
(661) 395-4011
www.bakersfieldcollege.edu/

Chabot College
25555 Hesperian Blvd.
Hayward, CA 94545
(510) 723-6600
www.chabotcollege.edu

College of San Mateo
1700 West Hillsdale Blvd.
San Mateo, CA 94402
(650) 574-6161
www.collegeofsanmateo.edu

Cuesta College
Highway 1
San Luis Obispo, CA 93403
(805) 546-3100
www.cuesta.edu

Foothill College
12345 El Monte Rd.
Los Altos Hills, CA 94022
(650) 949-7777
www.foothill.edu

Hartnell College
156 Homestead Ave.
Salinas, CA 93901
(831) 755-6700
www.hartnell.edu

Los Angeles Trade Technical College
400 West Washington Blvd.
Los Angeles, CA 90015
(213) 763-7000
www.lattc.edu

Merced College
3600 M St.
Merced, CA 95348
(209) 384-6000
www.merced.cc.ca.us

Palomar College
1140 West Mission
San Marcos, CA 92069
(760) 744-1150
www.palomar.edu

San Diego City College
1313 Park Blvd.
San Diego, CA 92101
(619) 388-3400
www.sdcity.edu/

Santiago Canyon College
8045 East Chapman
Orange, CA 92869
(714) 628-4900
www.sccollege.edu

Colorado

Arapahoe Community College
5900 South Santa Fe Dr.
Littleton, CO 80160
(303) 797-4222
www.arapahoe.edu

Front Range Community College
3645 West 112th Ave.
Westminster, CO 80031
(303) 466-8811
www.frontrange.edu

Pikes Peak Community College
5675 South Academy Blvd.
Colorado Springs, CO 80906
(719) 576-7711
www.ppcc.edu

Pueblo Community College
900 West Orman Ave.
Pueblo, CO 81004
(719) 549-3200
www.pueblocc.edu

Connecticut

Gateway Community College
60 Sargent Dr.
New Haven, CT 06511
(203) 285-2000
www.gwctc.commnet.edu

Naugatuck Valley Community College
750 Chase Pkwy.
Waterbury, CT 06708
(203) 575-8040
www.nvcc.commnet.edu

Northwestern Connecticut Community College
Park Pl. E
Winsted, CT 06098
(860) 738-6300
www.nwcc.commnet.edu

Norwalk Community College
188 Richards Ave.
Norwalk, CT 06854
(203) 857-7060
www.ncc.commnet.edu

Three Rivers Community College
7 Mahan Dr.
Norwich, CT 06360
(860) 823-2800
www.trcc.commnet.edu

Delaware

Delaware Technical and Community College—Owens
Route 18, Seashore Hwy.
Georgetown, DE 19947
(302) 856-5400
www.dtcc.edu/owens/

Delaware Technical and Community College—Stanton-Wilmington
400 Stanton-Christiana Rd.
Newark, DE 19702
(302) 454-3900
www.dtcc.edu

Delaware Technical and Community College—Terry
100 Campus Dr.
Dover, DE 19901
(302) 857-1000
www.dtcc.edu/terry

District of Columbia

N/A

Florida

Atlantic Technical Center
4700 Coconut Creek Pkwy.
Coconut Creek, FL 33063
(754) 321-5100
www.atlantictechcenter.com

Brevard Community College
1519 Clearlake Rd.
Cocoa, FL 32922
(321) 632-1111
www.brevardcc.edu

D. G. Erwin Technical Center
2010 East Hillsborough Ave.
Tampa, FL 33610
(813) 231-1800
www.erwin.edu

Florida Community College
at Jacksonville
501 West State St.
Jacksonville, FL 32202
(904) 632-3000
www.fccj.edu

George Stone Career Center
2400 Longleaf Dr.
Pensacola, FL 32526
(850) 941-6200
www.georgestonecenter.com

Gulf Coast Community College
5230 West Hwy. 98
Panama City, FL 32401
(850) 769-1551
www.gulfcoast.edu

Hillsborough
Community College
39 Columbia Dr.
Tampa, FL 33606
(813) 253-7000
www.hccfl.edu

Indian River Community College
3209 Virginia Ave.
Fort Pierce, FL 34981
(772) 462-4722
www.ircc.edu

Lee County High Tech Center
Central
3800 Michigan Ave.
Fort Myers, FL 33916
(239) 334-4544
www.hightechcentral.org

Lively Technical Center
500 North Appleyard Dr.
Tallahassee, FL 32304
(850) 487-7555
www.livelytech.com

Manatee Technical Institute
5603 34th St. W
Bradenton, FL 34210
(941) 751-7900
www.manateetechnical
   institute.org/

Mid Florida Tech
2900 West Oak Ridge Rd.
Orlando, FL 32809
(407) 855-5880
www.mft.ocps.net

Okaloosa Applied
Technology Center
1976 Lewis Turner Blvd.
Fort Walton Beach, FL 32547
(850) 833-3500
www.okaloosa.k12.fl.us/oatc

Palm Beach Community College
4200 Congress Ave.
Lake Worth, FL 33461
(561) 967-7222
www.pbcc.edu/

Pinellas Technical
Education Center
901 34th St. S
St. Petersburg, FL 33711
(727) 893-2500
www.myptec.org

Pinellas Technical Education
Center–Clearwater
6100 154th Ave. N
Clearwater, FL 33760
(727) 538-7167
www.myptec.org

Radford M. Locklin
Technical Center
5330 Berryhill Rd.
Milton, FL 32570
(850) 983-5700
www.santarosa.k12.fl.us/ltc/

Ridge Career Center
7700 State Rd. 544
Winter Haven, FL 33881
(863) 419-3060
www.polk-fl.net/ridge

Saint Johns River
Community College
5001 Saint Johns Ave.
Palatka, FL 32177
(386) 312-4200
www.sjrcc.edu

Santa Fe Community College
3000 Northwest 83rd St.
Gainesville, FL 32606
(352) 395-5000
www.sfcc.edu

Seminole Community College
100 Weldon Blvd.
Sanford, FL 32773
(407) 708-4722
www.scc-fl.edu

South Florida
Community College
600 West College Dr.
Avon Park, FL 33825
(863) 453-6661
www.southflorida.edu

Tallahassee Community College
444 Appleyard Dr.
Tallahassee, FL 32304
(850) 201-6200
www.tcc.fl.edu

Tom P. Haney Technical Center
3016 Hwy. 77
Panama City, FL 32405
(850) 747-5500
www.bay.k12.fl.us

Traviss Career Center
3225 Winter Lake Rd.
Lakeland, FL 33803
(863) 499-2700
www.travisstech.org

Washington-Holmes
Technical Center
757 Hoyt St.
Chipley, FL 32428
(850) 638-1180
www.whtc.us

Westside Tech
955 East Story Rd.
Winter Garden, FL 34787
(407) 905-2018
www.westside.ocps.net

Georgia

Albany Technical College
1704 South Slappey Blvd.
Albany, GA 31701
(229) 430-3500
www.albanytech.edu

Altamaha Technical College
1777 West Cherry St.
Jesup, GA 31545
(912) 427-5800
www.altamahatech.edu

Appalachian Technical College
100 Campus Dr.
Jasper, GA 30143
(706) 253-4500
www.appalachiantech.edu

Athens Technical College
800 US Hwy. 29 N
Athens, GA 30601
(706) 355-5000
www.athenstech.edu

Atlanta Technical College
1560 Metropolitan Pkwy. SW
Atlanta, GA 30310
(404) 225-4603
www.atlantatech.org

Augusta Technical College
3200 Augusta Tech Dr.
Augusta, GA 30906
(706) 771-4000
www.augustatech.edu

Bainbridge College
2500 East Shotwell St.
Bainbridge, GA 39819
(229) 248-2500
www.bainbridge.edu

**Central Georgia
Technical College**
3300 Macon Tech Dr.
Macon, GA 31206
(478) 757-3400
www.centralgatech.edu

**Chattahoochee
Technical College**
980 South Cobb Dr.
Marietta, GA 30060
(770) 528-4545
www.chattcollege.com

Coosa Valley Technical College
One Maurice Culberson Dr.
Rome, GA 30161
(706) 295-6963
www.coosavalleytech.edu

East Central Technical College
667 Perry House Rd.
Fitzgerald, GA 31750
(229) 468-2000
www.eastcentraltech.edu

Flint River Technical College
1533 Hwy. 19 S
Thomaston, GA 30286
(706) 646-6148
www.flintrivertech.edu

Griffin Technical College
501 Varsity Rd.
Griffin, GA 30223
(770) 228-7348
www.griffintech.edu

**Heart of Georgia Technical
College**
560 Pinehill Rd.
Dublin, GA 31021
(478) 275-6589
www.heartofgatech.edu

Middle Georgia Technical College
80 Cohen Walker Dr.
Warner Robins, GA 31088
(478) 988-6800
www.middlegatech.edu

Moultrie Technical College
800 Veterans Pkwy. N
Moultrie, GA 31788
(229) 891-7000
www.moultrietech.edu

North Georgia Technical College
1500 Georgia Hwy. 197
Clarkesville, GA 30523
(706) 754-7700
www.northgatech.edu

Ogeechee Technical College
One Joe Kennedy Blvd.
Statesboro, GA 30458
(912) 681-5500
www.ogeecheetech.edu

Okefenokee Technical College
1701 Carswell Ave.
Waycross, GA 31503
(912) 287-6584
www.okefenokeetech.edu

Sandersville Technical College
1189 Deepstep Rd.
Sandersville, GA 31082
(478) 553-2050
www.sandersvilletech.edu

Hawaii

Hawaii Community College
200 West Kawili St.
Hilo, HI 96720
(808) 974-7611
www.hawaii.hawaii.edu

Heald College–Honolulu
1500 Kapiolani Blvd.
Honolulu, HI 96814
(808) 955-1500
www.heald.edu/campus/
campus_honolulu.asp

Honolulu Community College
874 Dillingham Blvd.
Honolulu, HI 96817
(808) 845-9211
www.honolulu.hawaii.edu

Kauai Community College
3-1901 Kaumualii Hwy.
Lihue, HI 96766
(808) 245-8311
www.kauai.hawaii.edu

Idaho

College of Southern Idaho
315 Falls Ave.
Twin Falls, ID 83301
(208) 733-9554
www.csi.edu

Eastern Idaho Technical College
1600 South 25th E
Idaho Falls, ID 83404
(208) 524-3000
www.eitc.edu

North Idaho College
1000 West Garden Ave.
Coeur D'Alene, ID 83814
(208) 769-3300
www.nic.edu

Illinois

**City Colleges of Chicago–
Richard J. Daley College**
7500 South Pulaski Rd.
Chicago, IL 60652
(773) 838-7500
www.daley.ccc.edu

Heartland Community College
1500 West Raab Rd.
Normal, IL 61761
(309) 268-8000
www.heartland.edu

Illinois Valley
Community College
815 North Orlando Smith Ave.
Oglesby, IL 61348
(815) 224-2720
www.ivcc.edu

John Wood Community College
1301 South 48th St.
Quincy, IL 62305
(217) 224-6500
www.jwcc.edu

Joliet Junior College
1215 Houbolt Rd.
Joliet, IL 60431
(815) 729-9020
www.jjc.edu

Kaskaskia College
27210 College Rd.
Centralia, IL 62801
(618) 545-3000
www.kaskaskia.edu

Kishwaukee College
21193 Malta Rd.
Malta, IL 60150
(815) 825-2086
www.kishwaukeecollege.edu

Prairie State College
202 South Halsted St.
Chicago Heights, IL 60411
(708) 709-3500
www.prairiestate.edu

Richland Community College
One College Park
Decatur, IL 62521
(217) 875-7200
www.richland.edu

Rock Valley College
3301 North Mulford Rd.
Rockford, IL 61114
(815) 921-7821
www.rockvalleycollege.edu

Southeastern Illinois College
3575 College Rd.
Harrisburg, IL 62946
(618) 252-5400
www.sic.edu

Southwestern Illinois College
2500 Carlyle Ave.

Belleville, IL 62221
(618) 235-2700
www.swic.edu

Triton College
2000 5th Ave.
River Grove, IL 60171
(708) 456-0300
www.triton.edu

Waubonsee Community College
Rte. 47 at Waubonsee Dr.
Sugar Grove, IL 60554
(630) 466-7900
www.waubonsee.edu

Indiana

Ivy Tech Community College–
Central Indiana
50 West Fall Creek Parkway
   N Dr.
Indianapolis, IN 46208
(317) 921-4800
www.ivytech.edu/indianapolis/

Ivy Tech Community College–
East Central
4301 South Cowan Rd.,
   Box 3100
Muncie, IN 47302
(765) 289-2291
www.ivytech.edu/muncie/

Ivy Tech Community College–
Kokomo
1815 East Morgan St.
Kokomo, IN 46901
(765) 459-0561
www.ivytech.edu/kokomo/

Ivy Tech Community College–
Lafayette
3101 South Creasy Ln.
Lafayette, IN 47905
(765) 269-5000
www.ivytech.edu/lafayette/

Ivy Tech Community College–
Northcentral
220 Dean Johnson Blvd.
South Bend, IN 46601
(574) 289-7001
www.ivytech.edu/southbend/

Ivy Tech Community College–
Northeast
3800 North Anthony Blvd.
Fort Wayne, IN 46805
(260) 482-9171
www.ivytech.edu/fortwayne/

Ivy Tech Community College–
South Central
8204 Hwy. 311
Sellersburg, IN 47172
(812) 246-3301
www.ivytech.edu/sellersburg

Ivy Tech Community College–
Southwest
3501 First Ave.
Evansville, IN 47710
(812) 426-2865
www.ivytech.edu/evansville/

Ivy Tech Community College–
Wabash Valley
7999 US Hwy. 41
Terre Haute, IN 47802
(812) 299-1121
www.ivytech.edu/terrehaute/

Iowa

Des Moines Area
Community College
2006 Ankeny Blvd.
Ankeny, IA 50023
(515) 964-6241
www.dmacc.edu

Eastern Iowa Community
College District
306 West River Dr.
Davenport, IA 52801
(563) 336-3309
www.eicc.edu

Ellsworth Community College
1100 College Ave.
Iowa Falls, IA 50126
(800) 322-9235
www.ellsworthcollege.com

Northeast Iowa Community
College–Calmar
1625 Hwy. 150
Calmar, IA 52132
(563) 562-3263
www.nicc.edu

Northwest Iowa
Community College
603 West Park St.
Sheldon, IA 51201
(712) 324-5061
www.nwicc.edu

Western Iowa Tech
Community College
4647 Stone Ave.
Sioux City, IA 51102
(712) 274-6400
www.witcc.edu

Hawkeye Community College
1501 East Orange Rd.
Waterloo, IA 50701
(319) 296-2320
www.hawkeyecollege.edu

Indian Hills Community College
525 Grandview
Ottumwa, IA 52501
(641) 683-5111
www.ihcc.cc.ia.us

Iowa Central Community College
330 Ave. M
Fort Dodge, IA 50501
(515) 576-7201
www.iowacentral.edu

Iowa Western
Community College
2700 College Rd., Box 4C
Council Bluffs, IA 51502
(712) 325-3200
www.iwcc.cc.ia.us

Kirkwood Community College
6301 Kirkwood Blvd. SW
Cedar Rapids, IA 52406
(319) 398-5411
www.kirkwood.edu

North Iowa Area
Community College
500 College Dr.
Mason City, IA 50401
(641) 423-1264
www.niacc.edu

Southeastern
Community College
1500 West Agency Rd.
West Burlington, IA 52655
(319) 752-2731
www.scciowa.edu

Southwestern
Community College
1501 West Townline St.
Creston, IA 50801
(641) 782-7081
www.swcciowa.edu

Kansas

Coffeyville Community College
600 Roosevelt
Coffeyville, KS 67337
(620) 251-7700
www.coffeyville.edu

North Central Kansas
Technical College
Hwy. 24
Beloit, KS 67420
(785) 738-2276
www.ncktc.edu

Northeast Kansas
Technical College
1501 West Riley St.
Atchison, KS 66002
(913) 367-6204
www.nektc.net

Northwest Kansas
Technical College
1209 Harrison St.
Goodland, KS 67735
(785) 890-3641
www.nwktc.edu

Wichita Area Technical College
301 South Grove
Wichita, KS 67211
(316) 677-9400
www.watc.edu

Kentucky

Ashland Community and
Technical College
1400 College Dr.
Ashland, KY 41101
(606) 326-2000
www.ashland.kctcs.edu

Big Sandy Community and
Technical College
One Bert Combs Dr.
Prestonsburg, KY 41653

(606) 886-3863
www.bigsandy.kctcs.edu

Bluegrass Community and
Technical College
470 Cooper Dr.
Lexington, KY 40506
(859) 246-2400
www.bluegrass.kctcs.edu

Bowling Green Technical College
1845 Loop Dr.
Bowling Green, KY 42101
(270) 901-1000
www.bowlinggreen.kctcs.edu

Elizabethtown Community and
Technical College
600 College Street Rd.
Elizabethtown, KY 42701
(270) 769-2371
www.elizabethtown.kctcs.edu

Gateway Community and
Technical College
1025 Amsterdam Rd.
Covington, KY 41011
(859) 441-4500
www.gateway.kctcs.edu

Hazard Community and Technical College
One Community College Dr.
Hazard, KY 41701
(606) 436-5721
www.hazard.kctcs.edu

Hopkinsville Community College
720 North Dr.
Hopkinsville, KY 42241
(270) 707-3700
www.hopkinsville.kctcs.edu/

Jefferson Community and Technical College
109 East Broadway
Louisville, KY 40202
(502) 213-4000
www.jefferson.kctcs.edu

Madisonville Community College
2000 College Dr.
Madisonville, KY 42431
(270) 821-2250
www.madcc.kctcs.edu

Maysville Community and
Technical College
1755 U.S. 68
Maysville, KY 41056
(606) 759-7141
www.maycc.kctcs.edu

Owensboro Community and
Technical College
4800 New Hartford Rd.
Owensboro, KY 42303
(270) 686-4400
www.octc.kctcs.edu

Somerset Community College
808 Monticello St.
Somerset, KY 42501
(877) 629-9722
www.somerset.kctcs.edu

Southeast Kentucky Community
and Technical College
700 College Rd.
Cumberland, KY 40823
(606) 589-2145
www.southeast.kctcs.edu

West Kentucky Community and
Technical College
4810 Alben Barkley Dr.
Paducah, KY 42002
(270) 554-9200
www.westkentucky.kctcs.edu

Louisiana

Delgado Community College
615 City Park Ave.
New Orleans, LA 70119
(504) 361-6410
www.dcc.edu

L. E. Fletcher Technical
Community College
310 St. Charles St.
Houma, LA 70360
(985) 857-3655
www.lefletcher.edu

Louisiana Technical College–
Alexandria
4311 South Macarthur Dr.
Alexandria, LA 71302
(318) 487-5439
www.ltc.edu

Louisiana Technical College–
Delta-Ouachita Campus
609 Vocational Pkwy.
West Monroe, LA 71292
(318) 397-6100
www.ltc.edu

Louisiana Technical College–
Florida Parishes
137 College St.
Greensburg, LA 70441
(800) 827-9750
www.ltc.edu

Louisiana Technical College–
Gulf Area
1115 Clover St.
Abbeville, LA 70510
(337) 893-4984
www.ltc.edu

Louisiana Technical College–
Lafayette Campus
1101 Bertrand Dr.
Lafayette, LA 70506
(337) 262-5962
www.ltc.edu/lafayette/default.
html

Louisiana Technical College–
Lafourche Campus
1425 Tiger Dr.
Thibodaux, LA 70301
(985) 447-0924
www.ltc.edu

Louisiana Technical College–
Morgan Smith Campus
1230 North Main St.
Jennings, LA 70546
(337) 824-4811
www.ltc.edu

Louisiana Technical College–
Shreveport-Bossier Campus
2010 North Market St.
Shreveport, LA 71107
(318) 676-7811
www.ltc.edu

Louisiana Technical College–
Sullivan Campus
1710 Sullivan Dr.
Bogalusa, LA 70427
(985) 732-6640
www.ltc.edu

Louisiana Technical College–
Teche Area
609 Ember Dr.
New Iberia, LA 70560
(337) 373-0011
www.techeareacampus.net

Louisiana Technical College–
T. H. Harris Campus
332 East South St.
Opelousas, LA 70570
(337) 948-0239
www.ltc.edu

Louisiana Technical College–
West Jefferson Campus
475 Manhattan Blvd.
Harvey, LA 70058
(504) 361-6464
www.ltc.edu

Louisiana Technical College–
Young Memorial Campus
900 Youngs Rd.
Morgan City, LA 70380
(985) 380-2436
www.ltc.edu

Nunez Community College
3710 Paris Rd.
Chalmette, LA 70043
(504) 278-7497
www.nunez.edu

Sowela Technical
Community College
3820 J. Bennett Johnston Ave.
Lake Charles, LA 70616
(337) 491-2698
www.sowela.edu

Maine

Eastern Maine
Community College
354 Hogan Rd.
Bangor, ME 04401
(207) 974-4600
www.emcc.edu

Kennebec Valley
Community College
92 Western Ave.
Fairfield, ME 04937
(207) 453-5000
www.kvcc.me.edu

Northern Maine
Community College
33 Edgemont Dr.
Presque Isle, ME 04769
(207) 768-2700
www.nmcc.edu

Southern Maine
Community College
2 Fort Rd.
South Portland, ME 04106
(207) 741-5500
www.smccme.edu

Washington County
Community College
One College Dr.
Calais, ME 04619
(207) 454-1000
www.wccc.me.edu

Maryland

Anne Arundel
Community College
101 College Pkwy.
Arnold, MD 21012
(410) 647-7100
www.aacc.edu

Baltimore City
Community College
2901 Liberty Heights Ave.
Baltimore, MD 21215
(410) 462-8300
www.bccc.edu

Cecil Community College
One Seahawk Dr.
North East, MD 21901
(410) 287-6060
www.cecil.edu

College of Southern Maryland
8730 Mitchell Rd.
La Plata, MD 20646
(301) 934-2251
www.csmd.edu

Howard Community College
10901 Little Patuxent Pkwy.
Columbia, MD 21044
(410) 772-4800
www.howardcc.edu

Prince George's
Community College
301 Largo Rd.
Largo, MD 20774
(301) 336-6000
www.pgcc.edu

Community College of
Baltimore County
7201 Rossville Blvd.
Baltimore, MD 21237
(410) 682-6000
www.ccbcmd.edu

Wor-Wic Community College
32000 Campus Dr.
Salisbury, MD 21804
(410) 334-2800
www.worwic.edu

Massachusetts

Berkshire Community College
1350 West St.
Pittsfield, MA 01201
(413) 499-4660
www.berkshirecc.edu

Holyoke Community College
303 Homestead Ave.
Holyoke, MA 01040
(413) 552-2700
www.hcc.mass.edu

Massasoit Community College
One Massasoit Blvd.
Brockton, MA 02302
(508) 588-9100
www.massasoit.mass.edu

Middlesex Community College
Springs Rd.
Bedford, MA 01730
(978) 656-3200
www.middlesex.mass.edu

Mount Wachusett
Community College
444 Green St.
Gardner, MA 01440
(978) 632-6600
www.mwcc.mass.edu

Northern Essex
Community College
100 Elliott St.

Haverhill, MA 01830
(978) 556-3000
www.necc.mass.edu/

Quinsigamond
Community College
670 West Boylston St.
Worcester, MA 01606
(508) 853-2300
www.qcc.edu

Springfield Technical
Community College
1 Armory Sq.
Springfield, MA 01105
(413) 781-7822
www.stcc.edu

Michigan

Alpena Community College
666 Johnson St.
Alpena, MI 49707
(989) 356-9021
www.alpenacc.edu

Jackson Community College
2111 Emmons Rd.
Jackson, MI 49201
(517) 787-0800
www.jccmi.edu

Kellogg Community College
450 North Ave.
Battle Creek, MI 49017
(269) 965-3931
www.kellogg.edu

Lansing Community College
419 North Capitol Ave.
Lansing, MI 48901
(517) 483-1957
www.lansing.cc.mi.us

Mott Community College
1401 East Court St.
Flint, MI 48503
(810) 762-0200
www.mcc.edu

Bay De Noc Community College
2001 North Lincoln Rd.
Escanaba, MI 49829
(906) 786-5802
www.baycollege.edu

Delta College
1961 Delta Rd.
University Center, MI 48710
(989) 686-9000
www.delta.edu

Glen Oaks Community College
62249 Shimmel Rd.
Centreville, MI 49032
(269) 467-9945
www.glenoaks.edu

**Grand Rapids
Community College**
143 Bostwick Ave. NE
Grand Rapids, MI 49503
(616) 234-4000
www.grcc.edu

Henry Ford Community College
5101 Evergreen Rd.
Dearborn, MI 48128
(313) 845-9600
www.hfcc.edu

**Kalamazoo Valley Community
College**
6767 West O Ave.
Kalamazoo, MI 49003
(269) 488-4100
www.kvcc.edu

Kirtland Community College
10775 North Saint Helen Rd.
Roscommon, MI 48653
(989) 275-5000
www.kirtland.edu

Lake Michigan College
2755 East Napier Ave.
Benton Harbor, MI 49022
(269) 927-3571
www.lakemichigancollege.edu

Macomb Community College
14500 East Twelve Mile Rd.
Warren, MI 48088
(586) 445-7999
www.macomb.edu

**Monroe County
Community College**
1555 South Raisinville Rd.
Monroe, MI 48161
(734) 242-7300
www.monroeccc.edu

Montcalm Community College
2800 College Dr.
Sidney, MI 48885
(989) 328-2111
www.montcalm.edu

Muskegon Community College
221 South Quarterline Rd.
Muskegon, MI 49442
(231) 773-9131
www.muskegoncc.edu

Northwestern Michigan College
1701 East Front St.
Traverse City, MI 49686
(231) 995-1000
www.nmc.edu

Oakland Community College
2480 Opdyke Rd.
Bloomfield Hills, MI 48304
(248) 341-2000
www.oaklandcc.edu

Schoolcraft College
18600 Haggerty Rd.
Livonia, MI 48152
(734) 462-4400
www.schoolcraft.edu

Southwestern Michigan College
58900 Cherry Grove Rd.
Dowagiac, MI 49047
(269) 782-1000
www.swmich.edu

**St. Clair County
Community College**
323 Erie
Port Huron, MI 48061
(810) 984-3881
www.sc4.edu

**Wayne County
Community College**
801 West Fort St.
Detroit, MI 48226
(313) 496-2600
www.wcccd.edu

Minnesota

Anoka Technical College
1355 West Hwy. 10
Anoka, MN 55303
(763) 576-4700
www.anokatech.edu

**Dakota County
Technical College**
1300 145th St. E
Rosemount, MN 55068
(651) 423-8301
www.dctc.mnscu.edu

**Dunwoody College of
Technology**
818 Dunwoody Blvd.
Minneapolis, MN 55403
(612) 374-5800
www.dunwoody.edu

Hibbing Community College
1515 East 25th St.
Hibbing, MN 55746
(218) 262-7200
www.hibbing.edu

Lake Superior College
2101 Trinity Rd.
Duluth, MN 55811
(800) 432-2884
www.lsc.edu

Leech Lake Tribal College
6945 Littlewolf Rd. NW
Cass Lake, MN 56633
(218) 335-4200
www.lltc.org

**Minneapolis Community and
Technical College**
1501 Hennepin Ave.
Minneapolis, MN 55403
(612) 659-6000
www.minneapolis.edu

**Minnesota State Community
and Technical College**
1414 College Way
Fergus Falls, MN 56537
(218) 736-1500
www.minnesota.edu

**Minnesota West Community
and Technical College**
1593 11th Ave.
Granite Falls, MN 56241
(320) 564-4511
www.mnwest.edu

**Northland Community and
Technical College**
1101 Hwy. #1 E
Thief River Falls, MN 56701
(218) 681-0701
www.northlandcollege.edu

Northwest Technical College
905 Grant Ave. SE
Bemidji, MN 56601
(218) 333-6600
www.ntcmn.edu

Ridgewater College
2101 15th Ave. NW
Willmar, MN 56201
(800) 722-1151
www.ridgewater.edu

Riverland Community College
1900 8th Ave. NW
Austin, MN 55912
(507) 433-0600
www.riverland.edu

Saint Cloud Technical College
1540 Northway Dr.
Saint Cloud, MN 56303
(320) 308-5000
www.sctc.edu

Saint Paul College—
A Community and
Technical College
235 Marshall Ave.
Saint Paul, MN 55102
(651) 846-1600
www.saintpaul.edu

Mississippi

East Central Community College
275 West Broad St.
Decatur, MS 39327
(601) 635-2111
www.eccc.edu

East Mississippi
Community College
1512 Kemper St.
Scooba, MS 39358
(662) 476-5000
www.eastms.edu/

Hinds Community College
501 East Main St.
Raymond, MS 39154
(601) 857-5261
www.hindscc.edu

Itawamba Community College
602 West Hill St.
Fulton, MS 38843
(601) 862-8000

Mississippi Delta
Community College
Hwy. 3 and Cherry St.
Moorhead, MS 38761
(662) 246-6322
www.msdelta.edu

Mississippi Gulf Coast
Community College
51 Main St.
Perkinston, MS 39573
(601) 928-5211
www.mgccc.edu

Northeast Mississippi
Community College
Cunningham Blvd.
Booneville, MS 38829
(662) 728-7751
www.nemcc.edu

Pearl River Community College
101 Hwy. 11 N
Poplarville, MS 39470
(601) 403-1000
www.prcc.edu

Missouri

Linn State Technical College
One Technology Dr.
Linn, MO 65051
(573) 897-5000
www.linnstate.edu

St. Louis Community College—
Florissant Valley
3400 Pershall Rd.
St. Louis, MO 63135
(314) 513-4200
www.stlcc.edu

Crowder College
601 Laclede Ave.
Neosho, MO 64850
(417) 451-3223
www.crowder.edu

Jefferson College
1000 Viking Dr.
Hillsboro, MO 63050
(636) 797-3000
www.jeffco.edu

Metropolitan Community College—
Business and Technology
6899 Executive Dr.
Kansas City, MO 64120
(816) 482-5210
www.mcckc.edu

Mineral Area College
5270 Flat River Rd.
Park Hills, MO 63601
(573) 431-4593
www.mineralarea.edu

Moberly Area
Community College
101 College Ave.
Moberly, MO 65270
(660) 263-4110
www.macc.edu

Ozarks Technical
Community College
1001 East Chestnut Expwy.
Springfield, MO 65802
(417) 447-7500
www.otc.edu

Three Rivers Community College
2080 Three Rivers Blvd.
Poplar Bluff, MO 63901
(573) 840-9600
www.trcc.edu

Montana

Miles Community College
2715 Dickinson
Miles City, MT 59301
(800) 541-9281
www.milescc.edu

Nebraska

Central Community College
3134 West Hwy. 34
Grand Island, NE 68802
(308) 398-4222
www.cccneb.edu

Metropolitan Community
College Area
30th and Fort St.
Omaha, NE 68111
(402) 457-2400
www.mccneb.edu

Mid Plains Community College
601 West State Farm Rd.
North Platte, NE 69101
(800) 658-4308
www.mpcc.edu

Northeast Community College
801 East Benjamin
Norfolk, NE 68702
(402) 371-2020
www.northeastcollege.com

Southeast Community College
301 South 68th Street Pl.
Lincoln, NE 68510
(402) 471-3333
www.southeast.edu

**Western Nebraska
Community College**
1601 East 27th St.
Scottsbluff, NE 69361
(308) 635-3606
www.wncc.net

Nevada

**Truckee Meadows
Community College**
7000 Dandini Blvd.
Reno, NV 89512
(775) 673-7000
www.tmcc.edu

New Hampshire

**New Hampshire Community
Technical College–Nashua**
505 Amherst St.
Nashua, NH 03063
(603) 882-6923
www.nashua.nhctc.edu

**New Hampshire
Technical Institute**
31 College Dr.
Concord, NH 03301
(603) 271-6484
www.nhti.edu

New Jersey

Brookdale Community College
765 Newman Springs Rd.

Lincroft, NJ 07738
(732) 224-2345
www.brookdalecc.edu

Burlington County College
601 Pemberton–Browns Mills
Rd.
Pemberton, NJ 08068
(609) 894-9311
www.bcc.edu

Camden County College
College Dr.
Blackwood, NJ 08012
(856) 227-7200
www.camdencc.edu

County College of Morris
214 Center Grove Rd.
Randolph, NJ 07869
(973) 328-5000
www.ccm.edu

Essex County College
303 University Ave.
Newark, NJ 07102
(973) 877-3000
www.essex.edu

**Hudson County
Community College**
70 Sip Ave.
Jersey City, NJ 07306
(201) 714-7100
www.hccc.edu

**Mercer County
Community College**
1200 Old Trenton Rd.
West Windsor, NJ 08550
(609) 570-4800
www.mccc.edu

Middlesex County College
2600 Woodbridge Ave.
Edison, NJ 08818
(732) 548-6000
www.middlesexcc.edu

**Passaic County
Community College**
One College Blvd.
Paterson, NJ 07505
(973) 684-6800
www.pccc.edu

**Raritan Valley
Community College**
111 Lamington Rd.
North Branch, NJ 08876
(908) 526-1200
www.raritanval.edu

New Mexico

**Central New Mexico
Community College**
525 Buena Vista SE
Albuquerque, NM 87106
(505) 224-3000
www.cnm.edu

Luna Community College
Hot Springs Blvd.
Las Vegas, NM 87701
(505) 454-2500
www.luna.edu

Navajo Technical College
Lower Point Road, SR 371
Crownpoint, NM 87313
(505) 786-4100
www.navajotech.edu

Clovis Community College
417 Schepps Blvd.
Clovis, NM 88101
(505) 769-2811
www.clovis.edu

**New Mexico State University–
Alamogordo**
2400 North Scenic Dr.
Alamogordo, NM 88310
(505) 439-3600
www.alamo.nmsu.edu

**New Mexico State University–
Dona Ana**
3400 South Espina
Las Cruces, NM 88003
(505) 527-7500
www.dabcc.nmsu.edu

**New Mexico State University–
Grants**
1500 Third St.
Grants, NM 87020
(505) 287-7981
www.grants.nmsu.edu

San Juan College
4601 College Blvd.
Farmington, NM 87402
(505) 326-3311
www.sanjuancollege.edu

New York

Onondaga Community College
4941 Onondaga Rd.
Syracuse, NY 13215
(315) 498-2622
www.sunyocc.edu

Adirondack Community College
640 Bay Rd.
Queensbury, NY 12804
(518) 743-2200
www.sunyacc.edu

Bramson Ort College
69-30 Austin St.
Forest Hills, NY 11375
(718) 261-5800
www.bramsonort.org

Broome Community College
PO Box 1017
Binghamton, NY 13902
(607) 778-5000
www.sunybroome.edu

Cayuga County
Community College
197 Franklin St.
Auburn, NY 13021
(315) 255-1743
www.cayuga-cc.edu

Clinton City College
136 Clinton Point Dr.
Plattsburgh, NY 12901
(518) 562-4200
www.clinton.edu

Corning Community College
1 Academic Dr.
Corning, NY 14830
(607) 962-9011
www.corning-cc.edu/

CUNY Bronx Community College
West 181st St. and University
  Ave.
Bronx, NY 10453
(718) 284-5100
www.bcc.cuny.edu

CUNY Queensborough
Community College
222-05 56th Ave.
Bayside, NY 11364
(718) 631-6262
www.qcc.cuny.edu

Dutchess Community College
53 Pendell Rd.
Poughkeepsie, NY 12601
(845) 431-8000
www.sunydutchess.edu

Erie Community College
121 Ellicott St.
Buffalo, NY 14203
(716) 842-2770
www.ecc.edu

Fulton-Montgomery
Community College
2805 State Hwy. 67
Johnstown, NY 12095
(518) 762-4651
www.fmcc.suny.edu

Hudson Valley
Community College
80 Vandenburgh Ave.
Troy, NY 12180
(518) 629-4822
www.hvcc.edu

Mohawk Valley Community
College–Utica Branch
1101 Sherman Dr.
Utica, NY 13501
(315) 792-5400
www.mvcc.edu

Monroe Community College
1000 East Henrietta Rd.
Rochester, NY 14623
(585) 292-2000
www.monroecc.edu

Nassau Community College
1 Education Dr.
Garden City, NY 11530
(516) 222-7355
www.ncc.edu

Niagara County
Community College
3111 Saunders Settlement Rd.
Sanborn, NY 14132
(716) 614-6222
www.niagaracc.suny.edu

Onondaga Community College
4941 Onondaga Rd.
Syracuse, NY 13215
(315) 498-2622
www.sunyocc.edu

Orange County
Community College
115 South St.
Middletown, NY 10940
(845) 344-6222
www.orange.cc.ny.us

Schenectady County
Community College
78 Washington Ave.
Schenectady, NY 12305
(518) 381-1200
www.sunysccc.edu

Suffolk County
Community College
533 College Rd.
Selden, NY 11784
(631) 451-4110
www3.sunysuffolk.edu

SUNY Westchester
Community College
75 Grasslands Rd.
Valhalla, NY 10595
(914) 606-6600
www.sunywcc.edu

Tompkins-Cortland
Community College
170 North St.
Dryden, NY 13053
(607) 844-8211
www.tc3.edu

Ulster County
Community College
Cottekill Rd.
Stone Ridge, NY 12484
(845) 687-5000
www.sunyulster.edu

North Carolina

Asheville-Buncombe Technical
Community College
340 Victoria Rd.
Asheville, NC 28801
(828) 254-1921
www.abtech.edu

Beaufort County
Community College
5337 Hwy. 264 E
Washington, NC 27889
(252) 940-6202
www.beaufortccc.edu

Bladen Community College
7418 NC Hwy. 41 W
Dublin, NC 28332
(910) 879-5500
www.bladen.cc.nc.us

Blue Ridge Community College
180 West Campus Dr.
Flat Rock, NC 28731
(828) 694-1700
www.blueridge.edu

Caldwell Community College
and Technical Institute
2855 Hickory Blvd.
Hudson, NC 28638
(828) 726-2200
www.cccti.edu

Catawba Valley
Community College
2550 Hwy. 70 SE
Hickory, NC 28602
(828) 327-7000
www.cvcc.edu

Central Carolina
Community College
1105 Kelly Dr.
Sanford, NC 27330
(919) 775-5401
www.cccc.edu

Central Piedmont
Community College
1201 Elizabeth Ave.
Charlotte, NC 28204
(704) 330-2722
www.cpcc.edu

Cleveland Community College
137 South Post Rd.
Shelby, NC 28152
(704) 484-4000
www.clevelandcommunity
   college.edu

Coastal Carolina
Community College
444 Western Blvd.

Jacksonville, NC 28546
(910) 455-1221
www.coastal.cc.nc.us

College of the Albemarle
1208 North Road St.
Elizabeth City, NC 27906
(252) 335-0821
www.albemarle.edu

Davidson County
Community College
297 Davidson Community
   College Rd.
Thomasville, NC 27360
(336) 249-8186
www.davidsonccc.edu

Durham Technical
Community College
1637 Lawson St.
Durham, NC 27703
(919) 686-3300
www.durhamtech.edu

Fayetteville Technical
Community College
2201 Hull Rd.
Fayetteville, NC 28303
(910) 678-8400
www.faytechcc.edu

Forsyth Technical
Community College
2100 Silas Creek Pkwy.
Winston-Salem, NC 27103
(336) 723-0371
www.forsythtech.edu

Gaston College
201 Hwy. 321 S
Dallas, NC 28034
(704) 922-6200
www.gaston.cc.nc.us

Guilford Technical
Community College
601 High Point Rd.
Jamestown, NC 27282
(336) 334-4822
www.gtcc.edu

Halifax Community College
100 College Dr.
Weldon, NC 27890
(252) 536-4221
www.halifaxcc.edu

Haywood Community College
185 Freedlander Dr.
Clyde, NC 28721
(828) 627-2821
www.haywood.edu

Isothermal Community College
286 ICC Loop Rd.
Spindale, NC 28160
(828) 286-3636
www.isothermal.edu

James Sprunt
Community College
133 James Sprunt Dr.
Kenansville, NC 28349
(910) 296-2400
www.sprunt.com

Johnston Community College
245 College Rd.
Smithfield, NC 27577
(919) 934-3051
www.johnstoncc.edu

Martin Community College
1161 Kehukee Park Rd.
Williamston, NC 27892
(252) 792-1521
www.martincc.edu

Mayland Community College
200 Mayland Dr.
Spruce Pine, NC 28777
(828) 765-7351
www.mayland.edu

McDowell Technical
Community College
54 College Dr.
Marion, NC 28752
(828) 652-6021
www.mcdowelltech.edu

Mitchell Community College
500 West Broad St.
Statesville, NC 28677
(704) 878-3200
www.mitchell.cc.nc.us

Montgomery Community College
1011 Page St.
Troy, NC 27371
(910) 576-6222
www.montgomery.edu

Nash Community College
522 North Old Carriage Rd.
Rocky Mount, NC 27804
(252) 443-4011
www.nashcc.edu

Pamlico Community College
5049 Hwy. 306 S
Grantsboro, NC 28529
(252) 249-1851
www.pamlicocc.edu

Piedmont Community College
1715 College Dr.
Roxboro, NC 27573
(336) 599-1181
www.piedmontcc.edu

Pitt Community College
1986 Pitt Tech Rd.
Winterville, NC 28590
(252) 493-7200
www.pittcc.edu

Randolph Community College
629 Industrial Park Ave.
Asheboro, NC 27205
(336) 633-0200
www.randolph.edu

Richmond Community College
1042 West Hamlet Ave.
Hamlet, NC 28345
(910) 410-1700
www.richmondcc.edu

Robeson Community College
5160 Fayetteville Rd.
Lumberton, NC 28360
(910) 272-3700
www.robeson.cc.nc.us

Rowan-Cabarrus
Community College
1333 Jake Alexander Blvd.
Salisbury, NC 28146
(704) 637-0760
www.rccc.cc.nc.us

Southeastern
Community College
4564 Chadbourn Hwy.
Whiteville, NC 28472
(910) 642-7141
www.sccnc.edu

South Piedmont
Community College
680 Hwy. 74 W
Polkton, NC 28135
(704) 272-7635
www.spcc.edu

Southwestern Community College
447 College Dr.
Sylva, NC 28779
(828) 586-4091
www.southwesterncc.edu

Stanly Community College
141 College Dr.
Albemarle, NC 28001
(704) 982-0121
www.stanly.edu

Surry Community College
630 South Main St.
Dobson, NC 27017
(336) 386-3204
www.surry.edu

Tri-County Community College
4600 East US 64
Murphy, NC 28906
(828) 837-6810
www.tricountycc.edu

Vance-Granville
Community College
PO Box 917
State Rd. 1126
Henderson, NC 27536
(252) 492-2061
www.vgcc.edu

Wake Technical
Community College
9101 Fayetteville Rd.
Raleigh, NC 27603
(919) 662-3400
www.waketech.edu

Wilkes Community College
1328 South Collegiate Dr.
Wilkesboro, NC 28697
(336) 838-6100
www.wilkescc.edu

Wilson Technical
Community College
902 Herring Ave.
Wilson, NC 27893
(252) 291-1195
www.wilsontech.cc.nc.us

North Dakota

Bismarck State College
1500 Edwards Ave.
Bismarck, ND 58506
(701) 224-5400
www.bismarckstate.edu

North Dakota State College
of Science
800 North 6th St.
Wahpeton, ND 58076
(701) 671-2403
www.ndscs.edu

Ohio

Belmont Technical College
120 Fox Shannon Pl.
Saint Clairsville, OH 43950
(740) 695-9500
www.btc.edu

Bowling Green State University–
Firelands
One University Dr.
Huron, OH 44839
(419) 433-5560
www.firelands.bgsu.edu

Central Ohio Technical College
1179 University Dr.
Newark, OH 43055
(740) 366-1351
www.cotc.edu

Cincinnati State Technical and
Community College
3520 Central Pkwy.
Cincinnati, OH 45223
(513) 569-1500
www.cincinnatistate.edu

Columbus State
Community College
550 East Spring St.
Columbus, OH 43215
(614) 287-5353
www.cscc.edu

Cuyahoga Community
College District
700 Carnegie Ave.
Cleveland, OH 44115
(800) 954-8742
www.tri-c.edu

Hocking College
3301 Hocking Pkwy.
Nelsonville, OH 45764
(740) 753-3591
www.hocking.edu

James A. Rhodes State College
4240 Campus Dr.
Lima, OH 45804
(419) 221-1112
www.rhodesstate.edu

Jefferson Community College
4000 Sunset Blvd.
Steubenville, OH 43952
(740) 264-5591
www.jcc.edu

Lakeland Community College
7700 Clocktower Dr.
Kirtland, OH 44094
(440) 525-7000
www.lakelandcc.edu

Lorain County
Community College
1005 North Abbe Rd.
Elyria, OH 44035
(440) 366-5222
www.lorainccc.edu

Marion Technical College
1467 Mount Vernon Ave.
Marion, OH 43302
(740) 389-4636
www.mtc.edu

North Central State College
2441 Kenwood Cir.
Mansfield, OH 44901
(419) 755-4800
www.ncstatecollege.edu

Northwest State
Community College
22600 SR 34
Archbold, OH 43502
(419) 267-5511
www.northweststate.edu

Owens Community College
30335 Oregon Rd.
Perrysburg, OH 43551
(567) 661-7000
www.owens.edu

Sinclair Community College
444 West Third St.
Dayton, OH 45402
(937) 512-3000
www.sinclair.edu

Stark State College of Technology
6200 Frank Ave. NW
North Canton, OH 44720
(330) 494-6170
www.starkstate.edu

Terra State Community College
2830 Napoleon Rd.
Fremont, OH 43420
(419) 334-8400
www.terra.edu

Washington State
Community College
710 Colegate Dr.
Marietta, OH 45750
(740) 374-8716
www.wscc.edu

Oklahoma

Eastern Oklahoma County
Technology Center
4601 North Choctaw Rd.
Choctaw, OK 73020
(405) 390-9591
www.eoctech.org

Gordon Cooper
Technology Center
1 John C. Bruton Blvd.
Shawnee, OK 74804
(405) 273-7493
www.gctech.org

Great Plains Technology Center
4500 West Lee Blvd.
Lawton, OK 73505
(580) 355-6371
www.gptech.org

Metro Technology Centers
1900 Springlake Dr.
Oklahoma City, OK 73111
(405) 424-8324
www.metrotech.org

Oregon

Blue Mountain
Community College
2411 NW Carden Ave.
Pendleton, OR 97801
(541) 276-1260
www.bluecc.edu

Chemeketa Community College
4000 Lancaster Dr. NE
Salem, OR 97305
(503) 399-5000
www.chemeketa.edu

Clackamas Community College
19600 South Molalla Ave.
Oregon City, OR 97045
(503) 657-6958
www.clackamas.edu

Columbia Gorge
Community College
400 East Scenic Dr.
The Dalles, OR 97058
(541) 506-6011
www.cgcc.cc.or.us

Lane Community College
4000 East 30th Ave.
Eugene, OR 97405
(541) 463-3000
www.lanecc.edu

Mt. Hood Community College
26000 SE Stark St.
Gresham, OR 97030
(503) 491-6422
www.mhcc.edu

Oregon Coast
Community College
332 SW Coast Hwy.
Newport, OR 97365
(541) 265-2283
www.occc.cc.or.us

Portland Community College
12000 SW 49th Ave.
Portland, OR 97219
(503) 244-6111
www.pcc.edu

Rogue Community College
3345 Redwood Hwy.
Grants Pass, OR 97527
(541) 956-7500
www.roguecc.edu

Pennsylvania

Community College of Allegheny County
800 Allegheny Ave.
Pittsburgh, PA 15233
(412) 323-2323
www.ccac.edu

Delaware County Community College
901 South Media Line Rd.
Media, PA 19063
(610) 359-5000
www.dccc.edu

Harrisburg Area Community College–Harrisburg
One HACC Dr.
Harrisburg, PA 17110
(717) 780-2300
www.hacc.edu

Lehigh Carbon Community College
4525 Education Park Dr.
Schnecksville, PA 18078
(610) 799-2121
www.lccc.edu

Luzerne County Community College
1333 South Prospect St.
Nanticoke, PA 18634
(570) 740-0200
www.luzerne.edu

Rosedale Technical Institute
215 Beecham Dr.
Pittsburgh, PA 15205
(412) 521-6200
www.rosedaletech.org

Puerto Rico

Universal Technology College of Puerto Rico
111 Comercio St.
Aguadilla, PR 00603
(787) 882-2065
www.unitecpr.edu

Instituto Tecnologico De Puerto Rico–Manati
State Road 2 Km. 47.7
Manati, PR 00674

(787) 854-2250

Instituto Tecnologico De Puerto Rico–Recinto De Guayama
Urb. Vives, Final
Guayama, PR 00785
(787) 864-0354

Instituto Tecnologico De Puerto Rico–Recinto De Ponce
4820 Candido Hoyos Urb.
Perla Del Sur
Ponce, PR 00717
(787) 843-1305

Instituto Tecnologico De Puerto Rico–Recinto De San Juan
Calle Alegria Final Urb.
Las Virtudes
Rio Piedras, PR 00924
(787) 767-5905

Rhode Island

Community College of Rhode Island
400 East Ave.
Warwick, RI 02886
(401) 825-1000
www.ccri.edu

South Carolina

Greenville Technical College
506 South Pleasantburg Dr.
Greenville, SC 29607
(864) 250-8111
www.greenvilletech.com

Midlands Technical College
1260 Lexington Dr.
West Columbia, SC 29170
(803) 738-8324
www.midlandstech.edu

Northeastern Technical College
1201 Chesterfield Hwy.
Cheraw, SC 29520
(843) 921-6900
www.netc.edu

Aiken Technical College
2276 Jefferson Davis Hwy.
Graniteville, SC 29829
(803) 593-9954
www.atc.edu

Florence-Darlington Technical College
2715 West Lucas St.
Florence, SC 29501
(843) 661-8324
www.fdtc.edu

Greenville Technical College
506 South Pleasantburg Dr.
Greenville, SC 29607
(864) 250-8111
www.greenvilletech.com

Horry-Georgetown Technical College
2050 Hwy. 501 E
Conway, SC 29526
(843) 347-3186
www.hgtc.edu

Midlands Technical College
1260 Lexington Dr.
West Columbia, SC 29170
(803) 738-8324
www.midlandstech.edu

Orangeburg Calhoun Technical College
3250 Saint Matthews Rd.
Orangeburg, SC 29118
(803) 536-0311
www.octech.edu

Piedmont Technical College
620 North Emerald Rd.
Greenwood, SC 29646
(864) 941-8324
www.ptc.edu

Spartanburg Community College
Business I-85
Spartanburg, SC 29303
(864) 592-4600
www.stcsc.edu

Tri-County Technical College
7900 U.S. Hwy. 76
Pendleton, SC 29670
(864) 646-1500
www.tctc.edu

Trident Technical College
7000 Rivers Ave.
Charleston, SC 29423
(843) 574-6111
www.tridenttech.edu

York Technical College
452 South Anderson Rd.
Rock Hill, SC 29730
(803) 327-8000
www.yorktech.com

South Dakota

Mitchell Technical Institute
821 North Capital St.
Mitchell, SD 57301
(605) 995-3023
www.mitchelltech.edu

Sisseton Wahpeton College
PO Box 689
Agency Village, SD 57262
(605) 698-3966
www.swc.tc

Tennessee

Nashville State Technical
Community College
120 White Bridge Rd.
Nashville, TN 37209
(615) 353-3333
www.nscc.edu

Northeast State Technical
Community College
2425 Hwy. 75
Blountville, TN 37617
(423) 323-3191
www.northeaststate.edu

Southwest Tennessee
Community College
737 Union Ave.
Memphis, TN 38103
(901) 333-5000
www.southwest.tn.edu

Tennessee Technology Center
at Jackson
2468 Technology Center Dr.
Jackson, TN 38301
(731) 424-0691
www.jackson.tec.tn.us

Tennessee Technology Center
at Knoxville
1100 Liberty St.
Knoxville, TN 37919
(865) 546-5567
www.knoxville.tec.tn.us

Tennessee Technology Center
at Morristown
821 West Louise Ave.
Morristown, TN 37813
(423) 586-5771
www.morristown.tec.tn.us

Tennessee Technology Center
at Ripley
127 Industrial Dr.
Ripley, TN 38063
(731) 635-3368

Texas

Alvin Community College
3110 Mustang Rd.
Alvin, TX 77511
(281) 756-3500
www.alvincollege.edu

Amarillo College
2011 South Washington
Amarillo, TX 79109
(806) 371-5000
www.actx.edu

Angelina College
3500 South First
Lufkin, TX 75902
(936) 639-1301
www.angelina.edu

Austin Community College
District
5930 Middle Fiskville Rd.
Austin, TX 78752
(512) 223-7000
www.austincc.edu

Central Texas College
6200 West Central Texas
  Expwy.
Killeen, TX 76549
(254) 526-7161
www.ctcd.edu

Coastal Bend College
3800 Charco Rd.
Beeville, TX 78102
(361) 358-2838
www.coastalbend.edu

College of the Mainland
1200 Amburn Rd.
Texas City, TX 77591

(409) 938-1211
www.com.edu

Collin County Community
College District
4800 Preston Park Blvd.
Plano, TX 75093
(972) 881-5790
www.ccccd.edu

Del Mar College
101 Baldwin Blvd.
Corpus Christi, TX 78404
(361) 698-1255
www.delmar.edu

Eastfield College
3737 Motley Dr.
Mesquite, TX 75150
(972) 860-7002
www.dcccd.edu

El Paso Community College
919 Hunter Dr.
El Paso, TX 79915
(915) 831-2000
www.epcc.edu

Grayson County College
6101 Grayson Dr.
Denison, TX 75020
(903) 465-6030
www.grayson.edu

Houston Community
College System
3100 Main St.
Houston, TX 77266
(713) 718-2000
www.hccs.edu

Kilgore College
1100 Broadway
Kilgore, TX 75662
(903) 984-8531
www.kilgore.edu

Lamar State College–Port Arthur
1500 Proctor St.
Port Arthur, TX 77640
(409) 984-6342
www.pa.lamar.edu

Laredo Community College
West End Washington St.
Laredo, TX 78040
(956) 721-5394
www.laredo.edu

Lee College
511 South Whiting
Baytown, TX 77520
(281) 427-5611
www.lee.edu

Mountain View College
4849 West Illinois
Dallas, TX 75211
(214) 860-8680
www.dcccd.edu

North Harris Montgomery Community College District
5000 Research Forest Dr.
The Woodlands, TX 77381
(832) 813-6500
www.nhmccd.edu

North Lake College
5001 North Macarthur Blvd.
Irving, TX 75038
(972) 273-3000
www.dcccd.edu

Paris Junior College
2400 Clarksville St.
Paris, TX 75460
(903) 785-7661
www.parisjc.edu

Richland College
12800 Abrams Rd.
Dallas, TX 75243
(972) 238-6106
www.dcccd.edu

San Antonio College
1300 San Pedro Ave.
San Antonio, TX 78212
(210) 733-2000
www.accd.edu/sac/sacmain/
    sac.htm

San Jacinto College–Central Campus
8060 Spencer Hwy.
Pasadena, TX 77501
(281) 476-1501
www.sjcd.edu

South Plains College
1401 South College Ave.
Levelland, TX 79336
(806) 894-9611
www.southplainscollege.edu/we
    bsite/home.php3

St. Philips College
1801 Martin Luther King Dr.
San Antonio, TX 78203
(210) 531-3591
www.accd.edu/spc/spcmain/
    spc.htm

Tarrant County College District
1500 Houston St.
Fort Worth, TX 76102
(817) 515-5100
www.tccd.edu

Texarkana College
2500 North Robison Rd.
Texarkana, TX 75599
(903) 838-4541
www.texarkanacollege.edu

Texas State Technical College–Harlingen
1902 North Loop 499
Harlingen, TX 78550
(956) 364-4000
www.harlingen.tstc.edu

Texas State Technical College–Marshall
2650 East End Blvd. S
Marshall, TX 75671
(903) 935-1010
www.marshall.tstc.edu

Texas State Technical College–Waco
3801 Campus Dr.
Waco, TX 76705
(800) 792-8784
www.waco.tstc.edu

Texas State Technical College–West Texas
300 Homer K. Taylor Dr.
Sweetwater, TX 79556
(325) 235-7300
www.westtexas.tstc.edu

Trinity Valley Community College
100 Cardinal Dr.
Athens, TX 75751
(903) 675-6200
www.tvcc.edu

Tyler Junior College
1400 East Fifth St.
Tyler, TX 75789
(903) 510-2200
www.tjc.edu

Vernon College
4400 College Dr.
Vernon, TX 76384
(940) 552-6291
www.vernoncollege.edu

Victoria College
2200 East Red River
Victoria, TX 77901
(361) 573-3291
www.victoriacollege.edu

Weatherford College
225 College Park Dr.
Weatherford, TX 76086
(817) 594-5471
www.wc.edu

Wharton County Junior College
911 Boling Hwy.
Wharton, TX 77488
(979) 532-4560
www.wcjc.edu

Utah

Ogden-Weber Applied Technology College
200 North Washington Blvd.
Ogden, UT 84404
(801) 627-8300
www.owatc.com

Salt Lake Community College
PO Box 30808
Salt Lake City, UT 84130
(801) 957-4333
www.slcc.edu

Uintah Basin Applied Technology College
1100 East Lagoon St. 124-5
Roosevelt, UT 84066
(435) 722-4523
www.ubatc.edu

Vermont

N/A

Virginia

Blue Ridge Community College
1 College Ln.
Weyers Cave, VA 24486
(540) 234-9261
www.brcc.edu

**Central Virginia
Community College**
3506 Wards Rd.
Lynchburg, VA 24502
(434) 832-7600
www.cvcc.vccs.edu

**Dabney S. Lancaster
Community College**
1000 Dabney Dr.
Clifton Forge, VA 24422
(540) 863-2815
www.dslcc.edu

Danville Community College
1008 S. Main St.
Danville, VA 24541
(434) 797-2222
www.dcc.vccs.edu

**Eastern Shore
Community College**
29300 Lankford Hwy.
Melfa, VA 23410
(757) 789-1789
www.es.vccs.edu

Germanna Community College
2130 Germanna Hwy.
Locust Grove, VA 22508
(540) 423-9030
www.germanna.edu

John Tyler Community College
13101 Jefferson Davis Hwy.
Chester, VA 23831
(804) 796-4000
www.jtcc.edu

**J. Sargeant Reynolds
Community College**
1651 East Parham Rd.
Richmond, VA 23228
(804) 371-3000
www.reynolds.edu

Lord Fairfax Community College
173 Skirmisher Ln.

Middletown, VA 22645
(540) 868-7000
www.lf.vccs.edu

**Mountain Empire
Community College**
3441 Mountain Empire Rd.
Big Stone Gap, VA 24219
(276) 523-2400
www.mecc.edu

New River Community College
5251 College Dr.
Dublin, VA 24084
(540) 674-3600
www.nr.edu

**Northern Virginia
Community College**
4001 Wakefield Chapel Rd.
Annandale, VA 22003
(703) 323-3000
www.nvcc.edu

**Patrick Henry
Community College**
645 Patriot Ave.
Martinsville, VA 24112
(276) 656-0311
www.ph.vccs.edu

**Paul D. Camp
Community College**
100 North College Dr.
Franklin, VA 23851
(757) 569-6700
www.pc.vccs.edu

**Piedmont Virginia
Community College**
501 College Dr.
Charlottesville, VA 22902
(434) 977-3900
www.pvcc.edu

**Rappahannock
Community College**
12745 College Dr.
Glenns, VA 23149
(804) 758-6700
www.rcc.vccs.edu

**Southside Virginia
Community College**
109 Campus Dr.
Alberta, VA 23821
(434) 949-1000
www.sv.vccs.edu

**Southwest Virginia
Community College**
PO Box SVCC
Richlands, VA 24641
(276) 964-2555
www.sw.edu

**Thomas Nelson
Community College**
99 Thomas Nelson Dr.
Hampton, VA 23666
(757) 825-2700
www.tncc.edu

Tidewater Community College
500 East Main St.
Norfolk, VA 23514
(757) 822-1122
www.tcc.edu

**Virginia Highlands
Community College**
100 VHCC Dr.
Abingdon, VA 24212
(276) 739-2400
www.vhcc.edu

**Virginia Western
Community College**
3095 Colonial Ave.
Roanoke, VA 24018
(540) 857-7200
www.virginiawestern.edu

Wytheville Community College
1000 East Main St.
Wytheville, VA 24382
(276) 223-4700
www.wcc.vccs.edu

Washington

Bates Technical College
1101 South Yakima Ave.
Tacoma, WA 98405
(253) 680-7000
www.bates.ctc.edu

Bellingham Technical College
3028 Lindbergh Ave.
Bellingham, WA 98225
(360) 752-7000
www.btc.ctc.edu

Blue Collar & Proud Of It

Big Bend Community College
7662 Chanute St.
Moses Lake, WA 98837
(509) 793-2222
www.bigbend.edu

Perry Technical Institute
2011 West Washington Ave.
Yakima, WA 98903
(509) 453-0374
www.perrytech.edu

Renton Technical College
3000 NE Fourth St.
Renton, WA 98056
(425) 235-2352
www.rtc.edu

Spokane Community College
1810 North Greene St.
Spokane, WA 99217
(509) 533-8020
www.scc.spokane.edu

Walla Walla Community College
500 Tausick Way
Walla Walla, WA 99362
(509) 522-2500
www.wwcc.edu

**Yakima Valley
Community College**
Sixteenth and Nob Hill Blvd.
Yakima, WA 98907
(509) 574-4600
www.yvcc.edu

West Virginia

**Mercer County Technical
Education Center**
1397 Stafford Dr.
Princeton, WV 24740
(304) 425-9551

**Community and Technical
College at WV University
Institute of Technology**
405 Fayette Pike
Montgomery, WV 25136
(304) 442-3071
www.wvutech.edu

**Pierpont Community and
Technical College**
1201 Locust Ave.
Fairmont, WV 26554
(304) 367-4692
www.fscwv.edu

**Southern West Virginia
Community and Technical
College**
Dempsey Branch Rd.
Mount Gay, WV 25637
(304) 792-7098
www.southern.wvnet.edu

**West Virginia State Community
and Technical College**
Cole Complex
Institute, WV 25112
(304) 766-3118
www.wvsctc.edu

Wisconsin

Blackhawk Technical College
6004 Prairie Rd.
Janesville, WI 53547
(608) 758-6900
www.blackhawk.edu

**Chippewa Valley
Technical College**
620 West Clairemont Ave.
Eau Claire, WI 54701
(715) 833-6200
www.cvtc.edu

Fox Valley Technical College
1825 North Bluemound Dr.
Appleton, WI 54912
(920) 735-5600
www.fvtc.edu

Gateway Technical College
3520 30th Ave.
Kenosha, WI 53144
(262) 564-2200
www.gtc.edu

Mid-State Technical College
500 32nd St. N
Wisconsin Rapids, WI 54494
(715) 422-5300
www.mstc.edu

**Milwaukee Area
Technical College**
700 West State St.
Milwaukee, WI 53233
(414) 297-6370
www.matc.edu

Moraine Park Technical College
235 North National Ave.
Fond Du Lac, WI 54936
(920) 922-8611
www.morainepark.edu

Nicolet Area Technical College
Hwy. G South
Rhinelander, WI 54501
(715) 365-4410
www.nicoletcollege.edu

Northcentral Technical College
1000 Campus Dr.
Wausau, WI 54401
(715) 675-3331
www.ntc.edu

**Northeast Wisconsin
Technical College**
2740 West Mason St.
Green Bay, WI 54307
(920) 498-5400
www.nwtc.edu

Wyoming

Northwest College
231 West 6th St.
Powell, WY 82435
(307) 754-6000
www.northwestcollege.edu

Elevator Installers and Repairers

The International Union of Elevator Constructors (IUEC) offers an extensive apprenticeship and training program that prepares participants for a career in this sector. Most elevator companies rely on the trades to find employees, and the industry is primarily licensed by the National Elevator Industry Education Program. Those interested in becoming an elevator installer or repairer should contact a local IUEC office for more information about the apprenticeship process.

International Union of Elevator Constructors (IUEC)
www.iuec.org/locals.asp

Alabama

Local 24–Birmingham
PO Box 11462
Birmingham, AL 35202
(205) 591-4185

Local 124–Mobile
PO Box 1021
Lillian, AL 36549
(850) 458-0124

Alaska

N/A

Arizona

Local 140–Phoenix
1841 North 24th St., Ste. 6
Phoenix, AZ 85008
(602) 273-0025

Arkansas

Local 79–Little Rock
PO Box 2081
Little Rock, AR 72203
(501) 944-6970
iuec-local79@sbcglobal.net

California

Local 8–San Francisco
690 Potrero Ave.
San Francisco, CA 94110-1328
(415) 285-2900
info@iuec8.org.
www.iuec8.org.

Local 18–Los Angeles
100 South Mentor Ave.
Pasadena, CA 91106

Colorado

Local 25–Denver
7510 West Mississippi Ave.,
  #130
Lakewood, CO 80226
(303) 937-8039
iuec25@qwestoffice.net

Connecticut

Local 91–New Haven
914 Main St., Room 203
East Hartford, CT 06108
(860) 289-8689
iuec91@sbcglobal.net

Delaware

N/A

District of Columbia

Local 10–Washington, DC
9600 Martin Luther King Hwy.
Lanham, MD 20706
(301) 702-1010
www.iuec10.com

Florida

Local 49–Jacksonville
1416 East 14th St.
Jacksonville, FL 32206
(904) 353-2570

Local 71–Miami
3800 NW 35th Ave.
Miami, FL 33142
(800) 238-7171
local71@iuec71.org
www.iuec71.org

Local 74–Tampa
8406 North Hwy. 301
Tampa, FL 33637
(813) 988-0950
local74@gte.net
www.iueclocal74.com

Local 139–Orlando
1912B Ledd Rd., Ste. C2
Orlando, FL 32810
(407) 291-7808
iueclocal139@bellsouth.net
www.iuec139.org

Georgia

Local 32–Atlanta
374 Maynard Terr. SE
Atlanta, GA 30316
(404) 378-6208
iuec32@aol.com
www.iueclocal32.com

Hawaii

Local 126–Honolulu
707 Alakea St., Ste. 205
Honolulu, HI 96813
(808) 536-8653
iuec126@hawaiiantel.net
www.iuec126.org

Idaho

N/A

Illinois

Local 2–Chicago
300 South Ashland Blvd.,
  Room 308
Chicago, IL 60607
(312) 421-1440
iueclu2@aol.com
www.iuec2.com

Local 55–Peoria
Peoria Labor Temple
400 NE Jefferson, Ste. 203
Peoria, IL 61603
(309) 671-5085
iuec55@ameritech.net

Indiana

Local 34–Indianapolis
2206 East Werges Ave.
Indianapolis, IN 46237
(317) 536-8173
spa196@aol.com
www.iuec34.org

Iowa

Local 33–Des Moines
2000 Walker, Ste. I
Des Moines, IA 50317
(515) 262-0120
iueclu33@aol.com
www.iuec33.com

Kansas

N/A

Kentucky

Local 20–Louisville
7711 Beulah Church Rd.
Louisville, KY 40228
(502) 231-0136
iueclou@bellsouth.net

Louisiana

Local 16–New Orleans
2540 Severn Ave. #105
Metairie, LA 70002
(504) 889-1105
iuecno16@aol.com

Maine

N/A

Maryland

Local 7–Baltimore
10014 Harford Rd.
Baltimore, MD 21234
(410) 661-1491
iueclocal7@aol.com

Massachusetts

Local 4–Boston
50 Park St.
Dorchester, MA 02122
(617) 288-1547
local4@iueclocal4.com
www.iueclocal4.com

Local 41–Springfield
PO Box 1456
Sterling, MA 01564

(978) 422-5110
iuec41@comcast.net
www.local41.org.

Michigan

Local 36–Detroit
1640 Porter St.
Detroit, MI 48232
(313) 961-0717
local36@sbcglobal.net

Local 85–Lansing
5800 Executive Dr.
Lansing, MI 48911
(517) 882-0100

Minnesota

Local 9–Minneapolis
433 Little Canada Rd. E
Little Canada, MN 55117
(651) 287-0817
iuec9@local9.com
www.local9.com

Mississippi

N/A

Missouri

Local 3–St. Louis
5916 Wilson Ave.
St. Louis, MO 63110
(314) 644-3933
iueclu3@aol.com

Local 12–Kansas City
6320 Manchester Ave., Ste. 44
Kansas City, MO 64133
(816) 358-1312
iuec@iuec12.com
www.iuec12.com

Montana

N/A

Nebraska

N/A

Nevada

Local 28–Omaha
3333 South 24th St., Ste. 1
Omaha, NE 68108
(402) 734-7632
iuec28@qwest.net

New Hampshire

N/A

New Jersey

N/A

New Mexico

Local 131–Albuquerque
2835 Pan American Fwy. NE
Albuquerque, NM 87107
(505) 292-8715
elevators131@hotmail.com

New York

Local 35–Albany
890 3rd St.
Albany, NY 12206
518-438-2487
iuec35@aol.com

Local 14–Buffalo
3527 Harlem Rd., Ste. 10A
Buffalo, NY 14225
(716) 833-5528
iueclocal14bflo@aol.com
www.buffalotrades.com

Local 1–New York
47-24 27th St.
Long Island City, NY 11101
(718) 767-7004
www.localoneiuec.com

Local 138–Poughkeepsie
44 Verbank Club Rd.
Verbank, NY 12585
(845) 266-3078

Local 27–Rochester
244 Paul Rd., Ste. 3
Rochester, NY 14624

(585) 436-6440
local27@iuec27.org
www.iuec27.org

Local 62–Syracuse
615 West Genesee St.
Syracuse, NY 13204
(315) 422-5219
iuec62@hotmail.com

North Carolina

Local 135–Charlotte
4200 Morehead Rd.
Concord, NC 28027
(704) 455-5313
iuec135@aol.com
iueclocal135.org

Local 80–Greensboro
PO Box 387
Hillsborough, NC 27278
(919) 596-6172
iuec80@cs.com

North Dakota

N/A

Ohio

Local 45–Akron
PO Box 429
Akron, OH 44309
(330) 753-3953
iueclocal45@aol.com

Local 11–Cincinnati
1579 Summit Rd.
Cincinnati, OH 45237
(513) 761-4787
iuec11@aol.com

Local 17–Cleveland
3250 Euclid Ave.
Cleveland, OH 44115
(216) 431-8088
iueclocal17@neohio.twcbc.com

Local 37–Columbus
23 West 2nd Ave.
Columbus, OH 43201
(614) 291-5859
iuec37@aol.com

Local 44–Toledo
2300 Ashland Ave., #206
Toledo, OH 43620
(419) 242-7902

Oklahoma

Local 63–Oklahoma City
3815 North Santa Fe Ave.,
 Ste. 126
Oklahoma City, OK 73118
(405) 521-9385
iueclocal63@sbcglobal.net

Local 83–Tulsa
1502 East 2nd St.
Tulsa, OK 74120
(918) 587-1662
iuec-local83@sbcglobal.net

Oregon

Local 23–Portland
PO Box 301535
Portland, OR 97294
(503) 252-5852
www.iueclocal23.org

Pennsylvania

Local 59–Harrisburg
2163 Berryhill St.
Harrisburg, PA 17104
(717) 564-2749
iuec59@itech.net

Local 5–Philadelphia
12273 Townsend Rd.
Philadelphia, PA 19154
215-676-2555
local5moneyman@aol.com

Local 6–Pittsburgh
2945 Banksville Rd.
Pittsburgh, PA 15216
(412) 341-6666
iuec6@earthlink.net

Local 84–Reading
RR 4, Box 4283
Moscow, PA 18444
(570) 842-5430
iuec84@comcast.net

Rhode Island

Local 39–Providence
65 Frigate St.
Jamestown, RI 02835
(401) 423-2293

South Carolina

N/A

South Dakota

N/A

Tennessee

Local 30– Memphis
3078 Directors Row
Memphis, TN 38131
(901) 345-6233
iuec30@bellsouth.net
www.iuec30.com

Local 93–Nashville
2001 Elm Hill Pike
Nashville, TN 37210
(615) 889-0001
local93@bellsouth.net
www.iueclocal93.com

Texas

Local 133–Austin
400 Josephine St.
Austin, TX 78704
(512) 478-9950
iuec133@aol.com

Local 21–Dallas
1924 Baird Farm Rd., Ste. 101
Arlington, TX 76006-6524
(817) 635-0680
iuec21@logixonline.com

Local 31–Houston
2626 Sutherland St.
Houston, TX 77023
(713) 926-9678
iueclocal31@hotmail.com
www.iuec31.org

Local 81–San Antonio
1946 La Manda Blvd.
San Antonio, TX 78201
(210) 226-1942
iueclocal181@aol.com

Utah

Local 38–Salt Lake City
139 South 1400 West
Salt Lake City, UT 84104
(801) 467-1051

Vermont

N/A

Virginia

Local 52–Norfolk
7442 Tidewater Dr.
Norfolk, VA 23505
(757) 588-4338
iuec52@earthlink.net

Local 51–Richmond
3801 Jefferson Davis Hwy.
Richmond, VA 23234
(804) 271-1112
iuec51@aol.com

Washington

Local 19–Seattle
2112 Thorndyke Ave. W
Seattle, WA 98199
(206) 282-4885
theoffice@iuec19.org
www.IUEC19.org

West Virginia

Local 48–Charleston
717 Lee St. E–Odd Fellows
  Bldg. #201
Charleston, WV 25301
(304) 343-8345
iuec48@citynet.net

Wisconsin

Local 132–Madison
PO Box 243
Cottage Grove, WI 53527
(608) 839-5585
iuec132@verizon.net

Local 15–Milwaukee
17125 West Cleveland Ave.
New Berlin, WI 53151
(262) 786-9982
IUEC15@yahoo.com

Wyoming

N/A

Fabricator and Assembler

Assemblers and fabricators can often enter the workforce without an official apprenticeship. Many fabricators are members of unions that do offer some training. The following unions are recommended resources for more information: International Association of Machinists and Aerospace Workers; the United Automobile, Aerospace and Agricultural Implement Workers of America; the International Brotherhood of Electrical Workers; and the United Steelworkers of America.

Resources

International Association of Machinists and Aerospace Workers
www.goiam.org

United Automobile, Aerospace and Agricultural Implement Workers of America
www.uaw.org

International Brotherhood of Electrical Workers
See: Electrician

United Steelworkers of America
www.uswa.org

Forklift Operator

Although it is not always necessary, having a commercial drivers license (CDL) can be beneficial when applying for jobs. These licenses are useful for forklift operating, as well as truck driving and transport or moving occupations. CDLs are issued by each state's Department of Motor Vehicles (DMV), and while each state has slightly different requirements, you must be twenty-one to transport hazardous material. Between the background check and tests required as part of the CDL application, you can expect to spend between $50 and $150 on fees.

Groundskeeping and Landscaping

One way into this field is through an entry-level position at a landscaping company. General laborers can advance in the industry with experience and hard work. There are also certification programs available for groundskeepers. These certifications are often beneficial when applying for jobs and could increase your salary potential. To advance further in this industry, degrees are available in landscape design, turf management, or horticulture.

Resources

ISA: International Society of Arborists—Tree Workers Certifications
www.isa-arbor.com/chapters/professional.aspx

Professional Grounds Management Society—Grounds Management Certification
www.pgms.org/cgmcertification.htm

Professional Grounds Management Society—Grounds Technician Certification
www.pgms.org/cgtcertification.htm

Tree Care Industry Association—Certified Tree-Care Professional
www.treecareindustry.org/public/ctsp_faqs.htm

Heating, Ventilation, Air-Conditioning, Refrigeration Installer

The training for heating, ventilation, air-conditioning, and refrigeration (HVAC) installers and mechanics often overlaps with that of plumbers, sheet metal workers, and electricians. Because of the combination of skills involved in HVAC work, there are a great many community and technical colleges offering training programs in this occupation. Many HVAC workers have also received training through apprenticeships offered by the plumbing and pipe-fitting industry.

Contractors often offer on-the-job training, and www.careervoyages.gov is an excellent resource for finding a program near you.

Resources

United Association of Journeyman and Apprentices of the Plumbing and Pipefitting Industry
www.ua.org

Plumbing-Heating-Cooling Contractors
www.phccweb.org

NCCER-Accredited HVAC Training Centers

Alabama

American Construction Training, LLC
3299 CR 25 Ste. A
Dothan, AL 36303
(334) 983-1677
www.heoschool.net

Construction Education Foundation of Alabama
6700 Oporto-Madrid Blvd.
Birmingham, AL 35206
(205) 956-0146
www.cefalabama.org

Diversified Employment Service Inc.
211-C Hwy. 43 S
Saraland, AL 36571
(251) 679-0018

Alaska

ABC of Alaska Inc.
360 West Benson Blvd., Ste. 200
Anchorage, AK 99503
(907) 565-5600
www.abcalaska.org

Northern Industrial Training LLC
6177 East Mountain Heather Way
Palmer, AK 99645-9505
(907) 557-6400
www.nitalaska.com

Arizona

Arizona Public Service
1611 South Main St.
Snowflake, AZ 85937
(928) 536-6232
www.aps.com

Arkansas

Arkansas Chapter AGC Inc.
523 East Capitol Ave.
Little Rock, AR 72202
(501) 376-6641
www.agcar.net

California

Calexico Community Action Council
2151 Rockwood Ave., Ste. 166
Calexico, CA 92231
(760) 357-6464

Center for Seabees and Facilities Engineering
3502 Goodspeed St., Ste. 1
Naval Base Ventura County, CA 93041
(805) 982-3615
www.npdc.navy.mil/csfe

Shasta Builder's Exchange Community Fund
2985 Innsbruck Dr.
Redding, CA 96003
(530) 222-1917
www.shastabe.com

Colorado

ABC Western Colorado Chapter
2754 Compass Dr., Ste. 305
Grand Junction, CO 81506
(970) 243-7950
www.wcoabc.org

T and D Services
1143 Michael Cir.
Meeker, CO 81641
(970) 260-3415

Connecticut

Construction Education Center Inc.
2138 Silas Deane Hwy., Ste. 101
Rocky Hill, CT 06067
(860) 529-5886
www.thinkconstruction.org

Delaware

N/A

Florida

ABC Florida Gulf Coast Chapter
2008 North Himes Ave.
Tampa, FL 33607
(813) 879-8064
www.abcflgulf.org

Builders Association of North Central Florida
2217 Northwest 66th Ct.
Gainesville, FL 32653
(352) 372-5649
www.bancf.com

The Southern Company
One Energy Place
Pensacola, FL 32503
(850) 444-6821

Tri-County Apprenticeship Academy
13830 Jetport Commerce Pkwy., Ste. 5
Fort Myers, FL 33913
(239) 225-0995
www.TCAAFL.com

Georgia

CEFGA–Construction Education Foundation of Georgia
3585 Lawrenceville Suwanee Rd., Ste. 301
Suwanee, GA 30024
(678) 889-4445
www.cefga.org

Guam

ABC Guam Contractors
718 North Marine Corps Dr., Ste. 203
Upper Tumon, GU 96913
(671) 647-4840
www.guamcontractors.org/

Hawaii

N/A

Idaho

Construction Education Foundation of Idaho (CEFI) Inc.
1649 West Shoreline Dr.
Boise, ID 83702
(208) 344-2531
www.cefidaho.org

Illinois

Institute for Construction Education
2353 Federal Dr.
Decatur, IL 62526
(217) 877-7523
www.iceschool.org

Indiana

N/A

Iowa

ABC of Iowa
475 Alices Road, Ste. A
Waukee, IA 50263
(515) 987-3790
www.abciowa.org

Kansas

N/A

Kentucky

Kentuckiana ABC
1810 Taylor Ave.
Louisville, KY 40213
(502) 456-5200 or
   (800) 411-5848
www.kyanaabc.com

Kentucky Department of Corrections
2439 Lawrenceburg Rd.
Frankfort, KY 40602
(502) 564-4795 ext. 229
www.corrections.ky.gov/

Western Kentucky Construction Association–AGC
2201 McCracken Blvd.
Paducah, KY 42001
(270) 744-6261
www.wkca.org

Louisiana

ABC Pelican Chapter
19251 Highland Rd, Training Center A
Baton Rouge, LA 70809
(225) 752-0088
www.abcpelican.org

Maine

N/A

Maryland

ABC Metropolitan Washington
4061 Powder Mill Rd., Ste. 120
Calverton, MD 20705
(301) 595-9711
www.abcmetrowashington.org

Associated Builders and Contractors Inc.–Chesapeake
100 West St.
Annapolis, MD 21401
(410) 267-0347
www.abc-chesapeake.org

Baltimore Metro Chapter ABC
1220-B East Joppa Rd., Ste. 322
Towson, MD 21286
(410) 821-0351
www.abcbaltimore.org

Cumberland Valley Chapter ABC
530 North Locust St.
Hagerstown, MD 21740
(301) 739-1190
www.abccvc.com

Massachusetts

George W. Gould Construction Institute
200 Wheeler Rd.
Burlington, MA 01803
(781) 270-9990
www.gwgci.org

Michigan

ABC Central Michigan Chapter
1501 Rensen St., Ste. C
Lansing, MI 48910
(517) 394-4481
www.abccmc.org

Construction Education Trust
31800 Sherman Ave.
Madison Heights, MI 48071
(248) 298-3600
www.cet-tech.com

Minnesota

N/A

Mississippi

Mississippi Construction Education Foundation
290 Commerce Park Dr., Ste. B
Ridgeland, MS 39157
(601) 605-2989
www.mcef.net

Missouri

Vatterott Educational Centers Inc.
8580 Evans Ave., Ste. A
St. Louis, MO 63134
(314) 264-1806
www.vatterott-college.edu

Montana

N/A

Nebraska

N/A

Nevada

ABC of Southern Nevada
5070 Arville St., Ste. 4
Las Vegas, NV 89118
(702) 227-0536
www.abclasvegas.org

New Hampshire

N/A

New Jersey

ABC New Jersey Chapter
720 King George Post Rd.,
Ste. 303
Fords, NJ 08863
(732) 661-1045
www.abcnjc.org

New Mexico

Valencia County Hispano Chamber of Commerce
1052 Main St., Ste. A
Los Lunas, NM 87031
(505) 450-1611

New York

United Service Workers Local 355–JATF
267 Knickerbocker Ave.
Bohemia, NY 11716
(631) 589-5880

North Carolina

Carolinas AGC Inc.
1100 Euclid Ave.
Charlotte, NC 28203
(704) 372-1450
www.cagc.org

North Dakota

AGC of North Dakota
422 North Second St.
Bismarck, ND 58501
(701) 223-2770
www.agcnd.org

Ohio

ABC Northern Ohio Chapter
9255 Market Place W
Broadview Heights, OH 44147
(440) 717-0389
www.nocabc.com

ABC Ohio Valley CEF
33 Greenwood Ln.
Springboro, OH 45066
(937) 704-0111
www.ovabc.org

Construction Craft Academy
9760 Shepard Rd.
Macedonia, OH 44056
(800) 442-0067
www.craftacademy.com

Oklahoma

AGC of Oklahoma– Building Chapter
605 Northwest 13th St., Ste. A
Oklahoma City, OK 73103-2213
(405) 528-4605
www.agcok.com

Oregon

N/A

Pennsylvania

ABC–Southeast PA Chapter
430 West Germantown Pike
East Norriton, PA 19403
(610) 279-6666
www.abcsepa.org

ABC Western Pennsylvania Inc.
3500 Spring Garden Ave.
Pittsburgh, PA 15212
(412) 231-1446
www.abcwpa.org

Associated Builders and Contractors–Eastern PA
1036 North Godfrey St.
Allentown, PA 18109
(610) 821-6869
www.abceastpa.org

Keystone Chapter ABC
135 Shellyland Rd.
Manheim, PA 17545
(717) 653-8106
www.abckeystone.org

New Castle School of Trades
4164 U.S. Route 422
Pulaski, PA 16143
(724) 964-8811
www.nctrades.com

Blue Collar & Proud of It

Rhode Island

ABC–Rhode Island Chapter
400 Massasoit Ave., Ste. 108
East Providence, RI 02914
(401) 438-8446
www.abcri.org

South Carolina

N/A

South Dakota

N/A

Tennessee

ABC–Mid-Tennessee Chapter
1604 Elm Hill Pike
Nashville, TN 37210
(615) 399-8323
www.abctennessee.com

Texas

ABC of Greater Houston Inc.
3910 Kirby Dr., Ste. 131
Houston, TX 77098
(713) 523-6258
www.abchouston.org

ABC Texas Mid Coast CEF
116 Jason Plaza
Victoria, TX 77901
(361) 572-0299
www.abcvictoria.vbxhosting.org

Associated General Contractors of El Paso
4625 Ripley Dr.

El Paso, TX 79922
(915) 585-1533
www.agcelpaso.org

Brock Group
1221 Georgia Ave.
Houston, TX 77536
(409) 658-5088
www.brockgroup.com

Central Texas ABC Chapter
3006 Longhorn Blvd., Ste. 104
Austin, TX 78758
(512) 719-5263
www.abccentraltexas.org

Saulsbury Industries D/B/A Construction Workforce Training Center
5308 Andrews Hwy.
Odessa, TX 79762
(432) 366-7676
www.cwtc-tx.com

The Victor Group
801 High Ridge Dr.
Friendswood, TX 77546
(281) 850-8079
www.thevictorgroup.net

Utah

N/A

Vermont

Vermont Construction Careers Council
148 State St.
Montpelier, VT 05602
(802) 223-2374
www.agcvt.org

Virginia

ABC Virginia
14120 Parke Long Ct., Ste. 111
Chantilly, VA 20151
(703) 968-6205
www.abcva.org

Washington

Construction Industry Training Council of Washington
1930 116th Ave. NE, Ste. 201
Bellevue, WA 98004
(425) 454-2482
www.citcwa.org

West Virginia

N/A

Wisconsin

ABC of Wisconsin Inc.
5330 Wall St.
Madison, WI 53718
(608) 244-6056
www.abcwi.org

Wyoming

Corinthian Colleges Inc.
1706 Bill Nye Ave.
Laramie, WY 82070
(307) 742-3530
www.cci.edu

Industrial Machinery Mechanic

International Association of Machinists and Aerospace Workers
http://www.goiam.org

United Auto Workers
www.uaw.org

United Brotherhood Carpenters and Joiners
www.carpenters.org

United Steelworkers of America
www.uswa.org

NCCER-Accredited Training Centers

Brock Services, Ltd.
Craft Training-In-House
  Assessment-In-House
343 East Center St.
Kingsport, TN 37660
(423) 229-1656

CTC of New York State
6369 Collamer Dr.
East Syracuse, NY 13057
(315) 463-7539
www.abcnys.org

Florida Masonry Apprentice and Educational Foundation
3710 Glynn Cottage Court
Green Cove Springs, FL 32043
(904) 838-6531
www.masonryeducation.org

Industrial Technical Services Inc.
150 Telfair Rd.
Savannah, GA 31415
(912) 927-8006 ext. 4487

New Mexico Building Branch, AGC
Craft Training–Public Assessment
1615 University Blvd. NE
Albuquerque, NM 87102
(505) 842-1462
www.agc-nm.org

The Swan Group Inc.
1221 Bellevue St.
Green Bay, WI 54302
(920) 217-4056
www.theswanhouse.org

Community Colleges

Note that millwork/millwright programs are specified within the listings.

Alabama

Gadsden State Community College
1001 George Wallace Dr.
Gadsden, AL 35902
(256) 549-8200
www.gadsdenstate.edu

George C. Wallace Community College–Dothan
1141 Wallace Dr.
Dothan, AL 36303
(334) 983-3521
www.wallace.edu

H. Councill Trenholm State Technical College
1225 Air Base Blvd.
Montgomery, AL 36108
(334) 420-4200
www.trenholmtech.cc.al.us

John C. Calhoun State Community College
6250 US Hwy. 31 N
Tanner, AL 35671
(256) 306-2500
www.calhoun.edu

Lawson State Community College–Birmingham Campus
3060 Wilson Rd SW
Birmingham, AL 35221
(205) 925-2515
www.lawsonstate.edu

Northwest Shoals Community College–Muscle Shoals
800 George Wallace Blvd.
Muscle Shoals, AL 35661
(256) 331-5200
www.nwscc.edu

Shelton State Community College
9500 Old Greensboro Rd.
Tuscaloosa, AL 35405
(205) 391-2347
www.sheltonstate.edu

Southern Union State Community College
750 Roberts St.
Wadley, AL 36276
(256) 395-2211
www.suscc.edu

Alaska

N/A

Arizona

Northland Pioneer College
2251 East Navajo Blvd.
Holbrook, AZ 86025
(928) 524-7600
www.npc.edu

Arkansas

Arkansas Northeastern College
2501 South Division
Blytheville, AR 72316
(870) 762-1020
www.anc.edu

Arkansas State University–Beebe
1000 Iowa St.
Beebe, AR 72012
(501) 882-3600
www.asub.edu

Arkansas State University–Mountain Home
1600 South College St.
Mountain Home, AR 72653
(870) 508-6100
www.asumh.edu

Black River Technical College
1410 Hwy. 304 E
Pocahontas, AR 72455
(870) 248-4000
www.blackrivertech.edu

East Arkansas Community College
1700 Newcastle Rd.
Forrest City, AR 72335
(870) 633-4480
www.eacc.edu

Ouachita Technical College
One College Cir.
Malvern, AR 72104
(501) 337-5000
www.otcweb.edu

Ozarka College
218 College Dr.
Melbourne, AR 72556

(870) 368-7371
www.ozarka.edu

Phillips Community College of the University of Arkansas
1000 Campus Dr.
Helena, AR 72342
(870) 338-6474
www.pccua.edu

Southern Arkansas University Tech
100 Carr Rd.
Camden, AR 71701
(870) 574-4500
www.sautech.edu

University of Arkansas Community College–Batesville
2005 White Dr.
Batesville, AR 72503
(870) 612-2000
www.uaccb.edu

University of Arkansas Community College–Hope
2500 South Main
Hope, AR 71802
(870) 777-5722
www.uacch.edu

California

Millwork/Millwright
Bakersfield College
1801 Panorama Dr.
Bakersfield, CA 93305
(661) 395-4011
www.bakersfieldcollege.edu

Cerritos College
11110 Alondra Blvd.
Norwalk, CA 90650
(562) 860-2451
www.cerritos.edu

College of the Redwoods
7351 Tompkins Hill Rd.
Eureka, CA 95501
(707) 476-4100
www.redwoods.edu

Cuesta College
Hwy. 1
San Luis Obispo, CA 93403
(805) 546-3100
www.cuesta.edu

El Camino Community
College District
16007 Crenshaw Blvd.
Torrance, CA 90506
(310) 532-3670
www.elcamino.edu

Fresno City College
1101 East University Ave.
Fresno, CA 93741
(559) 442-4600
www.fresnocitycollege.edu

Fullerton College
321 East Chapman Ave.
Fullerton, CA 92832
(714) 992-7000
www.fullcoll.edu

Hartnell College
156 Homestead Ave.
Salinas, CA 93901
(831) 755-6700
www.hartnell.edu

Laney College
900 Fallon St.
Oakland, CA 94607
(510) 834-5740
www.laney.peralta.edu

Long Beach City College
4901 East Carson St.
Long Beach, CA 90808
(562) 938-4111
www.lbcc.edu

Los Angeles Pierce College
6201 Winnetka Ave.
Woodland Hills, CA 91371
(818) 347-0551
www.piercecollege.edu

Los Angeles Trade
Technical College
400 West Washington Blvd.
Los Angeles, CA 90015
(213) 763-7000
www.lattc.edu

Palomar College
1140 West Mission
San Marcos, CA 92069
(760) 744-1150
www.palomar.edu

San Joaquin Delta College
5151 Pacific Ave.
Stockton, CA 95207
(209) 954-5151
www.deltacollege.edu

Santiago Canyon College
8045 East Chapman
Orange, CA 92869
(714) 628-4900
www.sccollege.edu

Sierra College
5000 Rocklin Rd.
Rocklin, CA 95677
(916) 624-3333
www.sierracollege.edu

Victor Valley College
18422 Bear Valley Rd.
Victorville, CA 92395
(760) 245-4271
www.vvc.edu

Colorado

N/A

Connecticut

N/A

Delaware

Delaware Technical and
Community College–
Stanton-Wilmington
400 Stanton-Christiana Rd.
Newark, DE 19702
(302) 454-3900
www.dtcc.edu

District of Columbia

N/A

Florida

Brewster Technical Center
2222 North Tampa St.
Tampa, FL 33602
(813) 276-5448
www.brewster.edu

Ridge Career Center
7700 SR 544
Winter Haven, FL 33881
(863) 419-3060
www.polk-fl.net/ridge

Taylor Technical Institute
3233 Hwy. 19 S
Perry, FL 32348
(850) 838-2545
www.taylortech.org

Georgia

Abraham Baldwin
Agricultural College
2802 Moore Hwy.
Tifton, GA 31793
(229) 391-5001
www.abac.edu

Albany Technical College
1704 South Slappey Blvd.
Albany, GA 31701
(229) 430-3500
www.albanytech.edu

Altamaha Technical College
1777 West Cherry St.
Jesup, GA 31545
(912) 427-5800
www.altamahatech.edu

Athens Technical College
800 US Hwy. 29 N
Athens, GA 30601
(706) 355-5000
www.athenstech.edu

Augusta Technical College
3200 Augusta Tech Dr.
Augusta, GA 30906
(706) 771-4000
www.augustatech.edu

Bainbridge College
2500 East Shotwell St.
Bainbridge, GA 39819
(229) 248-2500
www.bainbridge.edu

Central Georgia
Technical College
3300 Macon Tech Dr.
Macon, GA 31206
(478) 757-3400
www.centralgatech.edu

**Coastal Georgia
Community College**
3700 Altama Ave.
Brunswick, GA 31520
(912) 264-7235
www.cgcc.edu

Columbus Technical College
928 Manchester Expwy.
Columbus, GA 31904
(706) 649-1800
www.columbustech.edu

Coosa Valley Technical College
One Maurice Culberson Dr.
Rome, GA 30161
(706) 295-6963
www.coosavalleytech.edu

DeKalb Technical College
495 North Indian Creek Dr.
Clarkston, GA 30021
(404) 297-9522
www.dekalbtech.edu

East Central Technical College
667 Perry House Rd.
Fitzgerald, GA 31750
(229) 468-2000
www.eastcentraltech.edu

Flint River Technical College
1533 Hwy. 19 S
Thomaston, GA 30286
(706) 646-6148
www.flintrivertech.edu

Griffin Technical College
501 Varsity Rd.
Griffin, GA 30223
(770) 228-7348
www.griffintech.edu

**Heart of Georgia
Technical College**
560 Pinehill Rd.
Dublin, GA 31021
(478) 275-6589
www.heartofgatech.edu

Lanier Technical College
2990 Landrum Education Dr.
Oakwood, GA 30566
(770) 531-6300
www.laniertech.edu

**Middle Georgia
Technical College**
80 Cohen Walker Dr.
Warner Robins, GA 31088
(478) 988-6800
www.middlegatech.edu

Moultrie Technical College
800 Veterans Pkwy. N
Moultrie, GA 31788
(229) 891-7000
www.moultrietech.edu

North Georgia Technical College
1500 Georgia Hwy. 197 N
Clarkesville, GA 30523
(706) 754-7700
www.northgatech.edu

North Metro Technical College
5198 Ross Rd.
Acworth, GA 30102
(770) 975-4000
www.northmetrotech.edu

Northwestern Technical College
265 Bicentennial Trail
Rock Spring, GA 30739
(706) 764-3510
www.northwesterntech.edu

Okefenokee Technical College
1701 Carswell Ave.
Waycross, GA 31503
(912) 287-6584
www.okefenokeetech.edu

Sandersville Technical College
1189 Deepstep Rd.
Sandersville, GA 31082
(478) 553-2050
www.sandersvilletech.edu

Savannah Technical College
5717 White Bluff Rd.
Savannah, GA 31405
(912) 443-5700
www.savannahtech.edu

South Georgia Technical College
900 South GA Tech Pkwy.
Americus, GA 31709
(229) 931-2394
www.southgatech.edu

Valdosta Technical College
4089 Valtech Rd.

Valdosta, GA 31602
(229) 333-2100
www.valdostatech.edu

West Central Technical College
176 Murphy Campus Blvd.
Waco, GA 30182
(770) 537-6000
www.westcentraltech.edu

West Georgia Technical College
303 Fort Dr.
Lagrange, GA 30240
(706) 845-4323
www.westgatech.edu

Hawaii

N/A

Idaho

North Idaho College
1000 West Garden Ave.
Coeur D'Alene, ID 83814
(208) 769-3300
www.nic.edu

Millwork/Millwright
College of Southern Idaho
315 Falls Ave.
Twin Falls, ID 83301
(208) 733-9554
www.csi.edu

Illinois

**City Colleges of Chicago–
Richard J. Daley College**
7500 South Pulaski Rd.
Chicago, IL 60652
(773) 838-7500
www.daley.ccc.edu

**City Colleges of Chicago–Wilbur
Wright College**
4300 North Narragansett
Chicago, IL 60634
(773) 777-7900
www.wright.ccc.edu

College of Lake County
19351 West Washington St.
Grayslake, IL 60030
(847) 543-2000
www.clcillinois.edu

Danville Area
Community College
2000 East Main St.
Danville, IL 61832
(217) 443-3222
www.dacc.edu

Heartland Community College
1500 West Raab Rd.
Normal, IL 61761
(309) 268-8000
www.heartland.edu

Highland Community College
2998 West Pearl City Rd.
Freeport, IL 61032
(815) 235-6121
www.highland.edu

Illinois Central College
One College Dr.
East Peoria, IL 61635
(309) 694-5011
www.icc.edu

Illinois Eastern Community
Colleges–Olney Central College
305 North West St.
Olney, IL 62450
(618) 393-2982
www.iecc.edu/occ

Illinois Valley
Community College
815 North Orlando Smith Ave.
Oglesby, IL 61348
(815) 224-2720
www.ivcc.edu

John A. Logan College
700 Logan College Rd.
Carterville, IL 62918
(618) 985-3741
www.jalc.edu

Joliet Junior College
1215 Houbolt Rd.
Joliet, IL 60431
(815) 729-9020
www.jjc.edu

Kankakee Community College
100 College Dr.
Kankakee, IL 60901
(815) 802-8500
www.kcc.edu

Kaskaskia College
27210 College Rd.
Centralia, IL 62801
(618) 545-3000
www.kaskaskia.edu

Prairie State College
202 South Halsted St.
Chicago Heights, IL 60411
(708) 709-3500
www.prairiestate.edu

Rend Lake College
468 North Ken Gray Pkwy.
Ina, IL 62846
(618) 437-5321
www.rlc.edu

Richland Community College
One College Park
Decatur, IL 62521
(217) 875-7200
www.richland.edu

Indiana

Millwork/Millwright
Ivy Tech Community College–
  South Central
8204 Hwy. 311
Sellersburg, IN 47172
(812) 246-3301
www.ivytech.edu/sellersburg

Ivy Tech Community College–
Southwest
3501 First Ave.
Evansville, IN 47710
(812) 426-2865
www.ivytech.edu/evansville

Iowa

Des Moines Area
Community College
2006 Ankeny Blvd.
Ankeny, IA 50023
(515) 964-6241
www.dmacc.edu

Eastern Iowa Community
College District
306 West River Dr.
Davenport, IA 52801
(563) 336-3309
www.eicc.edu

Hawkeye Community College
1501 East Orange Rd.
Waterloo, IA 50701
(319) 296-2320
www.hawkeyecollege.edu

Iowa Central Community College
330 Ave. M
Fort Dodge, IA 50501
(515) 576-7201
www.iowacentral.edu

Marshalltown
Community College
3700 South Center St.
Marshalltown, IA 50158
(641) 752-7106
www.iavalley.edu

Western Iowa Tech
Community College
4647 Stone Ave.
Sioux City, IA 51102
(712) 274-6400
www.witcc.edu

Kansas

Johnson County
Community College
12345 College Blvd.
Overland Park, KS 66210
(913) 469-8500
www.jccc.edu

Kentucky

Ashland Community and
Technical College
1400 College Dr.
Ashland, KY 41101
(606) 326-2000
www.ashland.kctcs.edu

Big Sandy Community and
Technical College
One Bert Combs Dr.
Prestonsburg, KY 41653
(606) 886-3863
www.bigsandy.kctcs.edu

Bluegrass Community and
Technical College
470 Cooper Dr.
Lexington, KY 40506
(859) 246-2400
www.bluegrass.kctcs.edu

Bowling Green Technical College
1845 Loop Dr.
Bowling Green, KY 42101
(270) 901-1000
www.bowlinggreen.kctcs.edu

Elizabethtown Community and Technical College
600 College St. Rd.
Elizabethtown, KY 42701
(270) 769-2371
www.elizabethtown.kctcs.edu

Gateway Community and Technical College
1025 Amsterdam Rd.
Covington, KY 41011
(859) 441-4500
www.gateway.kctcs.edu

Henderson Community College
2660 South Green St.
Henderson, KY 42420
(270) 827-1867
www.hencc.kctcs.edu

Hopkinsville Community College
720 North Dr.
Hopkinsville, KY 42241
(270) 707-3700
www.hopkinsville.kctcs.edu

Jefferson Community and Technical College
109 East Broadway
Louisville, KY 40202
(502) 213-4000
www.jefferson.kctcs.edu

Madisonville Community College
2000 College Dr.
Madisonville, KY 42431
(270) 821-2250
www.madcc.kctcs.edu

Maysville Community and Technical College
1755 U.S. 68
Maysville, KY 41056
(606) 759-7141
www.maycc.kctcs.edu

Owensboro Community and Technical College
4800 New Hartford Rd.
Owensboro, KY 42303
(270) 686-4400
www.octc.kctcs.edu

Somerset Community College
808 Monticello St.
Somerset, KY 42501
(877) 629-9722
www.somerset.kctcs.edu

West Kentucky Community and Technical College
4810 Alben Barkley Dr.
Paducah, KY 42002
(270) 554-9200
www.westkentucky.kctcs.edu

Louisiana

Bossier Parish Community College
6220 East Texas
Bossier City, LA 71111
(318) 678-6000
www.bpcc.edu

Louisiana Technical College–Alexandria Campus
4311 South Macarthur Dr.
Alexandria, LA 71302
(318) 487-5439
www.region6.ltc.edu

Louisiana Technical College–Delta-Ouachita Campus
609 Vocational Pkwy.
West Monroe, LA 71292
(318) 397-6100
www.theltc.net

Louisiana Technical College–Natchitoches Campus
6587 Hwy. 1 Bypass
Natchitoches, LA 71458
(318) 357-3162
www.theltc.net

Louisiana Technical College–Northwest Louisiana Campus
814 Constable St.
Minden, LA 71055
(318) 371-3035
www.ltc.edu

Louisiana Technical College–River Parishes Campus
181 Regala Park Rd.
Reserve, LA 70084
(985) 536-4418
www.region3ltc.edu

Louisiana Technical College–Ruston Campus
1010 James St.
Ruston, LA 71273
(318) 251-4145
www.ltc.edu

Louisiana Technical College–Tallulah Campus
132 Old Hwy. 65 S
Tallulah, LA 71282
(318) 574-4820
www.theltc.net

Louisiana Technical College–Teche Area Campus
609 Ember Dr.
New Iberia, LA 70560
(337) 373-0011
www.techeareacampus.net

Maine

Kennebec Valley Community College
92 Western Ave.
Fairfield, ME 04937
(207) 453-5000
www.kvcc.me.edu

Maryland

N/A

Massachusetts

N/A

Michigan

Grand Rapids Community College
143 Bostwick Ave. NE
Grand Rapids, MI 49503
(616) 234-4000
www.grcc.edu

Henry Ford Community College
5101 Evergreen Rd.
Dearborn, MI 48128
(313) 845-9600
www.hfcc.edu

Kellogg Community College
450 North Ave.
Battle Creek, MI 49017
(269) 965-3931
www.kellogg.edu

Lansing Community College
419 North Capitol Ave.
Lansing, MI 48901
(517) 483-1957
www.lansing.cc.mi.us

Macomb Community College
14500 East Twelve Mile Rd.
Warren, MI 48088
(586) 445-7999
www.macomb.edu

Southwestern Michigan College
58900 Cherry Grove Rd.
Dowagiac, MI 49047
(269) 782-1000
www.swmich.edu

Minnesota

Hennepin Technical College
9000 Brooklyn Blvd.
Brooklyn Park, MN 55445
(952) 995-1300
www.hennepintech.edu

Mesabi Range Community and Technical College
1001 Chestnut St. W
Virginia, MN 55792
(218) 741-3095
www.mr.mnscu.edu

Minnesota State College–Southeast Technical
1250 Homer Rd.
Winona, MN 55987
(507) 453-2700
www.southeastmn.edu

Riverland Community College
1900 8th Ave. NW
Austin, MN 55912
(507) 433-0600
www.riverland.edu

Mississippi

East Central Community College
275 West Broad St.
Decatur, MS 39327
(601) 635-2111
www.eccc.edu

East Mississippi Community College
1512 Kemper St.
Scooba, MS 39358
(662) 476-5000
www.eastms.edu

Meridian Community College
910 Hwy. 19 N
Meridian, MS 39307
(601) 483-8241
www.meridiancc.edu

Northeast Mississippi Community College
Cunningham Blvd.
Booneville, MS 38829
(662) 728-7751
www.nemcc.edu

Missouri

Hannibal Career and Technical Center
4550 Mcmasters Ave.
Hannibal, MO 63401
(573) 221-4430
www.hannibal.tec.mo.us

Jefferson College
1000 Viking Dr.
Hillsboro, MO 63050
(636) 797-3000
www.jeffco.edu

State Fair Community College
3201 West 16th St.
Sedalia, MO 65301
(660) 530-5800
www.sfccmo.edu

Three Rivers Community College
2080 Three Rivers Blvd.
Poplar Bluff, MO 63901
(573) 840-9600
www.trcc.edu

Montana

N/A

Nebraska

Central Community College
3134 West Hwy. 34
Grand Island, NE 68802
(308) 398-4222
www.cccneb.edu

Nevada

N/A

New Hampshire

N/A

New Jersey

N/A

New Mexico

San Juan College
4601 College Blvd.
Farmington, NM 87402
(505) 326-3311
www.sanjuancollege.edu

New York

N/A

North Carolina

Davidson County Community College
297 Davidson Community College Rd.
Thomasville, NC 27360
(336) 249-8186
www.davidsonccc.edu

Gaston College
201 Hwy. 321 S
Dallas, NC 28034
(704) 922-6200
www.gaston.cc.nc.us

North Dakota

N/A

Ohio

N/A

Oklahoma

Great Plains Technology Center
4500 West Lee Blvd.
Lawton, OK 73505
(580) 355-6371
www.gptech.org

Tulsa Technology Center—
Broken Arrow Campus
4600 South Olive
Broken Arrow, OK 74011
(918) 828-5000
www.tulsatech.com

Oregon

Clackamas Community College
19600 Molalla Ave.
Oregon City, OR 97045
(503) 657-6958
www.clackamas.edu

Millwork/Millwright
Central Oregon
Community College
2600 NW College Way
Bend, OR 97701
(541) 383-7500
www.cocc.edu

Pennsylvania

Community College of
Allegheny County
800 Allegheny Ave.
Pittsburgh, PA 15233
(412) 323-2323
www.ccac.edu

Delaware County
Community College
901 South Media Line Rd.
Media, PA 19063
(610) 359-5000
www.dccc.edu

Harrisburg Area
Community College–Harrisburg
One HACC Dr.
Harrisburg, PA 17110
(717) 780-2300
www.hacc.edu

Reading Area
Community College
10 South Second St.
Reading, PA 19603
(610) 372-4721
www.racc.edu

Rhode Island

N/A

South Carolina

Aiken Technical College
2276 Jefferson Davis Hwy.
Graniteville, SC 29829
(803) 593-9954
www.atc.edu

Central Carolina
Technical College
506 North Guignard Dr.
Sumter, SC 29150
(803) 778-1961
www.cctech.edu

Greenville Technical College
506 South Pleasantburg Dr.
Greenville, SC 29607
(864) 250-8111
www.gvltec.edu

Northeastern Technical College
1201 Chesterfield Hwy.
Cheraw, SC 29520
(843) 921-6900
www.netc.edu

Orangeburg Calhoun
Technical College
3250 Saint Matthews Rd.
Orangeburg, SC 29118
(803) 536-0311
www.octech.edu

Spartanburg Community College
Business I-85
Spartanburg, SC 29303

(864) 592-4600
www.sccsc.edu

Tri-County Technical College
7900 U.S. Hwy. 76
Pendleton, SC 29670
(864) 646-1500
www.tctc.edu

Trident Technical College
7000 Rivers Ave.
Charleston, SC 29423
(843) 574-6111
www.tridenttech.edu

York Technical College
452 South Anderson Rd.
Rock Hill, SC 29730
(803) 327-8000
www.yorktech.com

South Dakota

Millwork/Millwright
Western Dakota Technical
Institute
800 Mickelson Dr.
Rapid City, SD 57703
(605) 394-4034
www.wdt.edu

Tennessee

Dyersburg State
Community College
1510 Lake Rd
Dyersburg, TN 38024
(731) 286-3200
www.dscc.edu

Northeast State Technical
Community College
2425 Hwy. 75
Blountville, TN 37617
(423) 323-3191
www.northeaststate.edu

Southwest Tennessee
Community College
737 Union Ave.
Memphis, TN 38103
(901) 333-5000
www.southwest.tn.edu

Tennessee Technology Center
at Athens
1635 Vo Tech Dr.
Athens, TN 37371
(423) 744-2814
www.athens.tec.tn.us

Tennessee Technology Center
at Crossville
910 Miller Ave.
Crossville, TN 38555
(931) 484-7502
www.ttcc.edu

Tennessee Technology Center
at Crump
3070 Hwy. 64 W
Crump, TN 38327
(731) 632-3393
www.crumpttc.edu

Tennessee Technology Center
Dickson
740 Hwy. 46
Dickson, TN 37055
(615) 441-6220
www.ttcdickson.edu

Tennessee Technology Center
at Elizabethton
426 Hwy. 91
Elizabethton, TN 37643
(423) 543-0070
www.elizabethton.tec.tn.us

Tennessee Technology Center
at Hartsville
716 McMurry Blvd.
Hartsville, TN 37074
(615) 374-2147
www.ttchartsville.edu

Tennessee Technology Center
at Hohenwald
813 West Main
Hohenwald, TN 38462
(931) 796-5351
www.ttchohenwald.edu

Tennessee Technology Center
at Jackson
2468 Technology Center Dr.
Jackson, TN 38301
(731) 424-0691
www.ttcjackson.edu

Tennessee Technology Center
at Livingston
740 High Tech Dr.
Livingston, TN 38570
(931) 823-5525
www.ttclivingston.edu

Tennessee Technology Center
at Mcminnville
241 Vo Tech Dr.
Mcminnville, TN 37110
(931) 473-5587
www.ttcmcminnville.edu

Tennessee Technology Center
at Memphis
550 Alabama Ave.
Memphis, TN 38105
(901) 543-6100
www.ttcmemphis.edu

Tennessee Technology Center
at Morristown
821 West Louise Ave.
Morristown, TN 37813
(423) 586-5771
www.ttcmorristown.edu

Tennessee Technology Center
at Murfreesboro
1303 Old Fort Pkwy.
Murfreesboro, TN 37129
(615) 898-8010
www.ttcmurfreesboro.edu

Tennessee Technology Center
at Paris
312 South Wilson St.
Paris, TN 38242
(731) 644-7365
www.ttcparis.edu

Tennessee Technology Center
at Shelbyville
1405 Madison St.
Shelbyville, TN 37160
(931) 685-5013
www.ttcshelbyville.edu

Tennessee Technology Center
at Whiteville
1685 Hwy. 64
Whiteville, TN 38075
(731) 254-8521
www.ttcwhiteville.edu

Walters State
Community College
500 South Davy Crockett Pkwy.
Morristown, TN 37813
(423) 585-2600
www.ws.edu

Texas

Grayson County College
6101 Grayson Dr.
Denison, TX 75020
(903) 465-6030
www.grayson.edu

Hill College
112 Lamar Dr.
Hillsboro, TX 76645
(254) 582-2555
www.hillcollege.edu

Lamar Institute of Technology
855 East Lavaca
Beaumont, TX 77705
(409) 880-8321
www.lit.edu

Texas State Technical College–
Marshall
2650 East End Blvd. S
Marshall, TX 75672
(903) 935-1010
www.marshall.tstc.edu

Texas State Technical College–
Waco
3801 Campus Dr.
Waco, TX 76705
(800) 792-8784
www.waco.tstc.edu

Utah

Davis Applied
Technology College
550 East 300 South
Kaysville, UT 84037
(801) 593-2500
www.datc.net

Ogden-Weber Applied
Technology College
200 North Washington Blvd.
Ogden, UT 84404
(801) 627-8300
www.owatc.edu

Vermont

N/A

Virginia

N/A

Washington

Bellingham Technical College
3028 Lindbergh Ave.
Bellingham, WA 98225
(360) 752-7000
www.btc.ctc.edu

**Lake Washington
Technical College**
11605 132nd Ave. NE
Kirkland, WA 98034
(425) 739-8100
www.lwtc.ctc.edu

West Virginia

N/A

Wisconsin

Blackhawk Technical College
6004 Prairie Rd.
Janesville, WI 53547
(608) 758-6900
www.blackhawk.edu

**Chippewa Valley
Technical College**
620 West Clairemont Ave.
Eau Claire, WI 54701

(715) 833-6200
www.cvtc.edu

Gateway Technical College
3520 30th Ave.
Kenosha, WI 53144
(262) 564-2200
www.gtc.edu

Lakeshore Technical College
1290 North Ave.
Cleveland, WI 53015
(920) 693-1000
www.gotoltc.edu

Mid-State Technical College
500 32nd St. N
Wisconsin Rapids, WI 54494
(715) 422-5500
www.mstc.edu

**Milwaukee Area
Technical College**
700 West State St.
Milwaukee, WI 53233
(414) 297-6370
www.matc.edu

Nicolet Area Technical College
Hwy. G South
Rhinelander, WI 54501
(715) 365-4410
www.nicoletcollege.edu

Northcentral Technical College
1000 Campus Dr.
Wausau, WI 54401
(715) 675-3331
www.ntc.edu

**Northeast Wisconsin
Technical College**
2740 West Mason St.

Green Bay, WI 54307
(920) 498-5400
www.nwtc.edu

**Southwest Wisconsin
Technical College**
1800 Bronson Blvd.
Fennimore, WI 53809
(608) 822-3262
www.swtc.edu

**Waukesha County
Technical College**
800 Main St.
Pewaukee, WI 53072
(262) 691-5566
www.wctc.edu

Western Technical College
304 6th St. N
La Crosse, WI 54602
(608) 785-9200
www.westerntc.edu

**Wisconsin Indianhead
Technical College**
505 Pine Ridge Dr.
Shell Lake, WI 54871
(715) 468-2815
www.witc.edu

Wyoming

**Western Wyoming
Community College**
2500 College Dr.
Rock Springs, WY 82902
(307) 382-1600
www.wwcc.wy.edu

Ironworker

Most ironworkers enter the field through the local office of the International Association of Bridge, Structural, Ornamental and Reinforcing Ironworkers. Apprenticeships typically last three to four years and are the most common method of gaining experience. Some do still learn on the job or through an independent contracting company. The type of ironworking offered by these unions is listed according to the following program key:

(AO) Architectural and Ornamental
(M) Mixed (controls all branches of trade except shopmen and navy yard riggers)
(ML) Metallic Lathers
(MR) Machinery Movers, Erectors, and Riggers
(O) Ornamental
(R) Rodmen
(RODRG) Rodman Riggers
(S) Structural
(SD) Stone Derrickmen
(SH) Shopmen
(SMR) Structural, Machinery Movers, and Riggers
(SO) Structural and Ornamental
(YR) Navy Yard Riggers

International Association of Bridge, Structural, Ornamental and Reinforcing Iron Workers Union–Locals

Alabama

92 Birmingham (M)
2828 4th Ave. S
Birmingham, AL 35233-2818
(205) 323-4551
localno92@bellsouth.net

798 Mobile (M)
7920 Crary Station Rd.
Semmes, AL 36575
(251) 645-2477
iwlu798@bellsouth.net

477 Sheffield (M)
506 North Nashville Ave.
Sheffield, AL 35660.
(256) 383-3334
iwlocal477@aol.com

Alaska

751 ANCHORAGE (M) (SH)
8141 Schoon St.
Anchorage, AK 99518
(907) 563-4766
iw751@alaska.net
www.ironworkersnw.org/local
  751.htm

Arizona

75 Phoenix (M)
950 East Elwood St.
Phoenix, AZ 85040
(602) 268-1449/1440

Arkansas

321 Little Rock (M)
1315 West 2nd St.
Little Rock, AR 72201
(501) 374-3705

California

155 Fresno (M)
5407 East Olive, Ste. 16
Fresno, CA 93727
(559) 251-7388

624 Fresno (SH)
5537 East Lamona Ave., Rm #4
Fresno, CA 93727
(559) 251-5621

844 Hercules (O)
1660 San Pablo Ave., Ste. C
Pinole, CA 94564

416 Los Angeles (R)
13830 San Antonio Dr.
Norwalk, CA 90650
(562) 868-1251
www.reinforcingironworker
  slocal416.org

433 Los Angeles (O) (SMR)
17495 Hurley St. E
City of Industry, CA 91744
(626) 964-2500

509 Los Angeles (SH)
13031 San Antonio Dr.,
  Ste. 203
Norwalk, CA 90650
(562) 868-9883

378 Oakland (M)
3120 Bayshore Rd.
Benicia, CA 94510
(707) 746-6100

118 Sacramento (M)
2840 El Centro Rd., Ste. 118
Sacramento, CA 95833
(916) 646-6976

229 San Diego (M)
5155 Mercury Point
San Diego, CA 92111
(858) 571-5238/5239

377 San Francisco (M)
570 Barneveld Ave.
San Francisco, CA 94124
(415) 285-3880
www.ironworkerslocal377.com

**790 San Francisco-Oakland
(SH)**
8130 Baldwin St.
Oakland, CA 94621
(510) 639-7333

Colorado

24 Denver (M) (SH)
501 West 4th Ave.
Denver, CO 80223
(303) 623-5386

Connecticut

15 Hartford (M)
20-28 Sargeant St.
Veeder Place, 3rd Floor
Hartford, CT 06105

832 Meriden (SH)
705 North Mountain Rd.
Newington, CT 06111
(860) 953-8276

424 New Haven (M)
15 Bernhard Rd.
New Haven, CT 06473
(203) 787-4154

Delaware

451 Wilmington (M)
203 Old DuPont Rd.
Wilmington, DE 19804
(302) 994-0946
ironworkerslu451@verizon.net

District of Columbia

5 Washington (SO)
9100 Old Marlboro Pike
Upper Marlboro, MD 20772-
  3627
(301) 599-0960

201 Washington (R)
1507 Rhode Island Ave. NE
Washington, DC 20018
(202) 529-9151

486 Washington (SH)
c/o Iron Workers International
1750 New York Ave. NW,
  Ste. 400
Washington, DC 20006
(202) 383-4846

Florida

317 North Florida Ave.
Deland, FL 32720
(386) 734-0721/7360
www.ironworkers846.com

597 Jacksonville (M)
9616 Kentucky St.
Jacksonville, FL 32218
(904) 764-3265
www.ironworkers597.com

272 Miami (M)
1201 NE 7th Ave.
Fort Lauderdale, FL 33304
(954) 524-8731
www.ironworkerslocal272.com

698 Miami (SH)
9616 Kentucky St.
Jacksonville, FL 32218
angeljdominguez@aol.com

808 Orlando (M)
200 East Landstreet Rd.
Orlando, FL 32824
(407) 859-9366
www.ironworkers808.com

397 Tampa (M)
10201 Hwy. 92 E
Tampa, FL 33610
(813) 623-1515
iwlu397@tampabay.rr.com

402 West Palm Beach (M)
1001 West 15th St.
Riviera Beach, FL 33404
(561) 842-7651
402i@bellsouth.net
www.ironworkerslocal402.org

Georgia

387 Atlanta (M)
109 Selig Dr. SW
Atlanta, GA 30336
(404) 505-0022
iwlocal387@aol.com
www.ironworkerslocal387.com

709 Savannah (M)
409 Grange Rd.
Port Wentworth, GA 31407
(912) 964-6931
djedenfield@yahoo.com

Hawaii

625 Honolulu (M)
94-497 Ukee St.
Waipahu, HI 96797
(808) 671-4344

742 Honolulu (YR)
PO Box 30711
Honolulu, HI 96820
(808) 423-1572

803 Honolulu (SH)
94-497 Ukee St.
Waipahu, HI 96797
(808) 671-4344

Idaho

732 Pocatello (M)
456 North Arthur
Pocatello, ID 83204
(208) 232-4873
www.iw732.com

Illinois

393 Aurora (M)
1901 Selmarten Rd.
Aurora, IL 60505
(630) 585-1600

590 Aurora (SH)
256 Madison St.
Batavia, IL 60510
(708) 879-1053

380 Champaign (M)
1602 East Butzow Dr.
Urbana, IL 61801
(217) 367-6014
iwlu380@aol.com

1 Chicago (S)
7720 Industrial Dr.
Forest Park, IL 60130
(708) 366-6695
www.iwlocal1.com

63 Chicago (AO)
2525 West Lexington St.
Broadview, IL 60155
(708) 344-7727/7728

136 Chicago (MR)
1820 Beach St.
Broadview, IL 60155-2863
(708) 615-9300

473 Chicago (SH)
5440 West St. Charles Rd.
Berkeley, IL 60163
(708) 544-2314

392 East St. Louis (M)
2995 Kingshighway
East St. Louis, IL 62201
(618) 874-0313
lu392jac@msn.com

444 Joliet (M)
2082 Oak Leaf St.
Joliet, IL 60436
(815) 725-1804
www.ironworkers444.com

112 Peoria (M) (SH)
3003 North Main
East Peoria, IL 61611
(309) 699-6489

498 Rockford (M)
5640 Sockness Dr.
Rockford, IL 61109
(815) 873-9180

111 Rock Island (M)
8000 29th St. W
Rock Island, IL 61201
(309) 756-6614

46 Springfield (M)
2888 East Cook St.
Springfield, IL 62703
(217) 528-4041/4042
www.ironworkers46.com

Indiana

730 Elkhart (SH)
25886 Lake Dr.
Elkhart, IN 46514-6233

103 Evansville (M)
5313 Old Booneville Hwy.
Evansville, IN 47715
(812) 477-5317
i.workers103@insightbb.com

147 Ft. Wayne (M)
1211 West Coliseum Blvd.

Ft. Wayne, IN 46808
(260) 484-8514
www.ironworkers147.org

726 Ft. Wayne (SH)
4302 Drury Lane
Ft. Wayne, IN 46807
(260) 456-7725

Ironworkers Local 147
1211 West Coliseum Blvd.
Ft. Wayne, IN 46808
(260) 484-8514

395 Hammond (M)
2820 165th St.
Hammond, IN 46323
(219) 844-5120/5121
webmaster@ironworkers
 395.com
www.ironworkers395.com

22 Indianapolis (M) (SH)
5600 Dividend Rd., Ste. A
Indianapolis, IN 46241-4302
(317) 243-8222
iwlocal22@sbcglobal.net
www.ironworkers22.net

292 South Bend (M)
3515 Boland Dr.
South Bend, IN 46628
(574) 288-9033

Iowa

577 Burlington (M)
16452 Hwy. 34
West Burlington, IA 52655
(319) 752-6951
iw577clp@mchsi.com

89 Cedar Rapids (M)
Teamsters Bldg.
5000 J St., SW
Cedar Rapids, IA 52404
(319) 365-8675

67 Des Moines (M)
1501 East Aurora Ave.
Des Moines, IA 50313
(515) 262-9366

493 Des Moines (SH)
1501 East Aurora Ave.
Des Moines, IA 50313
(515) 266-3194

21 Omaha, NE (M)
Iowa Suboffice
507 7th St., Insurance Centre,
  Ste. 319
Sioux City, IA 51101
(712) 252-1761

Kansas

24 Denver, CO (M) (SH)
Kansas Suboffice
1330 East 1st St., Ste. 107
Wichita, KS 67214
(316) 264-2424

Kentucky

769 Ashland (M)
2151 Greenup Ave.
PO Box 289
Ashland, KY 41105
(606) 324-0415

70 Louisville (M)
2441 Crittenden Dr.
Louisville, KY 40217
(502) 637-8796
ironwk70@bellsouth.net
www.glbctc.org/iw70.html

782 Paducah (M)
2424 Cairo Rd.
Paducah, KY 42001
(270) 442-2722
ironworkerslo782@bellsouth.net

Louisiana

623 Baton Rouge (M)
6153 Airline Hwy.
Baton Rouge, LA 70805
(225) 357-3262

710 Monroe (M)
1601 Southern Ave.
Monroe, LA 71202-4509
(318) 388-0286
iw710@jam.rr.com

58 New Orleans (M) (SH)
3035 Paris Ave.
New Orleans, LA 70119
(504) 943-6663

591 Shreveport (M)
5000 Greenwood Rd.
Shreveport, LA 71109
(318) 631-1461

Maine

7 Boston, MA (M)
Maine Suboffice
Hinckley Rd., PO Box 579
Clinton, ME 04927
(207) 426-9555

807 Winslow (SH)
Winslow Fire Station
16 Benton Ave.
Winslow, ME 04901

Maryland

16 Baltimore (M)
2008 Merritt Ave.
Baltimore, MD 21222
(410) 284-4750

568 Cumberland (M)
119 South Centre St.
Cumberland, MD 21502
(301) 777-7433

Massachusetts

7 Boston (M)
195 Old Colony Ave., PO Box 7
S. Boston, MA 02127-2457
(800) 730-4766

501 Boston (SH)
826 Washington St.
Braintree, MA 02184

Michigan

340 Battle Creek (M)
510 East Columbia Ave.
Battle Creek, MI 49015
(616) 451-8391

25 Detroit (M)
25150 Trans X Dr., PO Box 965
Novi, MI 48376-0965
(248) 344-9494

508 Detroit (SH)
36040 Michigan Ave.

Wayne, MI 48184
(734) 728-0202
local508@sbcglobal.net

831 Wayne (SH)
2339 Second St.
Weatland, MI 48186
(734) 722-5749

Minnesota

**512 Twin Cities, Minneapolis
and St. Paul (M)**
851 Pierce Butler Rte.
St. Paul, MN 55104-1634
(651) 489-1488
www.ironworkers512.com

**535 Twin Cities, Minneapolis
and St. Paul (SH)**
851 Pierce Butler Rte.
St. Paul, MN 55104
(651) 489-5718

Mississippi

469 Jackson (M) (SH)
1231 Morson Rd.
Jackson, MS 39209
(601) 922-1414

Missouri

10 Kansas City (M)
1000 E. 10th St.
Kansas City, MO 64106
(816) 842-8917
kc10ironworker@sbcglobal.net

520 Kansas City (SH)
7400 Ozark Rd.
Kansas City, MO 64129
(816) 924-2882

396 St. Louis (M)
2500 59th St.
St. Louis, MO 63110
(314) 647-3008

518 St. Louis (SH)
2500 59th St.
St. Louis, MO 63110
(636) 584-7276
iw518@yhti.net

Montana

732 Pocatello, ID (M)
Montana Suboffice
2 N. Oak
East Helena, MT 59635
(406) 442-3648

Nebraska

21 Omaha (M)
14515 Industrial Rd.
Omaha, NE 68144
(402) 333-0276

553 Omaha (SH)
PO Box 31051
Omaha, NE 68131

14515 West L St. (SH)
Omaha, NE 68137 (Millard Branch)

Nevada

416 Los Angeles, CA (R)
Nevada Suboffice
4425 East Colton Ave., Ste. 110
Las Vegas, NV 89115
(702) 434-7416

433 Los Angeles, CA (R)
Nevada Suboffice
100 Shiloah Dr.
Las Vegas, NV 89110
(702) 452-8445

118 Sacramento, CA (R)
Nevada Suboffice
1110 Gregg St.
Sparks, NV 89431
(775) 331-8696

27 Salt Lake City, UT (M) (SH)
Nevada Suboffice

790 San Francisco-Oakland, CA (SH)
Nevada Suboffice
1150 Greg St.
Sparks, NV 89431
(775) 358-1221

New Hampshire

7 Boston (M)
1671 Brown Ave.
Manchester, NH 03103-6725
(603) 623-3273

745 Portsmouth (YR)
Portsmouth Naval Shipyard
23 Blue Hills Dr.
Rochester, NH 03839
(603) 332-6760

New Jersey

350 Atlantic City (M)
PO Box 2670
Ventnor, NJ 08406
(609) 344-6313

399 Camden (M)
409 Crown Point Rd.
Westville, NJ 08093.

480 Elizabeth (M)
730 Federal Ave.
Kenilworth, NJ 07033
(908) 245-0027
ironworkerslocal480@verizon.net

483 Hackensack (M)
555 Preakness Ave., Ste. 6A
Paterson, NJ 07502
(973) 595-5544
www.ironworkerslocal483.com

45 Jersey City (M)
558 Newark Ave.
Jersey City, NJ 07306
(201) 653-3365

11 Newark (M)
1500 Broad St.
Bloomfield, NJ 07003
(973) 338-3777

373 Perth Amboy (M)
462 Market St.
Perth Amboy, NJ 08861
(732) 442-1495

68 Trenton (M)
2595 Yardville-Hamilton Square Rd.
Trenton, NJ 08690
(609) 586-6801

New Mexico

495 Albuquerque (M)
2524 Baylor SE
Albuquerque, NM 87106
(505) 242-9124

New York

12 Albany (M)
Labor Temple
890 Third St.
Albany, NY 12206
(518) 435-0470

361 Brooklyn (S)
89-19 97th Ave.
Ozone Park, NY 11416
(718) 322-1016
unionhall@local361.com
www.local361.com

6 Buffalo (M)
196 Orchard Park Rd.
West Seneca, NY 14224
(716) 828-1200
ironworkerlocal6@aol.com

576 Buffalo (SH)
1560 Harlem Rd., Ste. 11
Buffalo, NY 14206
(716) 895-5052

824 Gouverneur (SH)
21 Little York Rd.
Gouverneur, NY 13642
(315) 287-4540

470 Jamestown (SH)
4560 Brainard Rd.
Kennedy, NY 14747

417 Newburgh (M)
583 Rte. 32
Wallkill, NY 12589
(845) 566-8417
office417@hvc.rr.com

40 New York (S)–NY
451 Park Ave. S
New York, NY 10016
(212) 889-1320
bobwalsh@ironworkers.net

46 New York (ML) (R)
1322 Third Ave.
New York, NY 10021
(212) 737-0500
www.ml46.org

197 New York (SD)
25-19 43rd Ave.
Long Island City, NY 11101
(718) 361-6534

455 New York (SH)
40-05 Crescent St.
Long Island City, NY 11101
(718) 361-9455

580 New York (O)
501 West 42nd St.
New York, NY 10036
(212) 594-1662
dlusardi@local-580.com

9 Niagara Falls (M)
Niagara Nine Bldg.
412 39th St.
Niagara Falls, NY 14303
(716) 285-5738/5739
iwl9@verizon.net

33 Rochester (M)
154 Humboldt St.
Rochester, NY 14610
(585) 288-2630
local33@frontiernet.net

60 Syracuse (M)
500 West Genesee St.
Syracuse, NY 13204
(315) 422-8200
iwlu60@aol.com

612 Syracuse (SH)
3652 US Rt. 11
Pulaski, NY 13142
(315) 298-5998
abay519@usadatanet.net

440 Utica (M)
801 Varick St.
Utica, NY 13502
(315) 735-4531
iw440sec@adelphia.net

North Carolina

812 Asheville (SH)–TV
16 Runyon Dr.
Leicester, NC 28748
(828) 683-0698

848 Charleston, SC (M)–MA
North Carolina Suboffice
3300 US Hwy. 70E
Durham, NC 27703

North Dakota

512 Twin Cities of Minneapolis and St. Paul (M)
North Dakota Suboffice
2901 Twin City Dr., Ste. 104
Mandan, ND 55854
(701) 663-4266

Ohio

550 Canton (M)
618 High Ave. NW
Canton, OH 44703
(330) 455-5164

44 Cincinnati (SMR)
4850 Madison Rd.
Cincinnati, OH 45227
(513) 271-4444

372 Cincinnati (R)
4958 Winton Ridge Ln.
Cincinnati, OH 45232
(513) 761-3720

522 Cincinnati (SH)
1579 Summit Rd., Room 123
Cincinnati, OH 45237
(513) 821-0522

17 Cleveland (M)
1544 E. 23rd St.
Cleveland, OH 44114
(216) 771-5558
union@ironworkers17.org

468 Cleveland (SH)
3250 Euclid Ave., Room 270
Cleveland, OH 44115
(888) 818-2538
www.iwlu468.com

172 Columbus (M)
2867 South High St.
Columbus, OH 43207
(614) 497-0550
iw172@ds.net
www.ironworkers172.com

290 Dayton (M)
606 Hillrose Ave.
Dayton, OH 45404
(937) 222-1622
www.iron290.com

585 Vincennes (SH)–SL
PO Box 788
Grand River, OH 44045-0788

55 Toledo (M)
1080 Atlantic Ave.
Toledo, OH 43609
(419) 385-6613
office@ironworkerslocal55.com
www.ironworkerslocal55.com

499 Toledo (SH)
9969 Crabb Rd.
Temperence, MI 48182
(419) 349-7168
ironworkerslocal499@att.net

207 Youngstown (M)
694 Bev Rd.
Boardman, OH 44512
(888) 207-6064
www.iw207.com

Oklahoma

48 Oklahoma City (M)
1044 Southwest 22nd St.
Oklahoma City, OK 73109-1637
(405) 632-6154

584 Tulsa (M) (SH)
14716 East Pine
Tulsa, OK 74116
(918) 437-1446
ironworkers584@sbcglobal.net
www.tulsaironworkers.com

Oregon

29 Portland (M)
11620 Northeast Ainsworth Cir.,
Ste. 200

Portland, OR 97220
(503) 774-0777
www.ironworkers29.org

516 Portland (SH)
11620 Northeast Ainsworth Cir.,
Ste. 200
Portland, OR 97220-9016
(503) 257-4743
shopmens@pacifier.com
www.local516.org

Pennsylvania

36 Easton (M)
521 Fifth St.
Whitehall, PA 18052
(610) 774-0433

404 Harrisburg (M)
981 Peifers Lane
Harrisburg, PA 17109
(717) 564-8550

822 Lewisburg (SH)
528 Myrtle St.
Milton, PA 17847
(570) 742-9146

401 Philadelphia (SO)
11600 Norcom Rd.
Philadelphia, PA 19154
(215) 676-3000
ironworkers401@aol.com
www.local401.com

405 Philadelphia (RODRG)
2433 Reed St.
Philadelphia, PA 19146
(215) 462-7300

502 Philadelphia (SH)
168 West Ridge Pike, Ste. 113,
Limerick Office Court
Limerick, PA 19468
(610) 454-0877

3 Pittsburgh (M)
2201 Liberty Ave.
Pittsburgh, PA 15222
(412) 227-6767
www.iwlocal3.com

527 Pittsburgh (SH)
2945 Banksville Rd.
Pittsburgh, PA 15216
(412) 341-6180

420 Reading (M)
1645 Fairview St.
Reading, PA 19606
(610) 373-7090

489 Scranton (M)
144 Brown St.
Yatesville, PA 18640
(570) 655-9400

521 Scranton (SH)
PO Box 250
Olyphant, PA 18447

Rhode Island

523 Pawtucket (SH)
119 Arland Dr.
Pawtucket, RI 02861
(401) 728-4615

37 Providence (M)
845 Waterman Ave.
East Providence, RI 02914
(401) 438-1111

South Carolina

848 Charleston (M)
7326 Pepperdam Ave.
North Charleston, SC 29418
(843) 552-1554
iw848@bellsouth.net
www.iwt.cc

South Dakota

21 Omaha, NE (M)
South Dakota Suboffice
(goes through Iowa)
c/o Local 21 Iowa Suboffice
507 7th St., Ste. 319
Sioux City, IA 51101
(712) 252-1761

Tennessee

704 Chattanooga (M)
2715 Belle Arbor Ave.
Chattanooga, TN 37406
(423) 622-2111
ironwork704@aol.com

384 Knoxville (M)
1000 Buchanan Ave. NE
Knoxville, TN 37917
(865) 689-3371

167 Memphis (M)
2574 Lindawood Cove
Memphis, TN 38118
(901) 367-1676
iwlu167@bellsouth.net
www.ironworkers167.com

492 Nashville (M)
2524 Dickerson Rd.
Nashville, TN 37207
(615) 226-5435/5436
iwlu492@comcast.net

733 Nashville (SH)
2425 Diecherson Rd.
Nashville, TN 37207
(859) 250-2966

Texas

482 Austin (M)
2201 Riverside Farms Rd.
Austin, TX 78741
(512) 385-2500

536 Dallas (SH)
1801 Elm Ln.
Okmulgee, OK 74447-5424
(918) 660-4930

263 Dallas/Fort Worth (M)
604 North Great Southwest
Pkwy.
Arlington, TX 76011
(817) 640-0202
iwlu263@aol.com

135 Galveston (M)
216 Gulf Freeway N
Texas City, TX 77591
(409) 935-2421

84 Houston (M)
PO Box 5116
Houston, TX 77262
(713) 928-3361

66 San Antonio (M)
4318 Clark Ave.
San Antonio, TX 78223
(210) 532-5237

Utah

27 Salt Lake City (M) (SH)
2261 South Redwood Rd.
Salt Lake City, UT 84119
(801) 972-8997
www.ironworkers27.com

Vermont

7 Boston, MA (M)
Vermont Suboffice
93 St. Albans Rd.
Swanton, VT 05488-9782
(802) 868-7919
vtiw.union@verizon.net

Virginia

79 Norfolk (M)
Ironworkers Office Bldg.
5307 Virginia Beach Blvd.
Norfolk, VA 23502
(757) 461-7979/7900

781 Norfolk (SH)
5307 East Virginia Beach Blvd.
Norfolk, VA 23502
(757) 461-6211

228 Portsmouth (YR)
PO Box 2466
Portsmouth, VA 23702
(757) 558-0944
local228@verizon.net

28 Richmond (M)
530 East Main St., Ste. 510
Richmond, VA 23219
(804) 643-7685
iwlocal28@verizon.net

697 Roanoke (M)
5109 Hildebrand Ave., NW
Roanoke, VA 24012
(540) 366-1429
rwa697@aol.com

Washington

86 Seattle (M)
4550 South 134th Pl., #102
Tukwila, WA 98168
(206) 248-4246
local86@local86.org
www.local86.org

506 Seattle (SH)
c/o Iron Workers District Council
  of the Pacific Northwest, 10828
Gravelly Lake Dr. SW, Ste. 212
Lakewood, WA 98499
(253) 984-0514
local506@ironworkersnw.org
www.ironworkersnw.org/
  local506.htm

14 Spokane (M)
16610 East Euclid
Spokane, WA 99216
(509) 927-8288
www.ironworkersnw.org/
  local14.htm

West Virginia

301 Charleston (M)
2425 Hampshire Dr.
Charleston, WV 25312
(304) 342-5343

787 Parkersburg (M)
303 Erickson Blvd.
Parkersburg, WV 26101
(304) 485-6231

549 Wheeling (M)
2350 Main St.
Wheeling, WV 26003
(304) 232-2660

Wisconsin

825 LaCrosse (SH)
2030 SR 16
LaCrosse, WI 54601
(608) 781-3463

383 Madison (M)
Madison Labor Temple
Room 210, 1602 South Park St.
Madison, WI 53715
(608) 256-3162
iwlu383@itis.com

665 Madison (SH)
PO Box 826
Sun Prairie, WI 53590-0826
(608) 837-2863

8 Milwaukee (M)
12034 West Adler Lane
Milwaukee, WI 53214
(414) 476-9370
www.iwl8.org

811 Wausau (SH)
Wausau Labor Temple
Room 6, 318 South 3rd Ave.
Wausau, WI 54401

Wyoming

Wyoming Suboffice (SO)
344 North Walsh Dr.
Casper, WY 82609
(307) 237-9556

NCCER-Accredited Training Centers for Ironworking

Alabama

Diversified Employment Service Incorporated
211-C Hwy. 43 S
Saraland, AL 36571
(251) 679-0018

Alaska

N/A

Arizona

N/A

Arkansas

N/A

California

N/A

Colorado

N/A

Connecticut

Construction Education Center Inc.
2138 Silas Deane Hwy.,
Ste. 101
Rocky Hill, CT 06067
(860) 529-5886
www.thinkconstruction.org

Delaware

N/A

District of Columbia

N/A

Florida

N/A

Georgia

N/A

Hawaii

N/A

Idaho

N/A

Illinois

N/A

Indiana

N/A

Iowa

ABC of Iowa
475 Alices Rd., Ste. A
Waukee, IA 50263
(515) 987-3790
www.abciowa.org

Kansas

N/A

Kentucky

N/A

Louisiana

N/A

Maine

N/A

Maryland

Baltimore Metro Chapter ABC
1220-B East Joppa Rd.,
Ste. 322
Towson, MD 21286
(410) 821-0351
www.abcbaltimore.org

ABC Metropolitan Washington
4061 Powder Mill Rd., Ste. 120
Calverton, MD 20705
(301) 595-9711
www.abcmetrowashington.org

Massachusetts

N/A

Michigan

ABC Inc.–Saginaw Valley Chapter
4520 East Ashman Rd., Ste. G
Midland, MI 48642
(989) 832-8879
www.abcsvac.org

Minnesota

N/A

Mississippi

N/A

Missouri

N/A

Montana

N/A

Nebraska

N/A

Nevada

N/A

New Hampshire

N/A

New Jersey

N/A

New Mexico

N/A

New York

CTC of New York State
6369 Collamer Dr.
East Syracuse, NY 13057
(315) 463-7539
www.abcnys.org

North Carolina

N/A

North Dakota

N/A

Ohio

Construction Craft Academy
9760 Shepard Rd.
Macedonia, OH 44056
(800) 442-0067
www.craftacademy.com

Oklahoma

Integrated Service Company, LLC
1900 North 161st East Ave.
Tulsa, OK 74116
(918) 234-4150
www.inservusa.com

Oregon

N/A

Pennsylvania

Keystone Chapter ABC
135 Shellyland Rd.
Manheim, PA 17545
(717) 653-8106
www.abckeystone.org

Rhode Island

N/A

South Carolina

N/A

South Dakota

N/A

Tennessee

Construction Education Partnership
Simpson St. and Island Dr.
Kingsport, TN 37660
(423) 578-2710

Texas

ABC of Greater Houston Inc.
3910 Kirby Dr., Ste. 131
Houston, TX 77098
(713) 523-6258
www.abchouston.org

Associated General Contractors of El Paso
4625 Ripley Dr.
El Paso, TX 79922
(915) 585-1533
www.agcelpaso.org

The Victor Group
801 High Ridge Dr.
Friendswood, TX 77546
(281) 850-8079
www.thevictorgroup.net

Utah

N/A

Vermont

N/A

Virginia

N/A

Washington

N/A

West Virginia

N/A

Wisconsin

N/A

Wyoming

Wyoming Contractors Association AGC
2220 North Bryan Stock Trail
Casper, WY 82601
(307) 237-4400
www.wcagc.org

Logging

E ntry-level loggers generally train on the job with a specific logging company or through a forestry organization. The following organizations and associations are excellent resources for someone looking to get into the industry.

Loggers Council
555 Alabama St.
Montgomery, AL 36104
(334) 265-8733
www.alaforestry.org

Arkansas Timber Producers
Association
2311 Biscayne Dr., Ste. 207
Little Rock, AR 72227
(501) 224-2232
www.arkloggers.com

Associated California Loggers
555 Capitol Mall, Ste. 745
Sacramento, CA 95814
(916) 441-7940
www.calog.com

Associated Logging Contractors
Inc. Idaho
PO Box 671
Couer d'Alene, ID 83816
(208) 667-6473
www.idahologgers.com

Associated Oregon Loggers
PO Box 12339
Salem, OR 97309
(503) 364-1330
www.oregonloggers.org

Great Lakes Timber
Professionals Association
PO Box 1278
Rhinelander, WI 54501
(715) 282-5828
www.timberpa.com

Green River Loggers Council
PO Box 505
Beaver Dam, KY 42430

Louisiana Loggers Association

PO Box 5
Winnfield, LA 71483
(318) 628-4031

Louisiana Loggers Council
PO Box 5067
Alexandria, LA 71307
(318) 443-2558
www.laforestry.com

Michigan Association of
Timbermen
7931 South M-123
Newberry, MI 49868
(800) 682-4979
timbermn@up.net
www.timbermen.org

Mississippi Loggers Association
PO Drawer 659
Quitman, MS 39355
(800) 305-6023
www.msloggers.org

Montana Logging Association
PO Box 1716
Kalispell, MT 59903
(406) 752-3168
www.logging.org

New Hampshire Timber
Harvesting Council
54 Portsmouth St.
Concord, NH 03301
(603) 224-9699

Northeastern Loggers'
Association (represents New
England, New York, and
Pennsylvania)
PO Box 69
Old Forge, NY 13420
(315) 369-3078
www.northernlogger.com

Northern Arizona Loggers
Association
504 East Butler Ave.
Flagstaff, AZ 86001
(928) 774-9111

Professional Logging Contractors
of Maine
PO Box 400
Fort Kent, ME 04743
(888) 300-6614
www.maineloggers.org

South Carolina Timber
Producers Association
601 Carola Lane
PO Box 811
Lexington, SC 29127
(803) 957-9919

Southeastern Wood Producers
Association
PO Box 9
Hilliard, FL 32046
(904) 845-7133
www.sewpa.com

Texas Logging Council
PO Box 139
Bloomburg, TX 75556
(903) 728-5736

Virginia Loggers Association
33 Morewood Pl.
Palmyra, VA 22963
(434)-589-8609
www.valoggers.org

Washington Contract Loggers
Association
PO Box 2168
Olympia, WA 98507-2168
(800) 422-0074

Masonry

While it's still considered acceptable for masons to learn on the job, there are programs that specialize in masonry courses and techniques. Many such programs are offered through the International Union of Bricklayers and Allied Craftsworkers, the Associated Builders and Contractors (ABC), or the Associated General Contractors of America (AGC). Additional information on these training programs is available through the National Center for Construction Education and Research (NCCER) at www.nccer.org/findCenter.asp. The Masonry Contractors Association of America (MCAA) has also compiled a list of recommended continuing education programs.

Resources
International Union of Bricklayers and Allied Craftsworkers
www.bacweb.org

MCCA Recommended Training Programs

Alabama

Carver State Tech
414 Stanton St.
Mobile, AL 36617
(251) 473-8692

CEFA
250 Commerce Pkwy.
Pelham, AL 35124
(205) 682-9963

Chambers County Career
Tech Center
PO Box 318
Lafayette, AL 36862
(334) 864-8864

Hale County Technology Center
19875 Hwy. 69
Greensboro, AL 36744
(334) 624-3691

Reid State Technical College
PO Box 588
Evergreen, AL 36401
(251) 578-1313

Wallace Community College–
Selma
3000 Earl Goodwin Pkwy.
Selma, AL 36702
(334) 876-9357

Wallace Community College–
Sparks Campus
PO Drawer 580
Eufaula, AL 36027
(334) 687-3543

Alaska

N/A

Arizona

Arizona Masonry Contractors
Association
1803 North 40th St., Ste. 102
Phoenix, AZ 85008
(602) 262-0510

Arkansas

N/A

California

Masonry Industry
Training Association
PO Box 9966
Moreno Valley, CA 92552
(800) 995-4540

Colorado

CITC (Construction Industry Training Council)
646 Mariposa St.
Denver, CO 80204
(303) 893-1500

Rocky Mountain
Masonry Institute
686 Mariposa St.
Denver, CO 80204
(303) 893-3838

Connecticut

Mason Contractors Association of CT
One Regency Dr.
Bloomfield, CT 06002
(860) 243-3977

Delaware

N/A

District of Columbia

N/A

Florida

Florida Masonry Apprentice & Educational Foundation Inc.
PO Box 457
Boca Raton, FL 33429-0457
(561) 239-2462

Florida Masonry Apprentice & Educational Foundation Inc.- North
PO Box 1345
Green Cove Springs, FL 32043
(904) 284-7556

Florida Masonry Apprentice & Educational Foundation Inc.- South
861 Nectar Rd.
Venice, FL 34293
(941) 496-4929

South Florida Trowel Trades
3127 West Hallandale Beach Blvd.
Pembroke Park, FL 33009
(954) 985-3807

Georgia

Masonry Association of Georgia
2501 Lantrac Ct.
Decatur, GA 30035
(678) 518-1104

Hawaii

N/A

Idaho

SW Idaho Masonry Apprenticeship Committee
1300 East Franklin Rd.
Meridian, ID 83642
(208) 344-5438

Illinois

BAC Local #8 of Illinois
PO Box 6569
Champaign, IL 61825
(217) 356-0419

Bricklayers' Local 21 of Illinois
1950 West 43rd St.
Chicago, IL 60609
(773) 650-9002

Bricklaying and Masonry Trades JAC
1011 South Grand Ave.
Springfield, IL 62703
(217) 528-0993

Central Illinois Mason Contractors Association
5200 North Knoxville 303N
Peoria, IL 61614
(309) 692-2997

District Council Training Center
2140 Corporate Dr.
Addison, IL 60101
(630) 953-0835

Indiana

IUBAC of Indiana and Kentucky
2008 LaPorte Ave.
Valparaiso, IN 46383
(219) 464-2450

Prosser School of Technology
4202 Charlestown Rd.
New Albany, IN 47150
(812) 949-4266

Iowa

Bricklayers Local #3
2425 Delaware Ave.
Des Moines, IA 50317
(800) 792-7445

Ellsworth Community College
1100 College Ave.
Iowa Falls, IA 50126
(800) 322-9235 ext. 253

Western Iowa Tech Community College
4647 Stone Ave.
Sioux City, IA 51106
(712) 274-8733 ext. 3239

Kansas

Northeast Kansas Technical College
1501 West Riley
Atchison, KS 66002
(913) 367-5220

Kentucky

Construction Training Institute
4517 Poplar Level Rd.
Louisville, KY 40213
(502) 962-2945

Louisiana

BAC Local #6 JATC
3801 Canal, Ste. 211
New Orleans, LA 70119
(504) 483-9929

Maine

Southern Maine
Community College
6 Fort Rd.
South Portland, ME 04106
(207) 741-5800

Maryland

N/A

Massachusetts

IMI New England Regional
Training Center
84 Myron St.
West Springfield, MA 01089
(413) 737-5999

Mason Contractors Association
of MA
PO Box 47
Bridgewater, MA 02324
(508) 697-1120

Michigan

N/A

Minnesota

Alexandria Technical College
1601 Jefferson St.
Alexandria, MN 56308
(320) 762-4458

MN Concrete and Masonry
Contractors Association
26 Exchange St., Ste. 414
St. Paul, MN 55101
(651) 293-0892

Mississippi

N/A

Missouri

BAC Local #15–Springfield
Chapter
414 South Grant
Springfield, MO 65806
(573) 216-7159

BAC Local Union #15
Apprenticeship and
Training Fund
105 West 12th Ave.
North Kansas City, MO 64116
(816) 471-0880

Bricklayer Training Center
4350 Green Ash Dr.
Earth City, MO 63045
(314) 770-1066

Diaz Construction Company
705 Virginia Ave.
Kansas City, MO 64106
(816) 474-3800

Mason Contractors Association
of St. Louis
1429 South Big Bend
St. Louis, MO 63117
(314) 645-1966

Rolla Technical College
1304 East 10th St.
Rolla, MO 65401
(573) 458-0150

South Central Career Center
610 East Olden St.
West Plains, MO 65775
(417) 256-6152

Montana

N/A

Nebraska

Mason Training Institute
17610 Storage Rd.
Omaha, NE 68136
(402) 339-7007

Nebraska Concrete Masonry
Association
PO Box 7196
Omaha, NE 68107
(402) 330-5260

Nevada

N/A

New Hampshire

Associated Builders and
Contractors NH/VT Chapter
6 Dixon Ave.
Concord, NH 03301
(603) 226-4789

New Jersey

International Masonry Institute
3281 Rt. 206
Bordentown, NJ 08505
(609) 324-0500

Ocean County Vo-Tech School
850 Toms River Rd.
Jackson, NJ 08527
(732) 928-3830

New Mexico

N/A

New York

SUNY–Alfred State College
2530 South Brooklyn Ave.
Wellsville, NY 14895
(607) 587-4133

North Carolina

NC Mason Contactors
Association
PO Box 2412
Hickory, NC 28603
(828) 324-1564

North Dakota

Jost Masonry Construction Inc.
PO Box 42
510 Cotton Ave.
Burlington, ND 58722
(701) 838-6059

Ohio

Akron Bricklayers JAC
908 1/2 North Main St.
Akron, OH 43307
(330) 253-5173

Eastland Career Center
302 Edenberry Ln.
Pataskala, OH 43062
(740) 964-9300

Maplewood Career Center
7075 SR 88
Ravenna, OH 44266
(330) 296-2892

Mason Contractors Association
of Akron and Vicinity
76 East North St.
Akron, OH 44304
(330) 762-9951

Vanguard Career Center
1306 Cedar St.
Fremont, OH 43420
(419) 332-2626

Oklahoma

Indian Capital
Technology Center
Route 4, Box 3320
Stilwell, OK 74960
(918) 696-3111

Kiamichi Technology Center
Route 3, Box 177
Idabel, OK 74745
(580) 286-7555

Northeast Technology Center
PO Box 219
Afton, OK 74331
(918) 257-8324

Northwest AVTS
1490 South Elliott St.
Pryor, OK 74361
(918) 825-5555

Oregon

Masonry Institute of Oregon
3609 SW Corbett, Ste. 4
Portland, OR 97201
(503) 224-1940

Oregon, SW Washington Mason
Trades Apprenticeship and Training
12812 NE Marx St.
Portland, OR 97230
(503) 234-3781

Pennsylvania

BAC, Local 1 of Pennsylvania
and Delaware
2702 Black Lake Pl.
Philadelphia, PA 19154
(215) 330-0544

Career Technology Center
3201 Rockwell Ave.
Scranton, PA 18508
(570) 346-8471

Sun Area Career and
Technology Center
21st Century Dr.
New Berlin, PA 17855
(570) 966-1031

The Williamson Free School
of Mechanical Trades
106 South New Middletown Rd.
Media, PA 19063-5299
(610) 566-1776

York County School of Technology
2179 South Queen St.
York, PA 17402
(717) 741-0820

Rhode Island

N/A

South Carolina

Pettit Construction Co. Inc.
PO Box 307
Roebuck, SC 29376
(864) 576-4762

South Dakota

Boxelder Job Corps
PO Box 110
Nemo, SD 57759-0110
(605) 348-3636

Tennessee

Resource Valley Construction
Training Council
4700 Western Ave., Ste. 101
Knoxville, TN 37921
(865) 602-2311

Tennessee Technology Center
821 West Louise Ave.
Morristown, TN 37813
(423) 586-5771

Texas

P and S Masonry
PO Box 649
Hamilton, TX 76531
(254) 386-8975 ext. 205

San Antonio Masonry
Contractors Association
PO Box 791042
San Antonio, TX 78279
(830) 606-5556

South Texas AGC
518 South Enterprise Pkwy.
Corpus Christi, TX 78405
(361) 289-0996

South Texas Masonry
Contractors Association
5205 Agnes St.
Corpus Christi, TX 78406
(361) 289-1072

Texas Masonry Council
314 East Highland Mall Blvd.,
Ste. 510
Austin, TX 78752
(512) 374-9922

Utah

Ogden/Weber
Technology College
200 North Washington Blvd.
Ogden, UT 84404
(801) 627-8345

Vermont

N/A

Virginia

Blue Ridge Masonry Association
PO Box 12744
Roanoke, VA 24028
(540) 389-4823

Masonry Institute
PO Box 707
Falls Church, VA 22043
(886) 529-7994

Washington

N/A

West Virginia

Fred Eberle Technical Center
Route 5, Box 2
Buckhannon, WV 26201
(304) 472-1259

Mercer County Technical
Education Center
1397 Stafford Dr.
Princeton, WV 24740
(304) 425-9551

South Branch Career and
Technical Center
401 Peirpont St.
Petersburg, WV 26847
(304) 257-1331

Wisconsin

Milwaukee Area
Technical College
1200 South 71st St.

West Allis, WI 53214
(414) 456-5367

Southwest WI Technical College
1800 Bronson Blvd.
Fennimore, WI 53809
(800) 362-3322

Wisconsin Indianhead
Technical College
1900 College Dr.
Rice Lake, WI 54868
(800) 243-9482 ext. 5281

Wyoming

N/A

Mining

There is no set way into the mining industry, but the United Mine Workers of America (UMWA) assists with individuals who are interested in mining with job training and placement. UMWA runs career centers around the country, specifically in areas where there is a mining presence.

United Mine Workers of America (UMWA)

Career Centers

Administrative Office
640 Jefferson Ave.
Washington, PA 15301
(800) 826-2338 or (724)
223-9332

Pennsylvania and Northern West Virginia Satellite Offices
199 Dunn Station Rd.

Prosperity, PA 15329
(724) 627-6259
Lucernemines, PA 15754
(888) 472-8330 or (724)
479-8692

Fairmont Satellite Office
310 Gaston Ave.
Fairmont, WV 26554
(304) 363-7500

Beckley, WV Office
Mining Technology and Training
Center, Beckley, WV Campus
2306 South Fayette St.
Beckley, WV 25801
(877) 798-8692 or
(304) 253-3772

UMWA District Offices

International
8315 Lee Hwy.
Fairfax, VA 22031
(703) 208-7200

Districts

District 2
Pennsylvania, New York,
  Eastern Canada
113 Roberts Rd., Ste. B
Grindstone, PA 15442
(724) 785-8692

Hazelton, PA
(570) 455-3621

Lucernemines, PA
(724) 479-8692

Glace Bay, NS
(902) 849-8692

District 12
Illinois, Indiana, Western
  Kentucky, Missouri, Iowa,
  Kansas, Oklahoma, Arkansas,
  Louisiana, Texas
3695 South Sixth St.
Springfield, IL 62703
(217) 529-8301
umwa12@springnet1.com

Benton, IL
(618) 439-7225

Madisonville, KY
(270) 821-2774

District 17
Southern West Virginia, Eastern
  Kentucky, Virginia, Tennessee
1300 Kanawha Blvd. E
Charleston, WV 25301
(304) 346-0341

Pikeville, KY
(606) 437-7376

Castlewood, VA
(276) 762-5537

Beckley, WV
(304) 252-0611

Chapmanville, WV
(304) 855-2280

Welch, WV
(304) 436-4123

District 20
Alabama, Florida, Georgia,
  Mississippi
275 Forest Rd., Ste. 100
Hueytown, AL 35023
(205) 744-9853
umwadistrict20@bellsouth.net

District 22
Western United States
525 East 100th South
Price, UT 84501
(435) 637-2037/2066
umwadistrict22@emery
  telcom.net

District 31
Northern West Virginia, Ohio

310 Gaston Ave.
Fairmont, WV 26554
(304) 363-7500

Bridgeport, OH
(740) 635-7600

Canada
33 Gallant St
Glace Bay, NS, Canada
  B1A 1T2
(902) 849-8692
www.umwa@ns.sympatico.ca

Regions

Region I
113 Roberts Rd., Ste. B
Grindstone, PA 15442
(724) 785-8693
umwaregion1@verizon.net

Region II
1300 Kanawha Blvd. East
Charleston, WV 25301
(304) 343-0259
region2@umwa.org

Region III
1530 North Main
Benton, IL 62812
(616) 439-6373

Region IV
6525 West 44th Ave.
Wheat Ridge, CO 80033
(303) 425-7110
Region4@umwa.org

State, Local, and District Mining Associations and Organizations

The Mine Safety and Health Administration maintains a list of state-by-state mining organizations and associations. While they will not all offer training, they serve as a resource for information about the industry. More information can be found at www.msha.gov/minelink/states.htm.

Mining Colleges and Universities

Many mining workers and supervisors start off in community colleges or other schools that teach mine safety, engineering, and management.

Colorado School of Mines
1500 Illinois St.
Golden, CO 80401
(303) 273-3220
www.mines.edu

University of Kentucky
Mining Engineering
230 Mining and Mineral
  Resources Building
Lexington, KY 40506-0107
(859) 257-8026
www.engr.uky.edu/mng

Michigan Technological University
Mining Engineering
630 Dow Environmental Engineering and Sciences Building
1400 Townsend Dr.
Houghton, MI 49931
(906) 487-2610
www.mg.mtu.edu

Montana Tech
www.mtech.edu/mines/
  mine_eng
North Campus
1300 West Park St.
Butte, MT 59701
(406) 496-4101

South Campus
25 Basin Creek Rd.
Butte, MT 59701
(406) 496-3707

University of Nevada, Reno
Department of Mining Engineering
Mackay School of Earth Sciences and Engineering
College of Science
900 North Virginia St.
Reno, NV 89503
(755) 784-6961

New Mexico Institute of Mining and Technology
801 Leroy Pl.
Socorro, NM 87801
(575) 835-5011
www.nmt.edu

South Dakota School of Mines and Technology
501 East Saint Joseph St.
Rapid City, SD 57701
(605) 394-2511 or (800)
  544-8162
www.sdmines.sdsmt.edu/sdsmt

West Virginia University–Department of Mining Engineering
365 Mineral Resources Building
PO Box 6070
Morgantown, WV 26506
(304) 293-7680
www.mine.cemr.wvu.edu

Pipe Layers, Plumbers, Pipe Fitters, and Steamfitters

Pipe layers, plumbers, pipe fitters, and steamfitters usually learn the trade through formal apprenticeship programs either with the United Association of Plumbers and Pipefitters, independent contractors, or a technical college.

The United Association of Plumbers and Pipefitters–Union Locals

These union apprenticeships offer classroom and on-the-job training and are considered some of the best opportunities and training in the industry. For more information, see www.ua.joinua.asp.

Alabama

Local 52
PO Box 211105
Montgomery, AL 36121
(334) 272-9500

Local 91
3648 9th Ave. N
Birmingham, AL 35222
(205) 591-2721

Local 119
2458 Old Shell Rd.
Mobile, AL 36607
(251) 476-0625

Local 372
3888 Greensboro Ave.
Tuscaloosa, AL 35405
(205) 758-6236

Local 377
PO Box 6084
Huntsville, AL 35813
(256) 772-0616

Local 498
PO Box E
Gadsden, AL 35904
(256) 546-6791

Local 760
PO Box 2678
Muscle Shoals, AL 35662
(256) 383-7900

Alaska

Local 262
1751 Anka St.
Juneau, AK 99801
(907) 586-2874

Local 367
610 West 54th Ave.
Anchorage, AK 99518
(907) 562-2810

Local 375
3568 Geraghty St.
Fairbanks, AK 99709
(907) 479-6221

Arizona

Local 469
3109 North 24th Street, Bldg. A
Phoenix, AZ 85016
(602) 956-9350

Arkansas

Local 29
701 Spradley Rd.
Van Buren, AR 72956
(479) 474-8004

Local 155
1223 West Markham
Little Rock, AR 72201
(501) 374-4943

Local 706
PO Box 30
El Dorado, AR 71731
(870) 863-6169

California

Local 38
1621 Market St.
San Francisco, CA 94103
(415) 626-2000

Local 62
11445 Commercial Pkwy.
Castroville, CA 95012
(831) 633-6091

Local 78
1111 West James M. Wood
   Blvd.
Los Angeles, CA 90015
(213) 688-9090

Local 114
93 Thomas Rd.
Buellton, CA 93427
(805) 688-1470

Local 159
1308 Roman Way
Martinez, CA 94553
(925) 229-0400

Local 228
1246 Putman Ave.
Yuba City, CA 95991
(530) 673-8690

Local 230
6313 Nancy Ridge Dr.
San Diego, CA 92121
(858) 554-0586

Local 246
1303 North Rabe Ave., #101
Fresno, CA 93727
(559) 252-7246

Local 250
18355 South Figueroa St.
Gardena, CA 90248
(310) 660-0035

Local 342
935 Detroit Ave.
Concord, CA 94518
(925) 686-5880

Local 343
401 Nebraska St.
Vallejo, CA 94590
(707) 644-4071

Local 364
223 South Rancho Ave.
Colton, CA 92324
(909) 825-0359

Local 393
6150 Cottle Rd.
San Jose, CA 95123
(408) 225-3030

Local 398
4959 Palo Verde., Ste. 200-C
Montclair, CA 91763
(909) 625-2493

Local 403
3710 Broad St.
San Luis Obispo, CA 93401
(805) 543-2416

Local 442
4842 Nutcracker Ln.
Modesto, CA 95356
(209) 338-0751

Local 447
5841 Newman Ct.
Sacramento, CA 95819
(916) 457-6595

Local 460
6718 Meany Ave.
Bakersfield, CA 93308
(661) 589-4600

Local 467
1519 Rollins Rd.
Burlingame, CA 94010
(650) 692-4730

Local 483
2525 Barrington Ct.
Hayward, CA 94545
(510) 785-8483

Local 484
1955 North Ventura Ave.
Ventura, CA 93001
(805) 643-6345

Local 494
1042 East Wardlow Rd.
Long Beach, CA 90807
(562) 490-4717

Local 582
3904 West First St.
Santa Ana, CA 92703
(714) 775-5563

Local 709
12140 Rivera Rd.
Whittier, CA 90606
(562) 698-9909

Local 761
1305 North Niagara St.
Burbank, CA 91505
(818) 843-8670

Colorado

Local 3
17100 East 32nd Pl.
Aurora, CO 80011
(303) 739-9300

Local 58
229 East Moreno Ave.
Colorado Springs, CO 80903
(719) 633-4052

Local 145
3168 Pipe Ct.
Grand Junction, CO 81504
(970) 245-2012

Local 208
6350 North Broadway
Denver, CO 80216
(303) 428-4380

Connecticut

Local 676
81 Market Square, Room #1
Newington, CT 06111
(860) 666-4447

Local 777
1250 East Main St.
Meridien, CT
(203) 317-4750

Delaware

Local 74
201 Executive Dr.
Newark, DE 19702
(302) 636-7400

Local 782
26705 Sussex Hwy.
Seaford, DE 19973
(302) 629-3521

Florida

Local 123
4923 West Cypress St.
Tampa, FL 33607
(813) 636-0123

Local 234
5411 Cassidy Rd.
Jacsonville, FL 32254
(904) 786-0941

Local 295
743 North Beach St.
Daytona Beach, FL 32114
(386) 253-9972

Local 366
2300 West Nine Mile Rd.
Pensacola, FL 32534
(850) 479-9166

Local 519
14105 Northwest 58th Ct.
Miami Lakes, FL 33014
(305) 362-0519

Local 592
3950 West Pensacola St.
Tallahassee, FL 32304
(850) 575-3552

Local 630
1900 North Florida Mango Rd.
West Palm Beach, FL 33409
(561) 689-8400

Local 719
2502 South Andrews Ave.
Fort Lauderdale, FL 33316
(954) 522-2532

Local 725
13185 Northwest 45th Ave.
Opa Locka, FL 33054
(305) 681-8596

Local 803
2447 Orlando Central Pkwy.
Orlando, FL 32809
(407) 851-9240

Local 821
106 Ponce de Leon St., Ste. B
Royal Palm Beach, FL 33411
(561) 422-9821

Georgia

Local 72
PO Box 17806
Atlanta, GA 30316
(404) 373-5778

Local 150
1211 Telfair St.
Augusta, GA 30901
(706) 724-8846

Local 177
PO Box 246
Brunswick, GA 31521
(912) 265-1890

Local 188
2337 East Victory Dr.
Savannah, GA 31404
(912) 354-5520

Hawaii

Local 675
1109 Bethel St., LL
Honolulu, HI 96813
(808) 536-5454

Iowa

Local 33
2501 Bell Ave.
Des Moines, IA 50321
(515) 243-3244

Local 125
PO Box 1091
Cedar Rapids, IA 52406
(319) 365-0413

Idaho

Local 296
575 North Ralstin, Ste. A
Meridian, ID 83642
(208) 288-1296

Local 648
456 North Arthur, Ste. 4
Pocatello, ID 83204
(208) 232-6806

Illinois

Local 23
4525 Boeing Dr.
Rockford, IL 61109
(815) 397-0350

Local 25
4600 46th Ave.
Rock Island, IL 61201
(309) 788-4569

Local 63
116 Harvey Ct.
East Peoria, IL 61611
(309) 699-3570

Local 65
PO Box 3038
Decatur, IL 62524
(217) 877-3440

Local 93
31855 North US Hwy. 12
Volo, IL 60073
(815) 759-5900

Local 99
406 Eldorado Rd.
Bloomington, IL 61704
(309) 663-2337

Local 101
137 Iowa Ave.
Belleville, IL 62220
(618) 234-5504

Local 130
1340 West Washington Blvd.
Chicago, IL 60607
(312) 421-1010

Local 137
2880 East Cook St.
Springfield, IL 62703
(217) 544-2724

Local 149
PO Box 725
Savoy, IL 61874
(217) 359-5201

Local 160
PO Box 187
Murphysboro, IL 62966
(618) 684-4521

Local 281
11900 South Laramie Ave.
Alsip, IL 60803
(708) 597-1800

Local 353
6304 West Development Dr.
Peoria, IL 61604
(309) 633-1353

Local 360
5 Meadow Heights
  Professional Park
Collinsville, IL 62234
(618) 346-2560

Local 422
2114 I-80 South Frontage Rd.
Joliet, IL 60436
(815) 725-0278

Local 439
PO Box 887
East St. Louis, IL 62203
(618) 624-6096

Local 501
1295 Butterfield Rd.
Aurora, IL 60502
(630) 978-4501

Local 551
PO Box 156
West Frankfort, IL 62896
(618) 937-1363

Local 553
2 South Wesley Dr.
East Alton, IL 62024
(618) 259-6787

Local 597
45 North Ogden Ave.
Chicago, IL 60607
(312) 829-4191

Local 653
154 South Chestnut
Centralia, IL 62801
(618) 532-3351

Indiana

Local 136
2300 St. Joseph Industrial
  Park Dr.
Evansville, IN 47720
(812) 423-8043

Local 157
8801 East Milner Ave.
Terre Haute, IN 47803
(812) 877-1531

Local 166
2930 West Ludwig Rd.
Fort Wayne, IN 46818
(260) 490-5696

Local 172
4172 Ralph Jones Ct.
South Bend, IN 46628
(574) 273-0300

Local 210
PO Box 11939
Merrillville, IN 46411
(219) 942-7224

Local 440
3747 South High School Rd.
Indianapolis, IN 46241
(317) 856-3771

Local 661
RR 5
4401 South Eaton Ave.
Muncie, IN 47302
(765) 282-7344

Iowa

Local 33
2501 Bell Ave.
Des Moines, IA 50321
(515) 243-3244

Local 125
PO Box 1091
Cedar Rapids, IA 52406
(319) 365-0413

Kansas

Local 441
1330 East First St., Ste. 115
Wichita, KS 67214
(316) 265-4291

Kentucky

Local 184
1332 Broadway
Paducah, KY 42001
(270) 442-3213

Local 248
PO Box 427
Ashland, KY 41105
(606) 325-2544

Local 452
525 Deroode St.
Lexington, KY 40508
(859) 252-8337

Local 502
1317 Berry Blvd.
Louisville, KY 40215
(502) 361-8492

Local 633
3128 Alvey Park Dr. W
Owensboro, KY 42303
(270) 683-1587

Louisiana

Local 60
PO Box 8428
Metairie, LA 70011
(504) 885-3054

Local 106
2013 Ryan St.

Lake Charles, LA 70601
(337) 436-4373

Local 141
7111 West Bert Kouns
   Industrial Loop
Shreveport, LA 71129
(318) 671-1175

Local 198
5888 Airline Hwy.
Baton Rouge, LA 70805
(225) 356-3333

Local 247
1211 Rapides Ave.
Alexandria, LA 71301
(318) 442-9923

Local 659
PO Drawer 2567
Monroe, LA 71207
(318) 322-4520

Maine

Local 716
PO Box 496
Augusta, ME 4332
(207) 621-0555

Maryland

Local 5
5891 Allentown Rd.
Camp Springs, MD 20746
(301) 899-7861

Local 486
7830 Philadelphia Rd.
Baltimore, MD 21237
(410) 866-4380

Local 489
2 Park St.
Cumberland, MD 21502
(301) 722-8515

Local 602
8700 Ashwood Dr.
Capitol Heights, MD 20743
(301) 333-2356

Local 669
7050 Oakland Mills Rd., #200
Columbia, MD 21046
(410) 381-4300

Massachusetts

Local 4
330 Southwest Cutoff
Worcester, MA 01604
(508) 799-7703

Local 12
1240 Massachusetts Ave.
Boston, MA 02125
(617) 288-6200

Local 104
168 Chicopee St.
Chicopee, MA 01013
(413) 594-5152

Local 537
35 Travis St., Unit 2
Allston, MA 02134
(617) 787-5370

Local 550
46 Rockland St.
Boston, MA 2132
(617) 323-0474

Michigan

Local 85
PO Box 6547
Saginaw, MI 48608
(989) 799-5261

Local 98
555 Horace Brown Dr.
Madison Heights, MI 48071
(248) 307-9800

Local 111
2601 North 30th St.
Escanaba, MI 49829
(906) 789-9784

Local 174
1008 O'Malley Dr.
Coopersville, MI 49404
(616) 837-0222

Local 190
7920 Jackson Rd., Ste. B
Ann Arbor, MI 48103
(734) 424-0962

Local 333
5405 South Martin Luther
King Blvd.
Lansing, MI 48911
(517) 393-5480

Local 357
11847 Shaver Rd.
Schoolcraft, MI 49087
(269) 679-2570

Local 370
G-5500 West Pierson Rd.
Flushing, MI 48433
(810) 720-5243

Local 636
30100 Northwestern Hwy.
Farmington Hills, MI 48334
(248) 538-6636

Local 671
309 Detroit Ave.
Monroe, MI 48162
(734) 242-5711

Local 704
32500 West Eight Mile Rd.
Farmington, MI 48336
(248) 474-7553

Minnesota

Local 11
4402 Airpark Blvd.
Duluth, MN 55811
(218) 727-2199

Local 15
708 South Tenth St.
Minneapolis, MN 55404
(612) 333-8601

Local 34
411 Main St., Room 215
St. Paul, MN 55102
(651) 224-3828

Local 417
1404 Central Ave. NE
Minneapolis, MN 55413
(612) 781-5804

Local 455
700 Transfer Rd.
St. Paul, MN 55114
(651) 647-9920

Local 539
312 Central Ave., #408
Minneapolis, MN 55414
(612) 379-4711

Local 6
PO Box 6375
Rochester, MN 55903
(507) 288-4172

Local 589
107 South 15th Ave. W
Virginia, MN 55792
(218) 741-2482

Mississippi

Local 436
1307 Jackson Ave.
Pascagoula, MS 39567
(228) 762-2972

Local 568
1237 Pass Rd.
Gulfport, MS 39501
(228) 863-1853

Local 619
PO Box 261
Vicksburg, MS 39181
(601) 638-2546

Local 714
PO Box 789
Brandon, MS 39043
(601) 936-0022

Missouri

Local 8
8600 Hillcrest Rd.
Kansas City, MO 64138
(816) 363-8888

Local 45
3003 Pear St.
St. Joseph, MO 64503
(816) 279-5534

Local 178
2501 West Grand
Springfield, MO 65802
(417) 869-0633

Local 268
1544 South 3rd St.
St. Louis, MO 63104
(314) 241-8023

Local 314
8510 Hillcrest Rd.
Kansas City, MO 64138
(816) 444-5113

Local 533
8600 Hillcrest Rd.
Kansas City, MO 64138
(816) 523-1533

Local 562
12385 Larimore Rd.
St. Louis, MO 63138
(314) 355-1000

Montana

Local 30
PO Box 30616
Billings, MT 59107
(406) 252-9371

Local 41
PO Box 3172
Butte, MT 59702
(406) 494-3051

Local 459
1026 South 5th St. W
Missoula, MT 59801
(406) 549-3479

Nebraska

Local 16
4801 F St.
Omaha, NE 68117
(402) 734-6274

Local 464
PO Box 45422
Omaha, NE 68145
(402) 333-5859

Nevada

Local 350
PO Box 1037
Sparks, NV 89432
(775) 359-2142

Local 525
760 North Lamb Blvd.
Las Vegas, NV 89110
(702) 452-1520

New Hampshire

Local 131
161 Londonderry Tpke.
Hooksett, NH 03106
(603) 669-7307

New Jersey

Local 9
2 Iron Ore Rd. at Rt. 33
Englishtown, NJ 07726
(732) 792-0999

Local 14
150 Main St.
Lodi, NJ 07644
(973) 473-5544

Local 24
986 South Springfield Ave.
Springfield, NJ 07081
(973) 912-0092

Local 274
PO Box 459
Ridgefield, NJ 07657
(201) 943-4700

Local 322
PO Box 73
Winslow, NJ 08095
(609) 567-3322

Local 475
PO Box 4187
Warren, NJ 07059
(908) 754-1030

Local 696
41-43 East Willow St.
Millburn, NJ 07041
(973) 379-7446

New Mexico

Local 412
510 San Pedro Dr. SE
Albuquerque, NM 87108
(505) 265-1513

New York

Local 1
158-29 George Meany Blvd.
Howard Beach, NY 11414
(718) 738-7500

Local 7
308 Wolf Rd.
Latham, NY 12110
(518) 785-9808

Local 13
1850 Mt. Read Blvd.
Rochester, NY 14615
(585) 338-2360

Local 21
1024 McKinley St.
Peekskill, NY 10566
(914) 737-2166

Local 22
3651 California Rd.
Orchard Park, NY 14127
(716) 662-3952

Local 73
PO Box 911
Oswego, NY 13126
(315) 343-4037

Local 112
PO Box 670
Binghamton, NY 13902
(607) 723-9593

Local 128
105 Clinton St.
Schenectady, NY 12305
(518) 357-9285

Local 200
2123 5th Ave.
Ronkonkoma, NY 11779
(631) 981-2158

Local 267
150 Midler Park Dr.
Syracuse, NY 13206
(315) 437-7397

Local 373
PO Box 58
Mountainville, NY 10953
(845) 534-1050

Local 638
32-32 48th Ave.
Long Island City, NY 11101
(718) 392-3420

Local 773
PO Box 1343
South Glens Falls, NY 12803
(518) 792-9157

North Carolina

N/A

North Dakota

Local 300
2901 Twin City Dr., Ste. 101
Mandan, ND 58554
(701) 663-0999

Ohio

Local 42
187 Woodlawn Ave.
Norwalk, OH 44857
(419) 668-4491

Local 50
7570 Caple Blvd., Ste. A
Northwood, OH 43619
(419) 662-5456

Local 55
980 Keynote Cir.
Brooklyn Heights, OH 44131
(216) 459-0099

Local 94
3919 13th St. SW
Canton, OH 44710
(330) 478-1864

Local 120
6305 Halle Dr.
Cleveland, OH 44125
(216) 447-3408

Local 162
1200 East Second St.
Dayton, OH 45403
(937) 222-8747

Local 168
201 Front St.
Marietta, OH 45750
(740) 373-7965

Local 189
1250 Kinnear Rd.
Columbus, OH 43212
(614) 486-2912

Local 219
644 East Tallmadge Ave.
Akron, OH 44310
(330) 253-9166

Local 392
1228 Central Pkwy., Room 200
Cincinnati, OH 45202
(513) 241-1760

Local 396
493 Bev Rd., Bldg. 3
Boardman, OH 44512
(330) 758-4596

Local 495
PO Box 1418
Cambridge, OH 43725
(740) 439-3623

Local 577
PO Box 577
Portsmouth, OH 45662
(740) 353-5869

Local 776
1300 Bowman Rd.
Lima, OH 45804
(419) 229-5176

Oklahoma

Local 344
4335 Southwest 44th St.
Oklahoma City, OK 73119
(405) 682-4571

Local 430
2908 North Harvard Ave.
Tulsa, OK 74115
(918) 836-0430

Local 798
PO Box 470798
Tulsa, OK 74147
(918) 622-1900

Oregon

Local 290
20210 Southwest Teton Ave.
Tualatin, OR 97062
(503) 691-5700

Pennsylvania

Local 27
1040 Montour West
  Industrial Blvd.
Coraopolis, PA 15108
(724) 695-8175

Local 47
186 Wagner Rd.
Monaca, PA 15061
(724) 775-2578

Local 354
PO Drawer I
Youngwood, PA 15697
(724) 925-7238

Local 420
14420 Townsend Rd., Ste. A
Philadelphia, PA 19154
(267) 350-4200

Local 449
1517 Woodruff St.
Pittsburgh, PA 15220
(412) 381-1133

Local 520
PO Box 6596
Harrisburg, PA 17112
(717) 652-3135

Local 524
711 Corey St.
Scranton, PA 18505
(570) 347-9214

Local 542
PO Box 58161
Pittsburgh, PA 15209
(412) 822-8040

Local 690
2791 Southampton Rd.
Philadelphia, PA 19154
(215) 677-6900

Local 692
14002 McNulty Rd.
Philadelphia, PA 19154
(215) 671-1692

Rhode Island

Local 51
11 Hemingway Dr.
East Providence, RI 02915
(401) 943-3033

South Carolina

Local 421
2556 Oscar Johnson Dr.
N. Charleston, SC 29405
(843) 554-3655

South Dakota

N/A

Tennessee

Local 17
4229 South Prescott
Memphis, TN 38118
(901) 368-0900

Local 43
3009 Riverside Dr.
Chattanooga, TN 37406
(423) 698-6991

Local 102
1216 Broadway NE
Knoxville, TN 37917
(865) 524-5806

Local 538
121 Spring St.
Johnson City, TN 37604
(423) 928-5751

Local 572
225 Ben Allen Rd.
Nashville, TN 37207
(615) 262-0893

Local 614
3746 Jackson Ave.
Memphis, TN 38108
(901) 386-8166

Local 718
109 Viking Rd.
Oak Ridge, TN 37830
(865) 986-5038

Texas

Local 68
PO Box 8746
Houston, TX 77249
(713) 869-3592

Local 100
3629 West Miller Rd.
Garland, TX 75041
(214) 341-8606

Local 142
3630 Belgium Ln.
San Antonio, TX 78219
(210) 226-1244

Local 146
2640 East Lancaster St.
Fort Worth, TX 76103
(817) 536-1979

Local 195
3184 Hwy. 69 N
Nederland, TX 77627
(409) 722-0434

Local 196
1505 West 7th St.
Amarillo, TX 79101
(806) 374-2895

Local 211
2535 Old Galveston Rd.
Houston, TX 77017
(713) 644-5521

Local 286
814 Airport Blvd.
Austin, TX 78702
(512) 385-0002

Local 389
125 FM 369 North
Iowa Park, TX 76367
(940) 692-9731

Local 529
PO Box 154009
Waco, TX 76715
(254) 754-3471

Local 629
2002 Ave. J
Lubbock, TX 79411
(806) 744-3835

Local 823
2811 South Hwy. 83
Harlingen, TX 78550
(956) 423-5210

Utah

Local 140
2261 South Redwood Rd.
Salt Lake City, UT 84119
(801) 973-1183

Vermont

Local 693
3 Gregory Dr.
South Burlington, VT 05403
(802) 864-4042

Virginia

Local 10
701 Stockton St.
Richmond, VA 23224
(804) 231-4233

Local 110
520 Naval Base Rd.
Norfolk, VA 23505
(757) 587-4768

Local 272
5304 South Palmyra Dr.
Virginia Beach, VA 23462
(757) 490-2301

Local 477
PO Box 2396
Suffolk, VA 23432
(757) 617-1180

Local 540
7812 Warwick Blvd.
Newport News, VA 23607
(757) 247-9089

Washington

Local 26
8501 Zenith Ct. NE
Lacey, WA 98516
(360) 486-9300

Local 32
595 Monster Rd. SW, Ste. 213
Renton, WA 98057
(425) 277-6680

Local 44
3915 East Main
Spokane, WA 99202
(509) 624-5101

Local 598
1328 Rd. 28
Pasco, WA 99301
(509) 545-1446

Local 699
2800 First Ave., Room 111
Seattle, WA 98121
(206) 441-0737

West Virginia

Local 83
177 29th St.
Wheeling, WV 26003
(304) 233-4445

Local 152
PO Box 862
Morgantown, WV 26505
(304) 292-8818

Local 521
2586 Guyan Ave.
Huntington, WV 25703
(304) 523-8489

Local 565
593 Cedar Grove Rd.
Parkersburg, WV 26104
(304) 485-5202

Local 625
3601 James St.
Charleston, WV 25312
(304) 744-3881

Wisconsin

Local 75
11175 West Parkland Ave.
Milwaukee, WI 53224
(414) 359-1310

Local 118
3030 39th Ave., Room 125
Kenosha, WI 53144
(262) 654-3815

Local 183
W175 N5700 Technology Dr.

Menomonee Falls, WI 53051
(262) 252-0183

Local 400
PO Box 530
Kaukauna, WI 54130
(920) 462-0400

NCCER-Accredited Training Sponsors for Plumbing

Alabama

ABC Mid Gulf Chapter
755-C McRae Ave.
Mobile, AL 36606
(251) 479-2441
www.abcmidgulf.com

Construction Education
Foundation of Alabama
6700 Oporto-Madrid Blvd.
Birmingham, AL 35206
(205) 956-0146
www.cefalabama.org

Diversified Employment
Service Incorporated
211-C Highway 43 S
Saraland, AL 36571
(251) 679-0018

North Alabama Craft Training
Foundation
152 Hollington Dr.
Huntsville, AL 35811
(256) 851-1566

Alaska

Associated General Contractors
of Alaska
8005 Schoon St.
Anchorage, AK 99518
(907) 561-5354
www.agcak.org

Council of Athabascan Tribal
Governments
Yukon Flats Center–Fort Yukon
Fort Yukon, AK 99740
(907) 662-3612
www.catg.org

Northern Industrial Training LLC
6177 East Mountain Heather
Way
Palmer, AK 99645-9505
(907) 557-6400
www.nitalaska.com

Arizona

Arizona Public Service
1611 South Main St.
Snowflake, AZ 85937
(928) 536-6232
www.aps.com

Arkansas

Arkansas Chapter AGC Inc.
523 East Capitol Ave.
Little Rock, AR 72202
(501) 376-6641
www.agcar.net

California

ABC Southern California Chapter
1400 North Kellogg Dr., Ste. A
Anaheim, CA 92807
(714) 779-3199
www.abcsocal.org

Calexico Community
Action Council
2151 Rockwood Ave., Ste. 166
Calexico, CA 92231
(760) 357-6464

Center for Seabees and Facilities
Engineering
3502 Goodspeed St., Ste. 1
Naval Base Ventura County, CA

93041
(805) 982-3615
www.npdc.navy.mil/csfe

Shasta Builder's Exchange
Community Fund
2985 Innsbruck Dr.
Redding, CA 96003
(530) 222-1917
www.shastabe.com

Colorado

ABC Western Colorado Chapter
2754 Compass Dr., Ste. 305
Grand Junction, CO 81506
(970) 243-7950
www.wcoabc.org

Construction Industry Training
Council of Colorado Inc.
646 Mariposa St.
Denver, CO 80204
(303) 893-1500

T and D Services
1143 Michael Cir.
Meeker, CO 81641
(970) 260-3415

Connecticut

Construction Education
Center Inc.
2138 Silas Deane Hwy.,
Ste. 101
Rocky Hill, CT 06067
(860) 529-5886
www.thinkconstruction.org

Industrial Management and
Training Institute Inc.
233 Mill St.
Waterbury, CT 06706
(203) 753-7910
www.imtiusa.com

Delaware

N/A

District of Columbia

N/A

Florida

ABC Florida Gulf Coast Chapter
2008 North Himes Ave.
Tampa, FL 33607
(813) 879-8064
www.abcflgulf.org

Builders Association of North
Central Florida
2217 Northwest 66th Ct.
Gainesville, FL 32653
(352) 372-5649
www.bancf.com

Georgia

CEFGA–Construction Education
Foundation of Georgia
3585 Lawrenceville Suwanee
Rd., Ste. 301
Suwanee, GA 30024
(678) 889-4445
www.cefga.org

Hawaii

ABC Hawaii Chapter
80 Sand Island Access Road
#119
Honolulu, HI 96819
(808) 845-4887
www.abchawaii.org

Idaho

N/A

Illinois

Associated Builders and Contractors, Illinois Chapter Inc.
1691 Elmhurst Rd.
Elk Grove Village, IL 60007
(847) 709-2960
www.abcil.org

Choice Construction Services
665 Hillcrest Blvd.
Hoffman Estates, IL 60195
(847) 483-4056
www.ietc-dupageco.com/Choice
    ConstructionSer

Indiana

N/A

Iowa

ABC of Iowa
475 Alices Rd., Ste. A
Waukee, IA 50263
(515) 987-3790
www.abciowa.org

Kansas

ABC Heart of America Chapter
6950 Squibb Rd., Ste. 418
Mission, KS 66202
(913) 831-2221
www.abcksmo.org

Kentucky

Kentuckiana ABC
1810 Taylor Ave.
Louisville, KY 40213
(502) 456-5200 or (800)
    411-5848
www.kyanaabc.com

Kentucky Department of
Corrections
2439 Lawrenceburg Rd.
Frankfort, KY 40602
(502) 564-4795 ext. 229
www.corrections.ky.gov/

Louisiana

ABC–Bayou Chapter
101 Riverbend Dr.
St. Rose, LA 70087
(504) 468-3188
www.abcbayou.org

Maine

N/A

Maryland

ABC Metropolitan Washington
4061 Powder Mill Rd., Ste. 120
Calverton, MD 20705
(301) 595-9711
www.abcmetrowashington.org

Baltimore Metro Chapter ABC
1220-B East Joppa Rd.,
    Ste. 322
Towson, MD 21286
(410) 821-0351
www.abcbaltimore.org

Cumberland Valley Chapter ABC
530 North Locust St.
Hagerstown, MD 21740
(301) 739-1190
www.abccvc.com

Massachusetts

George W. Gould
Construction Institute
200 Wheeler Rd.
Burlington, MA 01803
(781) 270-9990
www.gwgci.org

Michigan

ABC Inc. Saginaw Valley Chapter
4520 East Ashman Rd., Ste. G
Midland, MI 48642
(989) 832-8879
www.abcsvac.org

Associated Builders and
Contractors Inc.–Western
Michigan Chapter
580 Cascade West Pkwy.

Grand Rapids, MI 49546
(616) 942-9960
www.abcwmc.org

Construction Education Trust
31800 Sherman Ave.
Madison Heights, MI 48071
(248) 298-3600
www.cet-tech.com

Solomon Plumbing Company
29665 WK Smith Dr., Ste. A
New Hudson, MI 48165
(248) 486-1600
www.solomonplumbing.net

Minnesota

**Construction Education
Foundation of Minnesota**
10193 Crosstown Cir.
Eden Prairie, MN 55344
(952) 941-8693
www.mnabc.com

Mississippi

**Mississippi Construction
Education Foundation**
290 Commerce Park Dr., Ste. B
Ridgeland, MS 39157
(601) 605-2989
www.mcef.net

Missouri

**Independent Plumbing
Contractors Association**
800 Maryville Centre Dr.,
  Ste. 211
Chesterfield, MO 63017-5942
(314) 275-8100

Vatterott College
8580 Evans Ave., Ste. A
St. Louis, MO 63134
(314) 264-1806
www.vatterott-college.edu

Montana

N/A

Nebraska

**ABC Nebraska
Cornhusker Chapter**
2602 Harney St.
Omaha, NE 68131
(402) 344-4258
www.abcnebraska.org

Nevada

ABC of Southern Nevada
5070 Arville St., Ste. 4
Las Vegas, NV 89118
(702) 227-0536
www.abclasvegas.org

ABC–Sierra Nevada Chapter
240 South Rock Blvd., Ste. 121
Reno, NV 89502
(775) 358-7888
www.abcsierranv.org

**Nevada Center for Vocational
Education and Research**
1227 Kimmerling Rd.
Gardnerville, NV 89460
(775) 265-2818

New Hampshire

N/A

New Jersey

ABC New Jersey Chapter
720 King George Post Rd.,
  Ste. 303
Fords, NJ 08863
(732) 661-1045
www.abcnjc.org

New Mexico

ABC New Mexico Chapter
3540 Pan American Fwy.
  NE, Ste. F
Albuquerque, NM 87107
(505) 830-4222
www.abcnm.org

New York

CTC of New York State
6369 Collamer Dr.
East Syracuse, NY 13057
(315) 463-7539
www.abcnys.org

North Carolina

N/A

North Dakota

AGC of North Dakota
422 North Second St.
Bismarck, ND 58501
(701) 223-2770
www.agcnd.org

Ohio

ABC Northern Ohio Chapter
9255 Market Pl. W
Broadview Heights, OH 44147
(440) 717-0389
www.nocabc.com

ABC Ohio Valley CEF
33 Greenwood Ln.
Springboro, OH 45066
(937) 704-0111
www.ovabc.org

Building Trades Institute, LLC
459 Orangepoint Dr., Ste. F
Lewis Center, OH 43035
(740) 548-8091
www.buildingtradesinstitute.com

Construction Craft Academy
9760 Shepard Rd.
Macedonia, OH 44056
(800) 442-0067
www.craftacademy.com

Oklahoma

**AGC of Oklahoma–
Building Chapter**
605 Northwest 13th St., Ste. A
Oklahoma City, OK 73103-2213
(405) 528-4605
www.agcok.com

Oregon

N/A

Pennsylvania

ABC Central, PA Chapter
898 North Eagle Valley Rd.
Milesburg, PA 16853
(814) 353-1999
www.abccentralpa.org

ABC Southeast, PA Chapter
430 West Germantown Pike
East Norriton, PA 19403
(610) 279-6666
www.abcsepa.org

ABC Western Pennsylvania Inc.
3500 Spring Garden Ave.
Pittsburgh, PA 15212
(412) 231-1446
www.abcwpa.org

Associated Builders and Contractors, Eastern PA
1036 North Godfrey St.
Allentown, PA 18109
(610) 821-6869
www.abceastpa.org

Keystone Chapter ABC
135 Shellyland Rd.
Manheim, PA 17545
(717) 653-8106
www.abckeystone.org

Rhode Island

Associated Builders and Contractors–Rhode Island Chapter
400 Massasoit Ave., Ste. 108
East Providence, RI 02914
(401) 438-8446
www.abcri.org

South Carolina

N/A

South Dakota

N/A

Tennessee

ABC Mid-Tennessee Chapter
1604 Elm Hill Pike
Nashville, TN 37210
(615) 399-8323
www.abctennessee.com

Construction Education Partnership
Simpson St. and Island Dr.
Kingsport, TN 37660
(423) 578-2710

Texas

ABC Merit Shop Training Program Inc. D/B/A Craft Training Center of the Coastal Bend
7433 Leopard St.
Corpus Christi, TX 78409
(361) 289-1636
www.ctccb.org

ABC of Greater Houston Inc.
3910 Kirby Dr., Ste. 131
Houston, TX 77098
(713) 523-6258
www.abchouston.org

ABC South Texas Chapter
10408 Gulfdale Rd.
San Antonio, TX 78216
(210) 342-1994
www.abcsouthtexas.org

Associated General Contractors of El Paso
4625 Ripley Dr.
El Paso, TX 79922
(915) 585-1533
www.agcelpaso.org

Central Texas ABC Chapter
3006 Longhorn Blvd., Ste. 104
Austin, TX 78758
(512) 719-5263
www.abccentraltexas.org

The Victor Group
801 High Ridge Dr.
Friendswood, TX 77546
(281) 850-8079
www.thevictorgroup.net

Utah

N/A

Vermont

N/A

Virginia

ABC Virginia
14120 Parke Long Ct., Ste. 111
Chantilly, VA 20151
(703) 968-6205
www.abcva.org

Washington

Construction Industry Training Council of Washington
1930-116 Ave. NE, Ste. 201
Bellevue, WA 98004
(425) 454-2482
www.citcwa.org

West Virginia

N/A

Wisconsin

ABC of Wisconsin Inc.
5330 Wall St.
Madison, WI 53718
(608) 244-6056
www.abcwi.org

Wyoming

Corinthian Colleges Inc.
1706 Bill Nye Ave.
Laramie, WY 82070
(307) 742-3530
www.cci.edu

Lifelong Learning Center
1013 West Cheyenne Dr., Ste. A
Evanston, WY 82930
(307) 789-5742
www.uintaeducation.org

Community Colleges with Programs in Plumbing

(Source: Career Voyages—www.careervoyages.com) Programs offering training or courses in specialties such as pipe fitting or sprinkler fitting are noted below.

Alabama

Bishop State Community College
351 North Broad St.
Mobile, AL 36603
(251) 690-6416
www.bishop.edu

George C. Wallace Community College–Dothan
1141 Wallace Dr.
Dothan, AL 36303
(334) 983-3521
www.wallace.edu

J. F. Ingram State Technical College
5375 Ingram Rd.
Deatsville, AL 36022
(334) 285-5177

Lawson State Community College–Birmingham Campus
3060 Wilson Rd. SW
Birmingham, AL 35221
(205) 925-2515
www.lawsonstate.edu

Alaska

Ilisagvik College
Narl Facility
Barrow, AK 99723
(907) 852-3333
www.ilisagvik.cc

Arizona

Central Arizona College
8470 North Overfield Rd.
Coolidge, AZ 85228
(520) 494-5444
www.centralaz.edu

Gateway Community College
108 North 40th St.
Phoenix, AZ 85034
(602) 392-5000
www.gwc.maricopa.edu

Tohono O'Odham Community College
Hwy. 86, Mile Post 115.5 N
Sells, AZ 85634
(520) 383-8401
www.tocc.cc.az.us

Arkansas

N/A

California

Allan Hancock College
800 South College Dr.
Santa Maria, CA 93454
(805) 922-6966
www.hancockcollege.edu

Bakersfield College
1801 Panorama Dr.
Bakersfield, CA 93305
(661) 395-4011
www.bakersfieldcollege.edu/

Chabot College
25555 Hesperian Blvd.
Hayward, CA 94545
(510) 723-6600
www.chabotcollege.edu

City College of San Francisco
50 Phelan Ave.
San Francisco, CA 94112
(415) 239-3000
www.ccsf.edu

College of San Mateo
1700 West Hillsdale Blvd.
San Mateo, CA 94402
(650) 574-6161
www.collegeofsanmateo.edu

College of the Sequoias
915 South Mooney Blvd.
Visalia, CA 93277
(559) 730-3700
www.cos.edu

Foothill College
12345 El Monte Rd.
Los Altos Hills, CA 94022
(650) 949-7777
www.foothill.edu

Los Angeles Trade Technical College
400 West Washington Blvd.
Los Angeles, CA 90015
(213) 763-7000
www.lattc.edu

Rio Hondo College
3600 Workman Mill Rd.
Whittier, CA 90601
(562) 692-0921
www.riohondo.edu

San Diego City College
1313 Park Blvd.
San Diego, CA 92101
(619) 388-3400
www.sdcity.edu

Colorado

N/A

Connecticut

N/A

Florida

Brevard Community College
1519 Clearlake Rd.
Cocoa, FL 32922
(321) 632-1111
www.brevardcc.edu

**Florida Community College
at Jacksonville**
501 West State St.
Jacksonville, FL 32202
(904) 632-3000
www.fccj.edu

George Stone Career Center
2400 Longleaf Dr.
Pensacola, FL 32526
(850) 941-6200
www.georgestonecenter.com

**Hillsborough
Community College**
39 Columbia Dr.
Tampa, FL 33606
(813) 253-7000
www.hccfl.edu

Indian River Community College
3209 Virginia Ave.
Fort Pierce, FL 34981
(772) 462-4722
www.ircc.edu

**Lee County High Tech
Center Central**
3800 Michigan Ave.
Fort Myers, FL 33916
(239) 334-4544
www.hightechcentral.org

Manatee Technical Institute
5603 34th St. W
Bradenton, FL 34210
(941) 751-7900
www.manateetechnical
   institute.org

Mid Florida Tech
2900 West Oak Ridge Rd.
Orlando, FL 32809
(407) 855-5880
www.mft.ocps.net

**Okaloosa Applied
Technology Center**
1976 Lewis Turner Blvd.
Fort Walton Beach, FL 32547
(850) 833-3500
www.okaloosa.k12.fl.us/oatc

Palm Beach Community College
4200 Congress Ave.
Lake Worth, FL 33461
(561) 967-7222
www.pbcc.edu

**Pinellas Technical
Education Center**
901 34th St. S
St. Petersburg, FL 33711
(727) 893-2500
www.myptec.org

**Radford M. Locklin
Technical Center**
5330 Berryhill Rd.
Milton, FL 32570
(850) 983-5700
www.santarosa.k12.fl.us/ltc

Santa Fe Community College
3000 Northwest 83rd St.
Gainesville, FL 32606
(352) 395-5000
www.sfcc.edu

Seminole Community College
100 Weldon Blvd.
Sanford, FL 32773
(407) 708-4722
www.scc-fl.edu

**South Florida
Community College**
600 West College Dr.
Avon Park, FL 33825
(863) 453-6661
www.southflorida.edu

Georgia

Altamaha Technical College
1777 West Cherry St.
Jesup, GA 31545
(912) 427-5800
www.altamahatech.edu

Atlanta Technical College
1560 Metropolitan Pkwy. SW
Atlanta, GA 30310
(404) 225-4603
www.atlantatech.org

**Middle Georgia
Technical College**
80 Cohen Walker Dr.
Warner Robins, GA 31088
(478) 988-6800
www.middlegatech.edu

Moultrie Technical College
800 Veterans Pkwy. N
Moultrie, GA 31788
(229) 891-7000
www.moultrietech.edu

Hawaii

N/A

Idaho

N/A

Illinois

N/A

Indiana

**Ivy Tech Community College–
Central Indiana**
50 West Fall Creek Pkwy. N. Dr.
Indianapolis, IN 46208
(317) 921-4800
www.ivytech.edu/indianapolis

**Ivy Tech Community College–
East Central**
4301 South Cowan Rd.
Box 3100
Muncie, IN 47302
(765) 289-2291
www.ivytech.edu/muncie

**Ivy Tech Community College–
Northcentral**
220 Dean Johnson Blvd.
South Bend, IN 46601
(574) 289-7001
www.ivytech.edu/southbend

**Ivy Tech Community College–
Northeast**
3800 North Anthony Blvd.
Fort Wayne, IN 46805
(260) 482-9171
www.ivytech.edu/fortwayne

**Ivy Tech Community College–
South Central**
8204 Hwy. 311
Sellersburg, IN 47172
(812) 246-3301
www.ivytech.edu/sellersburg

**Ivy Tech Community College–
Southwest**
3501 First Ave.
Evansville, IN 47710
(812) 426-2865
www.ivytech.edu/evansville

**Ivy Tech Community College–
Wabash Valley**
7999 US Hwy. 41
Terre Haute, IN 47802
(812) 299-1121
www.ivytech.edu/terrehaute

Iowa

Kirkwood Community College
6301 Kirkwood Blvd. SW
Cedar Rapids, IA 52406
(319) 398-5411
www.kirkwood.edu

Kansas

N/A

Kentucky

**Elizabethtown Community and
Technical College**
600 College St. Rd.
Elizabethtown, KY 42701
(270) 769-2371
www.elizabethtown.kctcs.edu

**Jefferson Community and
Technical College**
109 East Broadway
Louisville, KY 40202
(502) 213-4000
www.jefferson.kctcs.edu

Madisonville Community College
2000 College Dr.
Madisonville, KY 42431
(270) 821-2250
www.madcc.kctcs.edu

Louisiana

**Louisiana Technical College–
Jefferson Campus**
5200 Blair Dr.
Metairie, LA 70001
(504) 736-7072
www.ltc.edu

**Louisiana Technical College–
West Jefferson Campus**
475 Manhattan Blvd.
Harvey, LA 70058
(504) 361-6464
www.ltc.edu

Maine

**Northern Maine
Community College**
33 Edgemont Dr.
Presque Isle, ME 04769
(207) 768-2700
www.nmcc.edu

**Southern Maine
Community College**
2 Fort Rd.
South Portland, ME 04106
(207) 741-5500
www.smccme.edu

**Washington County
Community College**
One College Dr.
Calais, ME 04619
(207) 454-1000
www.wccc.me.edu

Maryland

N/A

Massachusetts

N/A

Michigan

N/A

Minnesota

Anoka Technical College
1355 West Hwy. 10
Anoka, MN 55303
(763) 576-4700
www.anokatech.edu

**Minnesota State Community
and Technical College**
1414 College Way
Fergus Falls, MN 56537
(218) 736-1500
www.minnesota.edu

**Minnesota West Community
and Technical College**
1593 11th Ave.
Granite Falls, MN 56241
(320) 564-4511
www.mnwest.edu

**Northland Community and
Technical College**
1101 Hwy. #1 E
Thief River Falls, MN 56701
(218) 681-0701
www.northlandcollege.edu

Northwest Technical College
905 Grant Ave. SE
Bemidji, MN 56601
(218) 333-6600
www.ntcmn.edu

Saint Cloud Technical College
1540 Northway Dr.
Saint Cloud, MN 56303
(320) 308-5000
www.sctc.edu

**Saint Paul College–A Community
and Technical College**
235 Marshall Ave
Saint Paul, MN 55102
(651) 846-1600
www.saintpaul.edu

Mississippi

Hinds Community College
501 East Main St.
Raymond, MS 39154
(601) 857-5261
www.hindscc.edu

Missouri

St. Louis Community College–
Florissant Valley
3400 Pershall Rd.
St. Louis, MO 63135
(314) 513-4200
www.stlcc.edu

St. Louis Community College–
Forest Park
5600 Oakland Ave.
St. Louis, MO 63110
(314) 644-9100
www.stlcc.edu

Montana

N/A

Nebraska

N/A

Nevada

N/A

New Hampshire

N/A

New Jersey

N/A

New Mexico

Central New Mexico
Community College
525 Buena Vista SE
Albuquerque, NM 87106
(505) 224-3000
www.cnm.edu

New Mexico State University–
Dona Ana
3400 South Espina
Las Cruces, NM 88003
(505) 527-7500
www.dabcc.nmsu.edu/

New York

N/A

North Carolina

Blue Ridge Community College
180 West Campus Dr.
Flat Rock, NC 28731
(828) 694-1700
www.blueridge.edu

Cleveland Community College
137 South Post Rd.
Shelby, NC 28152
(704) 484-4000
www.clevelandcommunity
college.edu

Fayetteville Technical
Community College
2201 Hull Rd.
Fayetteville, NC 28303
(910) 678-8400
www.faytechcc.edu

Forsyth Technical
Community College
2100 Silas Creek Pkwy.
Winston-Salem, NC 27103
(336) 723-0371
www.forsythtech.edu

Guilford Technical
Community College
601 High Point Rd.
Jamestown, NC 27282
(336) 334-4822
www.gtcc.edu/

Halifax Community College
100 College Dr.
Weldon, NC 27890
(252) 536-4221
www.halifaxcc.edu

Johnston Community College
245 College Rd.
Smithfield, NC 27577
(919) 934-3051
www.johnstoncc.edu

Southeastern
Community College
4564 Chadbourn Hwy.
Whiteville, NC 28472

(910) 642-7141
www.sccnc.edu

Wake Technical
Community College
9101 Fayetteville Rd.
Raleigh, NC 27603
(919) 662-3400
www.waketech.edu

North Dakota

North Dakota State College
of Science
800 North 6th St.
Wahpeton, ND 58076
(701) 671-2403
www.ndscs.edu

Ohio

N/A

Oklahoma

N/A

Oregon

N/A

Pennsylvania

Community College of
Allegheny County
800 Allegheny Ave.
Pittsburgh, PA 15233
(412) 323-2323
www.ccac.edu

Delaware County
Community College
901 South Media Line Rd.
Media, PA 19063
(610) 359-5000
www.dccc.edu

Luzerne County
Community College
1333 South Prospect St.
Nanticoke, PA 18634
(570) 740-0200
www.luzerne.edu

Thaddeus Stevens College of Technology
750 East King St.
Lancaster, PA 17602
(717) 299-7730
www.stevenscollege.edu

Rhode Island

N/A

South Carolina

N/A

South Dakota

N/A

Tennessee

N/A

Utah

Ogden-Weber Applied Technology College
200 North Washington Blvd.
Ogden, UT 84404
(801) 627-8300
www.owatc.com

Vermont

N/A

Virginia

N/A

Washington

N/A

West Virginia

Carver Career Center
4799 Midland Dr.
Charleston, WV 25306
(304) 348-1965
www.kcs.kana.k12.wv.us/carver

Wisconsin

Blackhawk Technical College
6004 Prairie Rd.
Janesville, WI 53547
(608) 758-6900
www.blackhawk.edu

Chippewa Valley Technical College
620 West Clairemont Ave.
Eau Claire, WI 54701
(715) 833-6200
www.cvtc.edu

Gateway Technical College
3520 30th Ave.
Kenosha, WI 53144
(262) 564-2200
www.gtc.edu

Lakeshore Technical College
1290 North Ave.
Cleveland, WI 53015
(920) 693-1000
www.gotoltc.edu

Mid-State Technical College
500 32nd St. N
Wisconsin Rapids, WI 54494
(715) 422-5300
www.mstc.edu

Moraine Park Technical College
235 North National Ave.
Fond Du Lac, WI 54936
(920) 922-8611
www.morainepark.edu

Nicolet Area Technical College
Hwy. G South
Rhinelander, WI 54501
(715) 365-4410
www.nicoletcollege.edu

Northcentral Technical College
1000 Campus Dr.
Wausau, WI 54401
(715) 675-3331
www.ntc.edu

Southwest Wisconsin Technical College
1800 Bronson Blvd.
Fennimore, WI 53809
(608) 822-3262
www.swtc.edu

Waukesha County Technical College
800 Main St.
Pewaukee, WI 53072
(262) 691-5566
www.wctc.edu

Chippewa Valley Technical College
620 West Clairemont Ave.
Eau Claire, WI 54701
(715) 833-6200
www.cvtc.edu

Gateway Technical College
3520 30th Ave.
Kenosha, WI 53144
(262) 564-2200
www.gtc.edu

Mid-State Technical College
500 32nd St. N
Wisconsin Rapids, WI 54494
(715) 422-5300
www.mstc.edu

Milwaukee Area Technical College
700 West State St.
Milwaukee, WI 53233
(414) 297-6370
www.matc.edu

Moraine Park Technical College
235 North National Ave.
Fond Du Lac, WI 54936
(920) 922-8611
www.morainepark.edu

Northcentral Technical College
1000 Campus Dr.
Wausau, WI 54401
(715) 675-3331
www.ntc.edu

Western Technical College
304 6th St. N
La Crosse, WI 54602
(608) 785-9200
www.westerntc.edu

Wyoming

N/A

Railroad Conductor and Yardworker

Most railroad companies have in-house training and typically require at least a high school degree for entry-level positions. The National Academy of Railroad Sciences (NARS) also conducts training for people looking to get into the industry. We've included information on the seven largest freight companies in the United States and Canada, which are great places to start a career in the railroads. There are many smaller companies around the country.

Class I Railroad Companies

BNSF Railway
www.bnsf.com/careers

Canadian National Railway
www.cn.ca/careers

Canadian Pacific Railway
www.cpr.ca

CSX Transportation
www.csx.com/?fuseaction=careers.main

Kansas City Southern Railway
www.kcsouthern.com

Norfolk Southern Railway
www.nscorp.com/nscportal/nscorp

Union Pacific Railroad
www.unionpacific.jobs

Brotherhood of Locomotive Engineers and Trainmen
www.ble.org

Other Resources

National Academy of Railroad Sciences (NARS)
12345 College Blvd.
Overland Park, KS 66210
(913) 319-2602 or (800) 288-3378
www.railroadtraining.com

Conductor Training Information
www.railroadtraining.com/careers_fastTrack_conductor.html

Roofer

While many roofers learn skills on-the-job, some learn through union-based apprenticeship programs.

National Roofing Contractors Association (NRCA)
The NRCA's website at www.nrca.net is an excellent resource for information on courses around the country, including ones online.

NCCER-Accredited Training Centers
Construction Craft Academy
9760 Shepard Rd.
Macedonia, OH 44056
(800) 442-0067
www.craftacademy.com

The Victor Group
801 High Ridge Dr.
Friendswood, TX 77546
(281) 850-8079
www.thevictorgroup.net

United Union of Roofers, Waterproofers, and Allied Workers
www.unionroofers.org

Alabama

176–Birmingham-Mobile
PO Box 729
Greenbrier, TN 37073
(615) 298-5215
(615) 643-4850

Alaska

190–Anchorage
825 East 8th Ave.
Anchorage, AK 99501
(907) 272-4311
Local190@alaska.com

Arizona

135–Phoenix
1917 East Washington St.
Phoenix, AZ 85034
(602) 254-7059
rooferslocal135@aol.com
organizer135@aol.com

135–Tucson
842 South 6th Ave.
Tucson, AZ 85701
(877) 314-4201
rooferslocal135@aol.com

Arkansas

20–Little Rock
6321 Blue Ridge Blvd., Ste. 202
Raytown, MO 64133
(816) 313-9420
roofer20@sbcglobal.net

California

27–Bakersfield
5537 East Lamona Ave., Ste. 1
Fresno, CA 93727
(559) 255-0933

36–Los Angeles
5380 Poplar Blvd.
Los Angeles, CA 90032
(323) 222-0251

81–Oakland
8400 Enterprise Way, Ste. 122
Oakland, CA 94621

(510) 632-0505
roofers@pacbell.net

220–Orange County
283 North Rampart St., Ste. F
Orange, CA 92868
(714) 939-0220

220–Riverside
1074 East LaCadena Dr., #9
Riverside, CA 92501
(909) 684-3645

81–Sacramento
8400 Enterprise Way, Ste. 122
Oakland, CA 94621
(510) 632-0505
roofers@pacbell.net

45–San Diego
3737 Camino del Rio S,
  Ste. 202
San Diego, CA 92108
(619) 516-0192
roofer_45sd@sbcglobal.net

40–San Francisco
150 Executive Park Blvd.,
  Ste. 3625
San Francisco, CA 94134-3309
(415) 508-0261
www.rooferslocal40.org

95–San Jose
293 Brokaw Rd.
Santa Clara, CA 95050
(408) 987-0440
Alt. (408) 987-0441
Fax: (408) 988-6180

81–Stockton
8400 Enterprise Way, Ste. 122
Oakland, CA 94621
(510) 632-0505
roofers@pacbell.net

Colorado

58–Colorado Springs
404 North Spruce St.
Colorado Springs, CO 80905
(719) 632-5889

Connecticut

12–Bridgeport
15 Bernhard Rd.

North Haven, CT 06473
(203) 772-2565
Fax: (203) 772-2574
rooferslocal12@juno.com

9–Hartford
114 Old Forge Rd.
Rocky Hill, CT 06067
(860) 721-1174
rooferslocal9@aol.com

Delaware

30–New Castle
6447 Torresdale Ave.
Philadelphia, PA 19135
(215) 331-8770

District of Columbia

30–Washington
6447 Torresdale Ave.
Philadelphia, PA 19135
(410) 288-4401
Fax: (215) 331-8325

Florida

**6–Fort Lauderdale, Miami,
Tampa, West Palm Beach**
(877) 467-6637

181–Jacksonville
Jacksonville, FL 32254
(904) 924-0062

Georgia

136–Atlanta
374 Maynard Terr. SE,
  Room 208
Atlanta, GA 30316
(404) 373-7081
rooferslocal136@bellsouth.net

Hawaii

221–Honolulu
2045 Kam IV Rd., Ste. 203
Honolulu, HI 96819
(808) 847-5757

Idaho

189–Boise, Lewiston
315 West Mission Ave. #24
Spokane, WA 99201
(509) 327-2322

200– Pocatello
915 Berryman Rd.
Pocatello, ID 83201
(208) 237-5758

Illinois

97–Champaign
PO Box 6569
Champaign, IL 61826
(217) 359-3922

11–Chicago
9838 West Roosevelt Rd.
Westchester, IL 60154
(708) 345-0970
info@local11roofing.com

92–Decatur
234 West Cerro Gordo St.
Decatur, IL 62525-1634
(217) 422-8953

32–Burlington, Galesburg Area, Rock Island
2827 7th Ave.
Rock Island, IL 61201
(309) 786-2117
Fax: (309) 786-7490

11–LaSalle
9838 West Roosevelt Rd.
Westchester, IL 60154
(708) 345-0970
info@local11roofing.com

69–Peoria
3917 Southwest Adams St.
Peoria, IL 61605
(309) 673-8033

112–Springfield
PO Box 13426
Springfield, IL 62791-3426
(217) 529-2229
office@roofurslocal112.com

Indiana

205–Anderson
PO Box 14
Chesterfield, IN 46017
(765) 378-0556
uur205@unionplus.net

106–Evansville
1201 North Baker Ave.
Evansville, IN 47710
(812) 424-8641
Rooferslocal106@aol.com

26–Hammond-Gary
25 West 84th Ave.
Merrillville, IN 46410
(219) 756-3713
roofers26@sbcglobal.net

119–Indianapolis, Lafayette
2702 South Foltz St.
Indianapolis, IN 46241
(317) 484-8990

23–South Bend
1345 Northside Blvd.
South Bend, IN 46615
(574) 288-6506

150–Terre Haute
1101 North 11th St.
Terre Haute, IN 47807
(812) 232-7010

Iowa

182–Cedar Rapids
750 49th St.
Marion, IA 52302
(319) 373-2575
info@rooferslocal182.com
www.rooferslocal182.com

142–Des Moines, Sioux City, Mason City
3802 6th Ave.
Des Moines, IA 50313
(515) 244-7017

182–Dubuque Area, Waterloo Area
750 49th St.
Marion, IA 52302
(319) 373-2575

info@rooferslocal182.com
www.rooferslocal182.com

Kansas

20–Kansas City, Topeka, Wichita Area
C/O 6321 Blue Ridge Blvd., Ste. 202
Raytown, MO 64133
(816) 313-9420
roofer20@sbcglobal.net
www.rooferslocal20.com

Kentucky

147–Louisville
PO Box 91696
Louisville, KY 40291
(502) 231-3344

106–Paducah
210 North Fulton Ave., Box 8
Evansville, IN 47710
(812) 424-8641

Louisiana

317–Baton Rouge
3260 Winbourne Ave.
Baton Rouge, LA 70805
(225) 355-8502

123–Lake Charles, New Orleans, Shreveport
4025 Rufe Snow Dr.
Ft. Worth, TX 76180
(817) 589-2351 or (800) 564-1575

Maine

33–Bangor
53 Evans Dr.
PO Box 9106
Stoughton, MA 02072
(781) 341-9192

Maryland

30–Baltimore
6447 Torresdale Ave.
Philadelphia, PA 19135
(410) 288-4401

34–Cumberland
PO Box 500
Ridgeley, WV 26753
Phone/Fax: (301) 724-4773
rooferslu34@hotmail.com

Massachusetts

33–Boston, New Bedford Area
53 Evans Dr.
PO Box 9106
Stoughton, MA 02072
(781) 341-9192

248–Springfield
63 1/2 Main St.
Chicopee, MA 01020-1836
(413) 594-5291

Michigan

70–Ann Arbor
PO Box 116
Howell, MI 48844-0016
(517) 548-6554
office@rooferslocal70.com

**70–Battle Creek–
Kalamazoo Area**
PO Box 116
Howell, MI 48844-0016
(517) 548-6554
office@rooferslocal70.com

**70–Grand Rapids Area, Lansing
Area, Muskegon Area**
PO Box 116
Howell, MI 48844-0016
(517) 548-6554
office@rooferslocal70.com

149–Detroit
1640 Porter St.
Detroit, MI 48216
(313) 961-6093
roofersunionlocal149@
ameritech.net

**149–Marquette, Saginaw–
Bay City Area, Port Huron Area,
Traverse Area**
(810) 687-1368

Minnesota

**96–Brainerd Area, Duluth–
Iron Range Area, Minneapolis–
St. Paul, Southeastern
Minnesota, St. Cloud**
9174 Isanti St. NE
Blaine, MN 55449
(763) 230-7663
www.rooferslocal96.com

Mississippi

176–Jackson Area
Greenbrier, TN 37073
(615) 298-5215

Missouri

**20–Jefferson City, Springfield,
St. Joseph**
6321 Blue Ridge Blvd.,
Ste. 202
Raytown, MO 64133
(816) 313-9420
roofer20@sbcglobal.net

2–St. Louis
2920 Locust St.
St. Louis, MO 63103
(314) 535-9683

Montana

229–Billings
PO Box 31866
Billings, MT 59107
(406) 245-5762

250–Butte
1822 Whitman Ave.
Butte, MT 59701
(406) 782-4654

189–Missoula
C/O 315 West Mission Ave. #24
Spokane, WA 99201
(509) 327-2322

Nebraska

142–Omaha
C/O 3802 6th Ave.
Des Moines, IA 50313
(515) 244-7017

Nevada

162–Las Vegas
4125 Arctic Spring Rd.,
Stes. 5 and 6
Las Vegas, NV 89115
(702) 453-5801
union@rooferslocal162.org
www.rooferslocal162.org

81–Reno
C/O 8400 Enterprise Way,
Ste. 122
Oakland, CA 94621
(510) 632-0505
roofers@pacbell.net

New Hampshire

N/A

New Jersey

30–Atlantic City
305 South Main St.
Pleasantville, NJ 08232
(609) 646-7888

4–Newark
385 Parsippany Rd.
Parsippany, NJ 07054
(973) 515-8500

10–Paterson
321 Mason Ave.
Haledon, NJ 07508
(973) 595-5562
roofer10@optonline.net

30–Trenton
1400 Genessee St.
Trenton, NJ 08610
(609) 394-2700

New Mexico

123–Albuquerque
4025 Rufe Snow Dr.
Ft. Worth, TX 76180
(817) 589-2351 or (800)
564-1575

New York

241–Albany
890 3rd St.
Albany, NY 12206
(518) 489-7646

203–Binghamton
32 West State St., 2nd Fl.
Binghamton, NY 13901
(607) 722-4073
roofers203@hotmail.com

74–Buffalo
2800 Clinton St.
West Seneca, NY 14224
(716) 824-7488

154–Nassau-Suffolk
370 Vanderbilt Motor Pkwy.,
  Ste. #1
Hauppauge, NY 11788
(631) 435-0655

8–New York City
467 Dean St.
Brooklyn, NY 11217
(718) 789-8700

22–Rochester
280 Metro Park
Rochester, NY 14623
(585) 235-0080

195–Syracuse
6200 SR 31
Cicero, NY 13039
(315) 699-1808
roofers195@aol.com

North Carolina

136–Charlotte
c/o 374 Maynard Terr. SE,
  Room 208
Atlanta, GA 30316
(404) 373-7081

North Dakota

96–Fargo; Moorhead, MN
9174 Isanti St. NE
Blaine, MN 55449
(763) 230-7663
www.rooferslocal96.com

Ohio

88–Akron, Canton
6968 Promway Ave. NW
North Canton, OH 44720
(330) 497-2848
roofers88@sbcglobal.net

42–Cincinatti
1010 Yale Ave.
Cincinnati, OH 45206
(513) 821-3689
rooferslocalno42@fuse.net

44–Cleveland
1651 East 24th St.
Cleveland, OH 44114
(216) 781-4844
roofers44@sbcglobal.net

86–Columbus
37 1/2 West 2nd Ave.
Columbus, OH 43201
(614) 299-6404
roofers86@sbcglobal.net

75–Dayton
6550 Poe Ave.
Dayton, OH 45414-2527
(937) 415-3869
rooferslocal75@sbcglobal.net

134–Toledo
4652 Lewis Ave.
Toledo, OH 43612
(419) 478-3785

71–Youngstown
2714 Martin Luther King Blvd.
Youngstown, OH 44510
(330) 746-3020
njw071@aol.com

Oklahoma

143–Oklahoma City
111 Northeast 26th St.
Oklahoma City, OK 73105
(405) 524-4243

Oregon

156–Eugene
4015 Main St., Ste. E
Springfield, OR 97478
(541) 744-1771
(877) 774-9647

49–Portland
5032 Southeast 26th Ave.
Portland, OR 97202
(503) 232-4807
JATC: (503) 546-4235
local49roof@msn.com

Pennsylvania

210–Erie
1701 State St.
Erie, PA 16501
(814) 453-4503
mgress210@choiceonemail.com

30–Philadelphia, Harrisburg
6447 Torresdale Ave.
Philadelphia, PA 19135
(215) 331-8770

37–Pittsburgh
230 Lincoln Ave.
Bellevue, PA 15202
(412) 766-5360

30–Reading, Allentown, Scranton
41 South Maple St.
Kutztown, PA 19530
(610) 683-3666

South Carolina

N/A

South Dakota

N/A

Tennessee

**176–Knoxville, Memphis,
Nashville, Chattanooga**
PO Box 729
Greenbrier, TN 37073
(615) 298-5215

123–Dallas–Fort Worth, Houston, San Antonio
4025 Rufe Snow Dr.
Ft. Worth, TX 76180
(817) 589-2351
(800) 564-1575

91–Salt Lake City
2261 South Redwood Rd., Ste. N
Salt Lake City, UT 84119
(801) 972-6830

N/A

30–Northern Virginia
6447 Torresdale Ave.
Philadelphia, PA 19135
(215) 331-8770

54–Bellingham, Seattle
2800 First Ave., Room 105
Seattle, WA 98121

(206) 728-7654
roofers54@qwestoffice.net

189–Spokane
315 West Mission Ave. #24
Spokane, WA 99201
(509) 327-2322

153–Tacoma
3049 South 36th St.,
  Room 214
Tacoma, WA 98409
(253) 474-0527
rooferslocal153@qwestoffice.net

189–Yakima
315 West Mission Ave. #24
Spokane, WA 99201
(509) 327-2322

185–Charleston
Elkview, WV 25071
(304) 346-9234

242–Parkersburg
728 Tracewell Rd.
Mineral Wells, WV 26150
(304) 489-2111
roofers242mg@aol.com

188–Wheeling
2003 Warwood Ave.
Wheeling, WV 26003

(304) 277-2300
Roofers188@verizon.net

96–Eau Claire,
Fond du Lac Area
9174 Isanti St. NE
Blaine, MN 55449
(763) 230-7663
rob@rooferslocal96.com
www.rooferslocal96.com

65–Milwaukee, Madison Area,
Racine-Kenosha Area
16601 West Dakota St.
New Berlin, WI 53151
(262) 785-9720

96–Wausau
9174 Isanti St. NE
Blaine, MN 55449
(763) 230-7663
www.rooferslocal96.com

58–Cheyenne, Casper
404 North Spruce St.
Colorado Springs, CO 80905
(719) 632-5889

Wastewater Treatment Plant and System Operators

An associate's degree or one-year certificate program in this field will increase your opportunities for employment and ultimately advancement. Wastewater and drinking water treatment plants require state-certified operators. Each state has different requirements for operators or operators-in-training. The following, provided by the New Hampshire Department of Environmental Services, are programs that offer training in water distribution, collection, solid waste, and more. Refer to the key to determine the programs available.

Programs

BPAT Backflow Prevention Assembly Tester
C Wastewater Collection
D Water Distribution
I Biological Industrial Wastewater
IN Inspectors
L Land Application/Biosolids
M Maintenance
P Physical/Chemical Industrial Waste
R Solid Waste
SWWS Small Wastewater System
VSWS Very Small Water System
WLA Water Laboratory Analyst
WT Water Treatment
WWLA Wastewater Laboratory Analyst
WWT Wastewater Treatment
X Cross-Connection

State Certification Contacts

Alabama

Alabama Water and Wastewater
Operator Certification Program
(WT, D, WWT, C)
Alabama Department of
  Environmental Management
PO Box 301463
Montgomery, AL 36130
(334) 279-3040
www.adem.state.al.us

Alaska

Alaska Department of
Environmental Conservation,
Division of Water
(WT, D, WWT, C)
Operator Training and Certification
PO Box 111800
Juneau, AK 99811
(907) 465-5140

www.dec.state.ak.us/water/
  opcert/index.htm

Arizona

Arizona Operator
Certification Program
(WT, D, WWT, C)
Arizona Department of
  Environmental Quality
1110 West Washington St.
Phoenix, AZ 85007
(602) 771-4638
www.azdeq.gov/environ/water/
  dw/opcert.html

Inter Tribal Council of Arizona Inc.
(WT, D, WWT, C, SWWS, WLA,
  WWLA)
2214 North Central Ave.,
  Ste. 100
Phoenix, AZ 85004-1448
(602) 258-4822

www.itcaonline.com/program
  _tws.html

National Environmental, Safety
and Health Training Association
(WT, WWT)
PO Box 10321
Phoenix, AZ 85064
(602) 956-6099
www.neshta.org

Arkansas

Arkansas Drinking Water
Advisory and Operators
Licensing Committee
(WT, D, VSWS)
Arkansas Department of Health
4815 West Markham St.
Little Rock, AR 72205
(501) 661-2623
www.healthyarkansas.com/eng
  /opcert/oper.htm

Arkansas Wastewater
Licensing Committee
(WWT, P)
Department of Environmental
 Quality
5301 North Shore Dr.
North Little Rock, AR 72118
(501) 682-0823
www.adeq.state.ar.us/water/
 branch_enforcement/wwl

Arkansas Solid Waste
Licensing Committee
Department of Environmental
 Quality
5301 North Shore Dr.
North Little Rock, AR 72118-
 5317
(501) 682-0583
www.adeq.state.ar.us/solwaste

California

California Water Treatment
Operator Certification
(WT, D)
1616 Capitol Ave., 2nd Floor
PO Box 997377
Sacramento, CA 95899
(916) 449-5642
www.cdph.ca.gov/certlic/occu
 pations/Pages/DWopcert.aspx

California State Water
Resources Control Board
(WWT)
Office of Operator Certification
PO Box 944212
Sacramento, CA 94244
(916) 341-5672

California/Nevada Section
AWWA Certification Program
(D, WLA, X, BPAT, Water
 Conservation)
10574 Acacia St., Ste. D6
Rancho Cucamonga, CA
 91730-5448
(909) 481-7200
certification@ca-nv-awwa.org
www.ca-nv-awwa.org

California Water Environment
Association
(C, P, WWLA, L, IN, M)

Technical Certification Program
7677 Oakport St., Ste. 600
Oakland, CA 94621
(510) 382-7800
www.cwea.org/cert.shtml

National Tribal
Environmental Council
(WT, D, VSWS)
PO Box 1496
Roseville, CA 95678-8496
(505) 379-1909
www.ntec.org/water.htm

Colorado

Colorado Water and Wastewater
Facility Operators Certification
Board
(WT, D, VSWS, WWT, C,
 SWWS, I, P)
2170 South Parker Rd.,
 Ste. 290
Denver, CO 80231
(303) 394-8994
ocpo@ocpoweb.com
www.cdphe.state.co.us/op/ocb

Rocky Mountain Water Quality
Analyst Association
(WLA, WWLA)
PO Box 29407
Thornton, CO 80229-0407
(303) 762-2539
certification@rmwqaa.org
www.rmwqaa.org

Connecticut

Connecticut Department of
Public Health–Drinking Water
Section
(WT, D, VSWS, X, BPAT)
410 Capitol Ave., MS #51 WAT
Hartford, CT 06134-0308
(860) 509-7333
www.ct.gov/dph/cwp/view.asp
 ?q=387328

Connecticut Certification of
Wastewater Treatment Facility
Operators
(WWT)
Bureau of Water Management
79 Elm St.

Hartford, CT 06106-5127
(860) 424-3755
www.ct.gov/dep/cwp/view.asp
 ?q=325582

Connecticut Wastewater
Laboratory Certification Program
(WWLA)
State of Connecticut DEP
Bureau of Water Management
79 Elm St.
Hartford, CT 06106
(860) 424-3755

Connecticut Certification of
Waste Management Operators
(R)
BMMCA
79 Elm St.
Harford, CT 06106
(860) 424-3248
www.ct.gov/dep/cwp/view.asp
 ?q=325466

Delaware

Delaware Office of Drinking Water
(WT, D, VSWS)
Blue Hen Corp. Center
655 South Bay Rd., Ste. 203
Dover, DE 19901
(302) 741-8630
www.dhss.delaware.gov/dhss/d
 ph/regs.html#W

Delaware Board of Certification
for Wastewater Operators
(WWT)
89 Kings Highway
Dover, DE 19901
(302) 739-9946
www.dnrec.state.de.us/water2000

District of Columbia

U.S. Army Corps of Engineers–
Baltimore District
(WT)
Washington Aqueduct Division
U.S. Army Corps of Engineers
5900 MacArthur Blvd. NW
Washington, DC 20016
(202) 764-2702
www.washingtonaqueduct.nab.
 usace.army.mil

**U.S. Environmental
Protection Agency**
Office of Ground Water and
  Drinking Water (4601)
Ariel Rios Building
1200 Pennsylvania Ave. NW
Washington, DC 20460
(202) 564-3750
www.epa.gov/safewater

Florida

**Florida DEP Water/Wastewater
Operator Certification Program**
(WT, WWT)
Bureau of Water Facilities Funding
2600 Blair Stone Rd., MS 3506
Tallahassee, FL 32399
(850) 245-7500
www.dep.state.fl.us/water/wff/ocp

**Florida Water and Pollution
Control Operators Association
Voluntary Certification Board**
(D, C, X, BPAT, L)
Brevard Community College
1519 Clearlake Rd.
Cocoa, FL 32922
(321) 433-0081
training@fwpcoa.org
www.fwpcoa.org

Florida Section AWWA
(BPAT)
1107 Southwest Bromelia Terr.
Stuart, FL 34997-7145
(772) 781-2529
www.fsawwa.org

Georgia

**Georgia State Board of
Examiners for Certification
of Water and Wastewater
Treatment Plant Operators and
Laboratory Analysts**
(WT, D, VSWS, WWT, C, SWWS,
  P, WLA, WWLA)
Professional Licensing
  Boards Division
237 Coliseum Dr.
Macon, GA 31217
(478) 207-2440
www.sos.georgia.gov/plb/water

**Georgia Association of Water
Professionals**
(BPAT)
2121 New Market Pkwy. SE,
  Ste. 144
Marietta, GA 30067
(770) 618-8690
www.gawp.org

Hawaii

**Hawaii Board of Certification of
Public Water System Operators**
(WT, D)
919 Ala Moana Blvd.,
  Room 308
Honolulu, HI 96814
(808) 586-4258
www.hawaii.gov/health/
  environmental/water/
  sdwb/socert/operatorcert.html

**Hawaii Board of Certification
of Operating Personnel in
Wastewater Treatment Facilities**
(WWT)
1350 Sand Island Pkwy.,
  Bldg. 3A
Honolulu, HI 96819
(808) 586-4294
www.hawaii.gov/health/
  environmental/water/
  wastewater/wtc_cert.html

Idaho

**Idaho Bureau of
Occupational Licenses**
(WT, D, VSWS, WWT, C, SWWS,
  WWLA, BPAT, L)
1109 West Main St., Ste. 220
Boise, ID 83702
(208) 334-3233
www.ibol.idaho.gov/wwp.htm

Illinois

**Illinois Drinking Water Operator
Certification Program**
(WT, D)
1021 North Grand Ave. E
PO Box 19276
Springfield, IL 62794

(217) 785-0561
www.epa.state.il.us/water/
  operator-cert/drinking-water

**Illinois Wastewater Operator
Certification Program**
(WWT, C, SWWS, I, P)
Illinois EPA, Compliance
  Assurance Section #19
1021 North Grand Ave. E
PO Box 19276
Springfield, IL 62794
(217) 782-9720
www.epa.state.il.us/water/
  operator-cert/waste-water

**Illinois Microwater
Laboratory Certification**
(WLA)
Illinois Department of
  Public Health
Division of Laboratories
PO Box 19435
Springfield, IL 62794
(217) 782-6562

**Illinois Cross-Connection Control
Device Inspector Certification
Program**
(X, BPAT)
Southern Illinois University–
  Edwardsville
Campus Box 1075
Edwardsville, IL 62026
(618) 650-2030
www.siue.edu/ERTC

Water Quality Association
(VSWS)
4151 Naperville Rd.
Lisle, IL 60532
(630) 505-0160
info@wqa.org
www.wqa.org

Indiana

**Indiana Department of
Environmental Management**
(WT, D, VSWS)
Office of Water Quality MC 66-34
100 North Senate Ave.
Indianapolis, IN 46204
(317) 308-3305
www.in.gov/idem/5091.htm

Indiana Department of
Environmental Management
(WWT)
Office of Water Quality
  MC 65-42
100 North Senate Ave.
Indianapolis, IN 46204
(317) 232-8791
www.in.gov/idem/5088.htm

Indiana Water Environment
Association
(C)
City of Fort Wayne
WPCM/STM Department
515 East Wallace St.
Fort Wayne, IN 46803-2365
(260) 427-5188
www.indianawea.org

Indiana Cross-Connection
Control Program
(X)
Office of Water Quality
  MC 66-34
100 North Senate Ave.
Indianapolis, IN 46204
(317) 308-3300

Iowa

Association of Boards
of Certification
(WT, D, VSWS, WWT, C, I, P,
  WLA, WWLA)
208 5th St., Ste. 201
Ames, IA 50010
(515) 232-3623
abc@abccert.org
www.abccert.org

Iowa Operator Certification
Program
(WT, D, VSWS, WWT)
Iowa Department of Natural
  Resources
401 Southwest 7th St., Ste. M
Des Moines, IA 50309
(515) 725-0284
www.iowadnr.com/water/opcert.
  html

Iowa Water Pollution Control
Association
(C)

District Superintendent
Iowa Great Lakes Sanitary
  District
303 28th St
Milford, IA 51351-7077
(712) 338-2626
iglsd@milfordcable.net
www.iawpca.org

Kansas

Kansas Water and Wastewater
Operator Certification
(WT, WWT)
Bureau of Water
1000 Southwest Jackson St.,
  Ste. 420
Topeka, KS 66612
(785) 296-2976
www.kdheks.gov/water/tech.html

Kansas Water Environment
Association Voluntary
Certification Program
(D, C, I, P, WLA, WWLA, L)
6209 Southwest 24th Terr.
Topeka, KS 66614
(785) 357-4780
www.kwea.net

Kentucky

Kentucky Board of Certification
of Wastewater System Operators
(WWT, WT, D)
Division of Compliance
  Assistance
300 Fair Oaks Ln.
Frankfort, KY 40601
(502) 564-0323 or
  (800) 926 -8111
www.dca.ky.gov

Kentucky Water and Wastewater
Operators Association Inc.
(WLA, WWLA)
897 North Middletown Rd.
Paris, KY 40361-9145
(502) 863-7819
www.kwwoa.org

Kentucky Division of Waste
Management
(R, L)

Solid Waste Branch
14 Reilly Rd.
Frankfort, KY 40601
(502) 564-6716
waste@ky.gov
www.waste.ky.gov/branches/sw

Louisiana

Louisiana Committee of
Certification for Water and
Wastewater Operators
(WT, D, WWT, C, Water
  Production)
PO Box 4489
Baton Rouge, LA 70821
(225) 342-7508
www.dhh.louisiana.gov/offices/
  ?ID=236

Louisiana Solid Waste
Operator Certification and
Training Program
(R)
Waste Permits Division
PO Box 4313
Baton Rouge, LA 70821
(225) 219-0967
www.deq.louisiana.gov/portal/ta
  bid/259/Default.aspx

Maine

Maine Board of Licensure of
Water Treatment Plant Operators
(WT, D, VSWS)
Maine Drinking Water Program
286 Water St., 3rd Floor
11 State House Station
Augusta, ME 04333
(207) 287-7485
www.medwp.com

Maine Wastewater Operator
Certification Program
(WWT)
State of Maine DEP
17 State House Station
Augusta, ME 04333
(207) 287-9031
www.state.me.us/dep/blwq/doce
  ng/opcrtpg2.htm

Maryland

Maryland State Board of Waterworks and Waste Systems Operators
(WT, D, WWT, C, I, P, L)
Maryland Department of the Environment
1800 Washington Blvd.
Baltimore, MD 21230
(410) 537-3167
www.mde.state.md.us/Permits/WaterManagementPermits

Massachussetts

Massachusetts Board of Certification of Operators of Drinking Water Supply Facilities
(WT, D, VSWS)
Massachusetts DEP
1 Winter St., 5th Floor
Boston, MA 02108
(617) 556-1166
www.mass.gov/dpl/boards/dw

Massachusetts State Board of Certification of Operators of Wastewater Treatment Facilities
(WWT, P)
DEP Central Region
627 Main St.
Worcester, MA 01608-2022
(508) 767-2781

Massachusetts Backflow Prevention Device Inspectors and Cross Connection Surveyor Certification Program
(X)
Drinking Water Program
1 Winter St., 5th Floor
Boston, MA 02108
(617) 556-1085

New England Water Environment Association Voluntary Certification Program
(C, WWLA)
InfraMetrix
601 Edgewater Dr., Ste. 362
Wakefield, MA 01880
(813) 740-2510
www.newea.org

New England Water Works Association
(X, BPAT)
125 Hopping Brook Rd.
Holliston, MA 01746
(508) 893-7979
www.newwa.org

Michigan

Michigan Advisory Board of Examiners
(WT, D, WWT, I, P)
Operator Training and Certification Unit
PO Box 30457
Lansing, MI 48909
(517) 373-4752
www.michigan.gov/deqoperatortraining

Michigan Water Environment Association Education and Certification Committee
(C, WWLA, L, Env. Compliance, M)
City of East Lansing WWTP
1700 Trowbridge Rd.
East Lansing, MI 48823
(517) 371-2240
www.mi-wea.org

Michigan Backflow Prevention Tester Certification
(X, BPAT)
525 West Allegan
Lansing, MI 48909
(517) 241-1242

Minnesota

Minnesota Department of Health
(WT, D, VSWS)
625 Robert St. N
Saint Paul, MN 55164
(651) 201-4652
www.health.state.mn.us/divs/eh/water/wateroperator

Minnesota Pollution Control Agency
(WWT, C, L, IN)
Training and Certification Unit
520 Lafayette Rd. N
Saint Paul, MN 55155
(651) 296-9269
www.pca.state.mn.us/water/wastewater.html

Mississippi

Mississippi Department of Health
(WT, D, BPAT)
Bureau of Public Water Supply
PO Box 1700
Jackson, MS 39215
(601) 576-7518
www.msdh.state.ms.us/msdhsite/_static/44,0,76.html

Mississippi Department of Environmental Quality
(WWT, C)
Office of Pollution Control
PO Box 2261
Jackson, MS 39225
(601) 961-5293
www.deq.state.ms.us/MDEQ.nsf/page/OT_opcert

Missouri

Missouri Department of Natural Resources
(WT, D, WWT, CAFO [Concentrated Animal Feeding Operations], Waste Management)
Operator Certification Section
Jefferson City, MO 65102
(800) 361-4827 or (573) 751-1600
www.dnr.mo.gov/env/wpp/opcert/oprtrain.htm

Missouri Department of Natural Resources Solid Waste Technician Certification
(R)
Solid Waste Management Program
PO Box 176
Jefferson City, MO 65102
(573) 751-5401
www.dnr.mo.gov/env/swmp/index.html

Missouri Backflow Prevention
Assembly Tester Certification
Program
(BPAT)
Public Drinking Water Branch
PO Box 176
Jefferson City, MO 65102
(573) 751-5331
www.dnr.mo.gov/pubs/pub98.pdf

Montana

Montana Water and Wastewater
Operators' Advisory Council
(WT, D, VSWS, WWT, P)
Public Water and Subdivisions
Bureau
PO Box 200901
Helena, MT 59620
(406) 444-2691
www.deq.mt.gov/wqinfo/opcert/
index.asp

Nebraska

Nebraska Department of Health
and Human Services
(WT, D, VSWS, BPAT)
200 South Silber Ave.
North Platte, NE 69101-4200
(308) 535-8135
www.dhhs.ne.gov/crl/rcs/water/
water.htm

Nebraska Wastewater Treatment
Plant Operator Certification
Program
(WWT, SWWS, P)
Wastewater Section
PO Box 98922
Lincoln, NE 68509
(402) 471-2580
www.deq.state.ne.us

Nevada

Native American
Water Association
(WT, D, VSWS, WWT, C, WLA)
1662 US Hwy. 395 N, Ste. 212
Minden, NV 89423
(775) 782-6636
NAWA@msn.com

www.nawainc.org

Nevada Bureau of
Safe Drinking Water
(WT, D)
NV Division of Environmental
Protection
901 South Stewart St.,
Ste. 4001
Carson City, NV 89701
(775) 687-9527
www.ndep.nv.gov/bsdw

Nevada Water Environment
Association
(WWT, C, I, P, WWLA, Industrial
Waste Inspector)
PO Box 190
Smith, NV 89430-0190
(775) 465-2045
www.nvwea.org

New Hampshire

New Hampshire Department
of Environmental Services
(WT, D, VSWS)
29 Hazen Dr.
PO Box 95
Concord, NH 03302
(603) 271-2410
www.des.nh.gov/dwgb

New Hampshire Wastewater
Operator Certification Program
(WWT)
29 Hazen Dr.
PO Box 95
Concord, NH 03302
(603) 271-3325
www.des.state.nh.us/wwe/
operator.htm

New Hampshire Solid Waste
Operator Training and
Certification Program
(R)
New Hampshire Department of
Environmental Services
29 Hazen Dr.
Concord, NH 03301
(603) 271-2928
www.des.state.nh.us/SWTAS

New Jersey

New Jersey Water Supply and
Wastewater Operators Board
of Examiners
(WT, D, VSWS, WWT, C, I, P)
New Jersey Department of
Environmental Protection,
Examinations and Licensing
Unit
PO Box 441
Trenton, NJ 08625
(609) 777-1013
www.nj.gov/dep/watersupply/
operatorcert.htm

New Mexico

New Mexico Utility Operators
Certification Program
(WT, D, VSWS, WWT, C,
SWWS, WWLA)
New Mexico Environment
Department
Surface Water Quality Bureau
PO Box 26110
Santa Fe, NM 87502
(505) 222-9575
www.nmenv.state.nm.us/swqb/
FOT

New Mexico Environmental
Finance Center
(WT, D)
New Mexico Tech
2445 Alamo Ave. SE, Ste. 300
Albuquerque, NM 87106
(505) 924-7034
www.nmefc.nmt.edu

New Mexico Solid Waste Facility
Operator Certification
(R)
New Mexico Environment
Department
100 East Manana Blvd., Unit #3
Clovis, NM 88101
(505) 762-3728
www.nmenv.state.nm.us/swb

New York

**New York State
Department of Health**
(WT, D, X, BPAT)
Flanigan Square
547 River St., Room 400
Troy, NY 12180
(518) 402-7654
www.health.state.ny.us/
environmental/water/drink
ing/operate/operate.htm

**New York Qualifications of
Operators of Wastewater Plants**
(WWT)
New York State DEC
625 Broadway, 4th Floor
Albany, NY 12233-3506
(518) 402-8092
www.dec.ny.gov/chemical/
8464.html

**New York Water Environment
Association Inc.**
(C)
525 Plum St., Ste. 102
Syracuse, NY 13204
(315) 422-7811
www.nywea.org

North Carolina

**North Carolina Water Treatment
Facility Operators Certification
Board**
(WT, D, X)
Division of Environmental Health
1635 Mail Service Center
Raleigh, NC 27699
(919) 733-0379
www.deh.enr.state.nc.us/oet/
operator_cert/op_cert_main2.htm

**North Carolina Water Pollution
Control System Operators
Certification Commission**
(WWT, C, SWWS, I, P, L)
Technical Assistance and
Certification Unit
1618 Mail Service Center
Raleigh, NC 27699
(919) 733-0026
www.h2o.enr.state.nc.us/tacu

North Carolina AWWA and WEA
(WWLA)
City of Greensboro
PO Box 3136
Greensboro, NC 27402
(336) 433-7229
www.ncsafewater.org/index.php
?Itemid=69

North Dakota

**North Dakota
Department of Health**
(WT, D, VSWS, WWT, C,
SWWS)
918 East Divide Ave., Fl. 3
Bismarck, ND 58501-1947
(701) 328-6626
www.health.state.nd.us/MF

Ohio

Ohio EPA–Certification Unit
(WT, D, VSWS, WWT, C,
SWWS)
PO Box 1049
Columbus, OH 43216-1049
(614) 644-2752
www.epa.state.oh.us/ddagw/op
cert.html

**Ohio Water Environment
Association**
(P, WWLA)
2307 Regency Ct.
Fairborn, OH 45324-6013
(937) 878-1924
www.ohiowea.org

**Ohio Division of Industrial
Compliance**
(BPAT)
Division of Industrial Compliance
Backflow Section
PO Box 4009
Reynoldsburg, OH 43068-9009
(614) 644-3153
www.com.state.oh.us/dic/
dicplumbing.htm

Oklahoma

**Oklahoma Department of
Environmental Quality**
(WT, D, WWT, C, WLA, WWLA)
Certification and Compliance
Section
PO Box 1677
Oklahoma City, OK 73101
(405) 702-8100
www.deq.state.ok.us/
WQDnew/opcert

Oregon

**Oregon Water Operator
Certification Program**
(WT, D, VSWS)
Department of Human Services
Drinking Water Program
PO Box 14450
Portland, OR 97293-0450
(971) 673-0426
www.oregon.gov/DHS/ph/dwp/

**Oregon Department of
Environmental Quality**
(WWT, C)
Water Quality Division
400 East Scenic Dr., Ste. 307
The Dalles, OR 97058-3450
(541) 298-7255, ext. 35
www.deq.state.or.us/wq/opcert/
opcert.htm

Pennsylvania

**Pennsylvania State Board for
Certification of Water and
Wastewater Systems Operators**
(WT, D, VSWS, WWT, C,
SWWS)
Operator Certification
PO Box 8454
Harrisburg, PA 17105-8454
(717) 772-5158
www.depweb.state.pa.us/
operatorcenter/site/default.asp

Rhode Island

Rhode Island Drinking Water Operator Certification Board
(WT, D, VSWS)
Rhode Island Department of Health
Office of Drinking Water Quality
3 Capitol Hill, Room 209
Providence, RI 02908-5097
(401) 222-7824
www.health.ri.gov/environment/ dwq/operator

Rhode Island Board of Certification of Operators of Wastewater Treatment Facilities
(WWT)
DEM–Water Resources
235 Promenade St.
Providence, RI 02908
(401) 222-3961
www.dem.ri.gov/programs/ benviron/water/licenses/ wwoper

South Carolina

South Carolina Environmental Certification Board
(WT, D, WWT, P, Well Driller)
110 Centerview Dr.
PO Box 11409
Columbia, SC 29211
(803) 896-4430
www.llr.state.sc.us/POL/ Environmental

Water Environment Association of South Carolina Voluntary Certification Committee
(C, L)
Lancaster County Water and Sewer District
PO Box 1009
Lancaster, SC 29721-1009
(803) 416-5257
www.weasc.org/CertOpport.htm

South Carolina Department of Health and Environmental Control
(BPAT)
Cross Connection Control Program Coordinator

2600 Bull St.
Columbia, SC 29201
(803) 898-3567
www.scdhec.net/environment/ water/dwbflow.htm

South Dakota

South Dakota Operator Certification Program
(WT, D, VSWS, WWT, C, SWWS)
DWP/DENR
Foss Building–Lower Level
523 East Capitol Ave.
Pierre, SD 57501-3181
(605) 773-4208
www.state.sd.us/opercert

Tennessee

Tennessee Water and Wastewater Operator Certification Board
(WT, D, VSWS, WWT, C, SWWS)
J. R. Fleming Training Center
2022 Blanton Dr.
Murfreesboro, TN 37129
(615) 898-8090
www.tennessee.gov/ environment/permits/opcert. shtml

Tennessee Cross-Connection Control Certification Program
(X, BPAT)
Division of Water Supply
6th Floor, L&C Tower
401 Church St.
Nashville, TN 37243
(615) 532-9199
james.t.aslinger@state.tn.us

Texas

Texas Operator Certification Program
(WT, D, WWT, C, X, BPAT, R)
Texas Commission on Environmental Quality
PO Box 13087
Austin, TX 78711
(512) 239-6300

www.tceq.state.tx.us/nav/ permits/licenses.html

Texas Water Utilities Association/Laboratory Analysts Section
Texas Water Utilities Association
1106 Clayton Ln., Ste. 112W
Austin, TX 78723-2472
(512) 459-3124 or
(888) 367-8982
www.twua.org

Utah

Utah Water Operator Certification Commission
(WT, D, VSWS, X, BPAT)
Division of Drinking Water
150 North 1950 West
PO Box 144830
Salt Lake City, UT 84114
(801) 536-4200
www.drinkingwater.utah.gov

Utah Wastewater Operator Certification Program
(WWT, C, SWWS)
Division of Water Quality
288 North 1460 West
PO Box 144870
Salt Lake City, UT 84114-4870
(801) 538-6062
www.waterquality.utah.gov/ OpCert

Vermont

Vermont Water Supply Division
(WT, D, VSWS)
Old Pantry Building
103 South Main St.
Waterbury, VT 05671-0403
(802) 241-3415
www.vermontdrinkingwater.org

Vermont Wastewater Facility Operator Certification Program
(WWT, Industrial Paper, Industrial Metals, Industrial Dairy)
Vermont DEC, Wastewater Management Division
Sewing Building

103 South Main St.
Waterbury, VT 05671-0405
(802) 241-2369
www.anr.state.vt.us/dec/ww/
wwmd.cfm

Virginia

**Virginia Board for Waterworks
and Wastewater Works
Operators**
(WT, D, VSWS, WWT)
9960 Mayland Dr., Ste. 400
Richmond, VA 23233-1463
(804) 367-2648
www.dpor.virginia.gov/
dporweb/www_main.cfm

Washington

**Washington Water Works
Operator Certification Program**
(WT, D, VSWS, X, BPAT, Basic
Treatment Operator)
Washington Department
of Health
PO Box 47822
Olympia, WA 98504-7822
(360) 236-3137
www.doh.wa.gov/ehp/dw/our_
main_pages/opcertification.htm

**Washington Wastewater
Operator Certification Program**
(WWT)

Washington Department of
Ecology, Water Quality
Program
300 Desmond Dr.
PO Box 47696
Olympia, WA 98504-7696
(360) 407-6449
www.ecy.wa.gov/programs/wq/
wastewater/op_cert

**Washington Wastewater
Collection Personnel Association**
(C)
170 South Kent Pl.
East Wenatchee, WA 98802-
5553
(509) 884-3695
www.wastewatercpa.com

**Washington Landfill and
Incinerator Operator Certification
Program**
(R, Solid Waste Incinerator)
Washington Department of
Ecology
PO Box 47600
Olympia, WA 98504-7600
(360) 407-6136
www.ecy.wa.gov/programs/swfa
/nav/cert.html

West Virginia

**West Virginia Office of
Environmental Health Services**

(WT, D, VSWS, WWT, C, SWWS,
BPAT)
Capitol and Washington St.
1 Davis Sq., Ste. 200
Charleston, WV 25301-1798
(304) 558-6993
www.wvdhhr.org/oehs/eed/swap
/training&certification

Wisconsin

**Wisconsin Water and
Wastewater Operator
Certification Program**
(WT, D, VSWS, WWT, SWWS,
WWLA, I, P)
PO Box 7921
Madison, WI 53707-7921
(608) 266-0498
www.dnr.state.wi.us/org/es/
science/opcert/water.htm

Wyoming

**Wyoming Department of
Environmental Quality,
Water Quality Division**
(WT, D, VSWS, WWT, C)
Herschler Building, 4W
122 West 25th St.
Cheyenne, WY 82002
(307) 777-6128
www.deq.state.wy.us/opcert.asp

Other Pertinent Organizations

American Water Works Association (AWWA)
www.awwa.org

State Wastewater Certification Regulations
www.wef.org/ConferencesTraining/WastewaterOperatorsCertification/
Certifregulations.htm

National Rural Water Association (includes a job listing)
www.jobtarget.com/r/candidates/bank/search.cfm?site_id=678

Welding

An apprenticeship or other formal training program is the best way to enter the welding world. The American Welding Society (www.aws.org) has compiled an online list of community and technical colleges below, all with highly regarded welding programs. A sampling is below.

NCCER-Accredited Training Centers for Welding

Some welders also get their start by joining a contracting organization or by contacting a company or organization that sponsors public training. The following training centers rely on the program developed by the National Center for Construction Education and Research (www.nccer.org).

Alabama

Diversified Employment
Service Inc.
211-C Hwy. 43 S
Saraland, AL 36571
(251) 679-0018

Alaska

Associated General Contractors
of Alaska
8005 Schoon St.
Anchorage, AK 99518
(907) 561-5354
www.agcak.org

Arizona

Arizona Builders Alliance
1825 West Adams
Phoenix, AZ 85007
(602) 274-8222
www.azbuilders.org

Arkansas

N/A

California

Corey Delta Constructors
925 Airpark Rd.
Napa, CA 94558
(707) 747-7500
www.coreydelta.com

John Lopez Welding School
5310 Norris Rd., Unit B
Bakersfield, CA 93308
(661) 399-6607
www.jlweldingschool.com

Watkins Construction
Company Inc.
3229 South 15th at I-45
Corsicana, TX 75151
(903) 874-7791
www.watkinsconstruction.com

Welltech National Training
Systems Inc.
2751 East El Presidio St.
Carson, CA 90810-1139
(310) 223-6062
www.welltechsafety.com

Colorado

Construction Industry Training
Council of Colorado Inc.
646 Mariposa St.
Denver, CO 80204
(303) 893-1500

T and D Services
1143 Michael Cir.
Meeker, CO 81641
(970) 260-3415

Connecticut

Construction Education
Center Inc.
2138 Silas Deane Hwy., Ste. 101

Rocky Hill, CT 06067
(860) 529-5886
www.thinkconstruction.org

Delaware

N/A

Florida

Commercial Diving Academy
8137 North Main St.
Jacksonville, FL 32208
(904) 766-7736
www.commercialdiving
    academy.com

The Southern Company
One Energy Place
Pensacola, FL 32503
(850) 444-6821

Georgia

N/A

Hawaii

N/A

Idaho

Construction Education
Foundation of Idaho (CEFI) Inc.
1649 West Shoreline Dr.
Boise, ID 83702
(208) 344-2531
www.cefidaho.org

Illinois

Institute for Construction
Education
2353 Federal Dr.
Decatur, IL 62526
(217) 877-7523
www.iceschool.org

Indiana

N/A

Iowa

N/A

Kansas

Ace Construction Corporation
301 Main St.
Towanda, KS 67144
(316) 536-2202
www.aceconstcorp.com

Kentucky

Kentucky Department of
Corrections
2439 Lawrenceburg Rd.
Frankfort, KY 40602
(502) 564-4795 ext. 229
www.corrections.ky.gov

Western Kentucky Construction
Association–AGC
2201 McCracken Blvd.
Paducah, KY 42001
(270) 744-6261
www.wkca.org

Louisiana

ABC Pelican Southwest Chapter
222 Walcot Rd.
Westlake, LA 70669
(337) 882-0204
www.abcpelicansw.net

ABC–Bayou Chapter
101 Riverbend Dr.
St. Rose, LA 70087
(504) 468-3188
www.abcbayou.org

Maine

ABC–Maine Chapter
45 Melville St. #2
Augusta, ME 04332
(207) 623-4500
www.abcmaine.org

Maryland

Cumberland Valley Chapter ABC
530 North Locust St.
Hagerstown, MD 21740
(301) 739-1190
www.abccvc.com

Massachusetts

George W. Gould
Construction Institute
200 Wheeler Rd.
Burlington, MA 01803
(781) 270-9990
www.gwgci.org

Michigan

N/A

Minnesota

N/A

Mississippi

Mississippi Construction
Education Foundation
290 Commerce Park Dr., Ste. B
Ridgeland, MS 39157
(601) 605-2989
www.mcef.net

Missouri

Vatterott College
8580 Evans Ave., Ste. A
St. Louis, MO 63134
(314) 264-1806
www.vatterott-college.edu

Montana

Montana Contractors'
Association
1717 11th Ave.
Helena, MT 59601
(406) 442-4162
www.mtagc.org

Nebraska

N/A

Nevada

N/A

New Hampshire

N/A

New Jersey

ABC New Jersey Chapter
720 King George Post Rd.,
Ste. 303
Fords, NJ 08863
(732) 661-1045
www.abcnjc.org

New Mexico

New Mexico Building Branch,
AGC
1615 University Blvd., NE
Albuquerque, NM 87102
(505) 842-1462
www.agc-nm.org

New York

CTC of New York State
6369 Collamer Dr.
East Syracuse, NY 13057
(315) 463-7539
www.abcnys.org

North Carolina

Carolinas AGC Inc.
1100 Euclid Ave.
Charlotte, NC 28203
(704) 372-1450
www.cagc.org

North Dakota

AGC of North Dakota
422 North Second St.
Bismarck, ND 58501

(701) 223-2770
www.agcnd.org

Ohio

ABC Northern Ohio Chapter
9255 Market Pl. W
Broadview Heights, OH 44147
(440) 717-0389
www.nocabc.com

ABC Ohio Valley CEF
33 Greenwood Ln.
Springboro, OH 45066
(937) 704-0111
www.ovabc.org

Construction Craft Academy
9760 Shepard Rd.
Macedonia, OH 44056
(800) 442-0067
www.craftacademy.com

Oklahoma

AGC of Oklahoma–
Building Chapter
605 Northwest 13th St., Ste. A
Oklahoma City, OK 73103-2213
(405) 528-4605
www.agcok.com

Integrated Service Company,
LLC
1900 North 161st East Ave.
Tulsa, OK 74116
(918) 234-4150
www.inservusa.com

Oregon

N/A

Pennsylvania

ABC Central, PA Chapter
898 North Eagle Valley Rd.
Milesburg, PA 16853
(814) 353-1999
www.abccentralpa.org

Rhode Island

N/A

South Carolina

N/A

South Dakota

N/A

Tennessee

N/A

Texas

ABC Merit Shop Training
Program Inc.
Craft Training Center of the
Coastal Bend
7433 Leopard St.
Corpus Christi, TX 78409
(361) 289-1636
www.ctccb.org

ABC of Greater Houston Inc.
3910 Kirby Dr., Ste. 131
Houston, TX 77098
(713) 523-6258
www.abchouston.org

ABC Southeast Texas
2700 North Twin City Hwy.
Nederland, TX 77627
(409) 724-7886
www.abcsetx.org

ABC Texas Mid Coast CEF
116 Jason Plaza
Victoria, TX 77901
(361) 572-0299
www.abcvicotia.vbxhosting.org

Saulsbury Industries D/B/A
Construction Workforce
Training Center
5308 Andrews Hwy.
Odessa, TX 79762
(432) 366-7676
www.cwtc-tx.com

The Victor Group
801 High Ridge Dr.
Friendswood, TX 77546
(281) 850-8079
www.thevictorgroup.net

Watkins Construction
Company Inc.
3229 South 15th at I-45
Corsicana, TX 75151
(903) 874-7791
www.watkinsconstruction.com

Utah

N/A

Vermont

N/A

Virginia

N/A

Washington

N/A

West Virginia

N/A

Wisconsin

N/A

Wyoming

Wyoming Contractors
Association AGC
2220 North Bryan Stock Trail
Casper, WY 82601
(307) 237-4400
www.wcagc.org

Blue-Collar Apprenticeship and Industry Training Resources for Canada

Overview

While some prospective apprentices simply find a company that is willing to take them on for training and eventual employment, most industries require the completion of a preapprenticeship training program. Those interested in pursuing a trade will find that apprenticeships are beneficial for improving job prospects. In Canada, the governments of each individual province have responsibility for training and certifying apprentices.

The Interprovincial Standards Red Seal Program

The Red Seal Program is an attempt to standardize the apprenticeship process by providing a cross-provincial testing and certification format. The program allows those who graduate from an apprenticeship program and pass a trade's Standards Examination to work anywhere that recognizes the Red Seal. More information can be found at www.red-seal.ca.

About This List

Listed below are individual programs offered at community colleges and trade schools. However, local union offices and trade organizations are also helpful resources for starting a career. Many of those are listed as well. In addition, most provinces have government-level apprenticeship counselors or staff (under **Apprenticeship Contacts** below) who may be able to assist you in your efforts.

ONTARIO

Apprenticeship Contacts

Ontario Employment Counselors
(800) 387-5656

Automotive Service Technician, Electrician, Elevating Devices Mechanic, Industrial Mechanic, Machinist, Plumber, Precision Metal Fabricator, Welder

Durham College–Whitby Campus
1610 Champlain Ave.
Whitby, ON L1N 6A7
(905) 721-3300
www.durhamcollege.ca

Carpentry

United Brotherhood of Carpenters and Joiners Union Locals
4203 Carpenters District Council of Ontario, Canada
5780 Timberlea Blvd., Ste. 103
Mississauga, ON L4W 4W8
(905) 238-3063

Local 397 Whitby, ON
459 Croft St.
PO Box 27
Port Hope, ON L1A 3V9
(905) 885-0885
local397@cogeco.net

Local 18 Hamilton, ON
1342 Stonechurch Rd.
East Hamilton, ON L8W 2C8
(905) 522-0752
local18@quickclic.net

Local 93 Ottawa, ON
5500 Canotek Rd., Unit 102
Ottawa, ON K1J 1K6
(613) 745-1513
www.local93.org

Carpentry, Electrical, Heavy Equipment Operator, Welding

Fleming College
599 Brealey Dr.
Peterborough, ON K9J 7B1
(705) 749-5530
(866) 353-6464
www.flemingc.on.ca

Civil Engineering Technology, Forestry Technician, Mining Techniques, Welding

Confederation College
Thunder Bay, ON P7C 4W1
(807) 475-6110
liaison@confederationc.on.ca

Electrical: International Brotherhood of Electrical Workers (IBEW) Union Locals

IBEW Local Union 115
40 Binnington Ct.
Kingston, ON K7M 8S3
(613) 547-4115
www.ibew115.on.ca

IBEW Local Union 586
1178 Rainbow St.
Gloucester, ON K1J 6X7
(613) 741-5664
www.ibew586.org

IBEW Local Union 339
440 Balmoral St.
Thunder Bay, ON P7C 5G8
(807) 625-4339
loc339@tbaytel.net

IBEW Local Union 353
1377 Lawrence Ave.
East North York, ON M3A 3P8
(416) 510-3530
www.ibew353.org/

Electrician, Construction Craft Worker, Heavy Equipment Techniques, Mechanical Techniques—Industrial Millwright, Welding

Northern College of Applied Arts and Technology
Timmins, ON P4N 8R6
(705) 235-3211
info@northern.on.ca

Ironworkers

International Association Union Locals
Local 700 Windsor, Ontario
R.R. #3, 4069 County Rd. #46
Maidstone, Ontario N0R 1K0
(519) 737-7110
www.ironworkerslocal700.com

Local 721 Toronto, Ontario
909 Kipling Ave.
Etobicoke, ON M8Z 5H3
(416) 236-4026
www.iw721.org

Local 736 Hamilton, Ontario
1955 Upper James St.
Hamilton, Ontario L9B 1K8
(905) 679-6439 or
(905) 570-8703

Local 759 Thunder Bay, Ontario
915 Alloy Dr.
Thunder Bay, ON P7B 5Z8
(807) 345-8151

Local 786 Sudbury, Ontario
97 St. George St.
Sudbury, ON P3C 2W7
(705) 674-6903/6586
ironworkerslocal786@bellnet.ca

Local 765 Ottawa, Ontario
101–30 Concourse Gate
Nepean, ON K2E 7V7
(613) 225-0573
local765@bellnet.ca

Plumbing

United Association Union Locals
Local 46
936 Warden Ave.
Scarborough, ON M1L 4C9
(416) 759-9351
www.ualocal46.org

UA Local 71
904 Lady Ellen Place
Ottawa, ON K1Z 5L5
(613) 728-5583
ualocal71@on.aibn.com

Plumbing, Electrical

Humber College–North Campus
205 Humber College Blvd.
Toronto, ON M9W 5L7
(416) 675-5000
enquiry@humber.ca
www.humber.ca

Roofing

**Ontario Industrial Roofing
Contractors Association**
940 East Mall, Ste. 301
Etobicoke, ON M9B 6J7
(888) 336-4722 or
(416) 695-4114
oirca@ontarioroofing.com
www.ontarioroofing.com

Welding

Canadian Welding Skills
1010 Ward St.
Bridgenorth, ON K0L 1H0
(705) 745-6226
www.weldingskills.com

**Northern Ontario Welding
School Inc.**
122 Saunders Rd., Unit 10
Barrie, ON L4N 9A8
(800) 858-4566
www.northontweldschool.com/
index.htm

The Institute of Technical Trades
749 Warden Ave.
Scarborough, ON M1L 4A8
(800) 461-4981
www.instituteoftechnicaltrades.
com

QUEBEC

Apprenticeship Contacts

emploiquebec.net/anglais/index.
htm

Heading for Success

www.headingforsuccess.com

Director of Apprenticeship

Emploi-Québec
800, Tour de la Place Victoria,
27th Floor
C.P. 100
Montréal, QC H4Z 1B7
(514) 864-2458
http://emploiquebec.net/anglais/
index.htm

Carpentry

**Aviron Québec,
Collège Technique**
270, boul. Charest Est
Québec, QC G1K 3H1
(418) 529-1321

**Métiers de la construction
de Montréal**
5205, rue Parthenais
Montréal, QC H2H 2H4
(514) 596-4590

**United Brotherhood of Carpen-
ters and Joiners Union Locals**
4037 Quebec Regional Council,
PQ, CANADA
8580 Boul. du Golf
Anjou, QC H1J 3A1
(514) 355-1141

134 Montreal, PQ
8580 Boul. du Golf
Anjou, QC H1J 3A1
(514) 355-1141

160 Quebec City, PQ
8580 Boul. du Golf
Anjou, QC H1J 3A1
(514) 355-1141

Truck Driving

CS des Monts-et-Marées
C.F.P. de Matane
455, rue Saint-Rédempteur
Matane, QC G4W 1K7
(418) 566-2500, poste 2500

CS du Fleuve-et-des-Lacs
C.F.P. du Fleuve-et-des-Lacs
30 B, rue Bérubé
Cabano, QC G0L 1E0
(418) 854-0720

CS de Charlevoix
C.F.P. de Charlevoix
(Pavillon Saint-Aubin)
50-1, rue Racine
Baie Saint-Paul, QC G3Z 2R2
(418) 435-6805

**École nationale de camionnage
et équipement lourd (E.N.C.E.L)**
1015, avenue Godin,
bureau 800
Vanier, QC G1M 2X5
(418) 683-5053/
(800) 663-5053

Electrical

Electricity—General
Institut technique Aviron de
Montreal
5460, avenue Royalmount
Ville Mont-Royal, QC H4P 1H7
(514) 739-3010

Automated Systems Electromechanics
Centre de technologie Rosemont
3737, rue Beaubien Est
Montreal, QC, H1X 1H2
(514) 376-4724

Electrical Power Line and Cable Workers
Montage de lignes électriques
CS des Navigateurs
C.F. en montage de lignes
42, Route Kennedy
Saint-Henri, Quebec G0R 3E0
(418) 834-2463

International Brotherhood of Electrical Workers (IBEW) Union Locals
Local 4881
Jarry St. E, Ste. 248
St. Leonard, QC H1R 1Y1
(514) 329-0568
localunion@ibew568.com

Railway Carmen/Women
  Note: Completion of an internal company apprenticeship program or three to four years of on-the-job training are usually required.

Industrial Construction and Maintenance Mechanics (DEP)
CS Sir-Wilfrid-Laurier SB
  (Laurentides)
CDC Laurier Lachute
171, rue Mary
Lachute, QC J8H 2C1
(450) 562-3721/
  (877) 688-2933 ext. 3315

Eastern Townships SB (Montérégie)
Cowansville Vocational
  Education Training Centre
180, rue Adélard-Godbout
Cowansville, QC J2K 3X9
(450) 263-7901

Mécanique d'entretien en commandes industrielles
CS Harricana
Centre de formation Harricana
850, 1re Rue Est
Amos, QC J9T 2H8
(819) 732-3223

CS de la Beauce-Etchemin
(CIMIC) Centre intégré de
  mécanique industrielle de la
  Chaudière
11700, 25e Ave.
Saint-Georges, QC G5Y 8B8
(418) 228-1993

Ironworkers

CS de la Pointe-de-l'Île
Centre de Formation des Métiers
  de l'Acier
9200, rue de l'Innovation
Anjou, QC H1J 2X9
(514) 353-0801

International Association Union Locals
Local 711 Montreal, Quebec
9950 Boul Du Golf
Anjou, QC H1J 2Y7
(514) 328-2808/
  (800) 461-0711
info@local711.ca
www.local711.ca

Plumbing

United Association Union Locals
Local 500
1299, des Champs-Élysées,
  Bureau 207
Chicoutimi, QC G7H 6P3
(418) 543-9045
www.local500.org

Roofing

Association des Maitres Couvreurs du Quebec
3001 Boul. Tessier
Laval, QC H7S 2M1
(888)-973-2322
www.amcq.qc.ca

NEW BRUNSWICK

Apprenticeship

  Information regarding New Brunswick's programs can be found at www.gnb.ca. The government encourages people to go through apprenticeships and articulates this on its website: "A pre-employment course is one

of the best avenues to enter into the apprenticeship program. Not only do you learn the basic knowledge of the occupation, but you may also be eligible to receive theory and practical credit towards your apprenticeship program."

Apprenticeship–General

Director of Apprenticeship and Certification—New Brunswick
Chestnut Complex,
  PO Box 6000
470 York St., 1st Floor
Fredericton, NB E3B 5H1
(506) 453-2260

Automotive Service Technician, Bricklaying, Carpentry, Electrical, Heavy Equipment Service Technician, Industrial Mechanic, General Machinist, Plumbing, Refrigeration and Air Conditioning, Sheet Metal Fabrication, Welding

New Brunswick Community College
College Admissions Service
6 Arran St.
Campbellton, NB E3N 1K4
(506) 789-2404/
  (800) 376-5353
nbcc.admission.ccnb@gnb.ca

Carpentry

United Brotherhood of Carpenters and Joiners Union Locals
4121 NB Regional Council of
  Carpenters, New Brunswick
277 Main St., Ste. 201
Fredericton, NB E3A 1E1
(506) 450-8830

1386 Province of New
  Brunswick
277 Main St., Ste. 201
Fredericton, NB E3A 1E1
(506)450-4024
nbrc@aibn.nb.ca

Electrical–General

National Joint Apprenticeship and Training Committee
IBEW Local 502 Training
  Trust Fund
1216 Sand Cove Rd.
Saint John West, NB E2M5V8
(506) 635-8535

International Brotherhood of Electrical Workers (IBEW) Union Locals
IBEW Local Union 37
138 Neill St.
Fredericton, NB E3A 2Z6
(506) 455-0037
ibew37@nb.aibn.com

IBEW Local Union 502
1216 Sand Cove Rd., Unit 27
Saint John, NB E2M 5V8
(506) 635-8535
ibew502@nbnet.nb.ca

Ironworking

International Association Union Locals
Local 809 St. John,
  New Brunswick
FST Walker, 895 Rte. 845
Kingston, NB E5N 1J4
(506) 763-2530

Local 842 St. John, New Brunswick
Ste. 214, Building B,
  580 Main St.
Saint John, NB E2K 1J5
(506) 634-7313

Plumbing

United Association Union Locals
Local 213
351 King William Rd.
Sprucelake Industrial Park
Saint John, NB E2M 7C9
(506) 635-1605
www.ualocal213.org/

Roofing

New Brunswick Roofing Contractors Association
PO Box 7242, Stn. A
  (7 Market Square)

Saint John, NB E2L 4S4
(506) 652-7003
www.nbrca.ca

MANITOBA

Apprenticeship Contacts
1010–401 York Ave.
Winnipeg, MB R3C 0P8
(204) 945-3337
(877) 978-7233
  (1-877-97-TRADE)
apprenticeship@gov.mb.ca

Carpenter, Electrician–Construction and Industrial, Heavy-Duty Equipment Technician, Industrial Welder, General Machinist, Motor Vehicle Mechanic, Plumber

Assiniboine Community College
School of Trades and
  Technology
(204) 725-8700
www.assiniboine.net

Carpenter, Electrician, Construction, Industrial and Power, Industrial Mechanic, Industrial Welder, Heavy-Duty Equipment Mechanic, Machinist and Tool and Die, Motor Vehicle Mechanic, Motor Vehicle Body Painter, Truck and Transport Mechanic

Winnipeg Technical College–Henlow Campus
130 Henlow Bay
Winnipeg, MB R3Y 1G4
(204) 989-6500
www.wtc.mb.ca

Carpentry

United Brotherhood of Carpenters and Joiners Union Locals
4208 Manitoba Reg. Council
  of Carpenters, MB
87 Cole Ave.
Winnipeg, MB R2L 1J3
(204) 774-1609
jrowe@council.mb.ca

343 Winnipeg, MB
611 Erin St.
Winnipeg, MB R3G 2W1
(204) 774-1609

Electrical

International Brotherhood of Electrical Workers (IBEW) Union Locals
IBEW Local Union 435
214-301 Weston St.
Winnipeg, MB R3E 3H4
(204) 985-4239
ibew435@mts.net

Ironworker

International Association Union Locals
Local 728 Winnipeg, Manitoba
895A Century St.
Winnipeg, MB R3H 0M3
(204) 783-7853
ironworkers728@mts.net

Plumbing

United Association Union Locals
Local 254
34 Higgins Ave.
Winnipeg, MB R3B 0A5
(204) 947-0497
www.ualocal254.ca

Roofing

Roofing Contractors Association of Manitoba
290 Burnell St.
Winnipeg, MB R3G 2A7
(204) 783-6365
www.rcam.ca

Welding, Carpentry, Industrial Electrical Maintenance, Plumbing

Red River College
School of Continuing and
  Distance Education
C116-2055 Notre Dame Ave.
Winnipeg, MB R3H 0J9
(204) 694-1789/
  (866) 242-7073
cde@rrc.mb.ca

Red River College
Winkler Campus (Welding Only)
100-561 Main St.
Winkler, MB R6W 1E8
(204) 325-9672
winkler@rrc.mb.ca

BRITISH COLUMBIA

Apprenticeship Contacts

British Columbia's official site:
www.aved.gov.bc.ca/
industrytraining

British Columbia Industry
Training Authority
1223-13351 Commerce Pkwy.
Richmond, BC V6V 2X7
(604) 214-8700
info@itabc.ca
www.itabc.ca

Aircraft Maintenance, Welding, Plumbing, Carpentry, Electrician

Northern Lights College
Campuses: Atlin, Chetwynd,
   Dawson Creek, Dease Lake,
   Fort Nelson, Fort St. John,
   Tumbler Ridge
Office of the Registrar
(250) 782-5251/
   (866) 463-6652
appinfo@nlc.bc.ca

Automotive Repair Technician, Carpentry, Electrical, Heavy-Duty Mechanic, Welding

Northwest Community College
Campuses: Hazelton,
   Houston Campus, Kitimat,
   Qay'llnagaay, Masset, Nass,
   Prince Rupert, Queen Charlotte
   City, Smithers, Terrace
(877) 277-2288

Boilermaking, Carpentry, Electrical, Plumbing, Ironworker

British Columbia Institute of
Technology—Burnaby Campus
3700 Willingdon Ave
Burnaby, British Columbia
   V5G 3H2
(604) 456-8100
www.bcit.ca/apprenticeship

Carpentry

United Brotherhood of Carpenters and Joiners Union Locals
4190 BC Regional Council
   of Carpenters
#210–2750 Quadra St.
Victoria, BC V8T 4E8
(250) 383-8116

Local 506 Vancouver, BC
#3 1583 Pemberton Ave.
North Vancouver, BC V7P 2S4
(604) 986-3466

Local 1598 Victoria, BC
#210–2750 Quadra St.
Victoria, BC V8T 4E8
(250) 383-8116
loc1598@telus.net
www.victoriacarpenters.com

Local 527 Nanaimo, BC
169 Comox Rd.
Nanaimo, BC V9R 3H9
(250) 753-9155

Electrical

International Brotherhood of
Electrical Workers (IBEW)
Union Locals
IBEW Local Union 993
873 Desmond St.
Kamloops, BC V2B 5K3
(250) 376-8755
ibew993@telus.net

IBEW Local Union 213
4220 Norland Ave.
Burnaby BC V5G 3X2
(604) 571-6500
ibew213@ibew213.org

IBEW Local Union 230
2780 Veterans Memorial Pkwy.,
   Room 204
Victoria, BC V9B 3S6
(250) 388-7374
www.ibew230.org

Electrical, Plumbing/Piping, Welding, Carpentry, Aircraft Structure

University of the Fraser Valley
33844 King Rd.
Abbotsford, BC V2S 7M8

(604) 504-7441 or
   (888) 504-7441

Ironworkers

International Association
Union Locals
Local 97 Vancouver, BC
4055 1st Ave.
Burnaby, BC V5C 3W5
(604) 879-4191
info@ironworkerslocal97.com

Local 643 Victoria, BC
Unit 105, PO Box 613
1497 Admirals Rd.
Victoria, BC V9A 2P8
(250) 727-5531
hughesharpe@shaw.ca

Local 712 Vancouver, BC
1026 Auckland St.
New Westminster, BC V3M 1K8
(604) 525-2199

Plumbing

United Association Union Locals
Local 324
919 Esquimalt Rd.
Victoria, BC V9A 3M7
(888) 382-0415
www.ualocal324.com

Roofing

Roofing Contractors Association
of BC
9734-201st St.
Langley, BC V1M 3E8
(604) 882-9734
roofing@rcabc.org
www.rcabc.org

Welding, Electrical, Plumbing, and Pipe Trades

Camosun College
Lansdowne Campus
3100 Foul Bay RD.
Victoria, BC V8P 5J2
(250) 370–3550 or
   (877) 554-7555
www.camosun.bc.ca

PRINCE EDWARD ISLAND

Apprenticeship Contacts

Charlottetown
Apprenticeship Office
3rd Floor Sullivan Building
PO Box 2000
16 Fitzroy St.
Charlottetown, PE C1A 7N8
(902) 368-4460

Summerside
Apprenticeship Office
Access PEI Summerside
120 Harbour Dr.
PO Box 2063
Summerside, PE C1N 5L2
(902) 888-8034

Automotive, Carpentry, Electrical, Heating, Ventilation and Air Conditioning, Plumbing, Power Engineering, Precision Machinist, Steamfitting/Pipe Fitting, Welding Fabrication, Wind Turbine Technician

Holland College
First Floor, 305 Kent St.
Charlottetown, PE
(902) 629-4217
(800) 446-5265
getready@hollandcollege.com

Carpentry

United Brotherhood of
Carpenters and Joiners
Union Locals
4199 NS and Prince Edward
   Island Regional Council
3597 Dutch Village Rd.
Halifax, NS B3N 2T1
(902) 454-5100
office@carpentersunion.ca
www.carpentersunion.ca

Electrical

International Brotherhood of
Electrical Workers (IBEW)
Union Locals
IBEW Local Union 1432
326 Patterson Dr.
Charlottetown, PE C1A 8K4
(902) 894-3269
ibew1432@pei.aibn.com

SASKATCHEWAN

Apprenticeship Contact

Saskatchewan Apprenticeship
and Trade Certification
Commission
2140 Hamilton St.
Regina, SK S4P 2E3
(306) 787-2444/
   (877) 363-0536
   The Saskatchewan Institute of
Applied Science and Technology
(SIAST) provides training for the
majority of the province's
apprentices. More information
can be found at www.
saskapprenticeship.ca.

Automotive Service Technician, Bricklayer, Carpenter, Electrician, Heavy-Duty Equipment Mechanic, Iron-worker (Structural), Machinist, Plumber, Steel Fabricator, Truck and Transport Mechanic

Saskatchewan Institute of
Applied Science and Technology
(SIAST)
SIAST Administrative Offices
400–119 4th Ave. S
Saskatoon, SK S7K 5X2
(306) 933-7331/
   (866) 467-4278
www.gosiast.com
Campuses: Prince Albert, Saskatoon, Moose Jaw, and Regina

Carpentry

United Brotherhood of Carpenters and Joiners Union Locals
Local 4041 Saskatchewan RC
   of Carpentry
418 50th St. E
Saskatoon, SK S7K 6L7
(306) 382-4355
ubc1985@shaw.ca

Local 1985 Province of
Saskatchewan, SK
418 50th St. E
Saskatoon, SK S7K 6L7
(306) 382-4355
ubc1985@shaw.ca
www.saskcarpenters.com

Electrical

International Brotherhood of
Electrical Workers
IBEW Local Union 2038
1802 McAra St.
Regina, SK S4N 6C4
(306) 757-0222
ibew.2038@sasktel.net

IBEW Local Union 319
PO Box 23053 Market Mall,
   Postal Outlet
Saskatoon, SK S7J 5H3
(306) 222-3906
pres-bm@ibew319.ca

Ironworker

International Association
Union Locals
Local 771 Regina,
   Saskatchewan
1138 Dewdney Ave. E
Regina, SK S4N 0E2
(306) 522-7932

Local 838 Regina,
Saskatchewan–WC
PO Box 28031, Westgate
Saskatoon, SK S7M 5V8
(306) 382-4570

Roofing

Saskatchewan Roofing
Contractors Association
1935 Elphinstone St.
Regina, SK S4T 3N3
(306) 721-8020
www.srca.ca

ALBERTA

Apprenticeship and Industry Training Contacts

Ste. 300, Willow Park Centre
10325 Bonaventure Dr. SE
Calgary, AB T2J 7E4
Career Services
(403) 297-6347
Apprenticeship
(403) 297-6457

7th Floor, Capital Health Centre
South Tower
10030 107 St.
Edmonton, AB T5J 4X7
Apprenticeship
(780) 427-8517

Red Deer, AB
(403) 340-5151

Automotive Service Technician,
Carpenter, Electrician, Heavy
Equipment Technician, Lock-
smith, Industrial Mechanic
(Millwright), Plumber, Welder

Red Deer College
100 College Blvd.
PO Box 5005
Red Deer, AB T4N 5H5
(403) 342-3300

Carpenter, Electrician,
Glazier, Millwright, Plumbing,
Refrigeration and Air
Conditioning, Welder

Southern Alberta Institute of
Technology (SAIT)
Main Campus
1301 16th Ave. NW
Calgary, AB T2M 0L4
(403) 284-7248/
  (877) 284-7248

Carpenter, Welder, Machinist,
Automotive Service Technician,
Auto Body Technician, Crane
and Hoisting Equipment
Operator, Ironworker

Northern Alberta Institute of
Technology (NAIT)
11762—106 St.
Edmonton, AB T5G 2R1
askanadvisor@nait.ca
www.nait.ca
(780) 471-6248/
  (800) 661-4077

Carpentry

United Brotherhood of Carpenters and Joiners Union Locals
4038 Alberta and Northwest Territories Regional Council
200-15210 123 Ave.

Edmonton, AB T5V 0A3
(780) 474-8599

Local 2103 Calgary, AB
301-10th St.
Northwest Calgary, AB T2N 1V5
(403) 283-0747
rc2103@home.com

Local 1325 Edmonton, AB
#133, 15210-123 Ave.
Edmonton, AB T5V 0A3
(780) 471-3200

Electrical

National Joint Apprenticeship
and Training Committee
(NJATC)
Electrical Industry Education
  Trust Fund
4224 93rd St., Room 1210
Edmonton, AB T6E 5P5
(780) 462-5729

International Brotherhood of
Electrical Workers (IBEW)
Union Locals
IBEW Local Union 254
3615—29th St.
NE Calgary, AB T1Y 5W4
(403) 250-555
ww.ibew254.ca

IBEW Local Union 348
PO Box 3500
Sherwood Park, AB T8H 2T3
(780) 417-3145
www.ibew348.ca

Ironworker

International Association
Union Locals
Local 720 Edmonton, Alberta
10504-122 St.
Edmonton, AB T5N 1M6
(780) 482-0720
info@ironworkers720.com
www.ironworkers720.com

Local 725 Calgary, Alberta
Room 104, 2915–21st St. NE
Calgary, AB T2E 7T1
(403) 291-1300

Local 805 Calgary, Alberta
#206A, 12904—50 St. NW
Edmonton, AB T5A 4L2
(780) 473-1956

Plumbing

United Association Union Locals
Local 496
5649 Burbank Rd. SE
Calgary, Alberta T2H 1Z5
(403) 252-1166
www.local496.ca

Roofing

Alberta Roofing Contractors
Association
2380 Pegasus Rd. NE
Calgary, AB T2E 8G8
(800) 382-8515/
  (403) 250-7055
info@arcaonline.ca
www.arcaonline.ca

NEWFOUNDLAND
AND LABRADOR

Apprenticeship Contacts

Department of Education
PO Box 8700
Confederation Building
100 Prince Philip Dr.
St. John's, NL A1B 4J6
(709) 729-5097
education@gov.nl.ca
www.gov.nl.ca/edu

Automotive Service Technician,
Carpenter–Construction/
Industrial, Electrician,

Insulator (Heat and Frost),
  Plumber, Roofer, Sheet Metal
  Worker, Steamfitter/Pipe Fitter,
  Welder
Academy Canada
Trades College
37-45 Harding Rd.
St. John's, NL A1C 5R4
(709) 722-9151

Bricklaying, Carpentry, Electrical Engineering, Heavy-Duty Equipment Technician, Industrial Mechanic (Millwright), Ironworker, Mining, Mobile Crane Operator, Plumber, Powerline Technician, Welder

College of the North Atlantic
(888) 982-2268
info@cna.nl.ca
Campuses: Bay St. George, Baie Verte, Bonavista, Burin, Carbonear, Clarenville, Corner Brook, Gander, Grand Falls–Windsor, Happy Valley–Goose Bay, Labrador West, Placentia, Port Aux Basques, Prince Philip Drive, Ridge Road, Seal Cove, St. Anthony

Carpentry

United Brotherhood of Carpenters and Joiners Union Locals
4245 Newfoundland and
Labrador Regional Council
PO Box 3040
Paradise, NL A1L 3W2
(709) 364-5430

579 St John's, NL
PO Box 3040
Paradise, NL A1L 3W2
(709) 364-5430
nfregcouncil@nlrc.ca
www.nlrc.ca

Electrical

International Brotherhood of Electrical Workers (IBEW) Union Locals
IBEW Local Union 512
PO Box 338
Grand Falls, NL A2A 2J7
(709) 489-7897
ibew.512@nl.rogers.com

Ironworker

International Association Union Locals
Local 764 St. Johns,
Newfoundland
38 Sagona Ave., Donovans

Industrial Park
Mt. Pearl, NL A1N 4R3
(709) 747-2111

NOVA SCOTIA

Apprenticeship
http://nsapprenticeship.ca

Aircraft Maintenance Engineer (Structures), Automotive Collision Repair and Refinishing, Automotive Service and Repair, Bricklaying Masonry, Carpentry Diploma, Heating, Ventilation, Air Conditioning and Refrigeration, Heavy-Duty Equipment/Truck and Transport Repair, Heavy Equipment Operator, Industrial Mechanical, Machining, Marine–Industrial Rigging, Mechanical Engineering Technology, Metal Fabricating and Plating, Plumbing, Refrigeration and Air Conditioning, Sheet Metal Worker, Steamfitting/Pipe Fitting, Utility Line Work, Welding

Nova Scotia Community College
NSCC Admissions
PO Box 220
Halifax, NS B3J 2M4
(902) 491-4911/
(866) 679-6722
admissions@nscc.ca

Carpentry

United Brotherhood of Carpenters and Joiners Union Locals
4199 NS and Prince Edward
Island Regional Council
Local 83 Halifax, NS
3597 Dutch Village Rd.
Halifax, NS B3N 2T1
(902) 454-5100
office@carpentersunion.ca
www.carpentersunion.ca

1588 Sydney, NS
24 Cossitt Heights Dr.
Sydney, NS B1P 7E8
(902) 562-5130
www.ubclocal1588.ca

Electrical

International Brotherhood of Electrical Workers (IBEW) Union Locals
IBEW Local Union 625
58 McQuade Lake Crescent
Halifax, NS B3S 1G8
(902) 450-5625
www.ibewlocal625.ca

IBEW Local Union 1852
187 Bay St.
Sydney, NS B1N 3B1
(902) 562-1357
www.ibew1852@eastlink.ca

Ironworker

International Association Union Locals
Local 752 Halifax, Nova Scotia
14 McQuade Lake Crescent
Bayers Lake Park, Ste. 103
Halifax, NS B3S 1B6
(902) 450-5615
iron.worker@ns.sympatico.ca
www.iwdcec.ca

Roofing

Roofing Contractors Association of Nova Scotia
Mount Uniacke, 7 Frederick
Ave., Box 141
Hants County, Nova Scotia
B0N 1Z0
(888) 278-0133/
(902) 866-0505
rcans@accesswave.ca
www.rcans.ca

TERRITORIES
YUKON

Carpentry, Electrical, General Mechanic, Pipe Trades, Welding
Yukon College
Admissions Office
Box 2799
Whitehorse, YT Y1A 5K4
(867) 668-8710/
(800) 661-0504

Electrical

International Brotherhood of
Electrical Workers
IBEW Local Union 1574
4133–4th Ave., Ste. 202
Whitehorse, YT Y1A 1H8
(867) 667-6552

NORTHWEST TERRITORIES

*Mining, Heavy Equipment
Operator, Pre-Employment
Carpentry, Heavy-Duty
Mechanics, Welding*

Aurora College
Aurora Campus
   (866) 287-2655
Thebacha Campus
   (866) 266-4966
Yellowknife Campus
   (866) 291-4866

NUNAVUT

Nunavut Artic College
Nunavut Arctic College Head
   Office
PO Box 230
Arviat, NU X0C 0E0
(867) 857-8600

Index

Index

Index